ADVERTISING AND THE MARKET PROCESS

A Modern Economic View

By
Robert B. Ekelund, Jr. and David S. Saurman

Foreword by
Israel M. Kirzner

PACIFIC RESEARCH INSTITUTE FOR
PUBLIC POLICY
San Francisco, California

Cloth ISBN 0-936488-20-4
Paperback ISBN 0-936488-21-2

Library of Congress Catalog Card Number 87-63450

Printed in the United States of America

Pacific Research Institute for Public Policy
177 Post Street
San Francisco, CA 94108
(415) 989-0833

Library of Congress Cataloging-in-Publication Data

Ekelund, Robert B.
    Advertising and the market process.

    Bibliography: p.
    Includes index.
    1. Advertising.   I. Saurman, David Scott.   II.   Title.
HF5821.E42   1988   659.1   87-63450
ISBN 0-936488-20-4
ISBN 0-936488-21-2 (pbk.)   OCLC: 17442849

For Marcia and in Memory of Ludwig H. Mai, whose infectious interest in economic policy was an inspiration to a generation of students.

ADVERTISING AND THE MARKET PROCESS:

A MODERN ECONOMIC VIEW

Robert B. Ekelund, Jr.
Auburn University

and

David S. Saurman
San Jose State University

Foreword by
Israel M. Kirzner

CONTENTS

8

Regulation, Fraud, Economic Stabilization, and Free Speech

9

LIST OF FIGURES

LIST OF TABLES

FOREWORD: ADVERTISING IN AN OPEN-ENDED UNIVERSE

This book explores the phenomenon of advertising in considerable detail. It presents and critically examines the "traditional" view in economics that saw advertising as a fundamentally baneful phenomenon, thwarting the tendency of competitive markets to allocate resources efficiently. This book presents, by way of refreshing contrast, an "emerging" view of advertising that recognizes the essential and constructive role it plays in the functioning of markets.

This emerging view is presented here with clarity, and with cogency; it draws upon an impressive literature and reports a wide range of research findings. I believe that the thoughtful reader of this book is likely, after carefully and candidly comparing these two views, to concur with the authors in their conclusions rejecting the traditional sweeping condemnations of advertising on both economic and ethical grounds. While advertising, like every other human activity, is certainly both prone to error and subject to abuse, the insights developed in this book reveal that the phenomenon of advertising as such, is neither the expression of any ethical failure of the market nor the evidence of resources being inefficiently deployed in defiance of consumer preferences.

Yet the very cogency with which Professors Ekelund and Saurman develop their case raises an obvious problem. If advertising is indeed so usefully important for the functioning of markets, why has traditional economics so consistently failed to recognize this? The authors have, quite correctly, cited the excessive preoccupation of economists with equilibrium analysis as being primarily responsible for their failure to grasp the real, beneficial character of advertising. In the following pages I shall try to identify a key element in the economics of advertising which has placed it, so to speak, in the "blind spot" of traditional economics. Once this key element is brought into unmistakable focus, the irrelevance of traditional equilibrium analysis for an understanding of advertising becomes abundantly apparent. So that, I shall argue, an appreciation of the true economic role of advertising, as it emerges from this volume, can lead, in turn, to a more profound and sensitive appreciation for the nature of economic understanding, no longer confined narrowly to the contemplation of states of hypothetical equilibrium. The key element in the economics of advertising to which I wish to draw attention is the *open-endedness* of the universe to which it relates. The concept of open-endedness deserves some elaboration.

THE OPEN-ENDED UNIVERSE AND THE CLOSED

Fundamental to all economic understanding is the analysis of *choice*. Whether probing the nature of individual economic activity or canvassing the options confronting the framers of societal economic policy, economics is deeply involved in the theory of choice. For the greater part economics has dealt with choice, we shall contend, within a framework appropriate to a *closed* world. A closed universe is, for present purposes, one in which relevant alternatives present themselves to the decisionmakers in definitely perceived form. The decisionmaker sees himself confronted by a limited number of clearly marked out possible courses of action, each leading to a definitely perceived outcome. The calculations, on the basis of which the choice among alternatives must be made, are not clouded by any sense of possible surprises (that might reveal the environment to have been different from that envisaged at the moment of choice). What characterizes choice in a closed universe is the circumstance that there is, within its framework, no scope for the decisionmaker to exercise any foresight, or creative imagination. Once the parameters of this closed universe have been identified, once the decisionmaker's preferences among the given set of alternative possible outcomes have been recognized, the decisionmaking process becomes strictly mechanical. Given these parameters and preferences, choice is completely predictable and determined.

The open-ended universe differs decisively in these respects from the closed. Decisionmaking in the open-ended universe occurs within a context in which key elements required for deliberate, calculative decisionmaking are totally absent. While some possible courses of action may be more or less clearly perceived, others are not seen at all. While some possible outcomes (of given courses of action) may be glimpsed, others are not recognized. The possibility of utter surprise is central to the open-ended universe. Such a universe provides ample scope for—in fact, it imperiously demands—the imagination, creativity, and prescience of the decisionmaker. Successful decisionmaking in such a universe is not at all a matter of scanning and comparing a series of given and known alternative outcomes. Successful decisionmaking, in the open-ended universe, consists rather in creatively anticipating the as yet unknown, in imaginatively filling in the missing contours of the apparently open-ended environment.

KNOWLEDGE, IGNORANCE, AND OPEN-ENDEDNESS

It is not sufficient, for the description of the open-ended universe, to identify it with imperfect knowledge, on the part of the decisionmaker, concerning aspects of his environment. As we shall emphasize, a closed universe need not imply omniscience with respect to one's environment; a closed universe merely requires that relevant courses of action be immune to surprise. Thus someone who requires a piece of information (let us say, concerning the climate in a foreign country to which he is considering a visit) knows that a time-consuming trip to the library is needed to acquire the needed information. His decision on whether or not to go to the library is fully consistent with the conditions for a closed universe. Moreover, even should he decide *not* to go to the library, his subsequent decisions (concerning the prospective visit to the foreign country) may nonetheless yet be made in a closed context. It is true that he lacks pertinent information (concerning the climate of the country) but he *knows* that he lacks this information. Within a wide range, he is subject to no surprises.

For the open-ended universe it is not enough that knowledge is incomplete; it is required that the decisionmaker *be ignorant of the extent of his own ignorance*. He is subject to genuine surprise. One so subject to surprise is not choosing between perceived alternatives about whose outcomes he has specifically incomplete information; he is, in important respects, making a choice without knowing what he is selecting, or what he is giving up.

LIFE IN THE OPEN-ENDED UNIVERSE

As has been pointed out by a number of writers, particularly by Ludwig von Mises, George Shackle, and Ludwig Lachmann, life in the open-ended universe is radically different from life in the closed universe described in textbooks of economic theory. To choose in the open-ended universe is to strike out boldly into a largely unseen world. To act as a producer, in an open-ended world, is not to fabricate a commodity for a perceived market; it is to create a commodity for a market the extent of which must be imagined; it is to create a commodity for a market into which any number of competing producers may be introducing novel products at prices that can only be guessed at. To act as a producer, in an open-ended world, is not to produce a commodity for waiting consumers; it is to try to sell one's product to potential customers who are unaware of what has been made available to them. In other words, potential consumers in the open-ended universe may be ignorant, not merely of the availability of commodities for which they may have urgent need, but also of that ignorance itself. Moreover potential consumers may be ignorant concerning the potential usefulness to them of known available commodities—and may, to boot, be ignorant of their ignorance in this respect as well.

Confronted with markets made up of such "utterly" ignorant potential consumers, producers cannot content themselves with producing goods; nor can they even be content with making relevant information (concerning the availability of these products) available to potential customers. After all, customers who are unaware that they lack vitally important information are in no obvious way motivated to acquire that information—even if it is made costlessly available to them. It is necessary for the producer *to grab the attention of his prospective customers* and somehow to get them to see the product he has prepared for them (or at least to see the information available concerning such products). And it is in regard to the task of attention-grabbing that the economics of an open-ended world must differ most radically from that of a closed universe.

THE GRABBING OF ATTENTION IN A CLOSED UNIVERSE

Economists have learned well Adam Smith's lesson concerning the invisible hand. Economists understand that the butcher's eagerness to help produce my dinner is rooted in and motivated by his knowledge of my own eagerness to have dinner. When economists observe an act of production, no matter how bizarre it may appear, they are thereby alerted to the existence of some anticipated consumer eagerness (outlandish though this preference may seem to the rest of us) to which the producer proposes to cater. This training preserves economists, to a considerable extent, from the error of concluding that producers are somehow ungoverned by the imperatives of consumer sovereignty. But this very training renders it understandable why traditional economists have failed properly to grasp the nature of advertising. It is this very training that has rendered the *activity of grabbing attention* virtually incomprehensible to traditional economists in any but a socially baneful light. The matter is quite easy to see.

For the activity of seeking to grab attention seems, at first glance, to be simply impossible to be subsumed under Smith's invisible hand. It seems impossible to argue that my frantic efforts to grab your attention is in response to your eagerness that your attention be grabbed away from whatever you are now concentrating your attention upon. In fact it seems quite clear that you have definitely chosen to bestow your attention on something else; that you do *not* wish to read the advertising message that I wish you to read. It is, in fact, precisely because you have demonstrated your preference to concentrate on reading something else (say, a book) that motivates me to mobilize all the wiles of Madison Avenue somehow to turn your attention away from what *you* had decided you wished to read, toward what *I* would like you to read.

But of course this conclusion that my efforts to grab your attention violate the invisible hand insights obtains its validity only because it assumes a closed environment. For such a world, indeed, advertising represents a kind of *aggression* in which a powerful advertiser wrenches

the consumer away from the purchases which *he* deems the most efficient use of his budget and somehow manipulates him into buying
what the advertiser wishes him to purchase.

Moreover, in this same closed universe, it becomes easy to see how
disinterested "objective" observers of such a scene might be "scientifically" convinced that the products which the advertiser wishes to
ram down the throats of consumers are in fact wasteful or even harmful—and that the consumer himself will soon regret having suc-
cumbed to the advertiser's blandishments.

Grabbing Attention in the World of Open-Endedness

Once we escape the confines of the closed world of textbook economics, however, the activity of grabbing attention can be understood
much more sympathetically. To grab a consumer's attention may just
possibly be to do something for which that consumer will be eternally
grateful *even though, at the moment, it appears to violate his own
expressed preferences*. The advertiser has, without violating the consumer's property rights, stimulated the latter's imagination to the point
that he recognizes now an opportunity of which he had previously
been totally unaware. *The advertiser has, as it were, injected a pleas-
ant surprise into the world of the consumer*. The consumer finds that
his world, his range of options, is a little richer than he had dared
anticipate.

The advertiser, it should be emphasized, has not *responded* to
preexisting consumer demand, but neither has he, necessarily, violated that preexisting pattern of demand by invasively altering it through
psychological manipulation. He has merely opened the consumer's
eyes to see what he had earlier failed to notice. In a closed environment, eyes cannot be opened (since they were never closed). The only
way consumer behavior could be modified, under closed-world
conditions, would be by *engineering* a change of preferences. Advertising, from the closed-world perspective, is naturally seen as constituting such engineering, and hence as unethically and inefficiently
unfaithful to the original preferences. But open-endedness means that
consumers' eyes *are* likely to be closed, offering scope for entrepreneurial action to bring to consumer notice that which has hitherto
escaped them. To widen horizons is not to be unfaithful to what was
seen earlier, it is to *add* to what was seen earlier.

Nor can the outside observer, in the open-ended universe, arrogate to himself the authority to pronounce "scientifically" a particular advertising message or a particular advertised product as perverse or inconsistent with the consumer's true preferences. If the consumer himself does not yet know how much he might like a particular product (once a full display of its qualities might be imaginatively laid out by the entrepreneurial producer), it is all the more certain that no outside observer, no matter how knowledgeable, can know what the consumer's "true" preferences may be, once that consumer's world will have been enriched by the surprises injected by the advertiser.

A World of Competing Attention-Grabbers

Once we transcend the confines of the closed analytical universe, in fact, we can begin to appreciate more generally the benign character of social processes that are rooted in the open-endedness of the real world in which we live. The benign character of advertising emerges, then, as merely an example of a more general phenomenon. Once open-endedness has been recognized, we can understand the need for social processes that might stimulate the *discovery* of unknown opportunities and might reveal pleasantly surprising features of the environment that can be taken advantage of (as well as unpleasant surprises to be wary of). Hayek has taught us to see the *competitive process,* always central to markets, as just such a procedure for discovery. In the competitive process actions are taken that lead to the discovery of interpersonal (and technological) possibilities that no one had suspected. So that the outcome of the competitive process could never have been deliberately achieved without it.

Advertising, the activity of capturing consumer attention, is easily seen to be just one particular dimension of competitive activity. Competing advertisers, vying with each other for the consumer's attention, are inspired to devise attention-grabbing strategies that no one could have foreseen, disseminating information that no one could have known to have been needed (or perhaps even to be available), and stimulating the provision of goods and services the importance to consumers of which no one had suspected.

To be sure these strategies display features difficult to reconcile with the economics of a closed world. The phenomenon of advertising simply cannot fit a world in which consumers already know what they want. Nor can this phenomenon even fit a world in which consumers know what information they need to obtain, in order to know what they want. Advertising exists in a world in which people do not know what information they need to know.

Ethics, Economics, and the Open-Ended Universe

The world of economic activity is a seemingly chaotic one. The casual, untutored observer finds little that appears systematic in this world of vigorous competition and energetic entrepreneurial innovation. For much of its history the science of economics made important progress by abstracting from such apparently chaotic elements, and by therefore concentrating on only those features of the world that could fit into the model of a closed universe. Undoubtedly these contributions of economics were of enormous value and importance. Much that is central to the working of the market can indeed most easily be grasped by reference to the closed world model. But this approach to economic understanding has not been without its costs.

Principal among these costs has been the widespread tendency for economists to ignore and even to deny features of the world that do not fit into the closed world model. This has meant that economists have been inclined to interpret such features of the real world in terms of an ethics and an economics which is significantly inappropriate for them. Advertising, we have seen, is just such a feature. Its ethical and economic treatment at the hands of economists has suffered correspondingly. If the phenomenon of advertising (and other similar phenomena intrinsic to the open-ended universe) are to be adequately understood and evaluated, traditional economics must be regenerated, enriched and deepened to encompass concepts of discovery, surprise, and entrepreneurial competition. It is the outstanding merit of this volume that, in regard to the economics of advertising, it addresses this regenerative task with impressive comprehensiveness and scholarly excellence.

ISRAEL M. KIRZNER
Professor of Economics
New York University

PREFACE

Contemporary economists' views on the effects of advertising are acutely divided, much more so than twenty or twenty-five years ago. In a dynamic sense, economic opinion on advertising is changing as rapidly as any in the entire discipline. The traditional view among economists and critics—still the majority opinion—condemns much advertising as a generally wasteful, redundant, and inefficient activity basic to the creation of monopoly power and economic concentration. A rapidly growing minority of economists view advertising as a welfare-enhancing tool of the economic process providing market information, lower search costs, access to competitive markets, and foundations of the free political system.

Both views of advertising, but especially the emerging view, have received a great deal of attention in the recent technical economic literature written by professional economists. The best material on the emerging view has appeared in numerous technical journals, "think tank" research monographs (Cady 1976; Kelly and Maurizi 1978; Ornstein 1977; Scheidell 1978; Worcester and Neese 1978), and in general, but technical treatises on advertising issues directed toward the professional economist (Bachman 1967; Ferguson 1974; Lambin 1976; Simon 1970). This growing literature, while of extreme value and importance, deals with specific issues, most often in technical terms. No generally readable synthesis and analysis of the emerging minority position exists.

The purpose of this volume is to make the *emerging view* of the advertising process—what might be called a modern, new neoclass-ical, or neo-Austrian perspective—accessible to the general reader in business or government and to anyone related to marketing or eco-nomics. In addition, we seek to *apply* this view of the advertising process to recent and important requests or attempts to regulate the advertising process by the Federal Trade Commission, those related to the advertising of legal services, tobacco, alcohol, cereal products, eyeglasses, infant baby formula, contact lenses, etc. We do not spe-cifically address the academic economist specializing in industrial organization or market structures, though undergraduate (and even graduate) students in these areas may find important gaps in the lit-erature filled by this book. Our aim, moreover, is not to present an organized point-counterpoint discussion of the pros and cons of ad-vertising by critics and defenders. Our central focus is strictly upon the economic theory and evidence supporting the emerging view—that is, on *how* and *why* so many economists' assessment of adver-tising has been turned on its head over the past quarter century.

In order to accomplish our aims in the space of one volume our sculpture is, of necessity, chiseled in high relief. We make no pre-tense of giving "equal time" to the traditional and critical view of advertising, although the outlines of this position in terms of both theory and evidence are intertwined in our discussion. (These critical views have been aired elsewhere without apology or contrast.) For these reasons our characterization of the traditional position is at times, and of necessity, highly stylized. While we readily admit that truth is rarely discovered at the poles, it is our purpose to illuminate, in the clearest fashion possible, the arguments supporting the emerging new neoclassical or neo-Austrian analysis of advertising as a tool of the competitive process. To do this requires somewhat stronger colors than would typify a multivolume, full length treatise on the subject.

Using the most basic economic terminology possible, and as little technical discussion as is feasible, we draw a sharp contrast between the critical (traditional) and emerging (new neoclassical or neo-Aus-trian) positions on advertising. In addition to the historical develop-ment of advertising thought, special emphasis is placed on the real world relevance of these ideas and their contemporary policy impli-cations. Our approach is issue-oriented since that has been the focus of economists dealing with advertising for the last forty years. Re-search into this area has convinced us that contemporary economists dealing with competitive markets have provided a deep and sound rationale for advertising as an economic and social activity and that this position deserves to be understood. Our book is designed, moreover, so that those readers with a severe time constraint or those interested primarily in the economic rationale for and public policy aspects of advertising may omit Chapters 1, 2, 3, 6, and 7 for an uninterrupted policy orientation to the modern economic view of advertising activity.

We are most grateful for the sound suggestions of Professors Israel Kirzner (New York University), Keith Leffler (University of Washington), Charles Maurice (Texas A & M University), Robert D. Tollison (George Mason University), Richard S. Higgins (Federal Trade Commission), Richard Ault (Auburn University), and James Harris (Auburn University). Professor James Meehan (Colby College), more than anyone, has helped us improve vast portions of this manuscript and we are indeed in his debt. We wish to add special thanks to Chip Mellor and Greg Christiansen of the Pacific Research Institute for their encouragement and efforts throughout the numerous drafts of this book, and to the Institute for its support. A special thanks is due Ladd Jones, Mark Thornton, Gwen Reid, and Dan Jaffee, who read portions of the manuscript. Typists Bess Yellen and Pat Watson performed with usual efficiency.

RBE
DSS
Auburn, Alabama
January 1988

INTRODUCTION

Advertising is at least as old as the bazaar, but massive absolute increases in media expenditures over the post-World War II period have telescoped attention on its social and economic effects, especially in the United States. Social critics, politicians, regulators, and economists have asked a host of questions about the role of advertising. Does advertising have unethical social effects? Is it manipulative and damaging to consumers of products and services such as has been recently alleged in cases involving alcohol, tobacco, infant formula, children's video, legal services, etc.? Is advertising anti-competitive, welfare-inhibiting, so that it fosters monopoly? Are the mass of advertising messages duplicative and self-canceling, or is advertising demand-creative (in the aggregate sense) and therefore the possible subject of taxation for purposes of economic stabilization? Is advertising essential or antithetical to economic, social, and political freedom?

Traditional economic models of market functioning—those developed by Alfred Marshall and his orthodox successors—cast serious doubts upon the value of advertising. In this view advertising is characterized as either unnecessary to the competitive process (that is, wasteful of resources) or as inimical to economic welfare. Modern economic analysis, along with real world evidence, presents a radically different assessment of advertising's role and value. We characterize the modern view as positive, neo-Austrian, or new neo-classical, terms which must be clearly understood since a contrast between traditional and modern views on advertising is central to our discussion.

Traditional economic theory depicts markets in static or situational terms. Attainment of equilibrium is instantaneous once the factors underlying consumer and supplier decisions (demand and supply) are assumed and specified. Factors, or parameters, such as tastes, costs, or income may change either supply or demand, but the full impact of the change is felt instantaneously. A large part of the engine driving these (comparative static) results is an assumption of perfect knowledge and perfect information concerning prices among consumers and suppliers. Neither advertising nor entrepreneurship is necessary in this world to achieve equilibrium.

Modern economic analysis departs from the perfect information—perfect knowledge assumption *and/or* the placement of market discussions in static, situational terms. Part of the modern analysis of advertising originates within the static model with the new neoclassical realization that more realistic models of market behavior must include imperfect information, search time, and other transactions costs. The works of George Stigler, for example, are notable in this regard and they are fundamental to any analysis of the modern economics of advertising.

Another insightful approach to the economics of advertising, one which commands the attention of serious scholars of a modern approach, places the imperfect information—imperfect knowledge assumption within the context of a moving, dynamic, disequilibrium system of market functioning. This view is called the Austrian or neo-Austrian view of advertising. Within this world there is no divorce between selling costs and production costs, as in the traditional economic view. Information and knowledge about products cannot be separated from the very nature of products and services. Advertising is a provider of information about products but it is also much more. Far from being an appendage to the competitive-entrepreneurial process, it is inextricably interwoven with rivalrous competition. The flavor of this view is concisely developed in the analysis of competitive disequilibrium in the writings of Israel Kirzner:

> . . . selling effort (including advertising) that alters the opportunities perceived by consumers constitutes an entirely normal avenue of competitive-entrepreneurial activity. It is activity which would indeed be precluded by a state of equilibrium, since such a state is by definition

one in which maladjustments do not occur. In equilibrium there is no way available resources can be more successfully deployed (by exchange or production or both) to coordinate individual goals through any reshuffling of the kinds of opportunities offered to the market. Since selling effort, including advertising, modifies the kinds of opportunities available in the market (through altering the character of the opportunities as perceived by consumers, or through altering consumer awareness of these opportunities, or through altering consumer tastes), the opportunities perceived by entrepreneurs for profitable selling effort represent hitherto unexploited "misuses" of resources, characteristic of disequilibrium. The exploitation by entrepreneurs of these opportunities for profit is entirely of the same kind as entrepreneurial profit-making activity in general.[1]

Kirzner, correctly we believe, criticizes the static equilibrium notion of competition for its inability to tell us anything of the competitive process. The traditional static model, which is useful in some contexts, is incapable of depicting a role for entrepreneurship or for explaining the process of market entry. Married to the concepts of entry and the entrepreneurial role is the use of selling effort. Kirzner, then, along with some of his Austrian predecessors (e.g., Frederich von Wieser, Ludwig von Mises, and Frederich Hayek) finds a key role for selling effort and advertising in a disequilibrium world of less-than-perfect information.

The modern, positive, neo-Austrian (or simply Austrian), or new neoclassical view which we develop and apply in this book is a combination of contemporary work on the impact and economic role of information. It combines the insights of those, such as Stigler, who work within the confines of static analysis with the creative ideas of economists, such as Kirzner, who seek to explain advertising as a tool of entrepreneurship with less-than-perfectly informed market participants. In most cases, we use all of the terms positive, modern, new neoclassical, and Austrian, to identify contemporary economic theory which incorporates costly information as an essential feature of markets. Frequently, however, we will have specific reference to the Austrian conception of the market process—one in which advertising and other sales efforts are symptomatic of costly informa-

---

1. Israel Kirzner, *Competition and Entrepreneurship* (Chicago: University of Chicago Press, 1973), p.167.

tion and a disequilibrium process driven by competition and entrepreneurship.

The purpose of this book is to explain the theoretical and empirical underpinings of the new view of advertising, to show how they emerged, and to utilize them in analyzing actual and proposed advertising regulations. In Chapter 1, a brief historical development of advertising as a major force in business and economics provides the background for the twentieth century economic criticism of mass marketing. Economic arguments against advertising and their source in contemporary discourse are also presented. The alleged role of advertising in market malfunctioning is discussed in Chapter 2 as is a brief history of advertising thought within the general development of economic theory. The modern or new neoclassical rationale for advertising activity— wherein advertising's primary function is identified as a creator of information—is developed in Chapters 3 and 4. Actual evidence relating to the new neoclassical view of advertising's role in the economy is examined and evaluated in Chapters 5 and 6.

In Chapter 7 the modern view is extended to specific business advertising and marketing practices through a detailed examination of recent "case studies" of actual and contemplated regulation at the Federal Trade Commission. Chapter 8 extends the modern approach on advertising problems. Issues such as multinational corporate advertising in underdeveloped economies, fraud, the *macro*economic regulation of advertising, and the economic and political ambiguities in arguments to regulate advertising are evaluated from the perspective of the new neoclassical view. Chapter 9 is a brief recapitulation of the modern approach to advertising. At base, our argument is that advertising in the marketplace provides very clear and positive economic and social benefits to citizen-consumers—benefits far outweighing any actual or perceived costs in economic well-being. Economic benefits include low information costs, lower prices, narrowed price differences, smaller search costs,and more rapid introduction of new technology—that is, more robust economic development through the establishment of competition as a rivalrous process.

PART I

DEVELOPMENT OF AN ECONOMIC VIEW OF ADVERTISING

1

ADVERTISING AS AN ECONOMIC AND SOCIAL ISSUE

Advertising is the provision of messages or information about any aspect of commodities, services, or human activities. Broadly speaking, everyone advertises. Since man crawled out of caves and crisscrossed the grassy savannahs, he has advertised and absorbed advertising messages. Institutions, such as churches and schools advertise in the very basic sense of *communicating information*. Computer dating services, "matchmakers," and organized marriage markets in such nations as Japan are all aspects of information-provision and advertising. Our speech and dress advertise us as surely as the weekday serial commercials sell soap. Such transferral of information is a common part of everyday experience.

Advertising, more narrowly defined and the subject of this book, is a commercial activity associated with the sale of products and services within economic markets. Even more precisely, we define advertising as an economic (i.e., competitive) *activity* of market participants, principally sellers (buyers may and do, of course, also advertise). The primary aim of this book is to evaluate this activity in economic and social terms and, especially, its relevance to the competitive process. Here we set the stage by briefly tracing the development of advertising as an economic activity, by stressing its magnitude in modern societies, and by presenting a sketch of the principal issues relating to the activity in contemporary academic, political, and intellectual discussion.

3

THE DEVELOPMENT OF ADVERTISING AS A COMPETITIVE ACTIVITY

The early written record of advertising, like that of early man himself, is sparse and fragmentary. Trade presupposes primitive specialization and the advent of organized markets, but literacy was late in developing. It is known that both the ruling class Babylonians and the Egyptians conducted what today would be termed "institutional" advertising. Discovery of the Rosetta Stone—the key to the linguistics of the hieroglyphs—revealed that the early Egyptian kings were fond of advertising themselves and their accomplishments. (This activity was often at the expense of predecessors' monuments—the inscriptions of rivals or forebears were easily removed, making room for one's own accolades.)

Advertising in the modern sense, that is, written advertisements, was developed in ancient Rome, although criers and "symbol signboards" were common in Greece and elsewhere until the Industrial Revolution and are still used in modified form today. Moreover, the growth of literacy in Rome led to billboard advertising whereby buyers and sellers posted price and product information. Indeed, the Latin word *libel* stems from the custom of posting the names of absconded debtors—to "libel" someone was thus to advertise his name.

The development of early advertising waxed and waned with the development of literacy. Criers and trade symbols thus replaced written advertisements as literacy declined in the Middle Ages, and written advertisements reemerged with the development of printing and the spread of literacy in the fifteenth century. With respect to the interrelations of advertising and competition, the interim between the fall of Rome and the development of European city states contains some interesting incidents.

Early Regulation

In France, early non-print advertising was the object of government regulations and profit-seeking. Over a thousand years ago, town criers were chartered by the French government, with exclusive privileges granted. This well-known form of franchise also entailed entry control. Profit-seeking (obtaining an edge on the competition through favorable legislation) in France by the aristocracy was of course common right up to the nineteenth century. An early example shows how advertising controls could be used to affect competition and trade. In the thirteenth century, Parisian tavern keepers were required by law to use franchised town criers to advertise their wine. In 1258 Philip Augustus granted exclusive privileges to the criers by the following decree:

> Whosoever is a crier in Paris may go to any tavern he likes and cry its wine, provided they sell wine from the wood, and that there is no other crier employed for that tavern; and the tavern keeper cannot prohibit him.
>
> If a crier finds people drinking in a tavern, he may ask what they pay for the wine they drink; and he may go out and cry the wine at the prices they pay, whether the tavern keeper wishes it or not, provided always that there be no other crier employed for that tavern.
>
> If a tavern keeper sells wine in Paris and employs no crier, and closes his door against the criers, the crier may proclaim that tavern keeper's wine at the same price as the king's wine (the current price) that is to say, if it be a good wine year, at seven dinarii, and if it be a bad wine year, at twelve dinarii.
>
> Each crier to receive daily from the tavern for which he cries at least four dinarii and he is bound on his oath not to claim more.[1]

The edict only covered taverns, and while it must have provided employment and increased revenues for town criers, it attempted to provide legal checks on trade and prices. (Such legal checks, as we will illustrate in Chapter 6, probably reduced consumers' welfare.) Advertising may have increased tavern business, but it also likely reduced price dispersal and established a convenient means for the government to exact payments from the town criers' union.

Advertising and Literacy

Early government interferences with advertising were not limited to France. Several centuries after printing had been developed and crude print emerged, the English government, in spite of large-scale illiteracy of the general population, placed a tax on newspapers with an additional tax of three shillings sixpence on *every* advertisement (regardless of size). The tax was instituted in 1792 during Queen Anne's

---

1. Frank Presbrey, *The History and Development of Advertising* (New York: Greenwood Press, 1968), pp. 11–12.

reign and continued (with a few modifications) until 1853. Ostensibly the tax was to control libel, but one practical effect (apart from providing revenue to the Crown) was to *hamper* the spread of literacy—certainly at the margin. The marginal effect on literacy is manifest in the following estimates from the year 1850:

	Population	Number of Newspapers	Annual Circulation
United Kingdom	27,368,736	500	91,000,000
United States	23,191,876	2,302	422,600,000

The relative price of newspapers in England has been estimated at six to ten times higher than those in the United States.[2] The phenomena of "reading rooms" and clubbing (of newspaper expenses), a feature of English literature in these times, points to a slackened spread of literacy among the poorer classes. The advertising tax inadvertently supported the static English social structure.

Conditions relating to advertising in America took a decidedly different course as the above table reveals. Literacy spread relatively rapidly in the United States where advertising was untaxed. A free-wheeling environment existed for advertisers throughout the colonial period and over the entire nineteenth century. Yankee peddlers and P. T. Barnum (a great advertising innovator) are all part of the lore of the period. Mass marketing proceeded apace with the flowering of the Industrial Revolution and mass production of goods and services. It may be argued that a free advertising environment played an essential role in the emergence of the United States as a leading world industrial power and, indeed, as a homogeneous nation.

The Americanization of products took place in the post-Civil War period as diverse nationalities and languages began blending into one. Data on advertising revenues over this period for newspapers and periodicals, though sketchy and incomplete, reveal a phenomenal growth in mass marketing. Advertising revenues (unadjusted for inflation) in only these two media grew from about ten million dollars in 1867 to approximately one hundred million dollars in 1900 to nearly one billion dollars in 1925 according to census figures. Growth was especially pronounced in the post-World War I period. The development and mass marketing of the automobile and motion pictures account

2. Ibid, pp. 13–17.

for a large part of this growth. American society had always been a "mass consumption" culture in comparison to other industrialized nations. Thorstein Veblen's turn-of-the-century critique of American capitalism featured "conspicuous consumption" as *the* leading characteristic of U.S. society and advertising heightened and accentuated this trait. Along with it, however, came modern production methods and cost-saving technology. The economic growth of America in terms of real output of goods and services is related to an aggregate mass consumption preconception, and advertising and mass marketing played a major role in the process.

The Growth of Advertising

Advertising expenditures have grown tremendously in dollar terms since 1945 in the United States as figure 1–1 shows. The increasing advertising expenditures in the recent past reveal its growing and undeniable importance in our economy. Table 1–1 provides a comparison of advertising expenditures in selected countries. It shows *per capita* advertising expenditures for selected countries, both developed and developing, in U.S. dollars for 1981 (the last year reported), advertising expenditures as a percentage of gross national product, and total advertising expenditures. Table 1–2 shows the percentage *change* in expenditures on advertising (all media) for a recent five-year period between 1976 and 1981 for a different selected set of countries. The clear leader in terms of absolute dollars and percentage of GNP is the United States. In 1981, America spent about 2 percent of GNP, or sixty-one billion dollars, on all reported advertising. When combined with all other world expenditures on advertising, the total represents approximately 1.5 percent of all free world resources devoted to market sales activity. When one considers the percentage growth in advertising expenditures over the five-year period 1976–1981 (Table 1–2), it appears that advertising is growing in importance in less developed countries as well. The increasingly market-oriented economies of Taiwan, South Korea, and Japan are significant in this regard, although inflation is a factor in interpreting all increases over this period.

Criticism and misunderstanding of advertising's role in the competitive process rests on a traditional view of advertising in economic analysis. Before we assess the traditional view in Chapter Two, consider some contemporary criticism of advertising activity.

Figure 1–1.   Total Advertising Expenditures in the United States 1945–1983 (Constant 1986 Dollars).

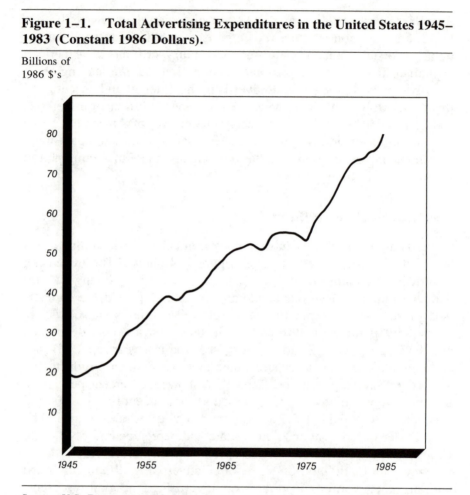

Billions of
1986 $'s

SOURCE: U.S. Department of Commerce, *Historical Statistics of the United States* (1975, p. 822) and *Statistical Abstract of the United States* (1985, p. 549).

WHY IS ADVERTISING PERCEIVED AS A PROBLEM?

Critical assessments of advertising stem from two basic sources. The first class of criticism relates to the (alleged and/or measurable) positive, or objective, economic defects or inefficiencies of advertising activity. The second, and far less tractable, area of attack rests upon ethical considerations. Normative, or subjective, arguments are often interrelated or even contradictory. Nevertheless, to understand the so-called advertising problem requires a careful delineation of the fun-

Table 1–1. Total Advertising Expenditures (in Millions of U.S. Dollars), Per Capita Advertising Expenditures (U.S. Dollars), and Advertising Expenditures as a Percentage of Gross National Product During 1981, Selected Countries.

Country	Total Advertising Expenditures	Per Capita Advertising Expenditures	Advertising Expenditures as a % of GNP
Argentina	$ 1,370	$ 48.76	1.99%
Bolivia	15	2.85	0.49
Brazil	2,589	20.75	0.97
Canada	3,529	145.84	1.39
Egypt	265	6.11	1.02
India	429	0.61	0.25
Japan	11,120	94.48	0.89
Keyna	31	1.78	0.41
Mexico	821	11.79	0.55
Nigeria	143	1.79	0.17
Sudan	9	0.49	0.12
Sweden	1,090	131.37	0.95
Thailand	120	2.46	0.35
United Kingdom	5,925	105.81	1.31
United States	61,320	266.61	2.29

SOURCE: *World Advertising Expenditures.* 17th ed. Starch Inra Hooper Group of Companies.

damental issues of resource allocation, market structure, economic welfare, and economic stabilization policies.

Advertising Is Anticompetitive and Duplicative

A number of positive economic issues related to advertising have focused on perceived economic wastes or inefficiencies in the activity. Indeed, economists themselves have traditionally been in the vanguard of those stressing advertising as wasteful activity.[3] The most cogent explanation for this criticism lies in economists' long honeymoon with the conclusion of a (static) perfectly competitive model in which advertising is regarded as superfluous. Long-run equilibrium in this model, propagated through turn-of-the-century Cambridge economist Alfred Marshall,[4] assesses the benevolent equalities of market

3. See E. F. Meade, "The Place of Advertising in Modern Business," *Journal of Political Economy* 9 (1901): 224–25; Vance Packard, *Hidden Persuaders* (New York: D. McKay Co., 1957) and *The Waste Makers* (New York: D. McKay Co., 1969).

4. See Alfred Marshall, *Industry and Trade* 3d ed (London: Macmillan and Co., 1920), and *Principles of Economics* 8th ed. (London: Macmillan and Co., 1920).

prices with marginal and average costs of production, an "optimum" rate of output or production, and the benign absence of economic profits (sometimes called economic rents). Products in this rarefied regime are homogeneous, and in a static context, there is no need for advertising. Since consumers are assumed to be perfectly informed at the outset (in a strict view of the model), advertising as information, possibly excepting price information, is unnecessary. This version of competition, in general, implies both efficiency and economic welfare maxima *without any advertising activity*.

The extension of "unnecessary" became "wasteful" or "useless" within a large part of the profession as economic analysis developed through the twentieth century. Proponents of this view of advertising got a boost with the modeling of more "realistic" forms of competition during the 1930s. Remaining within the static Marshallian framework of competitive theory, E. H. Chamberlin attempted to integrate advertising ("selling costs") and product differentiation into the theory of value (price) determination, a view which we will elaborate in Chapter 2. In *The Theory of Monopolistic Competition* (1933), Chamberlin argued that "selling costs" could be separated from real "production costs," thereby opening up the possible charge that selling costs are in some sense unnecessary for or wasteful in the provision of the good.[5] In a more modern *process* notion of competition—one

5. E. H. Chamberlain, *The Theory of Monopolistic Competition* (Cambridge, Mass: Harvard University Press, 1933), p. 117.

Table 1–2. Percentage Change in Advertising Expenditures: Radio, Television, and All Print Media for Selected Countries: 1976–1981.

Country	Percentage Change in Advertising Expenditures
Argentina	207%
Brazil	82
Canada	54
Japan	127
Mexico	80
South Korea	138
Taiwan	209
United Kingdom	167
United States	82
West Germany	90

SOURCE: *World Advertising Expenditures*. 17th ed., Starch Inra Hooper Group of Companies.

to be considered later in evaluating the static competitive theory—advertising is portrayed as a *tool* of competition.

Advertising Creates Industrial Concentration

In 1950, Nicholas Kaldor enlarged upon the above point. Advertising, in the famous Kaldor thesis, increases market concentration. Kaldor thought that in the defensive battle between firms to increase the demand for their products, "the larger firms are bound to gain at the expense of the smaller ones."[6] Firms who successfully establish strong "brand preference" for their products (and thereby increase sales) are in a better position to enlarge advertising expenditures, which leads to additional sales, etc. After advertising expenditures have "stabilized" within the product group, Kaldor suggests that "sales will have been concentrated among a smaller number of firms, and the size of the 'representative firm' will have increased." In this view such advertising campaigns lead to greater market power, and the expenditures themselves wax large as barriers to entry in certain areas. Advertising, in this sense, becomes part and parcel of the problem of market power, and it is at this point that economies of large-scale production—declining unit costs as output of the firm increases—become a relevant issue.

The Kaldor view is so important for our later assessment of advertising that it must be further explained. Under conditions of constant or diminishing returns to scale, advertising outlays not only will increase costs of production, but also will possibly intensify economic profits by limiting freedom of entry and increasing the range over which the monopolist can price. Moreover, it is not at all clear that, with increasing returns to scale (declining unit costs), consumers would be allowed to realize the cost savings brought about by the increase in output due to advertising. Consumers, in the Kaldor view, may be forced to pay *higher* prices owing to accretions to monopoly power *created* by monopoly power. Advertising, given the truth of Kaldor's hypothesis, contributes toward increases in market concentration and to the misallocation of economic resources. Economic problems and costs associated with monopolistic structures, then, as well as possible benefits emanating from these structures, must be attributed to advertising.

6. Nicholas Kaldor, "The Economic Aspects of Advertising," *Review of Economic Studies* 18 (1950): 13.

While the idea sounds plausible as a theory, and although there were some defenders of advertising (mostly advertising practitioners or marketing academics) in the early 1960s, it was not until the late sixties that economists began testing the relationship between advertising and concentration and advertising and profitability. Since that time, however, such activity has been a major if not *the* major empirical research effort of economists dealing with industrial organization and market structure. (Our assessment of these crucial issues is covered in Chapters 5 and 6.) There is, however, an important *macro*economic argument concerning advertising to be considered.

Advertising Creates "Mass Demand" and Should Be Regulated Countercyclically

Yet another criticism of advertising—macroeconomic in nature—is that advertising has some positive influence on aggregate demand. The *a priori* proposition that advertising might affect cycles of spending and saving first appeared in the wake of Keynesian economics in 1940, and the logical extension of this hypothesis—that *countercyclical regulation* of advertising expenditures could help promote economic stability—was expressed by Keynesian economist Alvin Hansen.[7] Since businessmen typically and traditionally link advertising expenditures to *past* sales levels, the fact that advertising expenditures closely follow the business cycle cannot reasonably be doubted. However, in order to argue that advertising is a *determinant* or "cause" of the business cycle (recessions and inflations), it must be shown that advertising, through "want creation" affects an *aggregate* consumption demand, that is, by increasing the propensity to consume. If changes in advertising expenditures, in other words, reduce savings on the upswing of the business cycle and increase private saving on the downturn, one would be able to say that procyclical advertising expenditures do *control* (in some sense) the business cycle. As with the concentration issue, economists have turned some attention to these matters in the 1970s. Chapter 8 weighs these matters in order to assess proposed regulation (through tax policies) on macroeconomic grounds.

---

7. Alvin Hansen, *Economic Issues of the 1960's* (New York: McGraw-Hill Book Co., 1969).

Advertising Is Unethical and Deceptive

Economists are not the only group to denounce business advertising. Social critics have been vocal in condemning advertising as wasteful and deceptive, and conducive to the misallocation of resources. All of these "ethical considerations" collapse into normative statements that are difficult for economists to evaluate. These matters, especially those relating to free speech and to free markets, will be analyzed in Chapter 8. At this point, however, consider some of these criticisms.

First, there has been an abiding suspicion on the part of those within and without the American university system that market mechanisms are incapable of monitoring "bad," "distasteful," or "harmful" products. Advertising is viewed as a major culprit in propagating such products, but there are numerous facets of this "ethical" argument.

Consider the argument that advertising is deceptive, that is, that flimflam men are able, continuously, to dupe consumers concerning the nature of goods or services. These consumers, it must be noted, are assumed to blithely continue consuming bad or injurious goods and services. Such vague and general charges against advertising become dubious when a new neoclassical view is considered. Empirically, consumers will not continue to purchase commodities that, on balance, *lower* their well-being. Thus, because of its role in market functioning and the effective self-regulation of market forces, advertising has remained fairly unregulated by government in spite of normative attacks on the authority.

The second stem of the argument is more difficult to assess. Since information may be viewed as a product produced under conditions of positive and increasing cost, consumers have been assumed to be either incapable or unwilling to invest in or purchase product information. Here we have the rationale for such items of federal legislation as the Pure Food and Drug Act passed in 1906. Consumers, the Act's defenders claim, must be protected through administrative decree from putrefied foods and harmful drugs. Implicit in these arguments is the supposition that government regulation by administrative action is the preferred, low-cost means of providing consumer protection. Ignored in these matters are two very important points: (1) the market functions in providing and maintaining information on a wide range of goods and services, especially given appropriate legal liability assignments, and (2) a product-monitoring administrative tribunal is not disinterested and impartial in regulating or retarding the introduction of products. The FDA, for example, has not been totally successful in keeping harmful products off the market. There is some evidence, moreover, that the FDA has capriciously withheld drugs with highly beneficial effects from the U.S. market. It is not, to be brief, a question of whether information (including informative advertising) must be provided to consumers. It is rather a case of who is the most efficient (low-cost) and welfare-enhancing provider—the government through regulation or a market with appropriate legal constraints attached to exchange transactions.

Yet another part of the "ethical" argument relates to highly normative criticisms. This might be termed the Galbraithian anti-consumption good, the some-things-are-bad-for-others argument. Social critics, such as John Kenneth Galbraith in his *Affluent Society* (1958), have argued that individuals in society *should* consume, for example, fewer Cadillacs and more education, fewer privately produced goods and more socially produced goods. A rationale for regulating advertising is thus set up since (Galbraith argues) the latter works primarily on behalf of private goods.

A recent variant of this argument is employed by groups advocating an international regulatory code to prevent the marketing and advertising of infant formula and other products in developing nations (see Chapter Eight) by certain multinational corporations. Another example is the proposed international regulation of soft drink advertising in these countries. Neither argument is based on the potential dangers inherent in the commodities themselves. Rather, the argument is that individual free choice may lead to less breastfeeding of infants and to more soft drinks consumed relative to other goods. The argument concludes that such choices are "bad," and that individuals should not be allowed such choices since they are incapable of making them "correctly" and that advertising as free speech should be regulated. There exists little or no empirical support for such regulation to suggest that infant formula, in and of itself, increases infant mortality rates in developing countries. Furthermore, such normative views are the origin of seemingly paternalistic social structures and interventions in these nations, as they have been to a more limited extent in U.S. regulatory experience. Ethical considerations may be analyzed in the context of new neoclassical views on information costs, concepts of free speech, and economic and political liberty, as they are throughout this book.

CONCLUSION

In this chapter we have explored, in abbreviated form, the long genesis of advertising as an economic activity, the growing importance of advertising in the U.S. and world economies, and the nature of some of the most common criticisms of advertising. Succeeding chapters delve far more deeply into all of these matters. It must be stressed at this point that, as economists, we are chiefly concerned with the impact of advertising within the broader context of *industry or market structure* and not with the effects of advertising on *individual* firms. While advertising's specific role in the sales strategy of individual businesses is a valid and important inquiry, the subject is wholly within the purview of marketing. Economists have always been far more concerned about the social effects of advertising on the overall allocation of resources and consumer welfare then they are about the well-known fact that advertising may alter the composition of resources or the profits of individual firms. In sum, this book evaluates the activity of advertising from an economic point of view. We begin, in Chapter 2, with the traditional economic assessment of advertising.

2

THE TRADITIONAL ECONOMIC CRITIQUE OF ADVERTISING

More than 150 years of economic analysis forms the basis for the traditional economic critique of advertising. This critique dominates opinion on advertising and provides the theoretical basis for much contemporary public policy. The traditional view is highly critical of contemporary advertising and is popular from the perspective of the intelligent layman. The purpose of the present chapter is to explore this critical view, both historically and logically, so that an alternative and more modern conception of advertising's role in the economic process may be formulated and more readily understood (in Chapters 3 and 4). Consider the economic analysis of advertising in historical context.

EARLY WRITERS

Early economic writings are distinguished by their *lack* of comments on the role of advertising. Francois Quesnay's eighteenth century work, the *Tableau Economique,* was the earliest attempt to describe logically the large-scale flows of products and services and incomes between major sectors of the economy. Yet nowhere in the *Tableau* is any mention of the "promotion" of these flows. David Hume, another eighteenth century writer, was concerned with the relationships of trade between two countries and the effects of trade on the quantities of gold owned by citizens. Specifically, Hume wanted to determine the effects that these actions would have on the general level of prices in both countries. Advertising does not enter his discourse either.

Adam Smith was, along with previous writers, concerned with basic *macroeconomic* relationships in economic systems. Smith, however, was also interested in *individual market outcomes*. A study of microeconomic relationships within markets is the area and level on which advertising and information problems may be approached, but Smith did not address the issues. The questions Smith addressed were the pertinent issues of that day—fundamental relationships of economic variables. Explaining the existence and reasons for advertising (which *did* exist at the time) was a much less important matter than was explaining the laborer's wage or the economic implications of the Corn Laws (laws regulating the importation of foreign grains into England). The situation continued throughout the classical period, with scholars such as David Ricardo, J. S. Mill, Robert Malthus, and Jeremy Bentham all producing volumes on economic issues and relationships without discussing advertising.

During the latter portion of the nineteenth century, especially after 1890, a number of economists began developing ideas and theories about the behavior of individuals, firms, and markets from a microeconomic perspective. This period, known as the neoclassical period, did not specifically explain the cause-and-effect relationships surrounding advertising and promotion. No neoclassical writer analyzed these topics in detail, partly because researchers were still in the process of trying to explain fundamental aspects of human economic behavior. It is important, however, that economists of this time established a formal microeconomic analysis and the tools used to analyze advertising in the twentieth century.

MARSHALLIAN DEVELOPMENTS: THE SOURCE OF CURRENT THOUGHT

The one neoclassical writer who did not ignore advertising was Alfred Marshall (1842–1924), although his treatment was terse. In his *Principles of Economics,* published in 1890, Marshall recognized that businesses did in fact advertise some products and that expenses for advertising are also part of the expenses that determine the cost of producing the advertised products.[1] He also noted that it may well be in the seller's interest to advertise.

Insight into modern controversy on advertising may be gained by considering the few short pages Marshall devoted to the topic in one of his lesser known works, *Industry and Trade,* originally published in 1919.[2] Here Marshall uncovered two possible effects of the advertising process that are part of the three major views held today concerning advertising's social desirability. Marshall observed that repetitive advertisements, produced primarily to combat rivals in the marketplace, involve a degree of a waste of society's scarce resources. He argued that such advertisements obscure less frequently advertised goods from the consumer's view and that large-scale advertising may force the costs of producing a product to be greater than would otherwise be the case. It was his view that heavily advertised goods are produced by using "too many" of the economy's scarce resources.

However, Marshall also reasoned that constructive advertisements and promotion could call the existence of goods and services or the location of goods and services to the attention of consumers. He also recognized the desirability of advertising in terms of conveying the existence or locations of products and, significantly, their qualities and capabilities. Thus, Marshall hit upon, but only in passing, two important consequences of advertising that play major roles in the new neoclassical analysis in the twentieth century. Those roles were (a) that advertising enables consumers to "satisfy their wants without inordinate fatigue or loss of time,"[3] and (b) that aside from actual purchase price, the costs consumers bear by making market transactions might be lowered through advertising. Marshall argued, moreover, that information concerning a product's quality could, in some instances, be conveyed before the consumer actually purchased the product, thus benefiting the consumer.

Economists can only regret, with perfect hindsight, that Alfred Marshall did not more fully apply his skillful perception and original insight into the economic theory of advertising and promotion. But

1. Alfred Marshall, *Principles of Economics* (London: Macmillan and Co., 1920), pp. 328–29.
2. Idem., *Industry and Trade,* 3d ed. (London: Macmillan and Co., 1920), pp. 304–07.
3. Ibid., pp. 304–05.

the characteristics of his theoretical system that at once hinted at a modern analysis of advertising and promotion also provided incentives for later scholars to ignore these issues as they built upon and refined his analytical tools. To make Marshall's theory of competition operable in determining the market price of a product, *perfect information on the part of buyers and sellers was assumed!* There is no impropriety in making this assumption in constructing a technical theory of how markets work—one which also performs well in explaining actual, real world results. Theory requires assumptions so that, in the end, it accurately describes real world events.

But the assumptions developed within the theory of competition in the first third of the twentieth century, those necessary to make the theory operate properly, drove researchers away from the role and dynamics of advertising to other investigations. With perfect information, why advertise prices or qualities? Could not advertising be treated as another ordinary input into the production process? Strict adherence to these assumptions even led some economists to conclude that advertising on the part of business may be superfluous at best and non-profit-maximizing or unwise behavior at worst. Thus, Marshall, his students, and his contemporaries did provide a refined, systematic, and logical system for analyzing microeconomic phenomena, but the resulting framework was technical, rigid, and sterile as far as its ability to attack issues and problems related to promotion, advertising, and information transference. It was a static world within which the dynamics of the competitive process remained hidden and collapsed in the notion of instantaneous equilibrium.

MONOPOLISTIC AND IMPERFECT COMPETITION

The refinement of neoclassical economics continued in the 1920s and 1930s as attempts were made to make static neoclassical theory more realistic and appealing to real world practitioners. At this juncture the concepts of advertising and promotion of products by firms entered the realm of economic theory in an important manner. In the same year, two independent works were published, Edward Chamberlin's *Theory of Monopolistic Competition* (1933) and Joan Robinson's *Economics of Imperfect Competition* (1933)[4] Both Robinson and Cham-

4. Edward Chamberlin, *The Theory of Monopolistic Competition* (Cambridge, Mass: Harvard University Press, 1933); Joan Robinson, *Economics of Imperfect Competition* (London: Macmillan and Co., 1933).

berlin were searching for an economic theory that was a middle ground between Marshall's theories of monopoly and competition. That is, both writers looked at the world, business firms in particular, and concluded that most firms neither fit the characteristics of a single-firm monopoly nor those of a competitive mold. Likewise, when viewing groups of firms, or industries, they reached the same conclusions: It would be difficult to classify industries as monopolistic or competitive since most industries exhibited characteristics of both extreme economic models. Both Chamberlin and Robinson noticed something else that did not square with received ideas.

Robinson and Chamberlin both wondered why we actually observe firms making expenditures on advertising and promotional activities. In answer to this question, they constructed economic theories of business firms that had some of the characteristics of monopoly and some of competition. They sought theories to explain, in logical fashion, why we observe business firms advertising—theories that would explain advertising and promotion from the viewpoint of the firm enhancing its own economic welfare or profits. Economists were finally at the threshold of an explanation for advertising.

The kernel of monopolistic or imperfect competition was that a *quasi-monopoly* firm could increase sales if it lowered the price of its output and vice versa. This is in stark contrast to the competitive firm which, if it raised its price above the market-determined price, would see sales drop to zero, but which would have no incentive to lower its price below market price since it can sell all it wants to at the market-determined price. In order to understand the traditional economic role of advertising we must examine why and how Robinson and Chamberlin obtained downward sloping demands for single firms in fairly competitive markets, not simply at the assumption that they are downward sloping.

Chamberlin noted that the products produced by firms within many industries were not homogeneous, or identical in all respects, as Marshall had assumed for his analysis of competition. Instead, Chamberlin assumed that, for a number of industries, the product produced by all firms will have some common characteristics. However, each firm will attempt to distinguish, in the eye of the consumer, its own product from those similar products produced by other firms in the industry. Each seller, because of some degree of "product differentiation" of his or her products from those of close competitors, will be able to vary price from market price and to alter sales somewhat. This was the element of monopoly that Chamberlin observed in competitive industries.

Chamberlin considered advertising an important method by which a firm could help differentiate its product from the products of other firms, given that such differentiation was feasible. Chamberlin further asserted that, by advertising, the individual firm could increase the price consumers would be willing to pay for any *given* amount of output or increase the demand for its product. Advertising would also lower the consumer's purchase sensitivity to price changes (elasticity) because it had the power of rearranging or manipulating the wants of the consumer. However, it is important to note that Chamberlin never asserted that advertising *created* monopoly elements in otherwise competitive industries. These elements were merely a consequence of monopolistically competitive industries.

Joan Robinson presented the reverse of this view. It was her premise that advertising was one cause of monopoly and of monopolistic practices in what would otherwise be competitive markets. While she did not try to construct a new view of markets and firms, as Chamberlin did, she viewed the world as populated by firms with varying degrees of monopoly power, and was more in line with traditional Marshallian economics than was Chamberlin. Her starting point was that "every individual producer has the monopoly of his own output" and, by implication, that the demand for each firm's output is not "perfectly elastic" as Marshall had asserted.[5] Each firm has some monopoly power gauged by the elasticity of demand. The technical details of Robinson's research are not important here, but her general views of advertising are relevant since they are the source of later ideas and public policy.

Advertising and promotion, through their abilities to influence consumer demands, helped create Robinson's view of most business firms as monopolies. She tells us that "the customer will be influenced by advertisement, which plays upon his mind with studied skill, and makes him prefer the goods of one producer to those of another because they are brought to his notice in a more pleasing or forceful manner."[6] The consumer is viewed as a passive actor in this scenario, with his or

5. Robinson, *Economics of Imperfect Competition*, p. 5.
6. Ibid., p. 90.

her decisions being manipulated or strongly influenced by the advertising medium. But this portrayal is, in and of itself, not the source of a loss of welfare. The undesirable part of advertising is, in Robinson's view, the fact that it produces monopolistically or quasi-monopolistically structured markets and firms which earn higher than normal profits, wherein consumers pay higher prices and obtain less output than under competitive conditions. Robinson argued that when "a firm finds the market becoming uncomfortably perfect (i.e., more competitive) it can resort to advertisement and other devices which attach customers more firmly to itself" should, for any reason, the monopoly power of a firm begin to erode.[7] The competitive process, so critical to the efficient functioning of a free enterprise market system, was depicted as being easily abrogated by the tool of advertising. Advertising was held to be one of the strongest anticompetitive measures a firm could employ on its behalf, preventing other firms from entering markets with lower priced products or goods of higher quality.

THE TRADITIONAL CRITIQUE OF ADVERTISING

Two major concepts about advertising emerged from Chamberlin's and Robinson's discussions: (1) that consumers are viewed as *passive actors* in the economic scheme of things, and (2) that advertising can manipulate, mold, and induce consumers into taking certain actions (buying the output of a particular firm, for example), whereas they would presumably be less inclined to do so in the absence of such advertising. This view of the consumer and his or her responses became the foundation for many of the results produced in the study of the effects of advertising in the 1950s and 1960s and for most contemporary public policy developments.

The development of static market models (especially by Robinson) was conducive to the development of the critical view of advertising's effects. Oligopoly is "in between" monopoly and competition but is tilted toward monopoly since there are presumed to be only a "few" firms in an oligopolistic market. It appears simple, moreover, for anyone to construct a list of industries that are oligopolistic—automobiles, cereals, oil, and so on. And oligopolistic markets do not produce the socially desirable results of a competitive market: Prices are higher and in some cases unresponsive to changes in the cost structure of

7. Ibid., p. 101.

the firm; the total amount of the product produced is lower than in a competitive market and it is produced at a higher cost; and profits are greater.

Models of imperfectly competitive firms, oligopolies included, were malleable. Certain concepts, such as advertising, could be discussed within their context without a hard and fast integration into the theory but only by assertion. The predominant (and lingering) view is that advertising is a weapon of firms in the continuous economic battle for profits. Most cause and effect analysis of the advertising phenomenon encompasses the sorting out of the technical reasons for a firm to advertise but, more importantly, it includes the effects such actions have on *market structure*, or the economic characteristics of an industry. What are the implications attributable to advertising in this kind of theoretical world?

BARRIERS TO ENTRY AND BRAND LOYALTY

Researchers of the 1950s acknowledged the fact that firms exist not out of any social responsibility felt by resource owners to other members of society, but in order to earn the largest possible profit for stockholders. It is well known that profits will tend to be reduced in industries, if they become inordinately large, by the entry of new firms into the product line. In order to maintain higher profits than would normally be the case in a free market, competitive entry into an industry earning large profits must somehow be prevented or impeded. A high level of profits over long periods of time would be observed after successful entry control. Thus, the issue of *barriers to entry* and their relationship to advertising arose.

If advertising could create an entry barrier, then advertising was a *cause* of market evolution and development along monopolistic lines. Monopolistic structures produced undesirable social consequences with a few firms in the market in possession of some degree of monopoly power. But how does the advertising of products create entry barriers that yield large, long-term profits to advertisers? Several hypotheses have been offered to answer this question. The first, and by far the simplest, is that advertising changes consumers' tastes and creates false values in the minds of consumers. That is, simply by advertising a product, a firm can either create a demand for the product or increase the existing demand, resulting in the ability to charge higher prices and, presumably, to increase profits.

This effect can be seen clearly by considering Figure 2–1. D_B represents the demand for some commodity before advertising and D_A reflects, according to the above argument, the demand curve for this commodity after advertising. The *demand curve* represents, for any given quantity of the commodity, the maximum per-unit price consumers would be both willing and able to pay in order to buy this particular amount of the good. It is apparent from Figure 2–1 that after the advertising of the product consumers would be willing and

Figure 2–1.   Increase in Consumer Demand Due to Advertising.

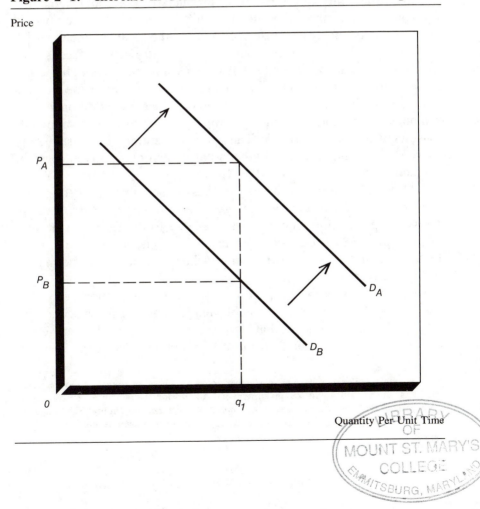

able to pay a greater price, P_A (greater than before advertising P_B) in order to purchase q units of the product and that the value of the product increases.[8] In other words, the hypothetical firm of Figure 2–1 has been successful in increasing the demand for its product through advertising's ability to change tastes and preferences of consumers in favor of the product. After a while, continuous advertising will have firmly entrenched these new, altered tastes on the part of consumers so much so that potential competitors dare not attempt to enter the market for fear of losses if they try.

Advertising, then, creates consumer loyalty to the particular brand that is advertised, as opposed to other brands of the same general class of products (soap, for instance, or automobiles). Over time, loyalty to the brand becomes stronger and stronger, so strong that other firms contemplating entry into this line of products face a troublesome disadvantage. Overcoming brand loyalty built up through the years would be an expensive process whose success would take an extended length of time. The firm or firms contemplating entry would face a cost disadvantage that the incumbent firm does not face. Though the potential entrant could produce a product at the same cost as the existing firm, it must be ready, willing, and able to bear the additional costs of a huge, continuous advertising campaign in order to try to convince consumers to switch brands. The *potential* entrant is consequently viewed as bearing a much higher total cost for any given level of production than does the existing firm.

Additionally, the established firm has presumably reached such a size as to be able to take advantage of *economies of scale,* through the use of production technologies available to the firm only at very large output rates. Thus, cost per unit of output, or average cost, is lower for firms that have firmly entrenched themselves in the market through advertising.

This same reasoning is not only applied to production costs, but also to advertising costs. The established firm also realizes economies of scale in advertising so that its per unit of output or average advertising costs are lower than those of a potential or actual new en-

---

8. Note that while advertising creates higher prices for a good or service, it also increases consumers' utility (at least in any given market). Advertising is not, however, welfare-enhancing when additions to total costs are juxtaposed with the increased utility. The traditional view concludes that the cost increase outweighs any utility increase with resulting *net* welfare reduction.

trant. The effect is that new firms face a cost disadvantage. Entry is discouraged or *an entry barrier is erected*. The existing firm in this situation has two advantages: (1) extensive brand loyalty is built up that is costly for potential competitors to overcome, and (2) the ability to advertise at lower costs, per unit of output, tends to discourage or prevent entry of new firms into the industry, or establishes a barrier to entry. This entry barrier is not, in itself, welfare inhibiting or inefficient. What is undesirable from an economic perspective is the effect on market prices and profits in an industry when entry is prevented.

In the traditional view, barriers to entry created by advertising short-circuit the competitive process. When this happens, prices and profits are invariably higher than in the competitive situation. From this perspective it appeared that advertising was not a socially desirable institution since it prevented markets from achieving a large degree of competitiveness, efficiency, and consumer welfare.

ADVERTISING AND DEMAND ELASTICITY

Another aspect of advertising and its effects on market structures was hypothesized in the 1950s and 1960s, also with roots in the analyses of Robinson and Chamberlin. This aspect of advertising plays down the cost-side effects and concentrates on the demand for the firm's output. For the static, perfect competitor, the demand for output is "perfectly elastic." That is, if the competitor raises prices, he loses all sales. At the same time he has no incentive to lower price *below* the market price as he will lose some revenue on each unit he then sells. In Figure 2–2, the demand for the competitor's product is horizontal, reflecting these circumstances. However, if a firm can create brand loyalty by advertising a product, then it has also distinguished its product in the minds of consumers. Advertising has thus been successful in differentiating this product from similar products. In the process consumers have become less responsive or sensitive to price changes. In the terminology of economics, advertising has "reduced the elasticity of demand." If the firm now raises its price, and it has differentiated its product through advertising so that D_A is the demand curve, the quantity bought by consumers will not fall to zero. It will decrease, *but not by as much as it would if the firm were a perfect competitor and raised prices*. In responding to changing market con-

Figure 2–2. Product Differentiation and the Effect of Advertising on Demand Elasticity.

Price

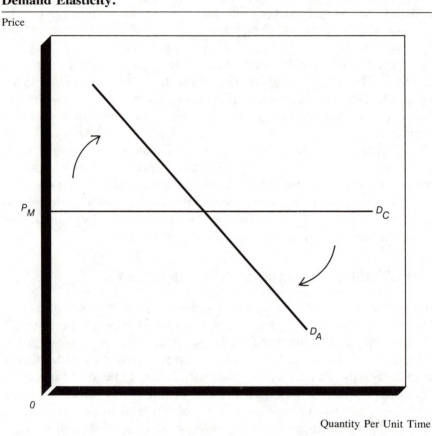

Quantity Per Unit Time

ditions, say a change in cost, the differentiating firm has less of an incentive to lower prices and more of an incentive to raise prices since the amounts consumers buy will not fall by much.

The last two points about how advertising affects firms and markets do not posit anything inherently socially undesirable about advertising. It is the *result* of advertising that is viewed as being less than desirable. Less-than-desirable results arise due to advertising's supposed anticompetitive effects. Advertising appears to make markets more monopolistic than competitive, although this conclusion is challenged by modern economic analysis.[9] Economists devised an index of monopoly power, or an indicator that would be able to measure how close to an actual monopoly any particular industry was. This concept, called a *concentration ratio,* measures the percentage of total industry output produced by a given number of firms in the industry. The higher the concentration ratio, or the smaller number of firms accounted for in the concentration ratio, the more monopolistic the industry is presumed to be.

The concentration ratio for an industry became a directly observable measure of monopoly power—something real and finite that could be expressed as hard evidence of monopoly power and of the undesirable side effects associated with it. The concentration ratio also adjusted well to the then-existing economic analysis of advertising. It was argued that advertising produced entry barriers and monopoly power, through brand loyalty, economies of scale (in both production and advertising costs) and/or product differentiation, which would lead one to conclude that markets exhibiting either of these characteristics would tend to have a relatively high concentration ratio. The idea that industries that are heavy advertisers also will tend to be highly concentrated, or that advertising causes concentration in markets, came to be the mainstream view of advertising.

The traditional economic critique of advertising was developed by many authors, but four stand out in terms of their influence on the methods of studying advertising. We have already mentioned Nicholas Kaldor who in 1949 expressed views that were to dominate thinking for years.[10] Kaldor looked back to the end of the nineteenth century and noted that, in England, the general trend of markets seemed to be that numerous local competitors of goods were transformed into national companies with an associated large increase in concentration in these markets. Kaldor then asserted that these large national firms were oligopolistic, i.e., noncompetitive, in nature, and that the cause of this transformation in the structure of British industry was the introduction of large-scale advertising. Manufacturers advertised to se-

9. Contemporary economic theory questions whether advertising differentiates products (helping to create monopoly market structures) or whether it permits firms to inform consumers of real product differences. Any welfare analysis of advertising's impact must come to grips with this question.

10. Nicholas Kaldor, "The Economic Aspects of Advertising," *Review of Economic Studies* 18 (1949): 1–27.

cure brand loyalty, products were standardized and produced on large scale, economies of scale resulted, and the industry became a concentrated, noncompetitive oligopoly. Markets previously characterized by many firms at each stage of the marketing process (suppliers of materials, transport, fabrication, delivery, etc.) now had only one large firm handling these functions and there were far fewer firms. On an individual firm level, Kaldor believed this process to be self-perpetuating. That is, once brand loyalty is established by a firm, economies of scale are realized by that firm and entry is impeded to some degree. The resulting profits are then reinvested in more advertising to secure an even stronger foothold on the market.

A foothold on the market was called a *market share,* and it was calculated as the percentage of total industry output accounted for by the sales of one firm. It was similar to the concentration ratio, but it purported to measure how close to a monopoly a single firm was, rather than the whole industry. Thus Kaldor provided the impetus and some of the tools necessary to serious inquiry into advertising and the performance of economic actors.

Along with Kaldor's work was the famous effort by Joe S. Bain in 1956.[11] Bain formalized and emphasized the role that advertising has in differentiating similar products produced by different firms, and argued that advertising-induced product differentiation yields entry barriers for new firms. It is significant, we think, that most of the studies connecting advertising, market concentration, market shares, and oligopoly are based on the works of Bain and Kaldor. William Comanor and Thomas Wilson must also be acknowledged for their contributions to the traditional critique of advertising.[12] Following Bain's (and to a lesser extent, Kaldor's) reasoning, Comanor and Wilson asserted, providing some empirical evidence, that economies of scale play a very crucial role in any analysis of advertising. The idea that advertising causes industrial concentration became even more firmly entrenched.

THE GALBRAITHIAN POSITION

These ideas were incorporated and taken to the extreme in a popularized, nonacademic fashion, by John Kenneth Galbraith in his books

11. Joe S. Bain, *Barriers to New Competition* (Cambridge, Mass: Harvard University Press, 1956).

12. William S. Comanor and Thomas S. Wilson, "Advertising, Market Structure, and Performance," *Review of Economics and Statistics* 49 (1967): 423–40.

The Affluent Society (1956) and *The New Industrial State* (1967).[13] Both of these books were nontechnical in terms of economic analysis, became popular with laymen, and reinforced the traditional analysis of advertising and its implications. Galbraith, as mentioned in Chapter 1, viewed advertising as a tool—a devious tool—whose purpose is to create wants and directly manipulate consumers' tastes in favor of products being advertised. Galbraith did not view advertising as merely influencing the tastes of consumers, but as actually *creating* them. Tastes are not formed independently by consumers themselves, but by producers who advertise. Additionally, Galbraith asserted that advertising expenses are more important to firms than any other type of expense.

> The even more direct link between production and wants is provided by the institutions of modern advertising and salesmanship. These cannot be reconciled with the notion of independently determined desires, for their central function is to create desires—to bring into being wants that previously did not exist. . . .Outlays for the manufacturing of a product are not more important in the strategy of modern business enterprise than outlays for the manufacturing of demand for the product. None of this is novel. All would be regarded as elementary by the most retarded student in the nation's most primitive school of business administration.[14]

Galbraith serves up the then-prevailing view of advertising. The implications of advertising and the large oligopolistic firms it produces is an industrialized sector in the economy, a *technostructure,* ever bent on hypnotizing society into purchasing its wares through advertising. Such a technostructure results in too many resources devoted to these activities and too few resources devoted to public activities or governmentally produced products and services. Further, according to Galbraith, the status quo will not be maintained by this process, but we will see the industrialized sector of the economy producing, over time, constantly rising proportions of gross national product. Galbraith's views about advertising, though more extreme, were and are consistent with the views of many contemporary academic scholars.

Traditional views on the economics of advertising are based pri-

13. John Kenneth Galbraith, *The Affluent Society* (Boston: Houghton Mifflin Co., 1958); Idem., *The New Industrial State* (Boston: Houghton Mifflin Co., 1967).
14. Galbraith, *The Affluent Society,* pp. 155–56.

marily upon the assertion that consumers, when confronted by advertising, react to it passively. Consumers are somehow persuaded by advertising (through some undescribed process) to be willing to pay a higher price for a product than would otherwise be the case. Firms advertise and consumers buy. As firms advertise more, consumers buy more. The end result of oligopoly, monopoly, and concentrated markets is higher prices and larger than normal profits.

CONCLUSION

In recent years we have observed government policies designed to exorcise advertising, or at least tame it, based on the mainstream traditional analysis. The Federal Trade Commission sets rules and regulations by which advertisers must play, and also enforces these rules through its own policing power. The Consumer Products Safety Commission was set up, in part, to help innocent consumers avoid unwise choices based upon persuasive advertising. The United Nations voted almost unanimously, the United States being the lone dissenter, to completely ban all advertising and promotion of infant formula in less-developed countries. Fraudulent advertising laws abound in the fifty states. While it is possible that some advertising regulation has had positive effects, an emerging view is that, in general, the traditional position is seriously flawed.

Advertising regulation as public policy has its basis in the traditional view of the economic theory of advertising—that advertising produces distortions and undesirable effects in markets. The problem is then one of the effectiveness of policy to achieve stated goals. Policy "effectiveness" also depends upon how accurately the traditional economic theory of advertising describes and predicts actual, real world economic phenomena.

Professor Galbraith and many other academics and policymakers are convinced of the accuracy of that view and of its applicability to public policy. As in any other field of research, the establishment of one set of views often leads to an antithesis, or to the development of a different set or collection of unified theories explaining and analyzing the same problem from a different perspective. And this is exactly what happened to the economics of advertising in the 1960s, 1970s, and early 1980s. A cohesive body of knowledge and research began to emerge that found its basis in the sovereign consumer. Galbraith himself challenged economists, relying on the refinements of Alfred Marshall's analysis. Said Galbraith: "This is not to say that the evidence affirming the dependence of wants on advertising has been entirely ignored. It is one reason why advertising has so long been regarded with such uneasiness by economists. *Here is something which cannot be accommodated easily to existing theory*" (italics added).[15]

Galbraith was correct. Economists had not rigorously integrated the theory of consumer behavior with advertising. Most economists accepted the traditional view of advertising and promotion in oligopoly and monopolistically competitive markets out of hand. Although advertising was not *easily* accommodated to existing theory, it was possible to do so and to obtain results and implications different from those of the traditional view. We now turn to new views which yield different implications about the manner in which consumers and owners of business firms behave in regard to advertising. Modern economic theory produces different conclusions concerning the impact of advertising on market processes, structure, prices, and profits. We call the new perspective the new neoclassical, modern, or positive economic rationale for advertising.

15. Ibid., pp. 156–57.

PART II

THE MODERN ECONOMIC RATIONALE FOR ADVERTISING

3

ENTRY BARRIERS, INFORMATION, AND THE RATIONAL CONSUMER

The economic assessment of advertising underwent enormous changes along with the rest of the discipline over the 1960s and the 1970s. A number of economists over recent decades reassessed the traditional and critical view of advertising which found little of economic value in the practice. The logical consistency and empirical (real world) validity of past thought on advertising was questioned but, more importantly, robust alternatives emerged. The present and following chapter assemble and develop the emerging economic rationale for advertising based upon a number of these new views.

THE EMERGING POSITIVE RESPONSE TO ADVERTISING'S CRITICS

The new neoclassical response to the traditional analysis of advertising is three-pronged. It relates to the so-called "passivity" of consumers, to the alleged incompatibility of advertising and competition, and to the development of models featuring the rational consumer.

First, a number of modern economists question whether consumers passively respond to advertising. Recall that in the traditional view, the consumer's reaction to the advertising messages of a firm is to increase the consumer's demand for the product or service advertised.

He or she is, after advertising, willing to pay a higher price for the commodity than before advertising. Modern economists take issue with such reasoning. The analyses are based upon a different theory of consumer behavior—that of the rational consumer. The *rational consumer* is an individual making self-interested choices or who makes choices that are expected to improve, or avoid the deterioration of, his or her own economic welfare. Within this view it is doubtful that rational consumers will respond zombie-like and in irrational fashion to television commercials with a willingness to pay higher prices for a given amount of an advertised product, given other considerations.

Developers of the positive position are working at the task that Galbraith considered difficult—the integration or reconciliation of concepts of the rational consumer and advertising. Is the existence of both logically consistent? Might advertising be explained on the basis of the consumer who consciously makes choices that attempt to improve his or her own economic welfare? An integration has been accomplished, and with it new and insightful economic implications of advertising are developing.

A second major view of the critics is challenged within the positive perspective—that advertising is inconsistent with competition. By depicting the consumer as a rational being, economists began the process of reconciling advertising with competition. They admit that advertising has no place in sterile and simplistic textbook models of perfect competition viewed as a situation. But the fact that advertising does not fit the characteristics or structure of *situational* pure or perfect competition does not prove or suggest that advertising indicates or supports monopolistic forms of market structure. When market functioning is viewed in process terms, advertising may be a force promoting competition or even an essential aspect of the competitive process. The existence of advertising may in fact be more logically consistent with competition than with monopoly or oligopoly when competition is viewed either as a process or even in more realistic "static" terms.

The third and most interesting aspect of the positive view is that its developers have fashioned new and alternative methods of analyzing advertising encompassing the consumer's importance as a rational economic actor. Great care, for example, has been given to describing and analyzing the rational consumer's choices and behavioral responses with regard to advertising. Does the consumer view all advertising in the same way or will different types of advertising have different effects? Were there new ways of looking at firms and their relationships to advertising?

Advertising, Demand Elasticity, and Competition

New neoclassical economists have gone to the core of traditional assertions about advertising. At the heart of the traditional approach is the assertion that advertising's incompatibility with competition meant that the economic tools of competition could not be used to analyze advertising. Overt rivalry (through advertising) was simply not a characteristic of competition in the situational sense. Hence, analyses of advertising gravitated towards market models of monopoly and oligopoly with the implied socially detrimental consequences. The early critique of this position is important, however, in that it brought these assertions into question by using the standard tools of economic analysis that produced the assertions in the first place.

A central implication of the critics, from Robinson forward, is that firms somehow make consumers less responsive (in terms of the amounts they purchase) or less sensitive to any given change in price through advertising. Thus, by advertising and lowering consumers' demand elasticity, the firm would be able to raise its price with a smaller drop in sales and larger profits than if it did not advertise. Since small demand elasticities were considered to be indicators of the degree of monopoly power, the conclusion is that advertising causes or creates monopoly power and its attendant economic problems. The key to this argument is that advertising *decreased* demand elasticity, i.e., reduced consumer sensitivity to price changes. Modern economic analysis questions this proposition.

New neoclassicals return to the basic principles of economics and note that one of the factors influencing consumer price sensitivity to a service or product is the number of other services or products that will substitute for it. If there is a relatively large number of substitutes available for some product, then an increase in its price will result in consumers shifting their purchases away from the good and buying substitute products instead. Consumers will be more sensitive to the product whose price has risen, and reduce purchases substantially. In this case the elasticity of demand will be relatively large. If advertising is a widespread phenomenon within an industry, and if people are acting in their own self-interest, then the possibility emerges that advertising may be making consumers aware of the fact that there are other similar products (substitute goods) available to them in the marketplace. Advertisers, within any given industry, also make consumers aware that substitute products are different to some extent. Far from making consumers unresponsive to price changes, advertising provides consumers with knowledge of other products which provides them with the real opportunity to be *more* sensitive to price changes.

Many modern economists assert that advertising can, at worst, leave consumers equally as sensitive to price changes as they would be in the absence of advertising. Advertising therefore may be perceived as a factor which actually increases demand elasticities, making industries more competitive than would otherwise be the case. With industries being pushed toward competition via advertising, lower prices, lower profits, more output, and less concentration could be expected. The primary point is that advertising, far from being an anticompetitive tool, as asserted by many traditional writers, may in fact be one of the essential forces pushing firms and industries in competitive directions.

Advertising and Entry Barriers

The criticism that advertising is a barrier to entry into industries has come under close scrutiny. The notion that advertising is a barrier arose only by viewing the consumer as one who is heavily influenced by advertising, but influenced in a manner which may not be to his or her benefit. The assertion that a firm "can resort to advertising and other devices which attach customers more firmly to itself," as Robinson believed,[1] evolved into the notion that advertising messages produce a type of "inertia" on the part of the consumer. Inertia, in this sense, means that the consumer would be unresponsive to the advertisements of other firms, thereby preventing or impeding the entry of new firms into the industry.

This analysis begs the question, however. Why would consumers become attached to one firm's product through the firm's advertising but remain impervious to the advertising of firms considering or con-

---

1. Joan Robinson, *Economics of Imperfect Competition* (London: Macmillan and Co., 1933), p. 101.

templating entering an industry? The notions of consumer inertia and attachment are logically inconsistent. One answer to this question couched in terms of the new neoclassical analysis is suggested by economists Richard Schmalensee (1982) and Keith Leffler (1981).[2]

First-mover advantages can accrue to the first firm in a market. Some advantages can occur with or without advertising, as Schmalensee observes. Leffler considers markets in which the first firm in the market has used advertising to provide consumers with information about a product. Over time, consumers, through purchase and use of the product induced in part by the information content of the first-mover's advertising, provide the first-mover with a large market share, sales, and perhaps profits. The informative advertising and resultant consumer purchases result in consumer experience with and knowledge of the good or service. Thus, even though potential entrants have the same tools of advertising and information provision available to them as does the first-mover, they may face difficulty entering the market. Their advertising *cum* information must induce consumers to switch from the first-mover's product. Yet consumers have gained experience or accumulated a large stock of knowledge about the first-mover's good (qualities, prices, locations, etc.) Potential entrants may find it costlier to enter and stay in a market than the first-mover or the pioneer. Both of these conclusions, however, arise from a treatment of the consumer as an efficient processor of information, making choices to use, use in part, or to ignore (not use) new information. Whether advertising produces an entry barrier or a higher cost of entry to potential entrants is, in no small part, a matter of semantics. Of more importance are the effects advertising has on the economic welfare of consumers.[3]

A recent empirical study puts the issue of advertising, entry barriers, and consumer welfare into sharper focus. Ioannis Kessides examines the mechanisms through which advertising in a market can

---

2. Richard Schmalensee, "Product Differentiation Advantages of Pioneering Brands," *American Economic Review* 72 (1982): 349–65; Keith B. Leffler, "Persuasion or Information? The Economics of Prescription Drug Advertising," *Journal of Law and Economics* 24 (1981): 45–74.

3. Leffler concludes that even when first-movers gain market power through informative advertising, consumers are the net beneficiaries of the advertising. This is so because advertising, if it increases sales, must do so by *at least* reducing what is known as the "full price" to the consumer. We develop a detailed description of the notion of "full price" later in this chapter.

affect entry decisions, apart from any considerations of consumer inertia (brand loyalty) or economies of scale.[4] Kessides suggests that in some markets, entrants must achieve a given level of consumer recognition through advertising in order to successfully penetrate the market. That is, there are start-up advertising costs associated with entry. Kessides also recognizes that not every entrant is successful and that the decision to enter a market is accompanied by the risk of a failed effort. These two facts, taken together, produce, in Kessides' view, an advertising-related entry barrier in the following fashion.

Initial advertising expenditures may be viewed as the purchase of productive capital by the firm, much like the purchase of buildings or machines. In the event of an unsuccessful entry attempt (a failure), buildings and machines have positive salvage value, but none of the goodwill or information generated by initial advertising expenditures may be salvaged or resold to other entrepreneurs. For firms already in the market, these costs are "sunk" or bygones that do not influence their activity. An advertising cost wedge, so to speak, exists between incumbent firms and potential entrants, with the cost advantage to incumbents. The greater inherent riskiness of newer versus older established products, coupled with the fact that "advertising capital" is nonsalvageable in the event of failure, produces an entry barrier. The barrier is the perceived higher cost (until, and if, the brand becomes established) of doing business on the part of potential entrants. In this view advertising entry barriers stem from the unique, nonsalvageable nature of the start-up advertising expenditures (in the event of failure), presumably resulting in an entry rate lower than what would exist in the absence of such costs.

Kessides' research illuminates the semantic nature of the term "entry barrier" as it is used in connection with advertising. In this view, the *existence* of advertising itself does not prevent entry. However, *one* of the characteristics of "advertising capital" raises the expected, perceived costs of entering and can therefore reduce entry from what it would be if advertising capital were salvageable. This, however, seems to be a socially unavoidable cost of doing business. In the event of failure, firms must also make nonsalvageable investments in employee training. Are these also entry barriers? We argue that the act

---

4. Ioannis N. Kessides, "Advertising, Sunk Costs, and Barriers to Entry," *Review of Economics and Statistics* 68 (1986): 84–95.

of entering an industry is not costless and that identifying these costs is a useful research endeavor. We also argue that advertising *per se* does not erect an entry barrier.

Kessides has shown *how* one unique characteristic of advertising capital produces an unavoidable fact of economic life, and that the act of entering an industry can exhaust resources. Entry will be reduced or less rapid than it would be were these costs not present. But these costs do exist, just as physical capital and employee training costs exist. As such, is advertising properly characterized as an entry barrier or should we appropriately recognize the nature of particular aspects of advertising? By taking the latter route, Kessides appears to move the analysis of advertising in fruitful directions.

Kessides finds that, on balance, the effect of advertising in reducing the risk of failure more than outweighs the above-mentioned entry cost effects. That is, in industries where advertising plays an important role, its *overall* impact is to facilitate, not to bar, entry. In fact, most positive writers argue that advertising, in general, would not be a barrier but a means or method of entry into a line of business. As firms advertise products to make consumers aware of the fact that new, competing products exist, advertising facilitates and lubricates the process of entry rather than impedes it. Even further, some economists (e.g., Telser[5]), following this line of argument, suggest that it is not advertising that produces higher cost products, but government prohibitions and limitations placed on industries' and firms' advertising that *creates* the inefficient production of goods and services. Advertising prohibitions, argues Yale Brozen, make it even more costly for firms to let consumers know that a new supplier is in the market.[6] Firms must then resort to other, more costly, methods of conveying information to consumers. It is likely that the prices of products would be even higher without advertising than with it.

Economies of Scale

Contemporary economists also question whether economies of scale in advertising create an entry barrier, i.e., whether the ability to ad-

---

5. Lester G. Telser, "Advertising and Competition," *Journal of Political Economy* 72 (1964): 537–62.

6. Yale Brozen, "Competition, Efficiency, and Antitrust," *The Competitive Economy* (Morristown, N.J.: General Learning Press, 1975).

vertise on a large scale at a relatively low average cost prevents new firms from entering an industry and competing away profits. In this view, new firms are faced with higher per unit of sales costs of advertising than older, established firms in the industry and are thereby prevented from entering and competing with older firms. This notion was attacked by George Stigler in defining open entry: "Free entry . . . may be defined as the condition that long-run costs of new firms if they enter the industry will be equal to those of firms already in the industry. This does not mean, as many infer, that a new firm can enter and immediately be as profitable as an established firm. We do not begrudge the new firm a decent interval in which to build its factory; we should be equally willing to concede a period during which production is put on a smooth-running schedule, trade connections are developed, labor is recruited and trained, and the like. These costs of building up a going business are legitimate investment expenses, and, unless historical changes take place in the market, they must be equal for both established and new firms."[7] Although this definition is inadequate, it will do if we exclude from long-run costs the capitalized value of such legal privileges as being allowed to have a utility franchise, a tobacco acreage allotment or marketing certificate, a certificate of public convenience and necessity, or one or several of a limited number of taxicab or liquor store licenses or bank charters.

Stigler's view is that it may indeed take time for a new firm in an industry to discover and build the best size of its plant, to organize itself in the most efficient manner, and to bear all the start-up costs of a business that are necessary to make it a going concern (including its advertising plan). A firm may have to suffer losses for a while after its initial entry into an industry, just as the established, existing firm may, and probably did, bear the same cost in its infancy. These economies of scale, either in advertising itself or because of advertising, cannot be viewed as preventing entry over the long term. Even if it were the case that a potential entrant could not produce at as low a per-unit cost as the existing firm, or advertise at as low a per-unit cost, we still could not label economies of scale as entry barriers since they do not *bar* entry of capable, efficient firms from an industry. This is a seemingly subtle point. There is more than a semantic dif-

---

7. George Stigler, "Monopoly and Oligopoly by Merger," *American Economic Review* 50 (1960): 27.

ference between a true entry barrier and the cost of entering an industry. The former *prevents* entry and the latter is always part of the entry process. Consider the following example.

Suppose that John and Gwen decided that they wanted to become professional singers, i.e., that they wished to enter the industry. Neither of them are very good singers. No one, in fact, would hesitate to judge them as poor, if not downright terrible singers. They would not be able to "produce" the same quality and quantity of "output" that a world-famous opera tenor or even the average nightclub singer could produce. They would not survive the market test of an "efficient firm" in this "industry" and would never be offered a role performing with the Metropolitan Opera or at Caesar's Palace in Las Vegas.

The point is that the existence of other vocalists infinitely more skilled at singing does not, in and of itself, eliminate or remove the opportunity to attempt to enter this industry. John and Gwen are not barred from entering the singing industry by the existence of better, more talented singers. They are especially not prevented from entering by the fact that singers hire agents to advertise their services and that nightclubs and opera companies advertise singers' appearances. They are not barred from entering this industry *by* anything. They *do not* enter, however, because they know they cannot produce a given quality output as efficiently as others can. There is nothing that existing singers are doing, including advertising, that establishes an *entry barrier* into this profession. The mere fact that the market weeds out inefficient (bad) performers is in line with what one would expect in an efficient market.

Could we expect that if Gwen and John were promising singers (who require only voice coaching or advice on how to stage a performance to bring them up to "star" caliber), they would be prevented from entering this industry because existing performers' skills and services are advertised? It is most unlikely. This reasoning is the thrust of Stigler's argument. The possibility of economies of scale in, or due to, advertising is not questioned. Stigler attacked the assertion that economies of scale, arising from whatever source, bar entry into product lines in a permanent fashion.

The conclusion that advertising is not an entry barrier has also been applied by modern positive economists to the concentration issue mentioned earlier. They reason that if advertising is not an entry barrier, then there is no reason to suspect that advertising *causes* concentration in industries, or a high degree of monopoly power in an industry. In this view, advertising, rivalry, and competition are all consistent with one another. Perhaps these sentiments are best represented by Yale Brozen who, speaking in reference to Robinson, states: "[S]he [Robinson] seizes on any action by firms such as . . . advertising and asserts that these acts are *the* anticompetitive forces which bring about this unnatural state of affairs. In this, she has followed the same path trod by the Antitrust Division and the Federal Trade Commission. Both have designated competitive actions as monopoly actions. Economists have joined this game and have come to believe that upside down is rightside up almost as frequently as the enforcers of antitrust law. They have been asserting for the last three decades that such means of entry such as . . . advertising are barriers."[8]

ADVERTISING AND CONSUMER INFORMATION: A MODERN APPROACH

The foundation of the modern defense of advertising is the analysis of the individual consumer. (Economists do not seek to represent the behavior of any specific consumer, but to set out general principles that describe and predict how a "representative" or average consumer will make choices.) The questioning of basic consumer behavior with regard to advertising had as its impetus one critical question: *Do consumers make choices in such a way so as to yield them the expected largest benefit?* More succinctly, do consumers, by and large, act and make choices in their own self-interest? Contemporary positive economists examine advertising and the consumer by assuming that consumers do in fact act in a rational manner. It is this assumption, for the most part, that produces the radically different explanations and predictions of the causes and effects of advertising on economic activity than those of traditional analysis.

The first question relates to the assertion that advertising forms tastes and preferences of consumers in favor of the product advertised. The general criticism of this notion was that economics does not, as a scientific body, address the question of how tastes and preferences are formed. This area is the realm of the sociologists, psychologists, and psychiatrists. If economics cannot answer the question of how

---

8. Yale Brozen, "Is Advertising a Barrier to Entry?" in *Advertising and Society* (New York: New York University Press, 1974), pp. 81–82.

tastes are formed, how can it hope to explain why they change, or predict when they will change, or even observe that tastes and preferences have indeed changed? Changes in behavior or choices of individuals may be observed, but to attribute this change in behavior to a change in tastes is a fruitless exercise at this stage of economists' knowledge of "taste development." This is so because any and every change in behavior may be explained on the basis of a change in tastes of the consumer. Further, if *everything* can be explained on the basis of taste changes, then nothing is explained. Even worse, if there is no set of principles that predict taste changes, how can the effect of certain proposed policies be predicted? We do not agree, of course, that taste changes are irrelevant in describing behavior related to advertising. It is simply the case, rather, that a primitive knowledge of factors affecting taste changes leaves large holes in the economic analysis of advertising.

Many contemporary writers reason as follows: Given that economists cannot, at present, observe and measure tastes (or their changes), assume that consumers do have a set of tastes and preferences that stay relatively constant, and focus attention on those factors of the economic environment which appear to influence decisionmaking and choices that we *can* observe, i.e., those that will have a definite, logical impact on the consumer.[9] With the reliance on consumer tastes held in abeyance, the analysis of advertising is driven in a different direction.

The reasoning behind the early analyses of Robinson, Bain, Galbraith, Comanor and Wilson, and others (the traditionalists) was that the theory of competition assumed *perfect information* on the part of both firms and consumers, and that advertising would be superfluous. Since advertising did not fit in as an expected characteristic of a competitive market to these analysts, any industry in which advertising was observed could not be deemed a competitive market and was therefore classified and analyzed as an imperfect market, an oligopoly, a monopoly, or some form other than a competitive market. The analysis focused on how firms and industries (noncompetitive firms and industries) behave, assuming that their advertising played on the tastes of the nonrational consumer.

9. Modern development of a "household production function" is an attempt to confine the "problem" of taste change. See, e.g., George Stigler and Gary S. Becker, "De Gustibus Non Est Disputandum," *American Economic Review* 67 (1977): 76–90.

Positive theorists take a different approach to the problem. They are aware that advertising is not a characteristic one would expect to find in perfect competition where perfect knowledge abounds. But their response is not to deny the possibility that industries could in fact be competitive if firms advertised. They argue that we do not want to be as concerned with whether or not theories and the economic agents they represent (firms, consumers) both possess the same characteristics, but rather that the deeper concern lies in whether or not theories accurately describe and explain behavior and can logically predict behavior on the basis of current knowledge.

Traditional writers argued that advertising was inconsistent with perfect competition and its assumption of perfect knowledge. New neoclassical economists, rather than concluding that competition cannot coexist with advertising, asked the slightly different question of whether or not advertising could exist in an industry that was competitive. That is, does the existence of advertising deny the possibility of competition? A key to answering this question lies in whether the consumer is viewed as manipulated by advertisers, or as a rational consumer making self-interested choices on the basis of available information.

The answer also depends upon one's view and definition of competition. Competition may be alternatively defined as a *situation* premised upon certain conditions such as large numbers of buyers and sellers, perfect knowledge, etc., or as a *process* of rivalrous behavior. In this latter conception, largely developed by contemporary Austrian economists, perfect knowledge and information is not assumed.[10] In this more modern view, rivalrous, that is, competitive, behavior takes place through time as entrepreneurs and firms enter and exit markets. In this conception of the economic process, entrepreneurs and the rational consumer behave in a more realistic world where information and knowledge is imperfect. Eliminating the assumption of perfect (or costless) information and knowledge does not lead to consumer inaction, monopoly, and anticompetitive practices, but to a new, remodeled, and more descriptive theory of consumer behavior and competitive markets.

10. See, e.g., Israel Kirzner, *Competition and Entrepreneurship* (Chicago: University of Chicago Press, 1973), and "Advertising," in Tibor R. Machan, ed., *The Libertarian Alternative* (Chicago: Nelson-Hall, 1974).

Stigler's View

George Stigler's study of the economics of information produced insightful contemporary research on the analysis of advertising.[11] Stigler formally recognizes one obvious fact of life in this early contribution: Knowledge *is* power. Stigler recognized that, for any particular product (in general), one could observe different prices within any given geographical market area. While traditional economists accepted price dispersion (a set of different prices for the same product at different locations) as evidence supporting a noncompetitive market for the product, Stigler took a different path. He viewed the existence of price dispersion as evidence of the existence of ignorance on the part of consumers. By ignorance, Stigler does not imply stupidity on the part of consumers, but merely the fact that they are unaware of prices charged by some sellers or that they do not have full and complete information about the price distribution offered by sellers. If consumers did have complete price information, they would buy from the seller offering the lowest price, forcing other sellers to lower their prices—the competitive *process* at work.

To Stigler, moreover, the existence of this price dispersion did *not* imply a noncompetitive market. The question leading to this conclusion was how and why can these price dispersions exist in the first place if we view the consumer as one who attempts to make self-interested choices? Further, how can price dispersions persist over time? The answer is clear and simple to any consumer who has ever made a purchase: *The acquisition of information or knowledge about prices is costly.* Consumers want price information because they are rational, but something must be sacrificed in order to obtain price information.

In a simple framework, we can enumerate the costs consumers bear in searching for lower prices in terms of gasoline used in driving while looking for the lowest price. But the major costs of consumer search are usually time costs. That is, in order for the consumer to spend precious, scarce time (even the wealthiest among us only have twenty-four hours in a day) in searching for a product, he or she must not

11. George Stigler, "The Economics of Information," in *The Organization of Industry* (Homewood, Ill.: Richard D. Irwin, Inc., 1968).

be spending time either working and earning an income or enjoying leisure. We may then measure the costs consumers bear while searching for lower prices as the value of commodities (gas, tires, etc.) that are sacrificed in order to search and the value of time (the foregone income, the value to the consumer of foregone leisure) that is sacrificed. There are real costs consumers face in obtaining price and other relevant information, just as there are real costs consumers face in obtaining any other type of scarce economic resource.

Given that the search for low prices is costly, why does the rational consumer search? The answer is obvious: There are benefits to the consumer to search. And like the costs of search, the benefits to search are real and may be measured and enumerated. The benefits consumers expect from search, given all other factors, reduce to discovering a lower price for the product than the best price currently known by the consumer. Benefits and costs of consumer search explain why price distributions exist, *and the amount and limits of price dispersion.* In terms of positive economic analysis, one would not expect to see a uniform price for a product in a competitive industry.

Calculating the Costs and Benefits of Consumer Search

A contemporary model of consumer choice is revealing in this regard. In deciding how much of a product to consume or choose, or how much of any activity to engage in, the consumer will equate the marginal benefits accruing from additional units of the activity to the marginal cost of additional units of the activity in order to maximize the *net* benefit of the activity. Consider Figure 3–1, in which the marginal cost of searching for lower prices is represented by the line labeled MC_S. To simplify, assume the marginal cost of search to be constant for any amount of search, with search time measured on the horizontal axis. The additional cost of the tenth search, for example, is the same as the additional cost of the ninth search or the eleventh search or the twentieth search. Perhaps an additional search takes one hour, with the marginal cost of the search then equal to the consumer's wage rate (the income given up in order to engage in search).

The additional benefits obtained through more search decrease as the amount of search increases. Benefit to the consumer from search consists in finding a price lower than the lowest one currently known. Generally there will be some "lowest" price in the market reflecting

Figure 3–1.   Graphic Explanation of Optimal Consumer Search

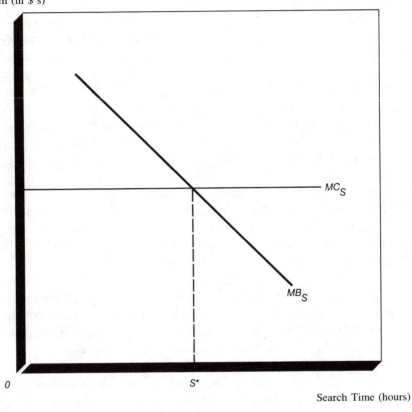

Marginal Cost &
Marginal Benefit of
Search (in $'s)

Search Time (hours)

the cost of producing the good. Then, as the consumer searches more and more, the prices he uncovers become closer and closer to this minimum price, and the *reduction* in price (MB$_S$) the consumer can expect from one more search gets smaller and smaller, or the marginal benefits decrease as the amount of search increases. In Figure 3–1, the "optimal" amount of search for this representative, rational consumer is shown as S*. Search time greater than S* yields fewer additional benefits in comparison with the additional costs—with welfare losses to the consumer. Additional search would be simply "not worth it." Search time less than S* yields additional benefits greater than additional costs, which would "pay" the consumer to search more. Thus, S* is the optimal amount of search to undertake for a consumer to maximize his or her own economic welfare.

Where then does advertising fit into all this? Very simply, the consumer may be viewed as being faced with two alternative methods of acquiring information about prices, through search or through advertising. A diagram similar to Figure 3–1 helps explain how price advertising affects consumer search. Suppose MC_S for this consumer is five dollars. One additional search (one hour) involves giving up five dollars worth of income. Let MB_S represent the marginal benefit to search *assuming that the consumer knows nothing* about existing prices. The optimal amount of search time for this consumer is then seven hours in Figure 3–2 ($MC_S = MB_S$).

Suppose, alternatively, that the consumer originally had knowledge of some (but not all) prices charged by some sellers and that the information was obtained through newspaper advertising. With such information the consumer cannot expect to find price differentials as large through search as in the first case because he already *knows* some prices from advertisements. Therefore, the additional benefit to any given amount of search (in terms of finding price reductions) is less in the second case where the consumer had price information. Marginal benefits to search in this second case may be depicted as MB_S', reflecting the fact that for any given amount of search time, additional benefits to search are less if consumers have some information ahead of time. The existence of advertising *reduces* the amount of time consumers spend in searching for lower prices. If consumers spend less time searching for lower prices, they necessarily have more time left over to devote to other, more desirable activities such as earning income (working) or enjoying leisure (consuming time).

The analysis of consumer search results in the consumer paying a certain number of dollars for the good or service in question, once optimal search uncovered the acceptable price. Obviously, this number of dollars, or what economists call a "money price," constitutes one part of the consumer's sacrifice in obtaining the good.

There is, however, for most purchases, a second sacrifice. In the example described in Figure 3–2, we show a consumer with a five dollars per hour time cost searching seven hours to find an optimal

Figure 3–2.   Effect of Advertising on Optimal Consumer Search.

Marginal Cost &
Marginal Benefit of
Search (in $'s)

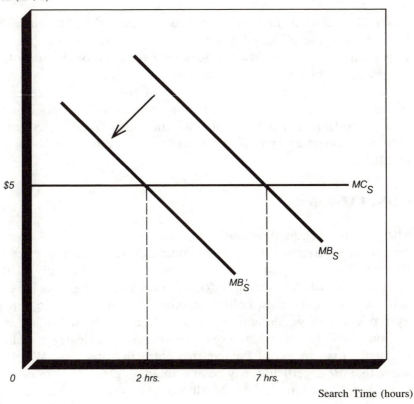

money price of a good, say $200. The total cost of this purchase, in an economic sense, is then the $200 money price *plus* the thirty-five dollars (five dollars per hour times seven hours of search) in search costs. The total of $235 represents the *full price* of the good or service purchased. Full price is the total value of resources sacrificed by a consumer (money price plus time costs) associated with the purchase of one unit of a good.

Full price (or at least the full price consumers expect to pay) is the relevant variable upon which consumers base purchase decisions. Money price may be relatively more important than time costs in some cases for some consumers, but this fact does not mean that full price is not the correct economic measure of resources sacrificed for a good or service.

We have argued (and will continue to argue) that, in general, advertising has the effect of lowering prices in the marketplace. The important point is that lower prices may occur through *either* lower money prices or lower time costs associated with the act of purchase, or both. We may expect certain kinds of advertising to lower both money price and time costs, while other modes reduce only one measure of cost. In either situation, the full price faced by consumers falls. Subsequent chapters focus on advertising's effects on both money and full prices.[12]

CONCLUSION

The present chapter develops a role for advertising based upon the microanalytic logic of the rational consumer acting in his or her self-interest. The basic point is that advertising is a commodity that, in general, provides information. Information as advertising, like ice cream and home computers, is both demanded by consumers and supplied by producers of goods and services. In the role of providing information about products, moreover, advertising (at least on balance) facilitates the process of competitive entry into markets. We do not argue that *all* advertising may be explained on grounds of information provision (for example, the Marlboro Man and Ronald McDonald convey no price information at all) or that advertising does not comprise a cost (sometimes a significant cost) of entering markets. Our purpose in the present chapter has simply been to underline the point that the modern theory of consumer behavior provides solid ground for an important role for advertising in the process of competition and the generation of consumer benefits. Chapter 4 expands upon the im-

---

12. A similar analysis could be developed by examining consumer search across a market of nearly homogeneous but "differentiated" products in order to find the best quality product relative to the price. The same principles that we have applied to price search would apply to quality search. There is not only a demand for price information, but also for quality information, and both types of information are provided, in part, through advertising. Costs of "misleading" or fraudulent advertising will be addressed in Chapter 8.

plications of rationality and problems related to information in understanding the dynamics and efficiency of contemporary competitive
systems.

4

INFORMATION AND COMPETITIVE MARKET STRUCTURE

The key to understanding the modern analysis of advertising is to understand its functions as a purveyor of messages and information. It is important to distinguish between advertisements that provide specific information and those that might be termed noninformational "messages." Specific information related to price, physical characteristics, or other attributes of services or products are obviously information-providing. Other less valuable "messages" (the Marlboro Man, Ronald McDonald) are generally perceived to provide no information about services or products, although they may still be welfare-enhancing and "informational" in a broader sense and, importantly, also have a role to play in the competitive process. The twofold purpose of the present chapter is to expand and explore the implications of the economics of information-provision for application later to such matters as fraud in the sale of various kinds of goods, and to show how advertising as a provider of information and messages is a *tool* of the competitive process.

DOES ADVERTISING PROVIDE INFORMATION EFFICIENTLY?

The demand for information has a number of important implications, many of which were discovered in early and important papers by No-

57

bel laureate Frederick Hayek.[1] How, for example, can one be sure that advertising conveys information to consumers in the most efficient, or least costly, manner? The answer is that, in some instances, it may not. There may be certain types of commodities and services (the stocks and bonds of corporations, for example) for which a substitute for advertising has arisen in the market (i.e., organized trading exchanges or locations, such as the New York Stock Exchange, or Chicago Board of Trade). There are, in all likelihood, relatively few buyers in relation to the medium that would circulate advertising for these instruments.

A similar device that develops in a market is a specialized trader. The specialized trader merely provides the service of connecting buyers and sellers of goods. A used car dealer is a prime example. However, in a competitive market system economy where transactions are *voluntary* exchanges at mutually agreed upon prices, any method of information transfer that evolves into continuous use (central trading houses, specialists, or advertising) by the unimpeded market generally will be the least cost/most efficient method. If the method were not efficient the arrangement would not last for long since it would be profitable for entrepreneurs to suggest and implement more efficient methods of information provision. Since advertising is the most frequently used of the above three methods, it may be concluded that, for most goods, it is the most efficient method we have for conveying the types of information advertising conveys.

An important question immediately arises. Why would any individual firm wish to advertise its prices and qualities simply to benefit consumers? The objective of firm owners is not to make economic life comfortable for consumers, especially if doing so involves spending firm resources. Firms seek to produce and sell output at a price that maximizes profits. Why would firms want consumers to have price information? It does not seem plausible that firms would be willing to supply information that would *lower* prices. The answer may be found in an individual firm's incentives to advertise.

One answer has been encountered already—that firms advertise to attach buyers to their products or, as Galbraith might suggest, to twist our wants and desires or to reshape our psyche in favor of a particular

---

1. Fredrich A. Hayek, "Economics and Knowledge," *Economica* 4 (1937): 33–54; Idem., "The Use of Knowledge in Society," *American Economic Review* 34 (1945): 519–33.

good. We believe that more logical explanations can be offered. Firms do not conduct business because they wish to raise the economic welfare of consumers. They seek profits, but in order to make profits, output must be sold. In a market economy, where the government does not divide up the consumer population and assign each consumer one and only one firm with which he or she can trade, it is in the interest of profit-maximizing firms to let consumers know that they exist, that they sell a particular good, and at what price or prices they stand ready to sell. Advertising certainly performs these functions, no matter whatever else it is asserted to do. This is especially the case in markets in which there is a high rate of buyer turnover, in which new buyers enter the market and old buyers leave with a high frequency.

Additionally, it may be reasonable to expect that the more a firm advertises, the more likely it is to contact consumers who were previously unaware of its existence or its prices, with possibly greater ensuing sales. There are benefits from advertising its product for any individual firm, but this does not imply that consumers' tastes are changed by advertising, or that advertising creates less price sensitivity among consumers in their purchases (reduces demand elasticity). The notion of advertising reducing consumer price sensitivity for a product is even more suspect when one recognizes that the firm's competitors are also providing consumer information through advertising.

It is sometimes useful to view advertising supplied by firms as part of the product itself. After all, firms do supply the goods and services consumers demand. It is doubtful that anyone objects to Hershey's selling wrappers with chocolate bars. The wrapper is part of the product. Consumers of chocolate want wrappers and are willing to pay for them if it benefits them. So too with advertising, only in a somewhat indirect fashion. Additional information about a product may be viewed as part of the product. Whether or not advertising by firms *causes* higher market prices is not the central issue. The important point is that observable, logical reasons exist why consumers want advertising and suppliers are willing to produce it.

Some socially beneficial common ground between the opposing forces of greedy sellers and greedy buyers may now be acknowledged. First, the total effort that consumers devote to information gathering can be reduced tremendously with the institution of advertising. An inexpensive method of gathering information has been substituted for an expensive method, freeing some of society's resources for other productive uses. On a much smaller scale, with a free market for advertising, we can be sure that advertising will not be free. Scarce economic resources must be used to convey information between parties. Firms have every incentive to place information or messages that are of the highest valued use to consumers in advertisements, for the goal is to attract buyers. Rational buyers will want what they feel to be their most valuable or highest valued information. Firms desire the greatest quantity of information conveyed, in general, for the advertising dollar. As Professor Stigler has noted: "Ignorance is like sub-zero weather: by a sufficient expenditure its effects upon people can be kept within tolerable or even comfortable bounds, but it would be wholly uneconomic entirely to eliminate all its effects. And, just as an analysis of man's shelter and apparel would be somewhat incomplete if cold weather is ignored, so also our understanding of economic life will be incomplete if we do not systematically take account of the cold winds of ignorance."[2]

SEARCH, EXPERIENCE, AND CREDENCE GOODS

Stigler's groundbreaking work on price search and on the theory of advertising as information provides a foundation for refinements of advertising theory as it relates to consumer behavior. Economist Phillip Nelson, for example, focused on a number of issues pertaining to how consumers behave in response to advertising and the implications and consequences of these responses for society.[3]

Nelson questioned the validity of theories concerning how advertising affects tastes. While rejecting the "changes in tastes" explanation, he raised important and provocative issues concerning the economics of advertising. First, it is a simple fact of life that tastes and preferences are not identical for all individuals. Tastes differ between people. (Bob is in hog heaven with pickled herring, while Mary could live life very well without it!) The very fact that tastes do differ among individuals leads to an important observation: Any product or

---

2. George Stigler, "The Economics of Information," in *the Organization of Industry* (Homewood, Ill.: Richard D. Irwin, Inc., 1968), p. 188.

3. Phillip Nelson, "Information and Consumer Behavior," *Journal of Political Economy* 78 (1970): 311–29; Idem., "Advertising as Information," *Journal of Political Economy* 82 (1974): 729–54.

service with a given set of physical characteristics is not necessarily subjectively valued the same by all consumers.

Richard and Sally may place a different valuation on smoked Virginia ham than would a devout Moslem, but the three of them would still be considering the very same ham. The physical quality of the ham is the same to all, yet the subjective valuations of that physical quality are different. Recognizing this fact makes individuals less prone to leap beyond the bounds of economic analysis to regard one set of tastes (or a change in tastes) as "bad" and some other set as "good."

The possibility of advertising-induced changes in tastes (supposedly for the "worse") has been discussed, but another possibility arises. Let us assume that consumers are rational and that they make choices in their (expected) best interest, and agree, for the moment, with the notion that advertising does change tastes. Is it not reasonable to conclude that by making the choice to confront advertising, consumers are actually *choosing* to have their tastes changed? Advertising can be easily avoided at low cost. Individuals can choose *not* to watch commercial television, or to ignore commercials, if they so desire. They can cheaply skip over ads in newspapers and look away from billboards. Or perhaps rational consumers are not choosing to have their tastes changed by confronting advertising but are, instead, expanding their horizons of methods available to satisfy their wants and desires. These hypotheses stand up as well, if not better, to the assault of those who argue that advertising merely changes tastes in some as yet unexplained fashion.

The theory of consumer search for low prices and advertising as information can also be used to explain quality discovery by consumers. Nelson addresses the issue in the same general manner as Stigler: Consumers are presumed to act in their own self-interest and advertising can be considered information that the consumer uses, along with other factors, in making decisions or choices. The problems faced by the consumer in this framework are different in kind than if the consumer were simply engaged in price search. Information about the quality of goods is more difficult (expensive) to obtain, in most cases, than is price information. Quality, whether it is measured by physical attributes or the subjective evaluation of physical attributes, is often discovered only *after* the sale while price is known with certainty *before* the transaction takes place. The problem for the consumer is one of authenticating quality. This means that all goods and services satisfying consumer wants may be categorized by characteristics. Consider, at the outset, only two categories in the taxonomy of goods characteristics: search goods and experience goods.[4]

Search Goods

Search goods are goods whose qualities can be determined prior to purchase. One can easily discern the intrinsic characteristics or qualities of a notepad or an umbrella before actually purchasing either item, and it is in this area that consumers have the greatest degree of market power. The advertising of quality characteristics of search goods is very easily (cheaply) authenticated by consumers. Advertisers of search goods have very little incentive to mislead consumers in the quality information they convey via advertising since actual purchases are made on the basis of observed, verifiable quality characteristics.

Sellers advertising beach umbrellas would find it difficult, if not impossible, to sell *ordinary* umbrellas to consumers expecting to find the *quality* beach umbrellas mentioned in the advertisement. Nonetheless, some misleading advertising of search goods might be expected. It may be the case that some qualities are better exaggerated in advertising than other qualities. The "sophistication" of a restaurant provides an example. Sophistication, like beauty, is in the subjective eye of the individual beholder. Even so, it may be the case that the cost of searching for a higher level of sophistication is fairly high, and that the firm has benefited from conveying misleading or false information via advertising of a search good.

An incentive does exist for providing misleading information to consumers in the case of search goods. Misleading advertising can be extremely costly to the producers, however, and strong incentives also exist to provide information about quality as accurately as possible. First, consumers obtain information not only from advertising, but also from one another, friends, and relatives, and a reputation for dispersing misleading information is certainly no asset to a business. Bad news travels fast, and the credibility of the seller would be adversely affected. Second, for some search goods there are costs involved in processing non-buying customers attracted with inaccurate

---

4. More properly, search and experience *components* characterize goods so that some goods may contain degrees of both components. We maintain, for simplicity, the fiction that all goods are either search or experience goods.

information. The real estate agent who advertises a modern home in a pastoral setting and shows customers a shack under a train trestle will have wasted costly time and gas on the trip. Finally, if repeat purchases are frequent, any future misleading information produced by the seller with advertising will be ignored by consumers. Should the content of the advertisements be changed, the new information will in all likelihood be heavily discounted. Thus, while some incentive exists to mislead consumers in search goods' markets, it appears that the costs of misleading far outweigh the benefits.

It is difficult to imagine consumers being made worse off by quality advertising for search goods. This form of information production has positive real value to the consumer in that it permits the consumer to conserve resources that would otherwise be devoted to discovering or uncovering information. Hence, rational consumers will demand the advertising of quality for these types of goods. *Choosing* to confront advertising and to make decisions on the basis of the chosen and easily authenticated information is a more reasonable way to view advertising of quality characteristics than concentrating upon subtle psychological alterations of consumers' tastes.

Experience Goods

Another general category of goods are those whose qualities and characteristics can be discovered *only after* the actual purchase of the good has occurred. These goods are called experience goods since the consumer must "experience" or sample them in order to ascertain either intrinsic quality or quality as subjectively perceived. Advertising of the qualities of experience goods provides the consumer with a kind of information, though the authenticity of the information is harder (more costly) to assess than in the case of search goods. But this difficulty *does not* imply that experience goods advertising ceases to be a form of information to consumers, for we may now distinguish between two different types or kinds of information, *direct and indirect*.

Direct information of quality, and therefore advertising of quality, appears more prevalent in search goods (e.g., seventeen-inch color television screens), but is a relatively small part of experience goods advertising. This is the case because direct information on experience goods is of relatively low value to consumers if the advertising is geared to providing quality information ("come and see our six-ounce cans of tuna fish!").[5] But where, then, is the informational content of indirect information in advertisements that extol brands of goods as "best" among brands, as "tastiest," as "most effective," *ad infinitum*? The full informational content of these types of advertisements, which critics charge are designed to psychologically dupe consumers, is contained in the knowledge that these goods or brands are *in fact advertised*. The fact that a brand advertises is itself (indirect) information.

Consumers are at least made aware of the existence of a product or service if they have observed an advertisement for it, even if the ad in question contains no information concerning price or intrinsic quality and is merely hyperbole. Viewing an ad on television promoting Miller Lite beer as "less filling" tells us little or nothing concerning price or physical quality, but does tell us that Miller Lite is for sale in the stores. This is not necessarily useless or valueless information. Knowledge of the existence of one more good or brand cannot make the consumer worse off, economically speaking.

The more frequently a brand or good is advertised, the more likely a consumer is to encounter the advertising information and alter his or her cache of knowledge, *and* the more likely a consumer will be to purchase both new and established products. Once purchased, the intrinsic and subjective qualities of an experience good can be accurately evaluated by the consumer, and thus the indirect informational content of the advertising can be assessed and used later. Important informational content can exist even for advertisements that appear to be of a psychologically persuasive (taste-changing) nature to most people, ads that could be termed "noninformative."

Leffler, in an analysis of prescriptive drug advertising, shows how

5. Some economists, such as Schmalensee, point out that, for *some* goods, advertising is only one aspect of quality determination, concluding that "the value of looking at consumers' acquisition and use of information" should be emphasized with less attention paid to advertising in general. In his 1982 study ("Product Differentiation Advantages of Pioneering Brands," *American Economic Review* 72 (1982): 349–65), Schmalensee based such arguments on the advantages of early entry (in a sequence of entries) in creating product differentiation and the subsequent difficulties of entering firms in convincing consumers of real product differences. Schmalensee also maintains that the concept of "experience goods" contains elements of circular reasoning. Here we ignore the intricacies of first entry models and focus instead upon the longer-run effects of the *process* of competition through time, a process wherein the notion of experience goods is more appealing.

such noninformative or repetitive advertising may benefit consumers.[6] Leffler views physicians as producing medical services for consumers by combining various "inputs," one of which is the prescription drug. The doctor's range of choices about which inputs to use to produce medical services may be very large. Hence, physicians' costs of remembering and appropriately selecting the proper drug for the given ailment from among many possible candidates may be high. One effect of noninformative advertising which establishes only a drug name and basic medical use can be to provide the physician with more rapid recall of the drug. This tends to lower the doctor's cost of making decisions about the complete package of care to provide the patient by saving time in the selection of drug therapy, and may even reduce the chance that an inappropriate drug is prescribed.[7]

Leffler's arguments can be extended to the consumer in general. We may view the consumer as one who makes purchases not simply to consume a good. That is, goods and services may not be an end in themselves. Consumers may be viewed as buying goods and services as inputs into the process of producing for themselves enjoyment or satisfaction or utility. The value of repetitive, noninformative advertising here is qualitatively the same as it is for Leffler's physicians and prescriptive drug analysis. It can lower the consumers'/ producers' recall costs concerning which inputs (goods and services) exist and which are most appropriate in producing output, enjoyment, or utility. In other words, the full price of the final consumption item for the consumer/producer may be lowered by this sort of advertising. Enjoyment is produced for the consumer at a lower time cost.

What of consumer sovereignty or consumer power in the markets for experience goods? Are not consumers at the mercy of profit-maximizing suppliers? At first blush it would seem to most that suppliers would be tempted to mislead consumers in advertising experience goods. Indeed, for experience goods there is a much greater incentive for

---

6. Keith B. Leffler, "Persuasion or Information? The Economics of Prescription Drug Advertising," *Journal of Law and Economics* 24 (1981): 46–74.

7. Leffler also argues, though, that such advertising may have the market effect of slowing the entry of lower-priced substitute drugs. Whether or not the response of such an effect in certain industries adversely affects consumers, and therefore implies that *on the whole* advertising makes consumers worse off than they would be in the absence of advertising, is another question altogether—a question that will be directly addressed in the next two chapters.

business to provide misleading and false advertising than in the advertising of search goods. But there are other particular features of this controversy that seem to have been ignored in popular discussion. The most common complaint by consumers, for example, is that the product does not live up to its expectations or to claims of its advertisers. A particular coffee may not, to some consumers, be the "richest" or "most enjoyable" they ever drank. For others, it may have been. Differential consumer tastes cannot be a basis of objective criticism or analysis. Businesses do have, in certain cases, an incentive to provide the consumer with misleading information regarding experience goods through advertising. This fact does not indicate that all, most, or even a significant portion of experience goods advertising is misleading nor that it *has the effect of* misleading the consumer. In instances where firms have the largest incentives to deceive consumers, consumers have the greatest incentives *not to be deceived*! Consumers who act in their own self-interest, rational consumers, are aware of the incentive firms have to deceive them through quality advertising and will take steps to try to minimize any deception.

From this simple fact a case may be made that consumers of experience goods are not the dupes of advertisers. One must also acknowledge that it is very difficult to fool all of the people all of the time. It is even more difficult to continually fool anybody all of the time if that person acts out of self-interest. Repeat purchases by consumers for many experience goods are commonplace, and intrinsic and subjective qualities can be quickly discovered. Deliberate provision of false or misleading information by a firm selling a frequently purchased product would tend to be self-defeating. In a market characterized by repeat purchases, consumers have a large degree of market power, in the sense that, if fooled once, purchase of the product is discontinued or reoriented to another brand.

Further benefits accrue to consumers in this area. First, does it pay to advertise poor or inferior brands or commodities? Even if agreement could be reached on what constitutes a bad product (rotten fruit? stale bread? radios without digital clocks?), there is not much of an incentive for firms to provide consumers with information about inferior goods for any length of time. Since higher quality goods and services tend to drive bad goods out of markets over time, consumers will not be regularly confronted with this kind of information.

Secondly, consumers whose tastes and preferences are best served by particular services or products will be the consumers who will most likely be in a position to observe the indirect information of these goods through advertisements. Producers have little incentive to advertise gourmet foods or cooking implements in *Sports Illustrated*, but there is great incentive to use *Gourmet Magazine*. To some degree, producers lower the cost to consumers of finding indirect information by placing it in the areas where it is most likely to be observed. Absorbing and processing this information can be a costly chore. The suppliers of advertising have an incentive to make the assimilation of indirect information less costly (easier, more enjoyable), just as the grocer has an incentive to make shopping for food more enjoyable (less costly) by providing a clean store, courteous check-out clerks, and air conditioning. The information an advertiser provides may be jointly supplied with entertainment (a television show, for example), or may take the form of entertainment itself, such as an award-winning commercial. These observations suggest that market power lies in the diffuse hands of consumers.

Credence Goods

Nelson's characterization of goods as possessing search or experience characteristics is helpful in understanding why firms advertise and the welfare implications of such advertising. We have argued that competition among sellers of these goods and services inhibits fraudulent advertising as a permanent fixture in markets. In discussing fraud and advertising, a third division in the taxonomy of goods and services may be made, those with *credence* characteristics.

Michael Darby and Edi Karni break down Nelson's experience category into two parts.[8] True experience goods, they argue, are goods for which the proper amounts to purchase are known before purchase and for which the qualities are accurately ascertained at low cost after purchase. Credence goods pose more of a problem for consumers. These are goods for which consumers face high costs in deciding the right amount to buy, determining the quality of what has been purchased, or some combination of the two. Examples of credence goods abound. Lack of specific knowledge makes us wonder if we "should" get a physical examination from a doctor every year and just how

---

8. Michael R. Darby and Edi Karni, "Free Competition and the Optimal Amount of Fraud," *Journal of Law and Economics* 16 (1973): 67–8.

"good" the physical was. Do we really "need" eight new spark plugs for a tune-up and how well are those new spark plugs performing? A large degree of imperfect knowledge on the part of consumers creates credence goods. Darby and Karni's research shows that even when there is competition among sellers, incentives exist to perpetrate fraud in the markets for credence goods. This is generally accomplished by selling customers "too much" of a good or service. Fraud is also achieved by selling a lower quality product or service than the consumer believes he or she is buying, with quality impossible or very costly to discover.

Darby and Karni do not address advertising directly while specifying market conditions that yield various degrees of persistent fraud under competition. They do suggest numerous complications associated with establishing and enforcing governmental quality standards, concluding that it is unclear whether governmental intervention is superior to the manner in which free markets cope with such prob-lems. Competitive markets, for example, offer warranties and guarantees, manufacturer-authorized repair, service contracts, leases, and a variety of other arrangements.

In short, the problems associated with credence goods should not be attributed to advertising. They stem, instead, from a lack of knowledge among consumers or from a high cost of monitoring and/or discovering quality. That these are problems that are difficult to dispose of socially is not in dispute. Consumer ignorance has its costs, just as market entry by a firm entails costs. While credence goods may be the likeliest candidates for fraud through false advertising, it is not clear that advertising in such markets works on balance to the detriment of consumers and society as a whole. Less clear is the desirability of the restrictions on advertising in markets for credence goods for exactly the same reasons cited in connection with search and general experience goods. The very nature of credence goods implies that some fraud, some of it abetted by advertising, will exist. Just how much fraud society "should" put up with in these markets will be addressed directly in Chapter 8.

QUALITY, DERIVED DEMAND, AND THE AUSTRIAN PERSPECTIVE

The traditional analysis of advertising asserts that the advertising of a single firm somehow (usually through a change of taste) increases consumer demand for the advertised good but also makes consumers less sensitive to price changes of the good. Advertising is a source of concentrated, noncompetitive markets; barriers to entry; abnormally high profits and prices; and other undesirable characteristics. Positive economists counter this idea with an alternative theory which also upsets received notions concerning firm and market structures.

Quality, Product Advertising, and Derived Demand

One of the most important yet simple points to arise respecting firm and market structure is raised by Nelson. One reason to advertise, according to the older view, was to differentiate a product in the consumer's eyes, to try to induce the consumer to see quality differences among brands or among slightly differentiated goods. Success in this area moves the firm closer to monopoly, with welfare-reducing side effects, than to competition. Nelson disagreed and argued that advertising does *not* differentiate products and produce monopoly. There are some products that are different to different consumers because of personally held subjective valuations (e.g., the value of a Virginia baked ham to a devout Moslem). Moreover, with respect to intrinsic quality, quality differentials can exist between brands whether or not those brands advertise. Advertising does not create quality differentials. It is therefore difficult to attribute market imperfections arising from quality differentials to advertising since the quality differentials would exist even in the complete absence of advertising.

One of the most important and related developments clarifying contemporary advertising research is the 1982 study of Isaac Ehrlich and Lawrence Fisher.[9] Ehrlich and Fisher note that consumers will, given tastes, incomes, etc., base purchase decisions on the *full price* of a good or service, recognizing that no consumer has perfect information about his or her market opportunities. Further, they recognize that advertising provides consumers information, even in the case of noninformative or repetitive advertising.

A *derived demand* for advertising follows from these facts. For example, firms demand electricity to make desired consumer goods and services. The demand for the electricity input is thus said to be a derived demand. It is derived from consumer demand for the final

9. Isaac Ehrlich and Lawrence Fisher, "The Derived Demand for Advertising: A Theoretical and Empirical Investigation," *American Economic Review* 72 (1982): 366–88.

product and the firm's decision that electricity provides, along with other inputs, the most efficient/least-cost method of supplying the final product. Advertising may be similarly treated. Its existence in markets can be shown to *derive from consumers'* desire to minimize the full price of the products and services they buy in a world where knowledge (information) is less than perfect. Advertising does not originate from firms' attempts to achieve monopolistic advantages over consumers and competitors, but from consumers' desire for cost-saving information which lowers the full price of their purchases.

Ehrlich and Fisher expand their analysis of derived advertising demand to examine the implications of advertising on market conditions. Their analysis reaches two important conclusions. First, advertising will be associated with *more* elastic consumer demands, which stands in direct contrast to the traditional view that advertising originated in the attempt to monopolize. Second, they find that advertising is, on balance, a socially efficient method of providing information in that it minimizes the full price paid by consumers. An implication of this finding is that when firms are prevented from advertising, inefficient means of providing information are employed (along with "wrong" amounts of information from consumers' standpoint). Full prices are higher than would otherwise be paid by consumers.

The traditional view that advertising makes consumer demands less price elastic may be reexamined within this same line of reasoning. (Remember, if demands become less price-elastic, then any given price increase will result in consumers' reducing their purchases by a relatively smaller amount than previously.) It is known from basic principles of economics that the larger the number of differentiated goods with similar uses, i.e., substitute goods, the greater will be the response by consumers to any given price change in terms of quantity purchased. It is obvious that consumers will be less price-sensitive to insulin, for example, than to Tide laundry detergent since Tide has many more substitutes than does insulin. In a world of imperfect knowledge the consumer must be aware of the existence of other goods and services, their prices, and their qualities for these other goods to affect the consumer's demand elasticity.

As discussed in the previous section, advertising generates just such information, direct and indirect, for both search and experience goods. But the key to understanding why advertising would make consumers more sensitive to price changes rests in a simple fact overlooked in traditional analysis. It is not the case in product lines where traditional analysis was applied that only *one* firm advertised. Ignored is the fact that consumers get information through advertising from a *number* of firms. With information being generated about all brands of a product, competition in advertising is observed. The general tendency is for consumer demands to become more price-elastic—more price-sensitive—with respect to any given brand.[10] If this important aspect of the problem is not ignored, if the consumer is viewed as rational but not in possession of full and perfect knowledge, different conclusions may be established.

Advertising not only of price but also of quality, far from producing monopolistic results, appears to make industries more competitive than they would be in the absence of advertising. At worst, advertising provides no information to consumers (an unlikely event) and it has *no* effect on the monopoly power of a firm.[11]

Is Advertising Compatible With Competition?

In any discussion of the competitiveness of markets, there is a single, most important criterion that should be examined. This criterion is whether or not firms are allowed to enter and leave the market at will. We believe this to be the core of what is meant by a competitive, free enterprise system. A free enterprise system means the freedom to establish firms, the freedom to go out of business if one desires, not the freedom to impede the actions of others. The market process by which consumer wants are satisfied, by which abnormal profits are competed away, and by which inefficient firms are eliminated from the market, crucially depends upon the ability of firms to leave and enter a market at will. This is the essence of competition.

The important issue for economic analysis is whether or not advertising inhibits or enhances entry into a market or product line. The

10. We may say that the effect is a "general tendency" since it also depends upon such factors as the pre-advertising information held by consumers and upon the characteristics of products and services advertised.

11. We do not mean to imply, moreover, that advertising will have negative welfare effects even if it reduces demand elasticity for some product or service. It may well be, as indicated earlier, that (in a static model of markets) increases in utility created by rises in and altered elasticity of differentiated product demand will outweigh the foregone resource costs of advertising.

economies of scale-barrier to entry argument may be seriously flawed. Advertising may be depicted as a short-term investment expenditure that most new firms in an industry must bear—a short-term cost differential with existing firms. A firm contemplating entry into an industry or product line must somehow be able to sell its output. In order to sell output there must be a buyer of output. And in order for there to be a buyer of output, a consumer must know at the very least that this new product or brand exists. To complete the logical circle, information and other messages about new brands or products can be efficiently transmitted to potential consumers through advertising. To be sure, there will be unavoidable costs associated with the entry process. Advertising may possess peculiar characteristics that force us to recognize that such expenditures, in part, comprise *one* of the start-up costs of market entry.[12] Overall, an abundance of strong arguments exist indicating that advertising enhances the competitiveness of markets to the advantage of consumers.

In this view a simple notion arises that is directly counter to traditional analysis. In the analysis of many contemporary economists, advertising is not a long-term barrier to entry. In a world of rational consumers where information is costly, advertising is a means of entry into industries and product lines. Thus, the ability to advertise lowers the cost of entry on balance. It also raises the probability of a successful entry. The conclusion that advertising makes markets less competitive than would otherwise be the case is suspect, since entry is a keystone of competition.

Yale Brozen carries this simple and cogent analysis one step further.[13] His thesis is that it is the prevention and/or limitation of advertising that is an anticompetitive, monopolistic practice. Any advertising limitations would in fact make it more difficult (expensive) for potential entrants to enter a product line. With limitations consumers would have, or know of, fewer substitute goods, and the existing firms in an industry would benefit in the sense that abnormally high profits would not be competed away as quickly or as completely. Not only would consumers pay higher prices due to a lack of competition, but also existing firms, in the absence of advertising

12. See the related discussion of barriers to entry concerning Kessides' recent work (1986) in Chapter 3.

13. Yale Brozen, "Is Advertising a Barrier to Entry?" in Yale Brozen, ed., *Advertising and Society* (New York: University Press, 1974), pp. 79–95.

created by some fiat, would compete among themselves to provide information about their own goods with methods that are costlier than advertising (dealer networks or expensive distribution systems, for example).

Consumers suffer both ways. Lack of entry and competition keep prices and profits higher than would otherwise be the case; inefficient methods of conveying information push costs and prices above levels that would otherwise exist. The bottom line: *advertising is a force that makes markets more competitive, not less competitive.* Methods of advertising prevention are seen for what they are—likely creators of entry barriers and forces of anticompetitive behavior.

Advertising and the Entrepreneurial Role: The Austrian Perspective

The most interesting modern assessment of advertising and its role in competition—one that we employ throughout this book—is that found in contemporary Austrian economics. Contemporary Austrian economics is an ongoing inquiry into free market processes that ranges from the pre-twentieth century writings of Carl Menger, Eugen Bohm-Bawerk, and Frederick Wieser to the contemporary investigations of Ludwig von Mises, Frederick A. Hayek, and Israel Kirzner. While market-oriented somewhat in the manner of orthodox (Marshallian) economics, the approach of the Austrians differs in some important respects. One of these different aspects concerns the role of advertising. Another relates to the process of acquiring and consuming information in a market economy.

No economist has broached the question of information in more telling ways than Nobel laureate Frederick Hayek. Hayek, in a criticism of Galbraithian notions of advertising, stressed the importance of information in the consumption of goods.[14] Galbraith argued that there was a "dependence effect," that is, consumption depended upon artificially created wants. In the modern view, of course, sovereign consumers determine what is to be produced, but Galbraith looked at the relation the other way around, contributing to his damnation of

---

14. Fredrich A. Hayek, "The Nonsequitur of the Dependence Effect," in E. Mansfield, ed., *Miroeconomics: Selected Readings* (New York: W. W. Norton and Co., 1979), pp. 7–11.

advertising. "Unimportant" private wants are expanded by advertising, whereas "important" public wants are neglected.

Hayek exploded this view by noting that very few of man's wants, with the possible exception of food, shelter, and sex, are innate. Rather, human wants, personality, and opinions are shaped by a *cultural environment*. One element of this environment, though certainly not the only one, is advertising. In a free market system producers may *attempt* to determine consumption for their particular product, but consumers will also be informed about competing products. The success of individual producers will depend upon the actions of other producers and upon a host of other factors affecting consumers of their products. The main point is that consumers *cannot* react without the information. No one would ever know if he had a taste for Mozart, Stravinsky, or the Beatles if desires and tastes were innate. In the words of Hayek, "to say that a desire is not important because it is not innate is to say that the whole cultural achievement of man is not important."[15] To the Austrians, advertising (among other factors) most surely affects tastes through its information content and it is in the fundamental interest of producers to provide such information.

Hayek's insights on information have been compared with a very important modern Austrian view of entrepreneurship. In the work of von Mises, and most centrally in the recent writings of Israel Kirzner, we find the entrepreneur as perceiver of profit opportunities and organizer of production.[16] The entrepreneur takes center stage in the competitive market process, and central to entrepreneurial activity is the ability to freely advertise.

The modern Austrians distinguish competition as a *process* from the traditional neoclassical view of competition as a *situation*. In the traditional conception, competition is treated as an equilibrium situation which, if disturbed, results in a new equilibrium instantaneously. A type of mathematical dynamics may be and has been added, of course, but neoclassical equilibrium is predetermined and predictable nonetheless. The Austrians, alternatively, have viewed competition as a rivalrous *process*. Competition takes on the businessman's definition of "rivalry against competitors for a prize." The *sine qua*

---

15. Ibid., p. 8.
16. Ludwig von Mises, *Human Action* (Chicago: Henry Regnery, 1966), pp. 257–323; Israel Kirzner, *Competition and Entrepreneurship* (Chicago: University of Chicago Press, 1973).

non of competition and the sole prerequisites for a laissez faire market economy, as discussed in the previous section of this chapter, is *freedom of entry*. Thus, competition is viewed as a continuous process in perpetual *dis*equilibrium. Economic profits are created and destroyed in perpetual fashion. The interesting part of this disequilibrium model is the role that entrepreneurship and advertising play in it.

The neo-Austrian view of the competitive process dovetails perfectly with J. A. Schumpeter's view of competition as "creative destruction."[17] Pre-Schumpeterian views of price theory depicted competition solely in terms of its price-reducing effects *for given products*. In Schumpeterian terms, as in those of the neo-Austrians, competition is most fruitfully viewed in dynamic terms wherein entrepreneurs experiment with "different" products. Through such activities as alterations in quality, changes in warranty length, and increases in product availability, sellers are *continuously* increasing the utility of products to consumers. Advertising is an essential means through which entrepreneurs are able to accomplish this increase in consumer welfare. As Schumpeter well knew, the process of competition, of which advertising is an inextricable part, meant that only temporary monopoly returns were possible through time.[18] To look at the economy in static terms, and to condemn activities that appeared to be monopolistic in a still picture view, was inherently misleading from the perspective of market dynamics. Advertising regulation (which we consider in the case studies of Chapters 7 and 8) or any other government regulation aimed at correcting perceived defects in the static market process was the real source of dynamic reductions in consumer welfare and economic growth.

Entrepreneurs are thus the prime movers of the economic process in the Austrian-Schumpeterian conception. In the presence of uncertainty, entrepreneurs perceive profit opportunities—that is, they recognize that there are differences between resource prices and the potential price of outputs of commodities and services. Within this perception, however, are the costs of *selling* output by informing customers of these goods and services. There are no distinctions between

17. Joseph A. Schumpeter, *Capitalism, Socialism and Democracy*, 3d ed. (New York: Harper & Row, 1950).

18. Ibid., pp. 87–99.

selling costs and production costs as Chamberlin had argued. Advertising (and other selling costs) do not connote monopoly but are part-and-parcel of the competitive process. They are, in effect, the *mode of entry* into markets in that they enable entrepreneurs to explain new products to consumers and to inform them on matters of price and quality differences. The bottom line is that information is purchased jointly with the product and is complementary with the "package" itself.

When competition is free (i.e., there is freedom of entry into markets) consumers may purchase from whom they choose. Deceit cannot be rewarded in the long run in a competitive market, but that fact does not mean that sellers cannot be deceitful in the short run. (Laws governing short-run deceit may, of course, be desirable.) At base, the success of a dynamic competitive system *requires* unfettered entry into markets, and a nonregulated freedom to advertise is prerequisite to free entry. Deceit and uncertainty are unfortunately part of our world, but long-term deceit is not possible except in the presence of restrictions on entry and advertising. Advertising, in the words of Kirzner, is ". . . an integral, inescapable aspect of the market economy."[19]

CONCLUSION

In the past three chapters we have come full circle in our survey of how the economic analysis of advertising originated, developed, and changed in the twentieth century. The traditional view of advertising, a popular and probably the majority view, has been examined along with the modern positive challenge to the traditionalist views. The differences are clear and may be summarized in two crucial points. The first and most obvious is the difference with which the two theories treat consumer behavior. Traditionalist critics of advertising depict consumers as cattle to be herded by psychological persuasion. Firms and consumers, moreover, are characterized as greedy individuals acting only in their own self-interest to society's detriment. The positive position, on the other hand, stresses the impact of and interactions between rational consumers and advertising within the market process. In this modern view, which blends Austrian process views

---

19. Kirzner, *Competition and Entrepreneurship*, p. 6.

of the market with new neoclassical advances in traditional theory, advertising is integral to competition and consumer welfare.

There is more to the economics of advertising than the statement that "advertising changes tastes." There are a number of reasons why consumers *want* advertising. There is in fact a demand for advertising. The demand for information and for noninformational messages through advertising originates in a market economy in which knowledge and information are not perfect. Information is both costly and beneficial. Advertising is exactly like any other scarce economic resource. In fact, in a world of imperfect knowledge and incomplete information on the part of consumers, it is impossible to conclude that consumers would be better off with severe restrictions on advertising. While there are gaps in our economic understanding of advertising, it appears that any general notion of the consumer as being manipulated by advertisers will not bear careful scrutiny.

Unfortunately, economic theory may only go so far in assessing the impact of advertising. A division between the "validity" of traditionalist and modern positive theoretical assessments of advertising can only be settled by a confrontation with the facts. Such evidence is examined in the next two chapters.

PART III

THE EVIDENCE ON ADVERTISING

5

BRAND LOYALTY, ENTRY, AND SCALE ECONOMIES

Traditional and modern approaches to the economic analysis of advertising raise important questions. Both theories arrive at different conclusions about how firms behave, about types of market behavior, and about whether prices and profits will be higher or lower in markets where the product is advertised heavily as opposed to markets where there is a dearth of advertising. While one theory may appear more reasonable, both explanations appear to have plausible components. This chapter considers evidence surrounding the direct effects of advertising on market participants, consumers and suppliers. Does advertising influence consumer decisions so as to create brand loyalty? Does it produce scale economies and impede entry of potential suppliers? Traditional and modern views of advertising must be compared from a "real world" empirical perspective.

THE EMPIRICS OF ADVERTISING

The scientific method is applicable to both physical and social sciences and it consists of two steps. The first is a theory to guide the scientist in answering questions about the world. Of equal importance is the matter of how well theory (the guide) accurately explains relationships. That is, not only must a theory be logically consistent, but it must also *accurately describe* and *predict* what it sets out to describe and predict. Is the theory consistent with actual real world

81

behavior, with observed data and facts? This is an equally important criterion of any theory in any scientific discipline, including economics.

Secondly, it is impossible to *prove* a theory. Statistical evidence can never prove anything. It can only provide varying degrees of confidence, sometimes a very large degree of confidence, that the theory has in fact described the true or correct relationships. Only logical analysis in economic investigations can disprove a theory by showing some contradiction or logical fallacy in it. Statistics and data can only present degrees of evidence for or against the validity or accuracy of a theory.

One last pitfall can exist. There may exist more than one method of testing a theory. Method A may be superior to method B in some situations but not in others, and the two methods may yield surprisingly different results. Suppose that we want to test some hypothesis concerning the prices of a particular product. Data on prices must be observed and subjected to the appropriate statistical analysis in order to amass evidence that either does or does not support the theoretical claims. It would clearly make a difference, however, if the price data were retail instead of wholesale, or listed price versus the transactions prices (the prices actually paid for new cars, for example). Some prices are adjusted for inflation; others are not. All of these product "prices" are in fact measuring the price of the product, but they measure price in six different ways. The measure of price must be chosen that best reflects relationships developed in the theory. Other measures may be chosen that may *not* best reflect theoretical relationships but that may yield more supportive results. With these warnings in mind, we can evaluate some of the more interesting evidence on the economics of advertising.

BRAND LOYALTY, ECONOMIES OF SCALE, AND ENTRY BARRIERS

Does advertising produce brand loyalty and economies of scale resulting in entry control in established industries or product lines? The traditionalists and the new neoclassicals or positive theorists developed opposing theories. Traditional analysis concluded that firms would advertise their product in order to "more strongly attach," in Robinson's words, "customers to their particular product or brand, reducing the tendency of consumers to shift purchases to other similar products or brands."[1] The ability of existing firms to mount large and successful advertising campaigns—to advertise at lower per-unit-of-sales cost—prevents new firms from entering the market. This is the barrier-to-entry hypothesis.

Positive economists argue that brand advertising would not necessarily generate the consumer responses and market effects described above. Advertising is a means by which the market facilitates information transferral, at least for consumer search goods. Knowledge of competitors' prices may breed consumer disloyalty. For experience goods, repetitive and noninformative advertising of brands may indeed have the partial direct effect of creating a type of brand loyalty. This kind of advertising may reduce cost to the consumer of producing satisfaction in that the consumer can quickly (inexpensively) recall desirable brands. For this to be the case, the consumer would be choosing to be brand loyal because the full price of the good would be lower. In this sense, brand loyalty is seen to be welfare enhancing.

And what of competitors' ads? In a narrow sense, brand loyalty *can* exist if it improves the consumer's welfare. More broadly, brand loyalty may be a market characteristic when there is competition in advertising for certain types of goods. Even more to the point, is observed market brand loyalty due to advertising or to other factors? Modern arguments that advertising is one tool available to new firms in penetrating or entering markets is different, both in method and result, from the traditional arguments.

Brand Loyalty

The notion that brand advertising by firms creates or generates brand loyalty is popular with the general public. Kaldor focuses on the issue: "Advertising makes the public 'brand conscious.' It is not so much a question of making the consumer buy things he would not have bought otherwise; but of crystallizing his routine habits, of making him conscious that keeping to a certain routine in consumption means not only buying the same commodities in a vague sort of way, but sticking to the same brand."[2] In an exhaustive, unique, and technical

---

1. Joan Robinson, *Economics of Imperfect Competition* (London: Macmillan and Co., 1933), p. 101.
2. Nicholas Kaldor, "The Economic Aspects of Advertising," *Review of Economic Studies* 18 (1949): 18.

volume of research, Jean Jacques Lambin provides a well-executed investigation into this issue.[3] Lambin recognizes the ambiguity of obtaining a measure of consumer loyalty, or even of isolating that portion of consumer behavior that is purportedly due to the notion of loyalty. Rather, he distinguishes between the (empirically) nebulous notion of "loyalty" and his measurable concept of "inertia" on the part of consumers. The distinction Lambin makes between loyalty and inertia is that loyalty implies a psychological commitment, preference, or taste, while inertia refers to routine buying done by the consumer to reduce any perceived risk or the costs involved in switching brands. This appears to be the closest observable measure of advertising changing tastes and creating loyalties. Given the new neoclassical explanation of why brand loyalty might arise, it is, of course, far from perfect.

Lambin, working with data from various European countries, estimated consumer inertia (or retention) rates for soft drinks, electric shavers, hair spray, gasoline, detergents, and cigarettes by their various brands. His findings indicate that there in fact is a statistically significant degree of consumer inertia (or brand loyalty) for the products and brands in the study. There is indeed a tendency toward consumer inertia in brand purchase decisions. Many of the products examined by Lambin, though, were products that people tend to purchase frequently. For these kinds of goods, there may be many reasons why consumer inertia would be detected, not the least of which would be that consumers minimize the full cost or price of their purchases. To conclude that advertising of these brands *causes* the inertia would be similar to convicting a suspect with only the prosecutor's opening statement to the jury as evidence. In our analogy, we have found only that consumer brand inertia seems to exist. Lambin states that it is entirely plausible that "the differential advantage of a brand . . . the creation of which is a natural goal of any entrepreneur . . . as reflected to some degree in consumer loyalty (inertia) is an outcome of many factors"[4]

Next, Lambin made a direct test of the hypothesis that advertising is the *cause* of observed consumer inertia, or more properly, that

3. J. J. Lambin, *Advertising, Competition, and Market Conduct* (Amsterdam: North-Holland Publishing Co., 1976).

4. Ibid., p. 117.

advertising intensity positively influences inertia. Three measures of advertising intensity were constructed and regression analysis was employed to see if, statistically, any or all measures could be considered a significant cause.[5] His three measures of advertising intensity were (a) brand advertising expenditures per capita, (b) brand advertising expenditures as a percentage of total industry advertising expenditures, and (c) the ratio of brand advertising to brand sales.

The results are interesting. For each measure of advertising or advertising intensity, advertising intensity increases produced not an increase in consumer inertia or brand loyalty, but a *decrease* in the measure of loyalty. These results run contrary to general perceptions and traditional theory pertaining to the manner in which advertising works and indicate that market-wide consumer inertia or brand loyalty should not be attributed specifically to measures of advertising intensities or to advertising itself.

Two effects are likely being observed in Lambin's empirical study. On the firm level, advertising may well play a role in explaining the existence of consumer inertia. When we move to the market level, it may be the case that competitors' advertising tends to reduce the degree of any consumer inertia associated with a particular brand. The issue is not whether brand loyalty or consumer inertia exists, but whether or not advertising creates and enhances brand loyalty, producing an entry barrier. We argue, with Lambin, that in the market setting the evidence suggests that advertising tends to *reduce* consumer inertia and that this tendency appears to be indirect evidence of competition. The presumption that creation of brand loyalty or inertia specifically through advertising is an entry barrier in industries cannot be supported or sustained utilizing Lambin's evidence.

5. Regression analysis is a formal statistical technique employed by economists, used to obtain an estimate of the true relationship between two variables by analyzing actual data which measure the variables. The theory sets out the direction of the relationship between the two variables. Changes in one variable are hypothesized to *cause* changes in the other, or *affect* the other. In regression terminology, the factor that causes change is an *explanatory* variable. The variable affected by this change is called the *dependent* variable. A *regression coefficient* is the goal of regression analysis and is merely a number. The number contains two pieces of information. The algebraic sign of the regression coefficient indicates whether the explanatory variable influences the dependent variable in a positive or negative fashion. The magnitude of the number indicates by how many units the dependent variable changes when the explanatory variable changes by one unit in which it is measured. It should be remembered that this number is an estimate of the theorized cause and effect.

Brand Advertising and Competition

Another aspect of the issue supports the position that advertising, brand advertising included, does not necessarily create brand loyalty. Rather, advertising provides information to less-than-perfectly informed consumers about such factors as price, quality, existence, and location. New neoclassical economists who view consumers as acting in their own self-interest conclude that advertising of all forms represents an avenue which firms use to *enter* industries or product lines. The notion that one firm permanently attaches customers to itself *solely through advertising* becomes suspect when one takes account of the fact that, in most industries or product lines, more than one firm sells a product and thus advertises. Competing advertisers exist. If one firm's ads work, why would one not expect a competitor's ads to work also? This line of argument leads to conclusions that are readily testable, i.e., comparatively easy to evaluate with the actual data produced in the real world.

One of the earliest tests of this topic was produced by Lester Telser.[6] Telser reasoned that if advertising were the source of brand loyalty as the traditional economists argued, then we could expect to see a particular phenomenon in certain markets over time. Specifically, for those products that advertised most intensively, the percentage of industry sales accounted for by each firm in an industry should change by a relatively small amount over time. If advertising is both an entry barrier and an effective generator of brand loyalty, relative sales positions of firms in the industry should not be altered, assuming the market undergoes no fundamental changes (e.g., technological innovations). For products that are not heavily advertised, the opposite would be expected.

Telser compared three industries—food products, soaps, and cosmetics and toiletries—and computed a measure of advertising intensity in each of these three broad categories as the ratio of total industry advertising outlays to total industry sales. From these calculations Telser concluded that advertising was relatively intensive in the toiletries-cosmetics industry, less intensive in the soap industry, and even less intensive in the food industry. The percentage of industry sales of

6. Lester G. Telser, "Advertising and Competition," *Journal of Political Economy* 72 (1964): 537–62.

each of the four leading brands in each of the three industries in 1948 was compared with the percentage of industry sales of the same four brands eleven years later. If advertising creates brand loyalty and prevents competition within industries, market shares of the leading brands should have *increased* or at best remained stable over time within an industry. Also, market shares should increase by more in the most advertising-intensive industry, or at least remain relatively more stable.

Telser's observations did not confirm this view. Market shares of the four leading brands in 1948 for each of the three industries decreased over the eleven years. Furthermore, market shares in the most intensively advertised industry, toiletries and cosmetics, decreased by *more* than market shares decreased in less intensively advertised industries. Market shares in the soap industry decreased by more than in the less advertising-intensive food industry. Telser's evidence does not support the position that advertising creates increasing market shares for firms and produces oligopolies and monopolies, but it is unclear why market shares changed. It is plausible to conjecture that entry into these industries took place, dissipating shares, and while the statistical correlation may in fact be spurious, Telser's study suggests that intensive advertising and shifting market shares are not incompatible in competitive markets.

Advertising and Rivalrous Competition

While Telser's early study of the effects on market shares of advertising intensity may be criticized as excessively broadbased, it provides insight into what actually happens in markets where advertising is employed in firms. J. J. Lambin has also studied the relationship of advertising to market share, but in markets which can be characterized as oligopoly markets.[7] Data for the study were collected from individual firms (not industries) and subjected to regression analysis. The results lend some credence to the view that, even in so-called oligopolistic markets, advertising is a competitive weapon of competition.

Lambin focused not solely upon the relationships of a single firm's sales or market shares and its own advertising, but also took account of the effects that the actions of other firms in the same industry would

---

7. Lambin, *Advertising, Competition and Market Conduct.*

have on that individual firm's sales or market shares. Although he was searching for "reaction" relationships and trying to substantiate characteristics of oligopolistic markets, his results and findings are more supportive of a process of competition among firms in markets where the number of firms is not large. That is, when viewed from a neo-Austrian perspective, rivalry is a characteristic of the competitive process with no implications for the type of market outcomes produced by the formal theory of oligopoly.

In trying to uncover a rivalrous relationship between firms in similar product lines, Lambin tried to explain statistically the level of sales and market shares of brands as being partially dependent upon the advertising of rivals or close competitors—other firms selling a similar good, but different brands—as well as on a measure of its own advertising. Lambin discovered that a firm's advertising *did* seem to influence its sales or market shares in a statistically significant and positive fashion.[8] Even if this finding stood alone, the positive theory of advertising would not be discredited since increasing sales and/or market shares over time would be consistent with the notion of advertising as a conveyor of information about goods, *other things being constant*. But, as Lambin viewed the matter, other things should be considered in markets with more than one firm. It would, for example, also be informative to examine or uncover the effect that rivals' advertising had on a firm's sales or market shares. He found that the advertising of other firms, whether we call them competitors or rivals, had a negative effect on any one firm's sales or market shares.

Table 5–1 shows a portion of Lambin's statistical results from several product lines. The numbers in the two columns represent esti-

---

8. The importance of statistical significance arises when it is remembered that regression analysis yields estimates of the direction and magnitude of theorized cause-effect relationships. Needed is something to indicate how confident the researcher can be that the estimate truly reflects the actual relationship—that the estimate really measures a *systematic* effect and not purely *random* relationships which the data may disguise as systematic effects. Statistical significance can be had only in degrees. That is, an estimate can be statistically significant at the 5-percent level. This simply means that the researcher is 95-percent sure or confident that the estimate really reflects the true relationship being investigated. In economic research, the 5-percent to 10-percent significance levels are generally required to be able to state that the estimate is actually different from zero and not the result of spurious data relationships. One last point is that regression results do not *prove* anything. We can never be 100-percent confident that an estimator captures true relationships. The best we can do is achieve degrees of confidence or significance.

Table 5–1. Effect of Advertising by Individual Firm and Its Rivals on Firm's Market Share, by Selected Product Group.

Product	Market Share Own Advertising Elasticity[a]	Market Share Rival's Advertising Elasticity
Electric Shavers	0.482[NS]	−0.471
	0.159	−0.153
	0.140[NS]	−0.249
	0.055[NS]	−0.346
Gasoline	0.028	−0.35
Hair Spray	0.087	−0.103
	0.035	−0.049
Deodorant	0.037	−0.059
Detergent	0.037	−0.069
	0.055	−0.098
	0.129	−0.286
	0.082	−0.093
Average[b]	0.111	−0.165

SOURCE: J. J. Lambin, *Advertising, Competition, and Market Conduct* (Amsterdam: North-Holland Publishing Co., 1976), p. 110.

[a]NS = Not statistically significant at 10 percent.
[b]Average excludes insignificant estimates.

mated elasticities.[9] The first column shows by what percentage Lambin's measures of a firm's market share increases given a 1-percent increase in his measure of the firm's advertising. The second column, where all numbers have negative signs, shows the percentage by which a firm's market share will decrease (note the negative signs) given a 1-percent increase in its rivals' advertising. The interesting conclusion is that in most cases the actual data appears to question the notion that firms can increase market shares by advertising, given that rivals or competitors are free to advertise. Table 5–1 shows that the effects of competitors' advertising generally outweigh the effects of a single

9. An elasticity is an economic measurement of how one variable responds to another. It measures the percentage by which a dependent variable will change when an explanatory variable changes by one percentage point. If, for example, a consumer responded to a 1 percent price decrease by buying .01 percent more units of some good, we would characterize that consumer as being insensitive, but not totally insensitive, to price changes. The measure of elasticity would be less than unity. If the elasticity is greater than unity, then the dependent variable can be classified as relatively responsive to changes in the explanatory variable. Like statistical significance, elasticity is a measure of degree.

firm's advertising. While an individual firm's advertising appears to be able to alter its market share, such advertising does not occur in a vacuum. Competitors, both old and new, also advertise. On balance this evidence suggests that, as long as all firms are free to advertise, advertising does not appear to fix market shares. Still other measures of advertising's effects are considered in Table 5–2.

Table 5–2 presents additional results on the relationship of market share stability and advertising. In Table 5–2, MSI_1 is a measure of market share fluctuations of all competing brands in a market over time while MSI_2 measures these flutuations for a single, specific brand. (The measures of advertising intensity are defined in Table 5–2.) Four of the six regression results in the table appear to indicate that advertising intensity does stabilize market shares as indicated by the negative signs of the estimated coefficients. But *none* of these four estimates is statistically significant. We cannot, therefore, draw any inference that increased advertising intensity, however measured, stabilizes market shares over time or that, more generally, advertising is incompatible with the competitive process. Indeed, when we look at the effect of firm advertising as a percent of industry-wide advertising on the stability of market shares, we find both *positive* and statistically *significant* regression coefficients in Table 5–2. Increased advertising intensity tends to destabilize market shares.

Table 5–2.   Effect of Advertising on Market Share Stability.

Dependent Variable		Constant	Explanatory Variable
MSI_1	=	5.200	−0.016 × BAPC
MSI_1	=	2.944	+9.826* × BPIA
MSI_1	=	4.260	−0.028 × BASR
MSI_2	=	1.996	−0.007 × BAPC
MSI_2	=	0.887	+5.149* × BPIA
MSI_2	=	2.386	−2.476 × BASR

SOURCE: J. J. Lambin, *Advertising, Competition, and Market Conduct* (Amsterdam: North-Holland Publishing Co., 1976), p. 120.

*Statistically significant at 5 percent.
BAPC: Firm brand advertising expenditures per capita.
BPIA: Firm brand advertising expenditures as a percent of industry advertising expenditures.
BASR: Firm brand advertising expenditure-to-firm-sales ratio.

Lambin measures market share instability or fluctuations by two methods which we have labeled MSI_1 and MSI_2. The evidence suggests that the opposite of the traditional scenario exists: *The more intensively all firms in industries advertise, the less stable are market shares or the more these market shares tend to change.* Lambin's evidence does not confirm commonly held notions concerning advertising, competition, monopoly, and oligopoly. If, as the traditional view implies, stable market shares signal a lack of competition (oligopoly or monopoly), then Lambin's results may in fact suggest that advertising is a phenomonon of the competitive process.[10]

Economies of Scale in Advertising

A significant amount of evidence on advertising and brand loyalty seems contrary to the notion that advertising creates loyalty and thus entry barriers. But there is additional statistical evidence on the existence of economies of scale. The idea that economies of scale, in the long run, should not be considered an entry barrier has already been carefully considered (Chapter 3). If advertising is an entry barrier, as the traditional view suggests, the case must first rest upon scale economies. The "scale" hypothesis may be investigated by considering two different methods. One method asks whether a one-dollar increase in advertising expenditures produces a greater than one-dollar increase in sales. If so, the existence of economies of scale arising from advertising may be indicated. For evidence, consider Lambin's study once more.

Table 5–3 shows both long- and short-term advertising-sales elasticities. The estimated coefficients in this table are interpreted as the percentage by which sales change given a one-percent change in advertising expenditures. For each of the seven product lines, whether one considers the shorter term or the longer term effects, a one-percent increase in advertising expenditures increases sales, but by *less than one percent* in each case. Lambin's results do not reveal econ-

---

10. In a dynamic demand context, with distributed lags, Schmalensee concluded that brand loyalty and inert consumers were not sufficient to provide firms with entry deterrence. Imperfect capital markets and insufficient collateral on the part of potential entrants are required to enable incumbents to deter entry in Schmalensee's model. Richard Schmalensee, "Brand Loyalty and Barriers to Entry," *Southern Economic Journal* 40 (1974): 587.

Table 5–3.   Sales Elasticities with Respect to Advertising Expenditures (Percent Change in Sales/Percent Change in Advertising Expenditures).

Product	Short-Run Elasticity	Long-Run Elasticity
Soft Drinks	0.057	0.415
Yogurt	0.031	0.363
Cigarettes	0.154	0.752
Electric Shavers	0.229	0.597
Gasoline	0.088	0.481
Hair Spray	0.045	0.436
Detergents	0.055	0.659

SOURCE: J. J. Lambin, *Advertising, Competition, and Market Conduct* (Amsterdam: North-Holland Publishing Co., 1976), p . 97.

All elasticities are significant at 5 percent.

omies of scale or increasing returns to advertising. Doubling the advertising dollar appears *not* to double sales, so that "large scale advertising has no built-in advantage of the power of a large purse. . . . This finding suggests that . . . advertising is not a key factor in the achievement of market power."[11] Not only is the economies-of-scale argument intuitively suspect, but also there is some evidence that suggests these economies of scale do not exist to begin with.

Alternatively, one may approach the scale economy issue by examining the relationship of advertising cost per dollar of sales in relation to total advertising expenditures. Increasing returns to advertising would then occur when the cost of advertising per dollar of sales falls or gets smaller as total advertising expenditures rise. This phenomenon is asserted to be prevalent especially for national advertisers reaching large audiences of consumers, as could be the case for network television advertising. A number of statistical studies—using both direct and complex methods—have been undertaken to investigate this issue. In most cases the results fail to confirm that advertising is related to economies of scale.[12]

Several authors have specifically investigated the notion that large national network advertisers reach television homes at a lower per

11. Lambin, *Advertising, Competition, and Market Conduct*, p. 98.
12. See, e.g., James M. Ferguson, *Advertising and Competition: Theory, Measurement, Fact* (Cambridge, Mass: Ballinger Publishing Co., 1974).

home cost than smaller advertisers.[13] All of the evidence in this area persistently rejects the idea that large advertisers have lower costs of advertising, per consumer or home-reached, than do smaller advertisers. Julian Simon (1969) also examined advertising cost data and concluded, in agreement with Lambin, that for any given firm advertising any given product, there is no evidence indicating economies of scale or increasing returns to advertising. Simon's data, which examine brand advertising in such areas as drugs, cigarettes, milk, and liquor, indicate that there are *decreasing* returns to brand ads, leading Simon to conclude that "increasing returns to repetition and size [of advertising] constitutes a monstrous myth."[14]

We do not pretend that the issue of whether economies of scale in advertising, or increasing returns to advertising expenditures, exist is settled within the economics profession. Research suggesting these effects has served as the target for other research pointing out the shortcomings of varying definitions, sub-par test design and implementation, and faulty interpretations of empirical results.[15] On the whole, the evidence cannot be said to support the idea that any scale barriers are produced through advertising.

Advertising and Entry Barriers: Summary

A good deal of evidence suggests that advertising does *not* produce entry barriers in industry. To do so, advertising must either produce

---

13. David M. Blank, "Television Advertising: The Great Discount Illusion, or Tonypandy Revisited," *Journal of Business* 41 (1968): 10–38; John L. Peterman, "The Clorox Case and Television Rate Structures," *Journal of Law and Economics* 11 (1968): 321–422.

14. Julian L. Simon, "Are There Economies of Scale in Advertising?" *Journal of Advertising Research* 5 (1969): 15–20.

15. The reader interested in surveying the pros and cons of this issue may begin with William S. Comanor and Thomas S. Wilson, "Advertising, Market Structure, and Performance," *Review of Economics and Statistics* 49 (1967): 423–40; and Joe S. Bain, *Barriers to New Competition* (Cambridge, Mass.: Harvard University Press, 1956). A review of several studies is in Richard Schmalensee, *The Economics of Advertising* (Amsterdam: North-Holland Publishing Co., 1972). Schmalensee's critique of Peles (Yoram Peles, "Economies of Scale in Advertising Beer and Cigarettes," *Journal of Business* 44 (1971): 32–37) should provide insight into the methodological and interpretative pitfalls that can exist. A guide to understanding the relevant terminology is also provided by Mark S. Albion and Paul W. Farris, *The Advertising Controversy: Evidence on the Economic Effects of Advertising* (Boston, Mass.: Auburn House Publishing Co., 1981).

a rather large degree of brand loyalty on the part of consumers or there must be increasing returns or economies of scale. Existing evidence does not, on balance, support either contention, but implies that the opposite relationships hold. Recall (from Chapter 4) the distinction between entry barriers and entry costs and the empirical results of Kessides (1986). An unusual characteristic of advertising expenditures (non-salvagability in the event of failure) does represent an entry cost. However, Kessides found this effect to be outweighed by the ability of advertising to make entry more successful. This positive theoretical economic view of advertising as integral to the competition process rests upon firm empirical or statistical ground.

Economists may even go further than merely casting doubt on the traditionalist hypotheses. A number of studies examine the issue of advertising's role of enabling new firms to enter industries and product lines. For example, prior to 1970 when a ban of television cigarette advertising was imposed, one new brand of cigarette, on average, successfully penetrated the industry each year. The cigarette industry was generally viewed as one in which advertising was an extremely effective entry barrier. However, between 1970 and 1974 no new brand was successful in entering the cigarette market. We do not argue that advertising, or the lack of it, tells the whole story. Surely industry growth or contraction, as well as other factors, are important. Yet the *ban* on cigarette advertising appears to have contributed to impeded entry.[16]

Evidence from the history of the cigarette industry pertaining to the reasons and motives for advertising by a firm is also instructive. Advertising in competitive industries is aimed partly at *potential* consumers and not merely at solidifying the loyalty of existing consumers. In the year before American Tobacco (also called the "Tobacco Trust") was broken into several smaller, competing companies, its total advertising expenditures on cigarettes were $4.2 million. The very next year, after the trust was dissolved, advertising expenditures more than doubled to $10.2 million. From this example, large-scale advertising would have to be classified as being associated with a larger degree of competition (after the trust was dissolved) as former trust members were forced to compete with one another.

16. J. J. Boddewyn, "Tobacco Advertising in a Free Society," in R. Tollison, ed., *Smoking and Society* (Lexington, Mass: D. C. Heath and Co.), pp. 309–32.

CONCLUSION

In 1956, Joe Bain's book *Barriers to New Competition* played a large part in crystallizing the hypothesis that advertising prevented or impeded entry into industries.[17] Bain isolates one industry group characterized by what he calls very "high" barriers that result only from advertising and promotion costs. The only industry cited as fitting into this category is the liquor distilling industry, in which "Entry on a relatively small scale . . . would encounter overwhelming disadvantages. . . . Large scale entry is not viewed as conceivable."[18]

James Ferguson (1967) examined the U.S. liquor industry to see whether it was the best example of an oligopoly where effective entry was prevented by advertising, as Bain suggested.[19] Ferguson discovered that roughly one third of the firms in the industry in 1965 had entered after World War II and twelve of the existing thirty-five registered distilleries producing whisky had entered the industry in the same period. Additionally, Ferguson cited the fact that the share of the market held by the leading twenty brands decreased over the period even though the share of total industry advertising represented by these twenty brands *increased* over his sample period. From 1951–1953 to 1960–1962, the market share of these leading twenty brands decreased by 14 percent while their share of industry advertising rose by 11 percent in the same period. The leading four brands in the liquor industry fared even worse from 1947 to 1967. Here the collective market share decreased from 75 percent to 54 percent.[20]

While it is the nature of statistical studies to be inconclusive, there appears to be small empirical support for the brand loyalty/economies-of-scale arguments that advertising creates entry barriers. A large body of existing evidence contradicts the widely held traditional view and supports theories that view advertising as a characteristic of the competitive process, not of oligopoly or monopoly. As suggested by neo-Austrian and other modern economists, advertising functions as a tool of entry, making markets more, not less, competitive.

17. Joe S. Bain, *Barriers to New Competition* (Cambridge, Mass: Harvard University Press, 1956).

18. Yale Brozen, "Is Advertising a Barrier to Entry?" in Yale Brozen, ed., *Advertising and Society* (New York: New York University Press, 1974), p. 89.

19. James M. Ferguson, "Advertising and Liquor," *Journal of Business* 40 (1967): 414–34.

20. Brozen, *Advertising and Society*.

6

CONCENTRATION OF INDUSTRY, PRICES, AND QUALITY

We have now evaluated statistical evidence on some of the commonly held beliefs regarding advertising and its direct effects on consumers and firms. The evidence surveyed contained interesting implications, two of which gave a modicum of support for traditional arguments: (1) that some advertising possesses unusual characteristics that give rise to certain entry costs, and (2) that, in some markets, brand or noninformative advertising may slow the entry of lower priced substitutes for a "first mover's" product. On the whole, however, available statistical evidence suggests that advertising, viewed from the perspective of market-wide effects, is consistent with a competitive environment and, indeed, is integral to the process of competition.

In this chapter we focus upon the indirect effects of advertising on markets. "Indirect" does not mean "of secondary importance" since these effects matter most to economists. Rather, the indirect effects of advertising relate to its impact on *market outcomes,* not to the more direct effects on the decisions of market participants.

We begin with the evidence on advertising and the concentration of industries, but the chapter also focuses on some interesting evidence concerning the effects of advertising on both the prices and quality of products and services. Traditional and modern approaches predict opposite effects on these important dimensions.

THE ADVERTISING-CONCENTRATION RELATIONSHIP

One of the oldest and most popular issues concerning the economic causes and consequences of advertising relates the intensity of advertising in specific industries to the degree of concentration found in those industries. The empirical debate over whether or not advertising *causes* concentration or high profit rates has raged for almost two decades, and this section discusses the results and predictions of the evidence. What does it mean to argue that advertising causes economic concentration? To answer this question, we first must know what is meant by concentration and how to decide if an industry is highly concentrated or not.

Industry concentration may be, and has been, measured in a variety of ways, chiefly by a number known as a *concentration ratio*. The concentration ratio is computed by finding the percentage share of the market held by the largest firms in that particular industry. Concentration ratios may be formed by using many different variables as measures of "the market" (i.e., sales, units of output, value of shipments, number of employees, and so on) and also by using different numbers of firms.

Generally the number of firms used to form a concentration ratio ranges from three to five of those firms accounting for the largest levels of sales or output in an industry. For example, if total sales in the beer industry during a period were $1,000,000, and the three firms with the largest sales accounted for $450,000 of total market sales, then the three-firm concentration ratio computed on the basis of dollar value of sales would be 0.45 or 45 percent. But if total sales of beer were 200,000 barrels, and the three largest firms charged different prices for their beer and accounted for 100,000 barrels sold, then the three-firm concentration ratio would be 0.50 instead of 0.45. Clearly, the variables we use to measure "the market" can influence the resulting concentration ratio. If there is only one firm in an industry so that the industry is a monopoly, then the concentration ratio would equal 1.00, or the firm would have 100 percent of the market. The higher the concentration ratio in an industry, given the number of firms, the "closer" this industry is to monopoly with all of the welfare-reducing properties that monopoly implies. This was an important hypothesis of the traditional view.

Traditional economics explains that advertising expenditure might produce *rising* concentration ratios in industries over time, or at worst, stabilize high concentration ratios. In this scenario, advertising produces monopolistic markets and *causes* concentration (or increasing concentration). The reasoning is that large firms have the advantage of increasing returns to scale or economies of scale in advertising, providing effective insulation from competition of new entrants. Evidence presented in the previous chapter suggested little support for the economies-of-scale-due-to-advertising argument, although the possibility exists that such effects may obtain in selected markets. Researchers have, for whatever reason, failed to uncover them. If such economies exist, however, they would result in market outcomes characterized by high levels of concentration.

The first attempt to test the advertising-concentration hypothesis was made by Nicholas Kaldor and Rodney Silverman in the 1940s.[1] They measured advertising intensity as the ratio of average advertising-to-sales ratios in 118 industries in England in 1938, and concentration by the number of firms necessary to account for 80 percent of industry advertising. Their findings initiated a still-raging controversy.

The Kaldor-Silverman study found that the most intensively advertising industries were those for which only a "few" firms, four to nine, accounted for 80 percent of total industry advertising. A large degree of advertising intensity was, in their study, associated with so-called oligopolistic industries. Later studies generally consisted of constructing different measures of concentration and advertising intensity and subjecting the different data to different methods of statistical analysis. Different authors achieved different results. (An interesting conclusion of the Kaldor-Silverman study, one that is generally forgotten by proponents of the view that advertising causes concentration, is that in situations where *fewer* than four firms accounted for at least 80 percent of the industry advertising expenditures, advertising intensities *diminished*.)

The exact methods other authors have used to remeasure and redefine data, and the reasons for using them, are important to those who wish to become serious students of this area of empirical economic analysis. For our purposes, they are of relatively minor im-

---

1. Nicholas Kaldor and R. Silverman, *A Statistical Analysis of Advertising Expenditure and Revenue of the Press* (Cambridge: Cambridge University Press, 1948).

portance. General results are of interest here and in most, but not all, cases researchers found little evidence in support of the thesis that advertising intensity increased concentration in industries, however measured. The general method followed in this research was to hypothesize the following sort of statistical relationship between concentration measures and advertising intensity:

CONCENTRATION = A CONSTANT + ADVERTISING
INTENSITY MEASURE

This implies that concentration (the dependent variable) is an *effect* caused by advertising intensity (the explanatory variable). Data are collected and used to measure concentration and advertising intensity. The statistical procedure of regression analysis is then applied to the data to obtain estimates of the degree by which a change in advertising intensity *causes* a change in the measure of concentration. Some degree of confidence that the estimate obtained from this procedure is the true measure of the actual relationship may also be had.

If, for example, regression analyses were performed using the above equation and the effect of advertising on concentration were estimated to be of the magnitude 0.5, then we would say that a one-unit increase in the advertising intensity measure causes one half of one unit increase in the concentration measure. If the estimate were a negative number, an increase in advertising intensity would appear to cause a decrease in concentration. The investigator must also have some way of determining whether or not the estimate is truly non-zero, or if a spurious relationship is being obtained. The statistical procedure yields tools that test for the "significance" of the estimate. Suffice it to say that the measure of whether or not the estimate is significant or insignificant is important. If the estimate is 0.5 but insignificant, one *cannot state scientifically* that the estimate of 0.5 is actually the true measure of how concentration levels respond to changes in advertising intensity. The data simply indicate that we have no sound evidence to state that advertising intensity affects concentration at all in any direction.

Table 6–1 shows some of the statistical results that have accumulated over the years from researchers subjecting different data and measures of the above equation to different statistical procedures in order to test the notion that advertising intensity causes concentra-

Table 6–1.   Summary of Research on Advertising's Effect on Market Concentration.

Author(s)	Sample Period	Concentration Ratio Measure	Advertising Measure	Statistically Significant
Telser (1964)	'47, '54, '58	4-Firm	A/S	NO
Mann *et al.* (1967)	'54, '58, '63	4-Firm	A/S of dominant firm	YES
Telser (1969)	'58	4-Firm	A/S of dominant firm	NO
Ekelund & Maurice (1969)	'54–'63	Change in 4-Firm	Change in A/S	NO
Ekelund & Gramm (1970)	'63	4-Firm	A/S	NO
Vernon (1971)	'64, '68	4-Firm	P/S	NO
Edwards (1973)	'64, '65	3-Firm	A/S	NO
Ornstein *et al.* (1973)	'63	4-Firm	AE	YES
Nelson (1975)	'58	4-Firm	A/S	MIXED
Strickland & Weiss (1976)	'63	4-Firm	A/S	YES

Source: Compiled from Stanley I. Ornstein, *Industrial Concentration and Advertising* (Washington, D.C.: American Enterprise Institute, 1977), pp. 68–73.

Notes: A/S = the advertising-to-sales ratio.
P/S = the promotion expenditures-to-sales ratio.
AE = absolute advertising expenditure.

tion in industry. While a few studies find that advertising intensity is a significant variable in explaining concentration, most studies show advertising activity to not have a significant effect on market concentration. At worst, one might conclude that the evidence suggests that the notion that advertising causes concentration is uncertain, with the preponderance of evidence suggesting no causal relationship at all.

In more recent research, Peter Asch examines the idea of whether changes in advertising intensity have produced relative changes in concentration in the U.S. over the period 1963 to 1972.[2] Dividing industries into producer and consumer products, and further dividing each into durable and nondurable products, Asch finds that in each of the four subdivisions, advertising intensity is not a statistically significant determinant of concentration, as the results of his regressions appearing in Table 6–2 show. Table 6–2 shows that the rather small increases in measured concentration that occurred in the U.S. from 1963 to 1972 (part B of Table 6–2) cannot be attributed to increasing advertising intensities, since none of the coefficients that measure advertising intensities (part A of Table 6–2) are significant. These results, along with others obtained by Asch, led him to conclude that "during 1963–1972 . . . industry advertising intensity played a largely insignificant role in changes in industry concentration. The associations suggest that *heavy advertising was at least as likely to accompany concentration decreases as increases. . . .* In the absence of better evidence however, it must be tentatively concluded that increasing concentration is not, in general, one of the evils *of* intensive industry advertising"[3] (emphasis added).

J. J. Lambin's study of European industry (1976) produced findings similar to those of Asch. In general, he found no significant relationship that would indicate that market concentration was being positively affected by advertising intensity.[4] Lambin uncovered partial evidence that, just as Asch hints, increasing advertising intensity may lead to decreasing concentration in industries—a result that is not inconsistent with the new neoclassical or positive view of advertising as a means of competition and entry. Other evidence produced by Lambin suggests that the market shares of firms within industries are relatively unstable in the face of heavy advertising intensities of competitors, implying that heavy advertising does not succeed in sheltering firms from the effects of competitors.[5]

The notion that heavy advertising causes industries to be highly concentrated has very little logical or empirical support in relation to the evidence that states this relationship not to be the case. There are

2. Peter Asch, "The Role of Advertising in Changing Concentration, 1963–1971," *Southern Economic Journal* 462 (1979): 288–97.

3. Ibid., pp. 294–95.

4. J. J. Lambin, *Advertising, Competition, and Market Conduct* (Amsterdam: North-Holland Publishing Co., 1976), p. 136.

5. Ibid., p. 121.

Table 6–2.   **Advertising Intensity and Changes in Market Concentration in the U.S. Between 1963 and 1972.**

Part A

The dependent variable in the following regression is the concentration ratio in 1973/ the concentration ratio in 1963, a measure of the *relative* change in the concentration ratio.

	Explanatory Variables			
	Concentration Ratio in 1963	Sales Growth Rate ('63 to '72)	Change in Advertising Intensity From '63	R^2
All Industries	−.004*	−.09*	.00007	.09
Producer Goods	−.003*	−.02	−.030	.08
Durables	−.003*	.07	−.030	.00
Nondurables	−.003*	−.02	−.030	.09
Consumer Goods	−.007*	−.27*	−.002	.16
Durables	.000	−.12	−.020	.01
Nondurables	−.010*	−.37*	.003	.20

Part B

Industry	
All Industries	1.069
Producer Goods	1.147
Durables	1.043
Nondurables	1.203
Consumer Goods	1.038
Durables	0.941
Nondurables	1.062

SOURCE: Peter Asch, "The Role of Advertising in Changing Concentration, 1963–1971," *Southern Economic Journal* 462 (1979): 295.

Note: *indicates statistical significance.

no data or evidence that consistently show that advertising, however measured, causes concentration. Indeed, there exists some evidence, albeit inconclusive, that just the opposite is the case. It may be the case that higher than average concentration in industries, however measured, *is the cause of,* not caused by, relatively heavy advertising intensities. In view of the preponderance of evidence it would be difficult to maintain that heavy advertising causes concentration in industries.

ADVERTISING AND PROFITS

Another area of concern is the supposedly abnormally high levels of profits that advertising either creates or enhances. The chain of reasoning is driven by the assumption of barriers to entry where competition and entry is somehow prevented or discouraged by existing firms through their advertising. The absence of competition produced by advertising then generates abnormally high profits for firms in the industry. Again, we focus on the outcome in the market, high profits, rather than the direct channel through which this outcome is produced.

What is meant by profits? Some individuals would define profits as equal to the revenues of a business, since some people sometimes forget about the costs of resources needed to produce commodities and services. This is obviously unacceptable. Accountants generally measure profits as total revenues from sales less total costs of producing output. The accounting view is lacking for purposes of economic analysis since it does not permit an accurate comparison of firms that are of different sizes and other characteristics.

For example, if IBM reported profits of $1,000,000,000 and AT&T reported profits of $500,000,000, many would conclude that IBM is more profitable (twice as profitable) than AT&T. This conclusion may be accurate for some purposes, but not in the terms of economic analysis. A better measure of profitability would be to look at the percentage rate of return that the firm earns on its assets, or the accountants "profits" divided by the value of the assets the firm must purchase or have in order to produce its output. If IBM owned, say, $10 billion in capital assets and AT&T owned $4 billion in capital assets, then AT&T would be the more profitable since its rate of return would be 12.5 percent as compared to 10 percent for IBM. The use of rates of return permits comparisons of a variety of firms and is the basis of economic research into issues of profitability. If a firm is earning large profits due to a lack of competition, its rate of return will be higher than the rates of return (on average) of other firms in other markets. It was this measure of profits or profitability, the rate of return on assets, that was used in the first serious study of the effect that advertising has on profits. As we shall see, however, the manner in which the rate of return is measured is also important in the study of advertising and profitability.

Initial research in this area was completed by two defenders of the traditional view of advertising, William Comanor and Thomas Wilson.[6] Their thesis was that concentration in an industry is a poor measure of the degree of monopoly since it measures only one dimension of an industry's structure, while monopoly power depends upon a number of factors. It may be inferred, according to Comanor and Wilson, that the higher the average rate of return on invested capital in an industry (their proxy measure of profits), the greater the degree of monopoly power that the industry possessed. For an industry to maintain a higher than average rate of return on capital or stockholder equity, it must be the case that new firms cannot enter the industry. If firms were to enter, prices would fall (revenues per unit of output sold would fall) and the higher than average rate of return would be competed downward. There must be, in other words, some abrogation of the competitive process.

The agent which discourages and prevents competitive entry is advertising, according to Comanor and Wilson. In brief, large existing firms have cost advantages over firms considering entering the industry, advantages which arise from the supposed consumer inertia and brand loyalty associated with the advertising of existing firms. Advantages also purportedly arise from the economies of scale in advertising and production which inhibit entry. New and smaller firms would face entry-inhibiting capital costs. In this manner the link was established between industries that exhibit high advertising-to-sales ratios ("relatively intensive" advertising) and industries that showed relatively high rates of return, or profits.

The results of their study are interesting, especially from the perspective of earlier analysis regarding the role of advertising as an entry barrier. Data from forty-one consumer goods industries and their regression analysis results show that, in general, the higher the advertising-sales ratio, or the more intensive the advertising in an industry, the larger will be the rate of return in the industry. In particular, industries that advertised most intensively had rates of return almost half again higher than other industries. Comanor and Wilson's study appeared to provide firm empirical support for the hypothesis

---

6. William S. Comaner and Thomas S. Wilson, "Advertising, Market Structure, and Performance," *Review of Economics and Statistics* 49 (1967): 423–40.

that high advertising intensity was at least one factor contributing to monopoly power.

An important oversight in this procedure came to the attention of Harry Bloch a few years later.[7] Bloch's point was this: In measuring the rate of return (r) a firm (or, on average firms in an industry) earns, one at first would subtract costs of production (C) from revenues (R) and divide this number by the value of capital assets or the net worth (NW) of the firm. Algebraically,

$$r = \frac{R - C}{NW}$$

This is essentially the procedure followed by Comanor and Wilson in their study. There is, however, a logical reason to believe and statistical evidence to suggest that some advertising does not only affect or provide information to consumers today, but into the *future* as well. Advertising is like any other capital item in that its effects or benefits can last into the future although it may be paid for today. Bloch argued that for purposes of economic and statistical analysis, advertising should not be treated totally as a current expense, as accountants treat advertising expenses in constructing balance sheets. Instead, such expenditures should be treated as a form of capital investment and amortized or depreciated over a period of time. Advertising, or its economic effects, last for some time and is an *investment* and not a current expense. Bloch also pointed out that a firm's tax payments are reduced by currently expensing the advertising expenditures, a fact that may further distort the calculated rate of return from its "true" value. (Note that a theoretical-analytical amortization of advertising in no way implies that advertising should not be treated as a current expense for tax purposes.)[8]

7. Harry Bloch, "Advertising and Profitability: A Reappraisal," *Journal of Political Economy* 82 (1974): 267–86.

8. Note that Bloch describes an *economic* effect of amortizing advertising over a longer period than one year. In economic terms—and for purposes of analysis—it is useful to consider advertising as an amortized and not a current expense. This clearly does not mean that advertising should be amortized for purposes of taxation. Variations in the effects of particular advertisements on particular firms make the "scientific" application of taxes to the impact of advertising practically impossible. Not enough is known about the "degeneration function" of particular advertisements to tax firms on this basis. Under such circumstances, current year expensing of advertising—i.e., in the year in which the expense is incurred—is likely the most equitable and "scientific" tax treatment of advertising expenses.

Bloch's research suggests that the rates of return used by Comanor and Wilson (and also by a subsequent Federal Trade Commission study which produced results similar to those of Comanor and Wilson *and* upon which public policy recommendations were made) be adjusted to reflect the idea that advertising is a capital asset which depreciates over time and not simply a current expense. Bloch found, in recomputing the rates of return, that "true" rates of return were smaller than accounting rates of return, and that accounting rates of return *overstate* profitability especially for relatively heavy advertisers. Specifically, Bloch's analysis shows that the measure of advertising intensity, the advertising-to-sales ratio, has no *statistically significant effect* on true profit rates of return.

The evidence is once more consistent with the theories of the new neoclassical or positive economists: Relatively high advertising intensities do not produce, yield, or cause firms to earn higher than average rates of return. This evidence does not suggest that intensive advertising makes markets or firms more monopolistic as characterized by persistently higher than average rates of returns. The extent of the bias may be understood by considering Table 6–3, which is a

Table 6–3.   Actual Profit Rates and Profit Rates Adjusted for Advertising Capital Depreciation: Selected Firms.

Company	Rates of Return (Percentages)		Advertising/ Sales Ratio	Average Advertising Asset (Millions of $)
	r	$\bar{r}$		
National Dairy Products	13.0	10.9	0.92	59.3
Joseph Seagram & Sons	14.2	10.5	2.06	101.6
General Foods	12.5	7.7	4.03	182.0
H. J. Heinz	6.7	4.8	1.45	41.1
Continental Baking Co.	12.3	8.9	1.16	19.4
Green Giant Co.	10.2	7.7	3.61	8.7

SOURCE: Harry Bloch, "Advertising and Profitability: A Reappraisal," *Journal of Political Economy* 82 (1974): 285.

Notes: r = the reported profit rate.

$\bar{r}$ = the reported profit rate adjusted by depreciating advertising expenditures.

Average advertising asset is the value of not yet depreciated advertising expenditures.

representative sample of the firms in Bloch's study, their actual and Bloch's "true" rates of return, advertising-to-sales ratios, and the value of advertising assets.

Bloch, however, was criticized by Comanor and Wilson for his methods of adjusting accounting rates of return to true rates of return by treating advertising as an asset in net worth and depreciating advertising over its expected functional life. In particular, Bloch assumed that advertising depreciated at a 5-percent annual rate for all firms in his sample. The basic criticism was that not all industry advertising effects last the same length of time. Rates of depreciation of advertising's effects can be expected to differ across industries, and the 5-percent rate of depreciation used by Bloch was unreasonably low. For example, the informational content of advertising messages for search goods which contain current, one-week only, sale prices may decay more rapidly than Ford Motor Company's current "superior quality" advertisements. These criticisms might weaken or invalidate the finding that high advertising intensity has no significant effect on profitability or rate of return on tangible invested capital.

In response to these criticisms, Robert Ayanian (1975) devised yet another method to judge the rate of depreciation of the effectiveness of advertising on an industry-wide basis that allows for differing depreciation rates for different industries.[9] His estimates of depreciation rates also avoid the criticism of being "too low" as they are all well above the rate of 5 percent assumed by Bloch. Ayanian subjected two forms of his and others' data to regression analysis and obtained the following statistical relationships:[10]

$$r = 12.45 + 0.242* \text{ percent} \times (A/S); \quad R^2 = .243$$
$$\bar{r} = 10.99 + 0.041 \text{ percent} \times (A/S); \quad R = .021$$

The first equation reveals, if we use the accounting rate of return (r) as a measure of profitability, that a 1-percent increase in the measure of advertising intensity [the advertising to sales ratio (A/S)], will cause the accounting rate of return to increase by about $24/100$ of one percent, with the asterisk indicating that this estimate is statistically signifi-

9. Robert Ayanian, "Advertising and Rate of Return," *Journal of Law and Economics* 18 (1975): 479–506.

10. Ibid., pp. 500–01.

cant. The R^2 is the percent of the variation in the accounting rate of return explained by the advertising-sales ratio—about 24 percent. (The 12.45 is simply a constant and can be ignored here.) The second equation shows that, if Ayanian's adjusted profit rate ($\bar{r}$) is used instead of actual accounting rates, a 1-percent increase in advertising intensity increases the true rate of return by only $^4/_{100}$ of one percent (not four percentage points), *but the estimate is statistically insignificant.* Note also that the R^2 is only 2 percent.

Ayanian's study directly answers criticisms aimed at Bloch and reaches much the same conclusions. When profitability is more carefully measured to account for the fact that the information content of advertising messages can last over a period of time and that advertising is in fact an investment and not a current expense, the scientific evidence indicates that *higher than average rates of return in industries cannot be attributed to advertising.*

Bloch and Ayanian directly address methodological problems of the traditional view, although new technical problems are raised. Two questions naturally come to mind. First, a positive correlation between accounting rates of return and advertising intensity does seem to exist. Are the *techniques* that accountants use in constructing profits (proper for their purposes) the source of this observed correlation? It is possible that researchers in economics have simply failed to uncover the profits-advertising linkages, should they truly exist. Next, if the accounting measure of rate of return is "faulty" and is the source of the advertising-profits correlation, would that fact necessarily imply an *absence* of entry barriers in heavily advertised industries?

Harold Demsetz addresses both of these issues in his 1979 study.[11] Demsetz shows that the accountant's measure of the rate of return on stockholder equity (a measure of a firm's profit rate) can be biased, either upward or downward, from the "true" measure of return. This bias depends upon, among other factors, how much advertising capital the firm has produced, how rapidly the firm adds to this advertising capital, and how rapidly advertising capital deteriorates or decays in the marketplace. The annual advertising-expenditures-to-stockholder-equity ratio, a measure of firm advertising intensity, can be constructed in order to investigate the first question posed above.

---

11. Harold Demsetz, "Accounting for Advertising as a Barrier to Entry," *Journal of Business* 52 (1979): 345–60.

Demsetz, as previous researchers, employs regression analysis to uncover an interesting result. In his data sample, the bias imparted to accounting rates of return of the individual firms varies. When advertising expenditures are expensed in the current period, rates of return are biased positively for some firms and negatively for others. Regression results show that advertising intensity affects the accounting rate of return in a positive, significant fashion *only* when this rate of return is positively biased from its true measure. (Demsetz obtains similar results using the advertising-sales ratio as the measure of advertising intensity.) When this bias is close to zero or negative, advertising intensity imparts no significant influence on profit rates. Demsetz concludes that it is the accounting artifact of expensing rather than amortizing advertising expenditures (capital) that yields the aforementioned biases in economic research. The accountant's method of handling advertising expenditures produces a *spurious* causal link between advertising intensity and profitability.

Demsetz also confronts the issue of what this bias represents. These "faulty" (from an economist's point of view) accounting practices can fail to reflect a genuine entry barrier that has not yet been discovered. They can also fail to reflect the welfare-enhancing value to consumers of information about the firm and its market.

The issue is addressed by first dividing firms in the sample into two groups. One group contains firms producing and selling final consumer goods, the other intermediate producer goods. Demsetz notes that the "advertising as entry barrier" hypothesis is usually reserved for industries characterized by hapless consumers facing large, market-powerful firms. Buyers of producer goods, on the other hand, are firms and businesses, presumably not swayed by the advertising effects of other businesses as are individual consumers. If the traditional hypothesis concerning advertising and entry barriers is correct, Demsetz argues, we should observe advertising intensity influencing profitability in the consumer goods sector to a significantly greater degree than in the producer goods sector.

The statistical effects of Demsetz's measure of advertising intensity on profitability are then reevaluated by dichotomizing firms producing consumer versus producer goods. The same statistical patterns mentioned earlier are observed for *both* types of goods. When current expensing of advertising creates a positive bias in the accounting rate of return measure, advertising intensity significantly increases the accounting rate of return measures. Were the brand loyalty-entry barrier hypotheses concerning advertising theoretically and empirically sound, we should observe a more pronounced and stronger influence of advertising intensity on profitability in the consumer goods group.

Demsetz concludes that the manner in which accountants treat advertising produces data which yield a spurious nexus between advertising intensity and profitability in economic research. He also concludes that such biases are less consistent with the advertising-as-entry-barrier school than with the view of advertising as enhancing consumer welfare and competition. The evidence does not support a popular notion of advertising as a source of monopoly power.

ADVERTISING, PRICES, AND QUALITY

A difficult concept for some is how advertising can have the effect of actually lowering, and not raising the money prices charged by firms for products and services. While the effect of lowered full prices may appear plausible, it seems reasonable to argue that the resources that go into advertising are not without cost and that they must be paid for. If advertising is an input into the production and distribution of goods and services, it will also enter as a factor in determining the costs of producing these goods and services. Thus, if products are marketed or advertised, costs are incurred that would not exist if there were no advertising at all. The use of advertising by firms must also increase the money prices of goods and services sold by firms. The argument, in one sense, is partially correct. But costs of production are not the *only* factor that determine what prices in fact emerge in markets.

An even more difficult notion to accept and understand is that advertising, or the lack thereof, may influence the *quality* of a product or service. A hamburger is a hamburger is a hamburger, and no amount of advertising can change the freshness of the bun or the sensation of taste to the consumer. However, as we will show, for some products and services quality is not an absolute, fixed characteristic determined either solely by the subjective valuations of consumers or fixed by producers in a vacuum. It is a characteristic that is both supplied and demanded in varying degrees. As such, product or service quality in some markets is closely intertwined with advertising activity. The amount of information consumers have about prices, qualities, availability, and characteristics of competing products plays a major role in determining prices charged and quality supplied by firms. Since information is transferred with advertising, consider some evidence concerning advertising, prices, qualities, and markets.

An interesting study in the statistical economic literature, written by Robert Steiner (1973), highlights the above point in research on the market for children's toys and television advertising.[12] Steiner points out that toy manufacturers advertised little on television until the Mattel Toy Company began purchasing time on The Mickey Mouse Club TV show in the mid-1950s. Since the audience of the Mickey Mouse Club was primarily composed of children, and since the ads proclaimed the merits of the advertised toys, giving little if any information on prices, allegations of devious advertising resulted. Critics charged that the minds of children were swayed to induce parental expenditure, all in the name of profit. (The charge remains popular as the discussion of "kiddie-video" shows; see Chapter 7.) Steiner points out that prior to the mid-1950s, a toy whose suggested retail price was $5 generally sold at around $4.95. After the Mattel ad campaign, along with increased advertising expenditures of other toy makers in cities where television advertising was relatively frequent, the price of the $5 toy charged by retailers had *fallen* to an average of about $3.50, with occasional sale prices of $3.00. In cities where there was little or no advertising, prices continued to average roughly $4.95.

This episode indicates that advertising (even in the face of a mild inflationary period during which prices could be expected to rise) may be viewed as an agent whose effect can be the substantial lowering of market prices. Price increases attributable to increased advertising costs have been minimal in many cases. Through its informational content, advertising produced a greater turnover in toys. Greater turnover permitted smaller profit margins and increased the number of known substitutes for consumers. This permitted greater price comparison shopping and limited or reduced the maximum price a retailer was able to charge *and still expect consumers to buy*.

Other cases are similar, but not identical, to the toy case. But instead of looking for something that occurred due to advertising, such as a drop in toy prices, one can look for things that have *not* hap-

12. Robert L. Steiner, "Does Advertising Lower Consumer Prices?" *Journal of Marketing* 37 (1973): 19–26.

pened. Recall that certain contemporary positive economists view advertising not as a barrier to entry into markets, not as an anticompetitive tool of monopolies and oligopolies, but as a device that makes markets more competitive. Evidence strongly supports this view. It is then a short step to reason through the following argument: If advertising is a means of competitive entry and lower prices, it would be in the economic interest of incumbent firms to somehow prevent advertising so as to eliminate or minimize competitive effects. After all, businesses are seeking to maximize profits, among other things.

The crucial question concerns the manner in which advertising is restricted. For one, all the firms in an industry could come to a gentleman's agreement not to advertise. But when profits are at stake, such agreements tend to break down quickly. The problem with the gentleman's agreement (apart from being illegal) is enforcement, and in most free societies one firm does not have the legal right to prevent another firm from advertising. The answer then lies in finding a method of preventing or discouraging advertising in such a way so as to guarantee that no or very little advertising will occur. The method must also make sure that if anyone does advertise, he will be caught, severely punished, and perhaps legally expelled from the industry.

The solution is to *pass a law,* and this is exactly what has been done in a number of industries. Laws, allegedly in the consumer's interest and strictly enforced by various levels of government, have been passed prohibiting advertising in certain industries. If advertising helps produce competitive results in markets, then it seems likely that a ban or prevention of advertising will likely produce anticompetitive or monopolistic outcomes. Specifically, new neoclassical economics leads one to expect prices to be higher than would otherwise be the case in industries where there is some degree of legal advertising prevention.

One of the most famous studies of this hypothesis analyzes the market for eyeglasses. This particular market provides a fertile area of analysis for several reasons. First, some states in the U.S. (over the period of study) did not ban advertising of eyeglasses and eye examination prices, but enough banned or inhibited advertising so that scientific comparisons could be made. Secondly, the states that did ban price advertising did so expressly in the public interest. Lee Benham (1972) examined the prices of eyeglasses and eye examinations charged in states that allowed or had few restrictions on advertising, and in states that did not allow advertising of these products and services in 1963.[13] Benham first subjected data to regression analysis to discern whether or not the effect of a prohibition on advertising would be a statistically significant factor causing prices to be higher in states where there existed effective prohibitions on advertising. After accounting for the effect other variables may have had on the price of glasses and exams (such as family income, age of customer, family size, and sex), Benham's results showed that advertising prohibitions were a statistically significant variable in causing prices to be higher in states prohibiting advertisements.

Consider Table 6–4, which reproduces some of Benham's results concerning price differentials. The upper half of Table 6–4 shows average prices in the two types of states when forty-eight states plus Washington, D.C. are included in the sample. Prices for glasses were 25 percent higher on average in states that restricted or banned advertising. The lower half of Table 6–4 is even more interesting. It compares the "worst" and the "best." That is, Washington, D.C. and Texas had virtually no advertising impediments on glasses or exams

13. Lee Benham, "The Effect of Advertising on the Price of Eyeglasses," *Journal of Law and Economics* 15 (1972): 337–52.

Table 6–4.   Effect of Advertising on Price of Eyeglasses and Eye Examinations (1963 Prices).

All States with Complete Restrictions on Advertising Price	*All States with No Restrictions on Advertising Price*	*Difference in Price*	*Percentage Difference in Price*
Eyeglasses			
$33.04	$26.34	$ 6.70	25%
Eyeglasses + Examination			
$40.96	$37.10	3.86	10%
North Carolina	*Washington, D.C. & Texas*		
Eyeglasses			
$37.48	$17.98	$19.50	108%
Eyeglasses + Examination			
$50.73	$29.97	20.76	69%

SOURCE: Lee Benham, "The Effect of Advertising on the Price of Eyeglasses," *Journal of Law and Economics* 15 (1972): 342.

in 1963 but North Carolina had wide-ranging advertising restrictions that had been in force for a number of years. The numbers speak for themselves. Benham's statistical results indicate that the *prohibition* of advertising had caused prices to be higher. These price differentials may seem small, but remember that they are all expressed in terms of 1963 dollars. When adjusted for general price inflation so that the price differentials are expressed in terms of 1988 purchasing power dollars, the numbers grow. For example, the price differential on the examination plus eyeglasses between North Carolina and Texas/ Washington, D.C. in terms of current prices is roughly $80.00. The study also indicates that the price differentials tend to be dramatically larger the greater the degree of difference in advertising laws.

In certain circumstances it may be difficult (costly) for groups of sellers to induce lawmakers to provide them with the competition-restricting legislation. Legislation is not the only method available to collusive groups of sellers that restricts the flow of information to consumers and reduces competition in the market. It may be the best method, but there are substitutes.

In later research, Lee and Alexandra Benham (1975) return to the market for eyeglasses and analyze the notion of what they termed "regulating through the profession."[14] Many professions have codes of ethics and conduct to which members of the profession must adhere or risk being officially excluded from membership. Sanctions may effectively prevent a supplier from transacting with consumers (local medical boards) or merely stigmatize the miscreant.

Professional associations probably have diverse objectives. The Benhams focus their attention on the American Optometric Association (AOA) and its state affiliates and suggest that one function of the AOA is to inhibit the flow of information available to consumers through the advertising of eyeglasses and eyecare by member optometrists. If advertising can be inhibited through private organizations, the same qualitative effect on prices (presumably to the benefit of association members) that legal advertising restrictions have could be obtained.

The Benhams observed that the AOA codes had declared such practices as advertising professional superiority, wider range of ser-

---

14. Lee Benham and Alexandra Benham, "Regulating Through the Professions: A Perspective on Information Control," *Journal of Law and Economics* 18 (1975): 421–47.

vices, and lower fees to be unethical and unprofessional conduct. Use of a brand name for a company or clinic was also taboo to the AOA. The state affiliate ethical codes reinforced the theme. For example, the Michigan Optometric Association rules in 1969 imposed a point system for membership. Table 6–5, a condensed form of the Michigan code, details how members achieved and maintained good standing. A minimum of eighty-five points out of one hundred was required yearly to maintain membership, with fully seventy points constituting information/advertising constraints. Twenty-twenty vision is not required to appreciate the intent of the Michigan code.

Given that the AOA and various state codes had the effect of severely limiting advertising activity on the part of members, the Benhams measured the effects of these information restrictions on the prices paid for eyewear. They argued that a good measure of the degree by which consumer information is suppressed can be had by calculating the percentage of optometrists in a state that are members of the AOA through the state affiliate organizations. In their data sample, taken in 1969, this fraction ranged from 43 percent to 93 percent. After adjusting for such factors as the purchaser's family size, age, sex, race (males tend toward better unaided vision than females, and blacks better than whites), city versus rural locations, and consumer income, results on price effects of AOA affiliation were obtained. The Benhams found that eyewear prices would rise by a statistically significant $36.40 (1988 purchasing power dollars) as the AOA membership rate rose from 43 percent to 91 percent. These results were

Table 6–5.   Michigan Optometric Association Membership Point Scale.

Activity by Association Members	Total Points
Not advertising (media, telephone books, window displays)	30
Not locating practice in an establishment whose primary public image is one of reduced prices and discount optical outlet	25
Limiting office identification sign to approved size and content	15
Participation in education activities (professional meetings)	14
Sufficient physical (laboratory and examining room) and functional (equipment) facilities	16

SOURCE: Lee Benham and Alexandra Benham, "Regulating Through the Professions: A Perspective on Information Control," *Journal of Law and Economics* 18 (1975): 425.

not as dramatic as Benham's previous study and Benham did not adjust for "quality" in either study, an issue we address below. However, the smaller magnitude of the more recent study's effects may reflect the possibility that the AOA advertising restriction mechanism is less efficient than legislation.

The Benhams' research also addressed two other issues closely related to markets and advertising. Their study indicated that individuals buy eyeglasses with greater frequency in areas where professional control (AOA membership) is lower. With lower prices in these areas, this is a reasonable conclusion. But *given the effects of price,* will "commercialism" in the provision of this facet of health care lead suppliers to fleece unsuspecting consumers with advertising-induced "unneeded" eyewear? An answer to this question was given by separating individuals in the sample into two groups. One group purchased eyewear from optometrists or physicians (professional sources) while the other bought from "commercial" sources. The statistical results indicated that, *given the effects of other factors, especially price,* consumers who shopped and lived in "commercial" environments did not purchase eyewear any more or less frequently than those who purchased in the "professional" advertising-restricted markets.

Carrying this line of reasoning one step further, advertising's critics argue that advertising preys on those least able to cope with it. That is, the credulous and ignorant purchase "unneeded" glasses. Professional control, such as the AOA's code of ethics, are needed to protect the less competent from commercialism, at least in health care.

The Benhams faced this argument directly and assumed that those less able to cope with the impact of advertising messages are individuals with a low level of education, as indicated by years of schooling. They again divided the sample data into two groups: those with more than thirteen and those with less than eight years of schooling. After adjusting for all other factors, they found that advertising/informational restrictions associated with the AOA codes *increased price by more to the less educated group* than the more educated group.

While data limitations restrict the ability to make broad generalizations from such studies, as the Benhams readily admit, it appears that professional codes of "ethics" show no signs of improving consumer welfare. From a number of vantage points, at least given the limited data sample of eyewear consumers, such restrictions tend to impair consumer well-being.

Advertising and Quality

The natural response of most people when confronted with the price-increasing effects of advertising prohibitions is to voice concern for the quality of goods or services. It is often argued that advertising restrictions really attempt to guarantee consumers a certain level of product or service quality. Advertising restraints are intended, in this view, to prevent charlatans and quacks from foisting inferior grade services and commodities on unsuspecting consumers. Such concerns are legitimate, especially when related to the professional services we buy. Eyesight, for example, is probably the most valuable of all human senses. Most of us who have less than perfect vision would probably find it difficult to distinguish subtle quality differences among the providers of vision care. Moreover, in the case of eyecare the quality of service would be difficult to judge *before* purchase with the distinct possibility that poor quality care could lead to permanent and costly damage to eyesight. A bad pizza may be cheaply thrown away. Low-quality eye care can damage vision forever. It would be informative then to measure the effect on the quality of such services that advertising restrictions have had. If restrictions actually produce a generally better quality of care along with higher prices, then there *might* be some positive social benefit associated with having such restrictions. If, on the other hand, legal advertising impediments do not improve quality, or if they reduce quality and increase prices, then laws of this kind work to the detriment of consumers. Higher prices *and* an inferior product are certainly not in the best interest of consumers.

One might imagine that measuring a slippery concept as the quality of eyecare services for the purpose of statistical analysis would be nearly impossible. However, the Federal Trade Commission's Bureau of Economics was able to do just that and to produce a study that contains surprising results.[15] With the cooperation of representatives of the American Academy of Ophthalmology, the American Optometric Association, and the Opticians Association of America, the

---

15. Gary D. Hailey, Jonathan R. Bromberg, and Joseph B. Mulholland, "A Comparative Analysis of Cosmetic Contact Lens Fitting by Ophthalmologists, Optometrists, and Opticians," *Report of the Staff of the Federal Trade Commission* (Washington, D.C.: Bureau of Consumer Protection and Bureau of Economics, 1983).

FTC was able to devise a method of measuring how well eyecare practitioners had "fit" contact lenses to patients. Thus, an index of the quality of a services was devised. Each of the three organizations provided qualified, professional practitioners to measure and grade certain characteristics of contact lens fit for a sample of contact lens wearers. Such characteristics as accuracy of prescription, incidence of corneal abrasion, and pathological corneal conditions, all of which indicate the quality of the fitting service, were measured in a manner designed to minimize inconsistency and subjective evaluations.

Subjects were asked to identify the fitter of his or her contact lenses. From this information, the FTC staff were able to identify lens wearers who were fit for their contact lenses by either "commercial" or by "noncommercial" optometric practices. Commercial practices were defined as those that advertised and/or employed a trade (or brand) name (a form of advertising). Noncommercial practices engaged in neither of these activities. Such activity is prohibited or inhibited in some states by statutes and licensing board regulations. In this manner the stage was set for a comparison of the quality of service provided by advertisers versus non-advertisers.

The results of the FTC's statistical analysis are interesting. The FTC found statistically significant differences (though at the 10-percent level) in the quality of hard contact lens fitting service among commercial and noncommercial optometrists. However, it was not the fitters who were restricted in their advertising abilities that had the higher quality-of-fit scores as advertising critics would suggest. Commercial optometrists, the ones who advertise in the yellow pages and in newspapers or television, the ones who operate practices under trade names or in mercantile locations (such as shopping malls), were the group that produced the greatest quality of hard contact lenses fitting. In the soft lens market, commercial fitters again scored higher on the quality scale than noncommercial fitters, though the difference was not statistically significant.

The FTC could find *no evidence whatsoever* for the notion that commercial practices such as advertising and the use of trade or brand names, even in a market where quality is extremely important yet difficult for consumers to judge, reduces the quality of the service provided to consumers. If anything, the FTC discovered the opposite to be the case. This, of course, makes sense when we recall the results of market advertising predicted by the modern analytical approach.

Advertising, by whatever method, lowers consumer search costs. Since at least some consumers have quality information (even though it may not be very good), the cost of finding or trying to find a relatively high (or higher) quality practitioner in a market where advertising activity exists to a relatively large degree is lower than in a market where advertising activity is not widespread. Suppliers know that reputations of poor service quality will, sooner or later, spread to consumers and in the process deplete the value of their advertising expenditures. In this type of market, buyers have relatively lower costs of switching suppliers (or avoiding low-quality suppliers) and finding higher quality care than they do in a market where a dearth of advertising information exists. Suppliers likewise face the prospect of losing more customers and losing them more rapidly if they try to sell low-quality care as well as depreciating the customer-attracting value of their advertising dollars. The FTC evidence seems to suggest that a higher quality of eyecare exists in markets where advertising activity is allowed. At worst, the evidence suggests that a lower quality of service is not prevalent in these markets. This conclusion is compatible with the modern view of the economics of advertising.

Two other items of interest surface in the FTC's contact lens study, both of which contradict the traditional view of the effects of advertising in markets and the effect on prices. The FTC staff designed a "standard package" that contact lens wearers normally purchase (the lenses, an eye exam, follow-up care, etc.), calculated the prices paid by study subjects for this given set of items and services, and then adjusted these prices for general cost-of-living differences of subjects residing in different parts of the United States. Statistical analysis of this data yields additional results worthy of attention.

Table 6–6 shows the average prices charged by commercial and noncommercial optometrists as well as ophthalmologists for both hard and soft lenses. Commercial optometrists charged the lowest prices of the groups for both kinds of contact lenses. This conclusion, coupled with the FTC's findings on quality, provides fairly persuasive evidence in support of the point that advertising and other associated commercial information-transferral activities work to the advantage of consumers.[16]

The FTC conducted one additional test. By examining contact lens

16. Ibid., p. 35.

Table 6–6.   Comparison of Prices Charged by Commercial and Noncommercial Optometrists and by Ophthalmologists (1988 Prices).

	Hard Lenses		*Soft Lenses*	
Type of Fitter	*Average Price Charged*	*Percent Above Commercial Optometrist Price*	*Average Price Charged*	*Percent Above Commercial Optometrist Price*
Ophthalmologists	$312.99	54%	$399.28	56%
Noncommercial Optometrists	$262.17	29%	$332.87	30%
Commercial Optometrists	$202.94	—	$255.48	—

SOURCE: Gary D. Hailey, Jonathan R. Bromberg, and Joseph B. Mulholland, "A Comparative Analysis of Cosmetic Contact Lens Fitting by Ophthalmologists, Optometrists, and Opticians," *Report of the Staff of the Federal Trade Commission* (Washington, D.C.: Bureau of Consumer Protection and Bureau of Economics, 1983), pp. C–F.

Note: Original source prices were measured over the period 1977–1979 and converted to 1988 prices by the authors through the use of the Consumer Price Index: All items, as measured in 1978 and 1988.

price data taken from cities where commercial optometrists were the dominant practitioners, the FTC was able to compare the average prices charged by eyecare practitioners in two ways. Prices charged by different types of practitioners within these relatively high intensity advertising areas could be compared to one another as well as merely comparing prices across these areas. Results indicate the power of competitive markets where the degree of competition is proxied by the (relative) ability to disseminate information through advertising. Ophthalmologists and noncommercial optometrists had a smaller upward influence on average price in areas that were relatively heavily commercialized. In the commercialized areas, lens prices charged by commercial and noncommercial optometrists were *not* significantly different. This contrasts sharply with Table 6–6, which shows that the noncommercial charge was about 30 percent higher than commercial optometrists' fees overall. The inference is clear. Sellers who do not advertise but operate in market areas where the extent of advertising and other commercial activities are fairly widespread are forced by competitive pressures to more closely match prices of other sellers who do advertise. Competitive advertising affects what the non-advertiser is able to do in the market.

It appears that the traditional view of advertising, in whatever form chosen to interpret it, is an empty box. Eyecare market studies strongly indicate that statutory impediments, be they laws, licensing requirements, or professional codes of conduct, that restrict information do not benefit consumers. At best, they produce higher consumer costs with no evidence of offsetting quality improvement or, worse, both higher costs and inferior quality.

Other Price Effects of Advertising

Another interesting study, one that examines advertising and retail drug prices, was conducted along the same lines as the Benham study but provides additional insight as to who benefits, consumers or suppliers, from advertising prevention. Like Benham, John Cady (1976) divides states into those that allow retail drug advertising and those that have laws prohibiting advertising.[17] While most people think of these laws as part and parcel of some code of ethics instituted to protect consumers or to guarantee some level of professional quality, the laws tend to be economic in nature. If the code of conduct and "points table" of the Michigan Optometric Association was not convincing enough, consider the following excerpt from the Maryland law regarding drug advertising: "The Board of Pharmacy is hereby granted power and authority . . . to suspend or revoke [a pharmacist's] license for advertising to the public by any means . . . the prices for prescriptions . . . or fees or services relating thereto or any reference to the price of said drugs or prescriptions whether specifically or as a percentile of prevailing prices, or by the terms 'cut-rate,' 'discount,' 'bargain,' or terms of similar connotation."[18]

There is not much said about consumer benefit in the statute, and its intent is clear—to prevent price advertising of prescription drugs. Cady found that prescription drug prices are higher by 5 percent in states that inhibit price advertising. If that does not seem like a large

---

17. John F. Cady, *Restricted Advertising and Competition: The Case of Retail Drugs* (Washington, D.C.: American Enterprise Institute, 1976). The reader should not confuse the type of drug advertising being discussed here with the drug advertising and promotion that Leffler (1981) analyzed. Leffler considered advertising and promotion expenditures by pharmaceutical companies aimed at physicians, not at pharmacy advertising aimed at the ultimate consumers, patients.

18. Ibid., p. 1.

difference, consider what it implies in terms of consumer expenditure on prescription drugs in the states that prohibit advertising.

Cady estimates that in 1975, the additional cost to consumers of these advertising regulations in terms of higher drug prices was about $380 million (about $820 million in 1988 dollars). Additionally, given the size of the pharmacy, measures of service levels (emergency deliveries, regular deliveries, recordkeeping, waiting areas, credit, and so on), which can be taken as examples of the quality of service, are generally no different in the two types of states. The actual evidence again suggests that advertising prohibitions do *not* benefit consumers by lowering prices. They increase prices above what they would have been in the absence of the advertising impediments. The quality and level of service are not significantly increased by such laws either, and may be decreased. It appears from the available evidence that consumers are made worse off by paying more than they would have for smaller amounts of (at best) equal quality than in the absence of such laws.

As a final example of the effect of advertising on prices, consider the posting of prices at a business establishment in plain view for customers. Since price posting supplies information to consumers prior to purchase in a relatively low cost fashion, it clearly falls within the definition of advertising. Thom Kelly and Alex Maurizi (1978) examined the phenomenon of service stations posting gasoline prices on billboards in plain view of customers and potential customers and the effects this form of advertising had on market prices of gasoline.[19] They obtained data from fourteen geographical areas of the country for two weeks in November of 1970. They surmised that the billboard posting of price would affect the average market price charged by tending to lower it, and that the higher the percentage of stations in a given area using billboards to post prices (the higher the posting or advertising intensity) the lower would be the average market price charged. Not only would the viewing of one sign (advertisement) alone give the consumer information about price, but also the viewing of one station's billboard and *being able to compare it to others cheaply* would limit somewhat the amount stations are able to charge consumers. Reading a price posted of $1.00 per gallon is useful, but it

19. Thom Kelly and Alex Maurizi, *Prices and Consumer Information: The Benefits from Posting Retail Gasoline Prices* (Washington, D.C.: American Enterprise Institute, 1978).

is even more useful to see a price of $1.00 posted at one corner and prices of $0.90 and $1.10 on billboards across the street.

After adjusting for such factors as family income in the area, gasoline taxes, whether or not trading stamps were offered, and whether the station was a major brand or an independent, Kelly and Maurizi found that the act of billboard advertising of prices significantly reduced the average price of gasoline charged, and that the intensity of posting prices in areas also tended to significantly reduce gas prices. For leaded regular gasoline, the combined effects of posting prices and of "billboard" intensity were to reduce gas prices on an average of 5.5 percent, while the combined effect on leaded premium gas was a price about 7.7 percent lower than it would have been in the absence of this type of advertising and advertising intensity.[20] Thus, billboard advertising appears to lower prices and to increase consumer welfare in certain markets. Though billboards are often singled out as eyesores by social critics, the information they contain yields net economic value to society. Completely ignored is the additional time saved by consumers in price-searching activities that billboard price advertising makes possible. Pro-competitive effects, moreover, have most likely had a far greater affect in lowering prices than any increase in costs brought about by advertising.

ADVERTISING AND DERIVED CONSUMER DEMAND

Before turning to an analysis of contemporary issues related to advertising (Chapters 7 and 8), we present some evidence concerning one last area. At the close of Chapter 4 we discussed the theory of advertising as developed by Ehrlich and Fisher (1982), which had its roots in the works of Nelson (1970, 1974). One basic inference we can draw from the Ehrlich-Fisher study is that advertising is consistent with, and can be expected to be an important characteristic of, competition and competitive markets. Recall that these economists argue that business advertising messages represent a derived demand. That is, the origin of advertising is the consumer's desire for information, which is the desire to reduce the full price of purchases. Competition, in the new neoclassical and Austrian views, generally provides advertising information in a form that will be efficient for the average

---

20. Ibid., p. 35.

consumer. Efficient information depends on market characteristics, especially the characteristics of consumers. These characteristics include the product or service being transacted, how frequently it is purchased, search or experience attributes, information consumers already possess, and so on.

David Laband (1986) examines the question of whether suppliers will in fact provide consumers information in the fashion outlined above—whether the market outcome, as far as the kinds of advertising that occur in the market are concerned, actually reflect the kind of information consumers desire.[21] Laband examines these issues with the aid of a rather unusual source of data—the Yellow Pages.

Laband argues, along the lines of Nelson and Ehrlich-Fisher, that one avenue of firm competition within industries is competition through supplying consumers with the most useful type of advertising. In particular he argues that consumers will, in varying degrees and depending on the circumstances, want information on product or service quality. And the greater the amount of quality information consumers want, the greater will be the incentive of firms to provide it. Thus, goods and services for which quality information would be of most benefit will be those goods and services whose advertisements emphasize quality characteristics relatively more than others.

The circumstances and market characteristics that identify goods for which we would expect to see ads of this type are not difficult to pinpoint. Consumers tend to rely on quality information provided by advertisements in buying relatively high priced and infrequently purchased items. For frequently purchased items, consumers already have a large stock of information that has been garnered through the act of purchase and consumption. Hence, additional quality information is of little additional value. Also, inexpensive goods entail a very low cost to the consumer of making a purchase "mistake" and buying something of unexpected low quality. We would then expect that advertisements of goods and services that are purchased infrequently and are comparatively high priced to contain the larger amount of quality information. Nelson's search good category seems to fit these kinds of purchases. Additionally, the stock of information on search goods that consumers already have will, in part, be a factor. Quality

21. David N. Laband, "Advertising as Information: An Empirical Note," *Review of Economics and Statistics* 68 (1986): 517–21.

information provision, or "signalling" in Laband's terminology, will be more prevalent in areas or markets where consumers have smaller existing stocks of information.

For purposes of his study, Laband measures quality-signalling by references in the Yellow Pages to licensure, certification, and professional membership association on the part of the vendor, as well as to ads listing the experience of the vendor.[22] Laband compared the Washington, D.C. and Baltimore Yellow Pages for ads of both low price-repeat purchase (corresponding to experience goods) and high price-infrequently purchased goods and services (search goods). In both localities, Laband finds the percentage of ads containing quality signalling to be significantly greater in his search goods, as opposed to experience goods, category. The differences run from four times greater to twelve times greater.

Comparison of the Yellow Pages ads of the two cities reveals even more. Laband contends that the average consumer in Baltimore has resided in that city more years than has the average Washingtonian. Consumers in Washington should then benefit *more* at the margin from Yellow Pages quality signalling than would the average consumer living in Baltimore. The Baltimore resident has a larger stock of existing quality information developed through actual past sampling of vendors, among other obvious means. In a competitive market setting, the benefits to Washingtonians of vendor quality signalling in the Yellow Pages provide the incentive for businesses in Washington to quality signal relatively more heavily than in Baltimore. Comparing search goods and services categories across the Yellow Pages lends evidence in support of the new neoclassical approach. A statistically significant larger fraction of ads in the Washington Yellow Pages convey seller quality information. Laband's evidence suggests that advertising, more particularly its form, character, and quantity, is heavily influenced by consumers. Further, his study is consistent with the view that market competition induces suppliers to provide the information to consumers that *consumers* deem most beneficial.

---

22. While we showed earlier in the chapter that quality of service was certainly not guaranteed by professional membership associations in the contact lens market, vendor associations may impart some minimum quality characteristics to consumers for the goods Laband studies.

CONCLUSION

Evidence on a wide-ranging number of issues regarding the economic effects of advertising has been covered in this and the previous chapter. A large quantity of evidence indicates that advertising, however measured and in whatever form, does not appear to be a tool used by monopolists or oligopolists in an attempt to raise prices or to increase profits.[23] Rather, accumulating evidence reveals that advertising is a characteristic of competition—a means of entry into markets, a vehicle for price reduction, and a benefit to consumers. In this role it is part and parcel of a rivalrous competitive process with profound implications for the functioning of a market economy. In Chapter 7 we evaluate, in light of the new neoclassical view, a number of recent cases before the Federal Trade Commission relating to advertising regulation.

23. We do not, of course, mean to imply that many other regulated commercial restrictions do not increase the price of goods and services. A recent empirical study of employment, location, branch office and trade name restrictions in optometry, for example, concludes that such commerical practices raised consumer costs by $4.7 million for eye examinations and eyeglasses in 1977: see Deborah Haas-Wilson, "The Effect of Commercial Practice Restrictions: The Case of Optometry," *Journal of Law and Economics* 29 (1986): 165–186. Methods of vertical coordination, such as exclusive distributorships, are also often cited as sources of monopoly in markets, but recent research casts doubt upon this proposition. In a study of exclusive distributorships and advertising restrictions in the beer industry Ekelund, *et al* find that higher beer prices are the result of the intensity of state advertising restrictions and other artificial constraints upon the competitive process and are not the result of exclusive arrangements between beer manufacturers and their distributors: see Robert B. Ekelund, Jr., *et al*, "Exclusive Territories and Advertising Restrictions in the Malt Beverage Industry," (manuscript, 1988).

PART IV

ADVERTISING AND CONTEMPORARY ISSUES

7

A MODERN ECONOMIC VIEW OF ADVERTISING: RECENT CASE STUDIES

Modern economic theory emphasizes a number of important aspects of advertising as its relates to consumers and to the competitive process. The new neoclassical/neo-Austrian model (1) characterizes advertising as a tool of the entrepreneur in creating and *sustaining* the competitive process, (2) underlines the cost-reducing informational aspects of advertising where the rational consumer is concerned, and (3) explicitly and implicitly maintains that advertising regulation (or restrictions on advertising in general) reduces the consumer welfare-enhancing properties of the competitive system. Translated into simple terms, restrictive regulation usually means reduced information, higher prices, lower production, and in some cases, lower quality.

RECENT ADVERTISING CASES BEFORE THE FEDERAL TRADE COMMISSION

In this chapter we put these concepts to work by applying them to recent (and pending) cases on advertising before the Federal Trade Commission. We will show that when advertising is viewed as an integral and dynamic part of the competitive process (*on both producer and consumer sides of the market*) most or all proposals to regulate advertising would likely yield a reduction in overall consumer welfare. Three diverse and fairly extreme cases—children's video, advertising of legal services, and the advertising of alcohol products—illustrate the usefulness of the modern theory of advertising as a vital cog in the process of competition.

Children's Video: The "Kid-Vid" Case

A 1978 staff report on television advertising to children urged the Federal Trade Commission to "eliminate harms arising out of television advertising to children" with the following conclusion: "We have shown that television advertising addressed to young children, who do not yet understand the selling purpose of commercials, or who lack the ability to comprehend or evaluate such commercials, or *a fortiori* to preschool children who have even greater perceptual difficulties as to advertising, is inherently unfair and deceptive. The inherent unfairness and deceptiveness are so great that only a ban can effectively remedy them."[1] The proposed ban, sponsored by nutritionists and a large number of other interest groups would ban television advertising of specified products deemed harmful to children during times which an audience would consist of predominately preschool-age children, or if "sugared products" were advertised when the audience was composed of older children. (Apparently some advertising of sugared products would be allowed if such advertising is balanced by nutritional information.)

The Logic of the Ban.   Upon what chain of logic do supporters of an advertising ban base their reasoning? We understand their arguments leading to the conclusion that advertising should be banned as flowing from the following propositions:

1. Children are captives of TV advertisers to the extent that an increase in advertising of "harmful products" will create an increase in the consumption of these products by children.
2. Sugar is the proven cause of a plethora of health problems, including obesity, poor dental health, poor general health, hypertension, and other maladies.
3. Children are the "real" consumers of these harmful products since

---

1. Ellis M. Ratner, et al., *FTC Staff Report of Television Advertising to Chilaren* (Washington, D.C.: U.S. Government Printing Office, 1978).

parents are actually pawns of their children. Parents finance and carry out the act of purchase, with children making the ultimate consumption decisions.

4. While the first amendment protects the rights of adults to encounter free speech, children are a special case requiring a broadening view of "deception" in advertising.

Closer consideration of these arguments reveals that they may be suspect and that the effect of such a proposal can be expected to be, at best, uncertain. In the first place, the staff report offers no evidence whatsoever suggesting the degree by which the consumption of sugared or similar "harmful" products are altered by the advertising of such products. Legal bans or other forms of formal restrictions on advertising, as we have noted at various points in our study, are likely to produce predictable economic effects. One of these effects is an increase in price, either money price or the time-cost component of full price, or both. Economists know that when price, however measured, increases consumption falls, given other determining factors. By what amount consumption falls here is important. Ignoring any other effects such a ban may produce, and accepting for the moment the notion that reduced consumption of this product enhances consumer welfare, it remains unclear that the supposed salutory effects of reduced consumption of sugared cereal outweighs the price effects on family economic welfare.

Consider next some of the direct effects on consumers which such a ban would likely produce. It is doubtful that many would place the products under discussion in the category of credence goods. That is, once sampled sufficiently, the incentives of producers to deceptively advertise are very small since the intrinsic qualities of these goods are easily and inexpensively discovered by the consumer. In spite of advertising, young children will usually not badger parents to buy foods that children have learned do not taste good. As such, the idea that these advertisements are deceptive from an economic standpoint is questionable. These products seem to fit more into the experience goods classification. We have discussed the benefits accruing to consumers that result from the market advertising of experience goods at length. Identical welfare implications are implied from the competitive advertising of breakfast cereals as from eyeglasses. With advertising, parents can easily discover what brands children enjoy as children and parents alike are periodically made aware of brands through advertising. Parents also use advertising as one means of sorting among products to buy for children. A ban on all advertising in this area would make it more costly to parents for some information about quality and characteristics of the product. Some parents (we would presume) do not wish their children to eat chocolate marshmallows with cereal for breakfast. An advertising ban would then make it more difficult for such parents to sort among brands and remember which brands contain unacceptable foods.

In short, proponents of a ban argue the ban would reduce consumption. We agree, but for, we suspect, different reasons. An advertising ban will not totally eliminate consumption because advertising is not solely responsible for the current level of consumption. Such a ban will raise the cost to the consumer of these products through the reduced information available in the market. This will, given other factors, reduce consumption. But important to the ban proponents' case is the size of the reduced consumption. The 1978 FTC report presents no reliable evidence concerning current price-consumption relationships. Reliable evidence, moreover, does not suggest anything about *intertemporal* trends of children's consumption patterns of sugared products (including candy and other sweets). Were we to hold in abeyance the dynamic effects of such a ban on the competitive process, and accept for the moment that consumption of these products is, on balance, bad for one's health, it remains unclear that a ban would, on net, be welfare-enhancing for consumers in the sense that it would be worth the resources needed to monitor and enforce it.

A second area of the report deals with health risks of the consumption of sugar. Nutritionists and other health authorities have long stressed the benefits of consuming grains, vegetables, and fruits. Additionally, there has been a long and well-publicized recognition that sugar consumption is related to dental cavities. While evidence in this area is fairly substantial, the staff report to the FTC offers only conjecture in relating sugar consumption to malnutrition, obesity, coronary heart disease, hypertension, insulin response, and diabetes.[2] However, such conjecture, even if correct, is not an argument for consumption and health-imposed restrictions by government and nu-

2. Ibid., pp. 142–56.

tritionists. Skin cancer is apparently related to exposure to the sun (and the association is currently being advertised along with sun screen and sun lotion products). Does this correlation mean that government should prohibit sun bathing? Our point is that it is the consumer who is in the better position to judge the *overall* economic value of goods and services. More to the point, what is the role of parents in providing for the nutrition and good health of their children?

The most insidious inference of the proposal to ban advertising aimed at children is that children, not parents, are the real consumers of harmful products. In this view children and parents are not rational consumers. The staff report cites "evidence" from psychologists such as Dr. Sidney Berman, former president of the American Academy of Child Psychiatry, who is "deeply concerned with the exploitation of children" for advertising purposes because it "encourage(s) confrontation and alienation on the part of children toward their parents and undermine(s) the parents' child rearing responsibilities."[3] And why are parents so unwilling to intervene in their children's TV viewing and to teach and provide good nutrition to their children? According to the report the unwillingness stems from "'profound feelings of helplessness' and from the fear that if they [the parents] deny their children so pervasive a childhood experience as children's programming, the children will become 'social outcasts or social isolates.'"[4] It may well be that allowing children to watch certain advertisements will create strife and alienation in the parent-child relationship. From a purely economic perspective, strife and alienation raise the cost of developing a desirable relationship between parents and children. However, parents can reduce the costs of strife by denying permission to watch such programming. In that event, ratings will be lower for strife-inducing advertisers, and market forces will tend to generate ratings-maximizing (that is, strife-minimizing) advertisements. Other aspects of the problem, however, are even more disturbing.

Government, in the form of FTC advertising regulation, is asked to intervene in the child-parent relationship—one that has been virtually sacrosanct in the courts since the foundation of the nation—by intervening in a market to remedy the alleged harmful effects of sugar

3. Ibid., p. 18.
4. Ibid., p. 26.

consumption. While the case may seem to present an innocuous intervention into that relationship, one can imagine similar applications of the "parents as pawns" argument that would not seem so innocuous in a free society. Even when the idea that consumption is, *on net,* harmful to health is accepted, consideration of only the simplest economics of the issue yields the conclusion that such regulation may make matters worse for consumers. Further analysis of this issue is required.

Recognizing that "kid-vid" advertising is not deceptive for adults using ordinary FTC standards relating to deception, the staff's recommendation to the Commission argues that "the State has a legitimate interest in curtailing speech that interferes with the paramount parental interest in the child-rearing process."[5] The staff argued, by analogy, that advertising of sugared cereals is an outside interference with the parent-child relationship and that the state had to "protect" that relationship by intervention. The analogy is to the Supreme Court case of *Ginsberg v. New York* in which the Court upheld a state restriction on the dissemination of sexually explicit materials to minors. Justice Fortas, who for other reasons dissented from the opinion of the Court, still argued that "The State's police power may, within very broad limits, protect . . . parents and their children from public aggression of panderers and pushers. This is defensible on the theory that they cannot protect themselves from such assaults."[6] The FTC staff then concluded that (a) since parents are unable to control the TV viewing *and* the nutritional habits of their children, and (b) since there is "increasing evidence that through continuous and massive food advertising directed to children, the advertising industry has successfully engineered itself into a position where it commands substantial power over the eating habits of young children,"[7] "kid-vid" advertising regulation, like that respecting sexually explicit materials, should be emplaced by government. Such logic, at least in our view, far from establishing a proper parent-child relationship, turns that relationship on its head. In this view, intervention *helps alter* the parent-child relationship. Is the matter of nutrition choice—admittedly an impor-

5. Ibid., p. 277.
6. Ibid., p. 278.
7. Ibid., p. 280.

tant issue—a matter for government? It is possible, even probable, that the food types under discussion are not on balance harmful to short- or to long-term health. Government intervention with advertising restrictions in the market is even more likely to produce economic harm, especially so if the majority of families are ones in which young children do not dictate diets to parents. If such interventions improve family welfare, then there must be other kinds of optimal interventions that would foster the child-parent relationship. And where does it end? In the metaphysical realm, for instance, would government have a role in restricting advertising should atheists determine that religious programming is deleterious to mental health?

Although the particular issue of nutritional products may not have been economically motivated, at least at the outset, market effects of a suggested ban may still be analyzed. The purely economic effects of an advertising ban on sugared and other non-nutritional products are germane, and misconceptions relate to the failure to view advertising in a dynamic perspective. Suppose, for example, that it could be proved that advertising creates a demand for non-nutritional products, that these products create health problems among children, and that parents are the quasi-dupes of their children in these matters. In this farfetched case, advertising regulation might make some sense from the purely static perception of market functioning. But when an essential role of advertising—that of the initiator and provider of information about new products—is considered, such an uncertain rationale would disappear. Products with lower sugar content would be more difficult and costly to introduce into the market. (The ban on TV cigarette advertising unquestionably slowed the introduction of low-tar and low-nicotine cigarettes and eliminated the public-service "equal time" ads, which reduced information about the health hazards related to smoking.) If these foods do have net nutritional content, the increased full price and reduced consumption effects of the restraints may be coupled with a decrease in average nutritional quality by suppliers, a result that parallels the eyewear studies. These results are by no means certain. However, the logic and evidence we have presented from other markets suggest that these effects are likely to arise when competition is restricted. Concerned parents have an incentive to invest time and other resources in determining the basic nutritional content of food, information that is often and necessarily produced jointly with TV advertising. If parents are unconcerned about the nutritional content of their children's diet, a ban on advertising will merely make current consumption patterns more rigid.[8]

Fortunately, the market process has worked to make parents and children more concerned with nutrition. Advertisers with more nutritious products to sell have a market incentive to emphasize these characteristics. Current concern with the diet and health of children and adults was not created by FTC regulation, but by rational consumers. This concern, manifested by the directions of market demand for food and other products, would be ignored by manufacturers and advertisers only at great costs to themselves. The dynamics of the market process, of which advertising is an integral part, tell us that when nutrition is demanded by adults, or by parents for children, nutritious products and information about them will be forthcoming. Advertising bans or other regulation can only prevent, impede, or forestall the development of and knowledge about such products.

Advertising Legal Services

Price and quality competition and market entry, according to the modern theory of advertising, is limited in degree when advertising is restricted by legal means. Throughout history, advertising bans, or at least severe restrictions, in the professions have been common. The most familiar bans in twentieth century America have involved medical and legal services. As early as 1887, Alabama became the first state in the union to explicitly condemn all form of self-laudation, newspaper press notices, or editorials in the market for legal services as an "evil tendency and wholly unprofessional."[9] Other states followed the trend and in 1908 the American Bar Association in its Canons of Professional Ethics, a guide to state and local bar associations,

---

8. Not only would consumption patterns become more rigid but, to the extent that advertising is an *allocator* of demand within the banned or restricted product groups, market shares would also tend to stabilize. From an interest group perspective, economic theory predicts that incumbents with high market shares would support the ban. As we will see, the same is true of advertising bans on legal services and on alcohol products.

9. Information in this section is derived from William A. Jacobs, et al., "Improving Consumer Access to Legal Services: The Case for Removing Restrictions on Truthful Advertising," Report of the Staff to the Federal Trade Commission (Washington, D.C.: Cleveland Regional Office, Bureau of Economics, Federal Trade Commission, 1984). Interestingly, the medical cartel was acquiring similar controls through state medical associations about the ame time.

condemned virtually all forms of advertising. Soon, nearly all state and local bars adopted the condemnation as part of their own code of legal ethics. Penalties for malfeasors were severe, often ending in harsh and embarrassing reprimands and even disbarment—loss of the license to practice law.

A condemnation of all advertising of legal services or any other service or commodity means, in economic terms, that consumers and potential consumers are deprived of a large portion of information concerning the existence of various kinds of legal assistance. Given the inability to advertise price differences, the price of legal services would likely be sustained above (and quantities provided to consumers below) competitive levels, especially those services for which the demand was relatively inelastic. By implication, profits higher than the opportunity cost of legal education, experience, etc. would likely also be earned in the legal profession. A ban on advertising, along with licensing restrictions, sanctions for code violators, effective entry control, and other restrictive practices in the legal profession, creates a market structure somewhat akin to a monopolistic cartel. Cartel managers—those establishing, policing, and enforcing restrictions—were the national, state, and local bar associations, but the important point is that they would have been ineffective at keeping recalcitrant lawyers in line *without the force of government sanctions and law*. Lawyers who wanted to compete through advertising were kept at bay by the inability to successfully find redress in the courts. When the force and support of law began to break down, the structure of rules governing market behavior established by the legal profession at the beginning of the twentieth century also began to dissolve.

A number of cases before the Supreme Court in the 1960s began to erode the proscription of advertising and other parts of the American Bar Association's Canons of Professional Ethics. Some of them were related to the provision of group legal services, price-fixing (minimum fee schedules for attorneys, outlawed, the Court said, by the Sherman Act), and advertising. Consumer groups, in particular, charged that low and middle income individuals found it difficult to know of the availability and the price of legal services—two items for which advertising is particularly well suited.

The Bates Case and Advertising in the Professions.   The American and, especially, the state and local bar associations attempted to retard drastic changes in the code. A large number of state bars continued to prosecute lawyers for media advertising which was not "false, deceptive, or misleading" under what would be currently accepted standards at the Federal Trade Commission. In perhaps the most important case, Arizona lawyers John Bates and Van O'Steen, partners in a law clinic, were brought to discipline by the Arizona State Bar for advertising the price and service availability of their clinic in the *Arizona Republic*. The most interesting part of the case were the six justifications offered by the Bar in support of continued restrictions (and by *amici curiae* filed by those potentially damaged by expanded, competitive advertising). These "justifications" are presented in the Staff report of the FTC:[10]

1. Price advertising will bring about commercialization which will have an adverse effect on professionalism.
2. Attorney advertising is inherently misleading.
3. Attorney advertising will adversely affect the administration of justice by stirring up litigation.
4. Attorney advertising will increase the cost of doing business, increase entry barriers to new attorneys, and drive up the prices of legal services.
5. Attorney advertising will adversely affect the quality of legal services.
6. Enforcement of anything less than a total ban would be too burdensome and difficult.

These six justifications for a proscription of advertising (other than a Yellow Pages listing) appear to express the bulk of all arguments used by certain professions to provide support for such competition-reducing restrictions throughout the twentieth century. In a landmark decision on advertising in the professions, commonly referred to as the *Bates* decision, the Supreme Court declared that a total ban on advertising contemplated in the Arizona State Bar's decision violated first amendment rights concerning commercial speech and that none of the six justifications listed above was a foundation for a total ban.[11] The Court, interestingly, invoked the argument that restrictions on

10. Ibid., p. 33.
11. See *Bates v. State Bar of Arizona,* 433 U.S. 350 (1977).

advertising eliminated an indispensable competitive element of the allocation of resources in a free enterprise system. State bars could still restrict false, deceptive, or misleading advertising, and other types in which the state had a "substantial" interest (i.e., where advertising is inherently misleading or of known subject to abuse), but the Court made it clear that it would uphold the rights of professionals to advertise in an informative, truthful manner. In fact, it did so in a unanimous affirmation of *Bates*.[12] The Court has made it clear that the free and truthful flow of information about the availability, price, and quality of legal services will not be thwarted.

As one might expect, the Court's clear and unequivocal decisions have not quelled the attempts by the ABA and state and local bars to maintain some of their anticompetitive restrictions. Recognizing the handwriting on the wall, the ABA (before *Bates*) began its own investigations into model codes, all of which contemplate retention of a regulatory approach which restricts or proscribes certain forms of truthful advertising. For example, in August 1983, the Model Rules of Professional Conduct adopted by the ABA prohibited the solicitation of clients (explicitly by direct mail, but implicitly by any media) by attorneys when the object or motive was pecuniary gain. Such a provision, taken literally, would proscribe all advertising and the Supreme Court has recognized the fact by reaffirmations of *Bates*.

The result of the ABA's equivocations and qualifications has been confusion (possibly an intended confusion) within the states and in the state codes of ethics. Enormous variations among state codes exist since the ABA neither disciplines lawyers, leaving that to the state and local bars, nor imposes ethical standards on other bars. Nevertheless, the ABA code serves as a model for state codes. According to the Federal Trade Commission staff report, a 1980 survey of state codes revealed the following diversity in advertising restrictions:[13]

1. Twenty-three states imposed geographic restrictions on print and broadcast media. (With this well-known competition reducing device, advertising is strictly limited to the locale of the lawyer).
2. Contingency fees could not be advertised in seven states.
3. Twenty-six states require that ads placed by lawyers be "dignified" and devoid of "self-laudatory" statements.

12. *In re R.M.J.*, 455 U.S. 191 (1982).
13. Jacobs, et al., *FTC Report*, pp. 32–54.

4. Trade names (such as the "ABC Legal Clinic") may not be used in thirty-six states.
5. Television advertising by lawyers is forbidden in twelve states.

While some of these restrictive regulations may have been dropped or modified by the state and local bar associations since 1980, it is clear that free enterprise in legal services is still not a reality in much of the United States. While the Supreme Court has made the law perfectly clear, the foot-dragging of the ABA and, especially, of the state and local bars has retarded competition for customers of legal services. Some states are clearly more restrictive than others. While Massachusetts and Wisconsin are fairly liberal in that lawyers may conduct any sort of advertising that is not misleading, unfair, or deceptive, states such as Mississippi, Kansas, and Alabama are severely restrictive. This suggests that the quantity and quality of legal services provided is lower and the price higher in those states and cities which have relatively more restrictive advertising.

This hypothesis, at least the one related to prices of various kinds of legal services, was tested under the aegis of the Federal Trade Commission. In survey data including seventeen cities conducted by the Survey Research Laboratory at Arizona State University and Louis Harris & Associates in 1980–1981 and 1981–1982, prices of various kinds of legal services in more restrictive states were compared with those in less retrictive states with the results summarized in Table 7–1 (which replicates Table D in the FTC staff report).[14] As the two parts of Table 7–1 indicate, prices in more restrictive states (grouped according to avertising restrictions), in at least two of the five state grouping comparisons, are significantly higher. For restrictions on specific types of advertising, prices also appear to be significantly higher for some services, but the statistical relationships for several of the services are less clear. There are ambiguous results respecting price-lowering effects of types of advertising restrictions on prices of simple wills. But given the alternatives to attorney prepared wills already available to consumers when the study was undertaken ("will kits" can be found at any bookstore), prices for simple wills were probably close to marginal cost and, therefore, may not be clearly responsive to advertising. Overall, however, the FTC-sponsored study

14. Ibid., p. 106.

Table 7–1. Effect of Advertising Restrictions on Prices of Legal Services.

(1) In More Restrictive States, Price Is:

Restriction[a]	Simple Will	Will with Trust	Bankruptcy	Divorce	Personal Injury
R1	*	*	*	*	*
R2	Higher	Higher	Higher	Higher	Higher
R3	Higher	Higher	*	Higher	Higher
R4	Higher	*	Higher	Higher	Higher
R5	*	*	Higher	*	Higher

(2) For Restrictions on Advertising Media or Content, Price Is:

Restriction	Simple Will	Will with Trust	Bankruptcy	Divorce	Personal Injury
No TV or Radio	Higher	*	Higher	Higher	Higher
No Trade Names	Higher	Higher	*	*	*
No Direct Mail	Lower	*	*	Higher	Higher
Limited Content	Lower	*	*	*	Higher

SOURCE: William W. Jacobs, et al., "Improving Consumer Access to Legal Services: The Case for Removing Restrictions on Truthful Advertising," Report of the Staff to the Federal Trade Commission (Washington, D.C.: Bureau of Economics and Cleveland Regional Office, 1984), p. 106.

[a]Prices were compared between more restrictive states and less restrictive states with respect to the *degree* of restrictions in the following manner: Restriction R1 compared Missouri and Mississippi (prohibited fee advertising) to the other 15 states in the sample; R2 compared Missouri, Mississippi, Oklahoma, and Alabama to the other 13 states (that did allow handbills and contingent fee advertising); R3 compared Missouri, Mississippi, Oklahoma, Alabama, Connecticut, and New Mexico to the other 11 states (that at this point allowed radio advertising); R4 compared Missouri, Mississippi, Oklahoma, Alabama, Connecticut, New Mexico, and Indiana to the other 10 states that permitted television advertising; R5 compared Massachusetts, Maryland, Michigan, Wisconsin, and California, states that had removed most advertising restrictions, to the other 12 states.

Note: * = No statistically significant difference.

appears to show that advertising restrictions on the most popular forms of legal services significantly raise the price of those services.

Interest Group Analysis.   The FTC, given the recalcitrance of many bar associations, has proposed a model code for various state and local associations to follow. The proposed code is simplicity itself: "A lawyer should not make a false or deceptive communication about the lawyer or the lawyer's services."[15] The few remaining details of the proposed code merely indicate that all advertising and personal communications will be permitted so long as they meet the ordinary FTC standards against "false and deceptive" advertising and that they do not involve "coercion, duress or harassment."

If we try to identify the economic winners and losers from the implementation of increased advertising and information provision on the part of the sellers of legal services, we will get an indication of the supporters and opponents of deregulation of advertising in the various states. The strongest opponents of competition in the provision of legal services tend to be established lawyers, many of them associated with old firms with established reputations. Any reduction in restrictions will probably mean reductions in profits that flow to these providers of legal services. While the "quality" dimension of providing services—experience, special talents, specialization, etc. —is important, such differentials *are* rewarded within a wholly competitive environment. We would expect that short-term profits, market-justified due to special skills, are in fact earned by individual lawyers and by individual firms due to expertise and successful past defense and plaintiff advocacy. This is, should be, and always will be the case in a dynamic competitive environment. Unduly large monetary returns stemming from *artificial restrictions* on consumer information will be eliminated by the deregulation of legal services advertising.

Naturally, the rational consumer would prefer an experienced lawyer for a specific task at the same price to a young or untested attorney. The truth is, however, that not all legal work requires a "Cadillac" lawyer. For some tasks, a "Chevrolet" lawyer will more than fill the bill. The question is, "How can young or untested lawyers, especially those not associated with established legal firms, compete with experienced attorneys?" An efficient manner for a young attorney to introduce his or her "product" to the market is through price and/or other forms of information. With advertising, consumers of legal services of all types may then make purchase decisions on the basis of price, quality, and other types of critical information. The provision of such information by advertising also means that search costs—those consumer costs associated with finding the right price/

15. Ibid., p. F-1.

quality combination for their own needs—are reduced. Other, comparatively inefficient, means of obtaining information need not be the only ones used.

Proponents of advertising deregulation of legal services will include some members of the legal profession. Young and untested lawyers, especially those who are not employed in the offices of established law firms, may be expected to support the code suggested by the Federal Trade Commission.[16] The big gainers, of course, are the consumers of legal services. Consumers may expect to pay lower prices and consume higher quantities of better quality service when lawyers are free to advertise in a nondeceptive, nonfraudulent manner. The competitive pricing of legal services will permit rational consumers to choose between legal services purchases and other goods that are produced under competitive conditions. The moral here is that the anticompetitive restrictions, supported by legal sanctions of government, cannot help but impede the maximization of the general welfare and the rational allocation of scarce resources.

Alcohol Advertising Regulations

Some groups believe that advertising is at the heart of two of America's most publicized health problems—alcoholism and cancer. The advertising of products related to these problems has been the subject of renewed efforts on the part of a number of groups who would ban or seriously restrict television advertising of alcohol products. ("Smokeless tobacco" products, such as snuff and chewing tobacco, have been partially regulated, along with cigarette advertising.)

In 1984, the Center for Science in the Public Interest, along with twenty-eight other groups and three individuals, petitioned the Federal

---

16. It is important to note that higher-than-competitive returns can exist in the long run only where entry is restricted. Given that entry restrictions in the legal profession are eliminated (or significantly liberalized), long-run *average* legal income will not be affected. However, where advertising is prohibited we may observe low returns to new lawyers and high returns to established ones. A relaxation in advertising restrictions will reduce income to older, more established, lawyers and they will be opposed by them. From a long-run perspective, young lawyers will not be benefited by the change since higher income in the short-run will be offset by lower incomes when these lawyers become established and must compete with new lawyers who can advertise. From a long-run perspective, then, it may be that the only lawyers favoring repeal will be those lawyers who believe that other lawyers will view advertising as "antiprofessional"—those, in other words, who see advertising as cartel-breaking or competitive behavior.

Trade Commission to regulate the marketing and advertising of alcohol. The petition, principally aimed at television advertising of beer
and wine (liquor advertisers "voluntarily" withdrew advertising from
TV more than a decade ago), cites alcohol as a "public health night-
mare" and a "national tragedy." The petition specifically links its use
to traffic deaths, industrial accidents, drownings, drug abuse through
interaction with alcohol, decreased birth weight, cancer of the tongue,
suicide, impotency, and early onset of postmenopausal menstrual ces-
sation in women.[17] Of particular concern to the petitioners is the effect
of advertising on the young and new consumers who are, according
to their logic, easily seduced and persuaded by the appeals of athletes,
rock stars, and entertainers hawking beer on television.

These public interest groups have urged the FTC to go beyond its
traditional standard on misrepresentation of the attributes of products.
They argue that the promotion of alcohol is *inherently* deceptive and
unfair since advertisers (and, of course, the manufacturers that hire
them) associate consumption with, among other things, a friend-filled,
happy, and successful lifestyle, winning athletic performance, and peer
approval. Most important of these charges it that such unsubstantiated
and unfair claims lead to increased consumption of alcohol products
and to alcohol abuse. At the outset, it is important to recognize that
alcohol is clearly subject to abuse and that its abuse creates enormous
problems, some of which (such as drunk driving) have a social
dimension.

The remedies sought for these alleged effects of advertising are
both bans and informational remedies. More specifically, the Omnibus Petition requests a total ban on advertising reaching small children, teenagers, and problem drinkers, explicitly condemning the use
of athletic, show business, or music celebrities, subliminal techniques, the linkage of consumption to success, and so on. Information
remedies sought include public service advertising and notational
warnings in print advertising.

Deception and Evidence on Alcohol Advertising.   In March 1985, the
Bureau of Consumer Protection and the Bureau of Economics at the
FTC issued a Memorandum to the Commission on the "Omnibus Pe-

---

17. Center for Science in the Public Interest, "Omnibus Petition for Regulation of Unfair
and Deceptive Alcoholic Beverage Advertising and Marketing Practices" (1984), pp. 1–4.

tition" recommending that the Commission deny the petition seeking specific FTC regulation of alcoholic beverage advertising and marketing. Attached to the memorandum is a staff report which investigates the issues brought in the petition.[18] The report is unequivocal: "Protection of the principles of consumer sovereignty rests at the heart of the Commission's exercise of its unfairness authority. In the context of alcoholic beverage advertising, these principles will not support a finding of substantial injury solely in the promotion of this lawfully marketed product. To hold otherwise would permit the Commission to substitute its own tastes for that of the marketplace. Thus, a finding that the challenged practices are unfair would require evidence that the practices are likely to lead to abuse. *It is abuse, not consumption per se, that leads to unavoidable consumer injury.*" (Emphasis supplied.)[19]

Those supporting the regulation of advertising in this instance were asking the FTC to go beyond forms of communication that were deceptive or those related to illegal activity. The regulation of communications that were not unlawful or misleading, forms clearly protected by the first and twenty-first amendments with only minor exceptions, were being proposed. If, for example, it could be demonstrated that regulating alcohol advertising served a "substantial government interest" and that the interest was directly advanced by the regulation, the FTC could step in. Increased abuse with social effects, in the case of alcohol, might have presented a case for FTC regulation. Advertising would not only have to be linked with consumption of alcohol in this case, but also directly with the abuse of alcohol.

What does economic analysis have to say about alcohol advertising, its link to consumption and abuse, and social welfare? From the perspective of economic analysis, alcohol advertising is similar to the "kid-vid" problem discussed earlier. From a narrow and purely economic standpoint, it is not at all clear that advertising prohibitions would make society better off. Assume, for the moment, that alcohol is a harmful product. Consumption makes people, on balance, worse off. Recognize also that advertising is not the creator of alcohol demand, but one factor that influences overall consumption. As in the

18. Bruce C. Levine, et al., *Memorandum to the Federal Trade Commission on Omnibus Petition for Regulation of Unfair and Deceptive Alcoholic Beverage Advertising and Marketing Practices* (1985).

19. Ibid., p. 12.

breakfast cereals analysis, advertising restrictions can be expected to raise the full price of alcoholic beverages to consumers by reducing the flow of the information content of ads. This will, of course, reduce the overall consumption of alcoholic beverages. It is still not clear that society is better off consuming a smaller amount at higher full prices.

The issue is cloudier still if we assume that alcohol users can be divided into two groups. For one group, alcohol is an economic good yielding positive net benefits. For abusers, it is deleterious. Advertising restrictions will affect the entire market and raise full price to both groups. If abusers do not reduce their consumption by much in the face of the price increase (as is likely), then the policy has not clearly produced net benefits for society. Abuse, and its attendant problems, has been only slightly reduced. For the other group, consumption of a good has decreased while price has increased. Non-abusers, a group which likely constitute a majority of alcohol consumers, will be worse off economically as a result of advertising proscriptions. This more realistic analysis yields a weaker case for social improvement through advertising restrictions.

There are additional considerations relating to the advertising-abuse relationship. We know of no reliable study *causally* linking advertising and abuse. One point often made is that the largest number of substance abusers are alcohol abusers. It seems plausible that the largest number of substance consumers are also alcohol consumers. We also know that there are abusers of other substances such as heroin, amphetamines, marijuana, and cocaine. These are substances that are not widely advertised or advertised at all. An interesting question revolves around the ratio of abusers to total consumers of advertised versus non-advertised substances. Does advertising produce a higher ratio of abusers to consumers? To our knowledge, there exists no evidence in this area. As such, the case for using alcohol advertising restrictions to address a substance abuse problem weakens further.

Economic theory and evidence also suggest that total alcohol consumption is not very responsive to the price of alcohol, at least in the short run, and that advertising is not a strong influence on money price. How, under these circumstances, does advertising enhance welfare? The answer is that advertising also acts as what economists call an allocator of demands among firms or brands in an industry. Even if the price-reducing effects of advertising do not increase consumption significantly within a product line, these effects direct purchases toward those specific products yielding greater, and away from those yielding less, consumer utility or satisfaction. Advertising may therefore be welfare-enhancing in an allocative role.

A parallel to the cigarette industry is instructive. The 1971 ban on the broadcast advertisements of cigarettes apparently had only a small effect on overall cigarette consumption.[20] In 1968, the Federal Communications Commission invoked the "fairness doctrine" with respect to broadcast cigarette ads, wherein public service announcements, shown to be somewhat effective at reducing demand, must be broadcast in proportion to cigarette ads. These announcements were sharply reduced with the end of TV cigarette advertisements. The ban, in other words, may have had the unintended effect of increasing overall consumption above what it otherwise would have been. Such ads that exist today in the alcohol area are aimed at both abusers and potential abusers. Will these ads, which inform consumers of the potential problems associated with alcohol consumption, and which are funded in no small part by alcohol suppliers, continue? Again, we cannot provide a concrete answer. A direct, causal link of advertising to alcohol abuse has not been established. It appears that advertising restrictions do not provide a satisfactory social response to the problem of alcohol abuse.[21]

The FTC staff report and the recommendation to the Commission thus argues that there are no legal grounds to ban or otherwise regulate advertising of alcohol products, at least within its jurisdiction. A ban or restrictions on alcohol advertising would also have additional important economic effects on the competitive process. In the first place, a ban would restrict the flow of information on the existence and price of products and, most significantly, of *new* products. For example, the trend to wines and beer with fewer calories and lower alcoholic content (currently in vogue) would be short-circuited by an advertising ban. To the extent that the purpose of a ban is to reduce alcohol abuse, this predictable effect would be counterproduc-

20. Ibid., App A., pp. 7–9.
21. We do not wish to imply that information concerning some dangerous products is necessarily supplied in adequate or optimal amount for all products. If it can be demonstrated that the market and/or the tort system fails in the provision of information for a potentially hazardous product, advertising regulation may be a possible solution. In most of these cases, however, products' safety and design and not advertising is the source of problems.

tive. Moreover, if advertising is an allocator of demand within product groups, beer and wine advertising increases the demand for lower alcohol drinks at the expense of hard liquor. If it is true that the young or uninitiated are most impressed by advertising, a ban might well increase the relative consumption of "more dangerous" forms of alcohol. To the extent that an advertising ban would raise the full price of beer or wine relative to hard liquor (as it apparently raises the price of legal services), economic substitution would reinforce this effect.

From an interest group perspective, moreover, a proposed ban on beer and wine advertising might contain interesting twists. The likely market effects of a ban would be to make market shares within the overall alcohol industry and within the sales of "brand-name" distributions of given categories more rigid. Interest-group economics would predict that there exist both proponents and opponents of regulatory bans or restrictions. To the extent that the TV advertising of beer and wine takes business away from liquor manufacturers, one would expect the latter to support the ban. Likewise, those beer and wine manufacturers with the largest market share at the time of the ban would find their competitive position enhanced, just as "established" lawyers would oppose the introduction of legal services advertising. On the other side, those beer and wine manufacturers with small shares of the current market, as well as potential entrants, would not support a ban on advertising. A ban would thus reduce information flowing to consumers about currently produced products and also forestall the entry of new products. Consumers would clearly be the big losers from a total or partial ban on alcohol advertising. Their market situation would be one of less information, reduced choice, and a strong likelihood of higher prices. Additionally, increased alcohol abuse could increase as a result of the ban.

This analysis does *not* mean that alcohol abuse is not a matter for individual (and in *some* cases, collective) concern in America. It simply means that advertising of legal alcohol products cannot be demonstrated to be, and is likely not, the cause of this problem.[22] Other avenues leading to the reduction of alcohol *abuse* might prove fruit-

---

22. It appears that an overwhelming number of alochol abusers come from homes with an alcoholic parent. To argue that such abusers are introduced to alcohol though advertising is preposterous since they take to alcohol despite the negative "advertising" obtained in the home. Another high-abuse class of alcoholics come from homes of non-drinking parents, suggesting that attempts to suppress information about alcohol can back-fire.

ful. Increased public awareness in the form of public service advertising (some of it currently sponsored and implemented by the alcohol industry itself)—a type of advertising that was proved to be effective in the cigarette industry—could be used effectively in promulgating the dangers of alcohol abuse. Higher minimum drinking ages coupled with increased penalties and enforcement related to drunk driving might also reduce the social affects of abuse. While public information campaigns may be beneficial, we should not forget that the prime responsibility for inculcating sound attitudes toward alcohol among the young rests with parents and other adults. Without such guidance, it is doubtful whether any action by government (including a return to Prohibition) will have any effect whatsoever on the formation of these attitudes. The competitive system will work impersonally under any circumstances. Its particular workings are a product, not a cause, of any moral system.

CONCLUSION: THE MORAL OF ADVERTISING RESTRICTIONS

The three case studies discussed in this chapter all reveal flaws in the traditional economic case and popular arguments against advertising. While we readily concede that some social costs might arise from some particular advertisements, a close examination of three cases—which present important difficulties to a pro-advertising position—does not yield a strong argument for advertising regulation. In the traditional and static economic critique, advertising was viewed as an appendage to the competitive system capable of reducing and constraining economic welfare. Within this mold, arguments that advertising restrictions would lower prices and/or improve consumer welfare flourished. But from the perspective of modern economics, one giving a starring role to the economics of information and to neo-Austrian dynamics, advertising is the single most important focus leading to an economic welfare-maximizing competitive system.

No one has better expressed the role of advertising as a key part of competitive dynamics than Israel Kirzner: "Competition means sometimes offering a better product, or perhaps an inferior product, a product which is more in line with what the entrepreneur believes consumers are in fact desirous of purchasing. It means producing a different model of a product, a different quality, putting it in a different package, selling it along with an offer of free parking, selling through salesmen who smile more genuinely, more sincerely. It means competing in many, many ways besides the pure price which is asked of the consumer in monetary terms."[23]

The bans or restrictions contemplated in the case studies of "kid-vid," legal services, and alcohol advertising would put severe limitations on this welfare-maximizing process. While some individuals in society might object to the consumption patterns of other individuals, they are not free to impose their own tastes on other rational consumers. To do so is the antithesis of democratic free choice. Progress in production, moreover, does not materialize or materializes less rapidly when market entry is legally restricted. At bottom, it is the failure to fully understand the economic role of advertising (what it does do and what it does not do) that often leads to the plea for restrictions.

Interestingly, advertising bans have historically, and apart from their other costly economic effects, often carried a "kicker" in the form of unintended consequences. In the contemporary and ongoing quest to regulate the advertising of "smokeless tobacco" (snuff and chewing tobacco), banned from TV in 1986, a startling but not surprising point emerged. In 1880 the per capita yearly consumption of cigarettes in the U.S. was 25; in 1983, it was 4,000 per capita. This growth was also associated with the decline (until the 1960s) in the use of smokeless tobacco. But cigarette smoking grew in popularity as a substitute for chewing and "spitting" due, at least partly, to the perceived health hazard of tuberculosis. Bans or antispitting laws created both a demand for "safer" cigarettes and a new cigarette-production technology to meet the demand. It is by no means clear, in other words, where advertising restrictions fall in terms of human welfare even *if* they are effective in keeping consumers from "harmful" commodities or activities.

While the purpose of the present chapter has been to illustrate the modern economic perspective on advertising through an examination of contemplated regulations, there are a number of broader social, political, and philosophic issues to consider. How, specifically, might advertising be viewed when related to such matters as fraud, free speech, macroeconomic stabilization, and multinational corporate activity? These are the subjects of Chapter 8.

23. Israel Kirzner, *Competition and Entrepreneurship* (Chicago: University of Chicago Press, 1973), p. 482.

8

REGULATION, FRAUD, ECONOMIC STABILIZATION, AND FREE SPEECH

The effects of advertising in the economy and upon market organization, as detailed in previous chapters, is a complex, much-debated, and often-misunderstood theoretical and empirical issue. A central theme of modern positive economic literature is that advertising is essential to the process of competition and consumer welfare, as we illustrated in earlier chapters. But advertising is linked to a number of other economic, political, and social issues, some of them related to the emerging modern theory of rivalrous competition and information theory. In the present chapter a potpourri of these matters is treated. Four topics are covered: (1) criticisms of advertising's role in less developed countries, (2) advertising and consumer fraud, (3) the role of advertising in macroeconomic stabilization, and finally, (4) the relation of advertising to free speech.

MULTINATIONAL CORPORATIONS AND ADVERTISING IN LESS DEVELOPED COUNTRIES

A great amount of discussion of the activities of multinational corporations (MNCs) has its roots in the writings of J. K. Galbraith.[1] That is, MNCs are viewed as large, powerful entities that act to im-

---

1. John K. Galbraith, *The Affluent Society* (Boston: Houghton Mifflin Co., 1958).

pose the tastes of developed countries on the residents of less developed countries (LDCs), altering traditional cultures, depleting the LDCs of resources, creating dependencies on products that people do not want or need, and earning extraordinarily large profits. Advertising plays a pivotal role in the process of creating dependence. Indeed, many professional economists adhere, with less drama, to Galbraithian notions of the goals and workings of MNCs in LDCs. And most of the work done in this area by professional economists can be clearly seen to have traditional economic analysis as a base.

The traditional economic view finds a basis in the assumption that MNCs are large firms, and it is but a short leap from "bigness" to the characterization of firms as either oligopolies or monopolies. The arguments continue along the same lines developed for domestic analysis, with only the scenery changed to that of an LDC. It has been suggested that the large MNCs take advantage of economies of scale in production and advertising, the holding of patents, and brand name capital (such as Coca-Cola) to take over foreign markets in LDCs and prevent domestic firms from producing in their own country. The MNC is viewed as the agent transferring a technology that the LDC does not need, producing and inducing purchases of goods that local residents do not want and, in the process, changing the tastes of local residents and inducing (undesirable) cultural change. The LDC is left with monopoly.

The traditionalist scenario is inadequate from both theoretical and empirical perspectives of the new neoclassical view of advertising. There are, of course, special problems in applying the theory to LDCs. While space and scope of this book preclude a wide-ranging and complete response to these special problems, several important issues may be addressed.

Economics and LDC Advertising

The traditional view that advertising creates monopoly does not fare well in light of the statistical evidence on advertising's role in the competitive process. Is economic analysis specific to one point in history or to one geographical location? While there is little specific evidence of a statistical nature concerning MNCs and LDCs, recall from Chapter 5 that the evidence from developed countries on the issue of advertising and economies of scale could certainly not be construed as generally supportive of the traditional view. Do such scale economies exist in LDCs? Does advertising in LDCs create them? There is no reason, a priori, to believe that scale economies can be linked to advertising. The mere fact that MNCs are large carries no implication that such firms are exempt from market forces or from the principles of economic behavior. MNCs are not leviathans controlling economic activity and outcomes in LDCs. Kindleberger puts matters into perspective: "Galbraith to the contrary notwithstanding, the corporation does not have the power to compel the individual to act, against his will, in ways it chooses. The state does. The state is sovereign. General Motors is not."[2]

Another argument is that MNCs do not act in the interest of the host country's consumers and residents, to the detriment of the host country. Few if any private firms in a free market take action directly aimed at improving the "interest" or well-being of the consumer. Firms are ordinarily in business to earn as large a profit as possible and will act in the consumer's interest only if such action will be in the firm's profit interest as well. Businessmen, whether in the United States, Europe, or Zimbabwe, cannot be generally characterized as altruistic.

The motive of self-interest does not imply, however, that the MNCs are unconstrained or that they do not end up serving the interests of consumers. They face consumer demands for final goods and services and advertising. It is in their interest to satisfy consumer demands, but through indirect routes. Multinational corporations exist and produce output solely because their products are demanded by consumers.

Whether MNCs serve consumer interests in the free market is a valid issue, but arguments that they generally possess large degrees or amounts of monopoly power rest on uncertain theoretical and empirical footing. Multinational corporations often face as much com-

---

2. Charles Kindleberger, "Size of Firm and Size of Nations," in John H. Dunning, ed., *Economic Analysis and the Multinational Enterprise* (New York: Praeger Publishers, 1974), p. 354. Monopoly outcomes have traditionally been the product of government-sanctioned trading companies, England's East India Company being only the most famous. While nationalistic goals of state power may have played a role in the development of such trade and the colonization that supported it, the monopoly structures it generated were facilitated and legitimized by legal and other governmental institutions. Indeed, the mercantile state's administration of LDCs is not understandable without recourse to the economic interest group analysis of government. See Robert B. Ekelund, Jr. and Robert D. Tollison, *Mercantilism as a Rent-Seeking Society: Economic Regulation in Historical Perspective* (College Station, Texas: Texas A&M University Press, 1981), pp. 111–46.

petition, international and local, as domestic firms. Coca-Cola is not the only seller of soft drinks throughout the world. Competition exists where governments allow it to exist. The competitive process works to constrain the economic power of MNCs in LDCs, just as the competitive process produces socially desirable economic results in developed countries.

What does the evidence tell us about the economic functioning of MNCs? Some studies utilizing aggregate data seem to indicate that MNCs appear fairly profitable in LDCs.[3] The meaning of "fairly profitable" is rather unclear, however, especially when one considers that studies indicating fair profitability do not attribute it to any real factor such as government restrictions on entry, patents, high-risk industries, or other such factors.

Other research has been more careful. A small number of studies have compared rates of return of MNCs and domestic firms that coexist in particular LDCs. These studies have been unable to find any statistically significant difference between rates of return of MNCs and local firms in countries such as Costa Rica, India and Colombia, and Uganda.[4] In fact, one study found that rates of return of domestic firms were slightly higher than those of MNCs in Guatemala.[5] The major point is that economic behavior, and therefore economic theory, knows no geographical bounds.

Baby Formula, Advertising, and the Third World

We argue that firms do not behave differently in Third World countries than they do in the economically developed world. Firms produce, advertise, and sell goods and services to consumers possessing diverse tastes and preferences. Of course, the types of goods trans-

3. Sanjaya Lall, "Financial and Profit Performance of MNC's in Developing Countries: Some Evidence from an Indian and Columbian Sample," *World Development* 4 (1976): 713–24.

4. L. Willmore, "Direct Foreign Investment in Central America Manufacturing," World Development (1976); Lall, "Performance of MNC's in Developing Countries"; I. Gershenberg, "The Performance of Multinational and Other Firms in Economically Less Developed Countries: A Comparative Analysis of Ugandan Data" (Discussion Paper 234, Institute of Development Studies, Nairobi, 1976.)

5. G. Rosenthal, "The Rule of Private Foreign Investment in the Development of the Central American Common Market" (1973). (Mimeo.)

acted in the Third World may differ somewhat as may the institutional setting and the constraints it imposes on market behavior. But the general manner in which markets function, the competitive process, is the same world-wide.

This realization allows us to address and analyze a recent controversy in the economics of advertising and LDCs concerning the advertising of infant formula and the welfare of Third World children. Economic growth and technological advancement in the 1960s and 1970s made possible the development of Third World markets for infant formula, a relatively inexpensive substitute for breastfeeding. The marketing of this product in LDCs by large MNCs was hotly debated in the United Nations and the U.S. Congress. In fact, the United Nations General Assembly voted overwhelmingly (the U.S. casting the sole dissenting vote) in 1981 to adopt a code developed by the World Health Organization restricting the marketing, and essentially banning the advertising, of infant formula in Third World countries. The issues surrounding the controversy, while perhaps not currently in vogue, provide an interesting case study in the economic analysis of advertising in LDCs.

The criticism of baby formula advertising in LDCs stems from one basic objection concerning the proper *use* of the product. That is, if baby formula is mixed with impure water, or otherwise improperly used, the results can lead to illness and possibly to the death of infants. Such criticism of products is not surprising. A number of goods, if not used properly, will produce dangerous or unwanted side effects (this fact is the basis of the FTC's Consumer Products Safety Division). What is surprising is the manner in which opponents of infant formula framed their argument. The solution to the problem of misuse, one is led to believe, is a total ban of all forms of advertising of infant formula in Third World countries. Economic theory leads one to question whether a ban on advertising will make the consumers of infant formula better or worse off.

The logic of the critical positions is the following: Large MNCs producing and selling infant formula advertise their product with billboards and free samples as well as other methods. Advertising is aimed at "uneducated" Third World mothers to induce them to use infant formula rather than breastfeed their children. Uneducated, and perhaps illiterate, mothers mix the formula with contaminated water or fail to mix the optimal proportions of formula and water, to the detriment of the newborn child.[6] Use of the formula causes the mother to cease lactating after a period, creating a "captive" consumer for the baby formula producer. Thus, if advertising in all its forms were prohibited, the problem would then be presumably eliminated, with the additional effect that MNCs would no longer be profiteering in infant mortality.

This reasoning has an origin in the view of the consumer taken by the traditional critics of advertising. The consumer is viewed as being affected by advertising so as to act in a manner detrimental to the consumer's own self-interest. (We presume that Third World mothers, like mothers elsewhere, consider the health and safety of their children to be in their own self-interest.) The effect is even more pronounced because the consumers in question are reportedly uneducated and illiterate.

Even if consumers are uneducated or illiterate, it is not clear that they knowingly behave in self-detrimental fashion. Literacy would not seem to be prerequisite to rationality in an economic sense. And if irrational behavior on the part of consumers is denied, then criticisms of such advertising deteriorate as rapidly as they did in the analysis of domestic consumers. Advertising is a method of conveying information about the prices, characteristics, and existence of available products to consumers. The modern approach leads us to believe that the advertising of infant formula, at worst, *informs* Third World mothers of the *existence* of a product that has potential in improving the health of their infants.

There is also good reason to believe, moreover, that advertising of infant formula causes *price* to be lower than it would be in the absence of advertising. A ban on advertising will not *lower* the price of this natural food substitute nor will it improve the already relatively low real incomes of LDC mothers. An infant formula advertising ban would also not improve the economic welfare of mothers who do not yet know of the existence of the product. Consumers of products are not

6. It is interesting to note that recent evidence produced by a scientific task force under the auspices of the Centers for Disease Control suggests that breastfeeding is not the only nor the primary determinant affecting infant mortality and health. Moreover, the task force casts substantial doubt on the notion that infant formula injures infant health by discouraging breastfeeding. Carol Adelman, "Closing the Book on Infant Formula Fears," *The Wall Street Journal* (June 19, 1983): 30.

made better off by restricting knowledge about the existence of products. On the ultimate basis of economic welfare, a prohibition of advertising is counterproductive.

Apart from these two economic effects of an advertising ban, there are other logical flaws in the advancing of such a ban. The goal of the proposed advertising ban is to dissuade mothers from using infant formula and/or to eliminate infant formula from markets in the Third World countries. The question then begs itself. Why, in LDCs with relatively high infant mortality rates due partly to malnutrition, is less food available for infants viewed as preferable to more food available? An advertising ban raises prices and reduces consumption and availability of infant formula. Supporters of formula advertising prohibition will, if successful, reduce nutrition available from one source without increasing nutrition currently available from other sources. Supporters also argued that viable substitutes exist for infant formula, such as wet nurses and breastmilk banks. We argue that these alternatives are economically no better than, and plausibly inferior to, formula. Mothers may find it difficult (costly) to discern the health of a wet nurse and thus the average quality of milk. Wet nurse milk may be a good example of a credence good. If so, the incentive of the nurse to disguise and misinform the mother-consumer concerning health and milk quality is real and dangerous. The efficacy of breast milk banks presumes that health officials in LDCs effectively monitor donors' quality, properly pasteurize milk to eliminate viruses, and maintain clean and efficient refrigeration storage. All of this seems comparatively unlikely given conditions in most Third World countries. Additionally, the expense of doing so makes banked breast milk a more expensive substitute of questionable quality. Carole Adelman indicates that fees for safe breast milk from milk banks in the U.S. are $2.50 per ounce, implying a total cost of $50.00 per day to feed an infant with bank milk.[7] Given incomes in Third World countries, an expenditure of this magnitude would likely preclude milk banks as viable substitutes on price alone. It is difficult to see how the proposed United Nations' ban makes LDC infants better off.

Additionally, an advertising ban hinders entry of new firms. With impeded entry, prices and long-term profits earned by firms currently selling in the infant formula industry will be higher than if entry could

---

7. Adelman, "Closing the Book on Infant Formula Fears."

be facilitated by advertising. One of the by-products of entry and competition through advertising could well be product improvement—a safer, more nutritious product. Firms not only enter and establish themselves by selling at lower prices, but also by selling improved quality. Improved quality can be detected, in part, by Third World mothers through monitoring and observing the health and growth of their own and other infants. Established sellers would be induced by competition to improve their product quality in order to forestall or prevent lost sales. An advertising ban, with its entry restricting property, could certainly not be expected to speed up formula quality improvement.

There is one other objection to infant formula advertising, one centered on the difficulty of assimilating existing information. The argument is one of illiteracy and not irrationality. Advertising of formula, in the form of free samples at hospitals or labels on the containers, provides information on proper use. The right proportions, the boiling of water prior to mixing, and other steps of precaution to ensure a nutritional food are provided in both printed and symbolic form. Firms provide this information, through advertising or otherwise, because it is in their interest to do so. They want consumers to continue buying the product. However, if the consumer cannot read, is uneducated, or for whatever reason does not or cannot prepare the mixture properly, impure formula may have a detrimental effect on the child.

Our earlier discussion of advertising as a derived demand suggests that firms will strive to provide advertising information than is amenable for use by consumers. The mere fact that a consumer is illiterate does not imply that certain styles of advertising cannot accurately convey important information. It is also curious that organizations supporting this advertising prohibition try to discourage infant formula consumption in LDCs by advertising *against* it. If the illiterate mothers of LDCs cannot understand proper usage instruction, in part through advertising and marketing campaigns, how can they hope to understand advertising encouraging them not to buy infant formula? Advertising is not the problem. Illiteracy and lack of information are. Third World infants would be better fed, or better off economically, if such organizations devoted anti-advertising resources to programs designed to educate mothers in the proper, most nutritious way to use the product.

Infant formula, in one sense, is qualitatively no different from eyeglasses, gasoline, or prescription drugs. Advertising restrictions on infant formula can be expected to produce economic results similar to those discussed earlier. At base, the effects of advertising by MNCs have been severely misinterpreted by those who supported a ban on advertising of infant formula. These groups are analytically correct on one point, which is that MNCs are out to earn as large a profit as possible in the infant formula market. In order to do this, however, the industry must provide food for Third World infants. Once we admit to economic rationality on the part of the mothers of the infants, *even though they may be illiterate*, the socially beneficial effects of advertising in a competitive market become clear. The bottom line is the same as for developed world consumers: Consumers are better off in a competitive market where the provision of information through advertising abounds than in a relatively noncompetitive market where information is much more difficult to obtain because it is prohibited.

CONSUMER FRAUD, DECEPTION, AND ADVERTISING

Proliferation of government activity in the area of regulation during the late 1960s and 1970s in the United States extended to advertising. Consumer advocate organizations arose and induced legislators, both on national and local levels, to pass laws affecting the advertising process. The Federal Trade Commission became very active over this period in a number of areas. New rules of the game were imposed on advertisers, most with the intent of eliminating (or reducing) consumer deception or fraud from advertising.

Consumer advocates often agree with the views of some traditional economists. Consumers are considered irrational and the subjects of manipulation by advertisers and producers. The term "consumer protection" itself implies that consumers are weak and defenseless in the marketplace and that they must be somehow protected from any fraud associated with advertising. This notion has led to myriad state regulations and to the fairly wide-ranging authority of the FTC to, in effect, establish deception through informal hearings (Trade Regulation Rules), place the burden of proving nondeception on the shoulders of the accused through "advertising substantiation" programs, and require "corrective" advertising in instances where it is deemed to be warranted by the FTC, not a court of law. However, consumers are not irrational and will not consciously act in a manner that is detrimental to their own self-interest. Consumers will not *continuously* buy empty cereal boxes (be defrauded) just because they are advertised on Saturday morning TV.

Another possible reason for the plethora of protective legislation and bureaucratic agencies is that, even though consumers are rational, they are without sufficient information to make beneficial choices. What is a "lack" of information? Consumers may be presumed to have the ability to assimilate information and use it to make wise choices, choices that make them economically better off. Is there a lack of information that prevents consumers from making proper choices? Specificity is needed in defining a "lack" of information, for in one sense there is a lack of information, but in another sense there is not.

Consumers are not stranded in a desert of ignorance. Information is obtained through advertising and the consumption of products and services, or sampling. But no consumer has complete, perfect, and current information on all products and services available, and for a very good reason. Information is not free as we have stressed through this book. Along with any product or activity that involves sacrificing something in order to obtain the product or engage in the activity, consumers balance costs and benefits of additional information in deciding on the amount of information to obtain. Figure 8–1 uses the simple marginal cost–marginal benefit approach to analyze this choice on the part of an individual. In this example the marginal cost of obtaining information (MC_I) is assumed to be constant. Each increment of information costs as much as the last. The marginal benefit of additional information (MB_I) is downsloping, again showing that each increment of information yields smaller and smaller benefits. For the rational individual, the optimal amount of information to obtain is I_0.[8] The individual would not choose to gather more information, say I_1, simply because it would not be worth it. Suppose that the difference between I_0 and I_1 were one unit of information. The additional cost of this unit would be greater than the additional benefit.

8. This model of individual behavior does not attempt to describe the *thought processes* of an individual. It does, however, provide a good description of how people *act* or *behave*. No one consciously calculates marginal costs and benefits before making a choice, but this theory will accurately describe and predict the end results of the choice process.

Figure 8–1.   Optimal Information Accumulation.

Marginal Cost &
Marginal Benefit
of Information
(in $s)

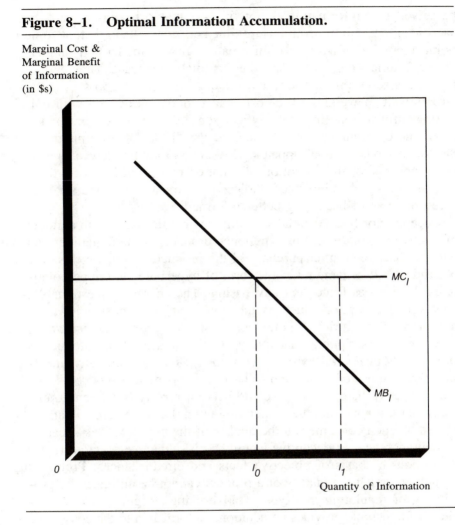

That given up would be of greater value than what is received. The individual's optimal amount of information (I_0) is less than the *maximum* amount of information the individual could obtain. Past some point, it does not pay to become more informed.

The previous analysis clarifies the meaning of insufficient information on the part of consumers. Viewed in a simplistic and misleading sense, there is a lack of information in that consumers do not possess all information that is available in the market. But once it is perceived that information is not free—valuable resources must be sacrificed to obtain it (even leisure time has value)—and that, at some point, the value of additional information grows smaller and smaller, then consumers cannot be described as totally ignorant. They choose to possess some information, and the quantity they do possess is the direct result of weighing the costs and benefits associated with collecting information. In an analytical sense, when all factors of the economic environment are considered, the "lack" of information on the part of consumers disappears. Consumers may be viewed as generally possessing an amount of information that is sufficient for them to make reasonably informed choices over most goods and services given the cost of becoming better informed.

Deceptive or fraudulent advertising may be discussed with a model of *optimal information*. For experience products, certain qualities can only be discovered after purchase of the product. Often, for this type of product, advertising takes the form of hyperbole, and hyperbole is often depicted as fraudulent advertising. The charge is questionable, however. Descriptions such as the "prettiest" or "most enjoyable" restaurant, a "luxurious" hotel, a "must see" movie, *ad infinitum*, may not be descriptions that live up to the quality of the product as *subjectively evaluated* by some consumers, but may actually understate the opinions other consumers have of the particular product. Thus, the same advertising message could be subjectively fraudulent to one consumer but not to another depending upon the subjective valuations placed by each consumer on the quality of the product. Classification of such messages as deceptive would be on subjective opinion, rather than upon the basis of objective facts and circumstances. Problems of authenticating the quality of a product cannot be mitigated by prohibiting or regulating this type of advertising. Regulation or prohibition of hyperbole provides no additional information to the consumer.

The definition of deceptive or fraudulent advertising must be objective in nature and content. A rule is needed that, when applied to any advertising message, will decide for us on an objective basis whether the message is deceptive. The construction of such a rule is difficult. Perhaps we could settle on a rule of the following nature: An advertisement is deceptive if it consciously and intentionally misrepresents characteristics of a product that are *objectively* measurable. These characteristics might include price, location, weight, quantity, technical capabilities, and many other attributes. There would be no problem classifying an advertisement for a "beachfront lot," when in fact the lot is six miles from the ocean, as deceptive or fraudulent. While some may disagree with this definition of what constitutes a deceptive advertisement, it will be used in the following policy discussion. It is worth remembering that conscious and intentional misrepresentations are central to the act of fraud.

Consider an overall, society-wide analysis of fraud from the perspective of the economist. One plain fact of life is that fraud or deception does exist. We may not like it, we may find it morally objectionable as we would theft or murder, but we must recognize that individuals and firms do exist who are willing to engage in deceptive advertising (as defined above). Truly deceptive advertising may be expected to exist more frequently in markets for credence goods which we discussed in Chapter 4. Consumers of credence goods face large costs of discovering and ascertaining product qualities, and in some cases the proper amounts of purchase. Although competition in credence goods markets have produced some viable solutions to these problems such as service contracts and warranties, markets are simply not perfect. With large benefits to fraudulent advertising of credence goods, we would expect the existence of such deception. The problem, from the economist's viewpoint, must be analyzed by recognizing that deceptive advertising is costly to society and that any effectual reduction in the amount of fraud requires society to devote scarce resources to deception-reducing activities. There is no free lunch. It is *costly* to eliminate some, or all, deceptive advertising. Society's problem is to decide what quantity of scarce resources to devote to the detection and elimination of fraud. Alternatively, society must allow some quantity of deception to exist given that prevention is costly, i.e., there is a socially "optimal" amount of fraud.

With some alteration, the model of marginal benefits and marginal costs may be used to analyze the problem from a societal perspective. Figure 8–2 shows the marginal cost society bears of various possible levels or units of fraud. Assume that additional units of perpetrated fraud entail higher and higher costs to members of society, or that the marginal cost to society of fraudulent activity (MC_F) rises as fraudulent activity increases. These costs entail substitution of other, less efficient forms of information than advertising when choosing products, the resources consumers devote to detecting and avoiding deceptive advertising, and a host of other costs.

Deceptive advertising and the perpetration of fraud is clearly costly to society as Figure 8–3 indicates. But preventing or reducing fraud is, unfortunately, not costless. Legislation must be enforced. Cheaters must be discovered. Penalties must be applied. These activities involve the use of society's scarce resources (policemen, prisons, courts, additional FTC employees, and so on) that could be used to produce other goods and services. Figure 8–3 contains a representation of the cost to society, in terms of the necessary resources sacrificed, of preventing successive units of fraudulent activity, or the marginal cost of preventing fraud (MC_{pf}).

In interpreting Figure 8–3, some adjustments are necessary. Con-

---

Figure 8–2.   Marginal Cost to Society of Fraud.

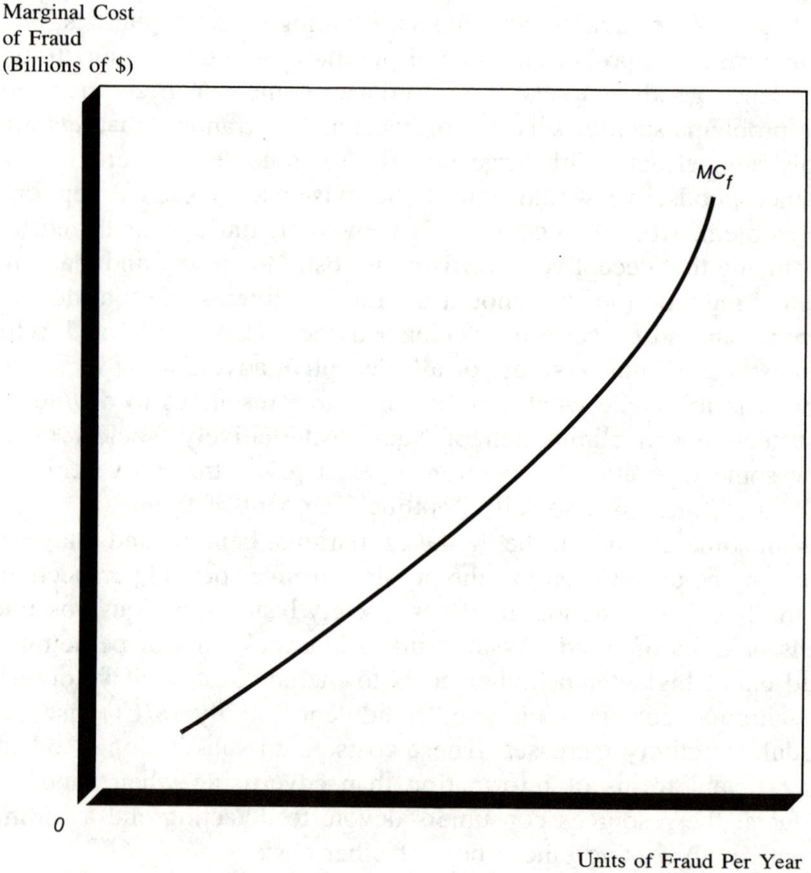

Marginal Cost
of Fraud
(Billions of $)

MC_f

0

Units of Fraud Per Year

Figure 8–3. Marginal Cost to Society of Preventing Fraud.

Marginal Cost of
Preventing Fraud
(Billions of $)

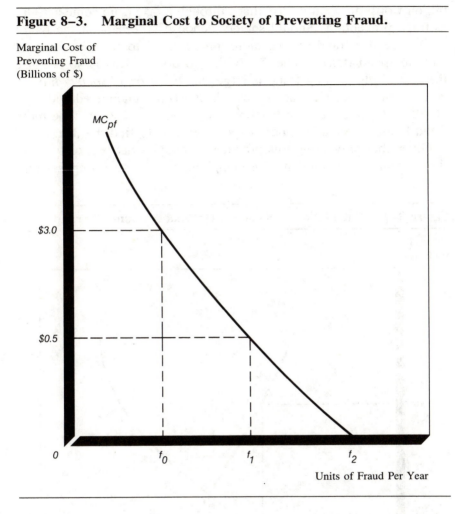

MC_{pf}

$3.0

$0.5

0

f_0 f_1 f_2

Units of Fraud Per Year

sider the level of fraudulent advertising f_2, a relatively high level that would exist if society devoted *no resources* to its prevention; hence the marginal cost of preventing no fraud is zero (the MC_{pf} curve intersects the horizontal axis at f_2, and the marginal cost of fraud prevention associated with the f_2 level of fraud is $0). Suppose society chose to eliminate or prevent one unit of fraud, or equivalently allow f_1 units of fraud to exist. The marginal cost of preventing one unit of fraud, of reducing the level of fraud from f_2 to f_1, would be $0.5 billion according to the figure. Society would have to reallocate $0.5

billion worth of resources (perhaps through a tax) from some activity to fraud prevention. Should society "choose" (perhaps at the ballot box) to reduce fraud by one more unit, from f_1 to f_0, society would have to spend (tax) another \$3 billion to do so. This is so because the cost of eliminating fraud is larger *the more fraud society has already eliminated*. The easy cases (cheapest) are uncovered and penalized first, the next easiest (more costly) next, and so on. The more fraud found, the harder (more expensive) it is to find the rest.

Given that preventing this practice is costly, what is society's optimal amount of fraudulent advertising? Figure 8–4 superimposes Fig-

Figure 8–4.   Calculation of Society's Optimal Amount of Fraud.

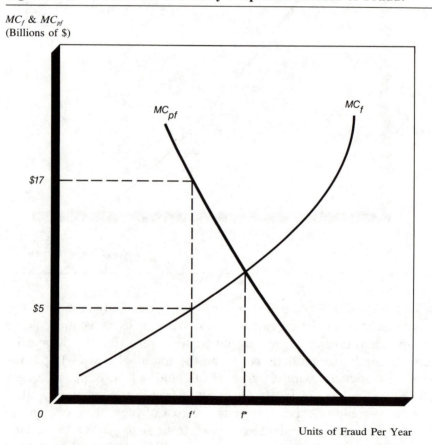

MC_f & MC_{pf}
(Billions of \$)

ures 8–2 and 8–3. Society *does* have an optimal amount of fraud, f^* in this case, when the cost of prevention is considered. Society should continue to eliminate fraudulent advertising until the marginal cost society bears from deceptive advertising is just equal to the additional cost of preventing deceptive advertising. To see why this is so, suppose society were considering the elimination of one more unit of fraud, contemplating a reduction in fraud from f^* to f. The reduction would entail the hiring of additional resources (for detection, enforcement of laws, etc.) that would cost an additional $17 billion in this example. But the removal of this one unit of fraud would yield lower damages to consumers due to fraud of only $5 billion. Is it worth it to society to tax itself $17 billion to prevent $5 billion worth of damage? Surely not.

When cost of prevention is considered, society has an efficient or optimal level of deceptive advertising to allow to exist. This conclusion is not an endorsement of fraudulent advertising. The idea of intentional deception in the marketplace, as well as anywhere else, is deplorable: it inhibits the otherwise smooth functioning of the market. Economists, however, are realistic in recognizing the real costs involved.[9]

Fraudulent Advertising and Consumer Protection

A major issue is the proclivity of consumer advocate groups to demand legislation and regulation with respect to fraudulent advertising (this issue is apart and distinct from the philosophical issue of freedom of speech discussed later in this chapter). Economists cannot say whether these laws are good or bad. Economists can analyze the laws as to their efficiency in achieving their stated goals and perhaps suggest alternative methods of goal achievement.

Consider again the concept of deceptive or fraudulent advertising and recall that a reasonable definition of fraudulent advertising involves a conscious and intentional attempt to misrepresent the characteristics of a product or service that are objectively measurable. While deceptive advertising does exist, it may appear to some that the extent of this phenomenon has been artificially magnified by those individuals and groups lobbying for extensive regulation of advertis-

9. Michael R. Darby and Edi Karni, "Free Competition and the Optimal Amount of Travel," *Journal of Law and Economics* 16 (1973): 67–88.

ing messages. Hyperbole cannot be classified as deception, nor can deception be interpreted as a product's failure to live up to the consumer's expectations regarding its want-satisfying properties (unless, of course, expectations are directly established by untrue descriptions of objective characteristics). This eliminates a number of off-the-cuff candidates for fraudulent advertising. But these are not the only reasons why the level and economic damage of deceptive advertising can be overestimated.

Critics of advertising only consider the incentives advertisers have to try to deceive consumers. But those instances and situations in which advertisers have the greatest pecuniary incentives to deceive consumers are the same instances and situations in which consumers have the greatest incentives not to be deceived. Not only must there be a lie for fraud to exist, but also there must be someone who believes the lie and backs up that belief with money. If consumers are self-interested, can they be expected to believe as many lies as the critics believe they do, especially when it is expensive to do so? This is unlikely. Additionally, one wonders how many times consumers will believe the lie. Advocates of advertising regulation would have us believe that they are the only ones who are able to detect deception. Consumers are demonstrably adept at detecting deceptive or fraudulent advertising, especially if they have been the victim of previous fraud.

The competitive process also functions in dealing with fraudulent advertising. Consider, for example, such credence good market institutions as warranties, manufacturer-certified service locations, franchise regulations governing the quality of the franchisee's service or product long-term service contracts, and others as indirect evidence. Such market characteristics evolve within the profit-maximizing competitive structure in society. Even if consumers are not particularly skilled at detecting fraud and fraudulent advertising in these markets, the competitive process nonetheless provides consumers with some positive protection.

The Design of Advertising Regulation

How well advertising regulation performs in terms of reducing fraud involves not only the costs of establishing regulations and the costs of enforcing them, but also the particular *type* of regulation under consideration. One form of FTC advertising regulation strongly favored in the past prevented advertisers of brand name items from mentioning the names of rival brands, or prohibited brand name comparative advertising. Since the presumed goal of regulation in this area is to make consumers better off economically with better information, it is difficult to understand the value of these regulations. Consumers have not benefited from such policies and economists generally supported their elimination. At present such regulation has been eliminated.

The design of advertising regulations, if we are to have them at all, is a very important issue. Even a (presumably) carefully designed advertising regulation may not be very effective in terms of reducing the economic damage to consumers that results from deceptive advertising. Mandatory labeling has, for decades, been an important and hotly debated economic issue. Market-originated labeling has been a part of sales of products for many years and mandatory labeling of some products carries important benefits to consumers. These savings come in the form of a reduced amount of resources spent by consumers on information. While the benefits of mandatory labeling are clear in some cases, costs may also accompany the price.

Phillip Nelson has examined this problem by considering the law that prohibits mislabeling of the fabric content of clothing.[10] The enforcement of this law leads some, but perhaps not all, consumers to believe that labels are accurate, providing an incentive for some manufacturers to mislabel, knowing full well that the law is costly to enforce, that they may or may not be caught, and figuring that their gains from mislabeling outweigh any expected penalties if they are apprehended. Without the regulation, a large proportion of consumers would be very distrusting of labels and tend to substitute other avenues of information for labels in discerning clothing content. Without the law, fraudulent labels would simply not fool a large number of consumers for a long time. The point is that it is not at all clear that this regulation does what it is intended to do. It may or may not reduce the economic costs of deceptive advertising. It may yield more specific and accurate information to some consumers, but at the expense of enforcement costs and some detected and undetected fraud

10. Phillip Nelson, "Comments on Advertising and Free Speech," in Allen Hyman and M. Bruce Johnson, ed., *Advertising and Free Speech* (Lexington, Mass.: Lexington Books, D.C. Heath and Co., 1977), pp. 1–32.

in cases where some consumers would otherwise not be so trusting of the label. Given that regulations of this type produce questionable or ambiguous results, real, definite, and measurable expenditure of resources instituting and enforcing such regulations should be carefully considered.[11]

One other problem arises with respect to the government regulation method of coping with deceptive advertising. Assume, with most consumer advocate groups, that consumers are the ill-informed and defenseless prey of shady advertisers. They are unable to evaluate advertising as to its truthfulness and as a result frequently make the wrong choices. Perhaps, as Nelson posits, the consumer is "confused"—sometimes too trusting and gullible, sometimes too mistrusting and skeptical.[12] Suppose that this characterization is an accurate description of consumers in general. Is the consumer better off under wide-ranging regulation of advertising as opposed to little or no regulation? The answer is unclear.

If consumers find it costly or are unable to judge for themselves whether or not an advertisement is deceptive by evaluating information in the ad, the product, and the terms of the transaction, can the same consumers be expected to understand the implications of government-imposed standards concerning deception? Do these consumers know the complexities of the Truth-in-Lending Act? Does any citizen completely understand the 2,000-page (1986 revised) Tax Code of the United States? Not only will these regulations be costly to enforce, but the door is opened to giving many consumers a false sense of security which would make them ripe for puffery. Darby and Karni have analyzed various schemes by which government can intervene in credence goods markets that are analogous and applicable to the kind of advertising regulation discussed here.[13] These range from government information-production to quality standards established by government regulation with violators detected by consumer "bounty hunters." They conclude that it is unlikely that government-sponsored

11. The value of FTC's Advertising Substantiation Program, in which the FTC had authority to conduct advertising "sweeps" forcing companies (without complaints) to verify ad content, has been questioned. For details, see Richard Higgins and Fred S. McChesney, "Truth and Consequences: The FTC's Ad Substantiation Program," *International Review of Law and Economics* 6 (1986): 151–68.

12. Nelson, "Comments on Advertising and Free Speech," p. 56.

13. Darby and Karni, "Free Competition and the Optimal Amount of Travel," pp. 83–86.

proposals could better address the fraud problem than the mechanisms of the private market.

Policing of the law expends resources, as do trials, and appeals of advertisers. Special exemptions would undoubtedly be granted by legislatures along with grandfather clauses for certain advertisers. The possibility that the regulatory agency will become a tool of the industry itself and used to restrict competition is very real. Consider the Civil Aeronautics Board (CAB) and the Interstate Commerce Commission (ICC) for evidence on this point. Prior to 1977, the CAB acted, according to a large number of economists, as a cartel manager for domestic airlines. Route restrictions, fare restrictions, entry restrictions, service restrictions imposed as consumer-oriented regulation were a direct cause of prices and profits well above competitive levels in this industry over a long period of time.

Even if consumers are too ignorant to act in their own self-interest, and we cannot presume that they are, it is not at all clear that wide-ranging advertising regulation would be beneficial to consumers. Advertising regulations have been viewed either as an anticompetitive tool increasing the profit of the industries regulated (e.g., eyeglasses, prescription drugs, gasoline) or as a barricade preventing the consumer from receiving both direct and indirect information. An essentially free market in advertising, with marginal and effective control of obvious fraud, would likely yield the largest benefits to consumers.

One idea, suggested by Nelson, would seem to be a low-cost method of improving efficiency in this market.[14] Suppose antifraud legislation were passed allowing advertisers of products and services to *voluntarily* choose to warranty their advertisements as to their truthfulness. Two classes of advertisements would then exist. Consumers could, at low cost, discover more credible advertisements by simply looking for the "warranty mark." However, advertisers who warranty their ads would so do with the full and complete knowledge that they could be held legally liable and accountable for deceptive or fraudulent advertising.

Enforcement court costs could be financed a number of ways, perhaps through a percentage of any penalties applied to advertisers who violate their warranties. Additionally, detection fees would not be paid by taxpayers not directly involved in the case. Any consumer who

14. Nelson, "Comments on Advertising and Free Speech," p. 56.

has discovered a warranty cheater could sue and obtain a discoverer's fee. To prevent a floodtide of wrongly accused warranty cheaters, the court could impose court costs on the plaintiff should the accused be proven innocent. This arrangement would allow for low-cost authentication of objective information in advertising (prices, location, quantities, etc.), but would not eliminate hyperbole and colorful claims to subjective qualities. It would also make detection of deception fairly easy and reduce the incentives advertisers have to deceive consumers.[15] In a sense, this is what Sears and Roebuck Company does with much of the merchandise it sells and advertises. "Satisfaction guaranteed or money back" and "rainchecks" on advertised products that are temporarily sold out are good examples of such warranties. Sears did not become the world's largest retailer by defrauding consumers.

Advertising and Fraud: Conclusion

One need not restrict the discussion of advertising, fraud, and regulation to the markets for the products and services most of us purchase and consume every day. The discussion is easily extended to voting in the political "market." Politicians often argue for strict regulation of the advertising media. The call for regulation from the elected caretakers of government is strange indeed when one considers that federal, state, and local governments most likely spend more than any other organization on advertising (no exact figures on federal, state, and local government advertising, curiously enough, seem to exist).

Bureaucrats and politicians are apparently not willing to live by the same regulations that they seek to impose on others. It is doubtful whether politicians would be willing to put a legal warranty on campaign statements, which are, after all, just another type of advertising. Recent legislation, passed by an incumbent Congress (existing firms) and signed by an incumbent President (an existing firm), severely restricts the amount that can be spent on advertising by challengers in elections (potential competitors). In no way does this suggest that

---

15. This solution is not perfect. The possibility exists that more private resources than justified by social gains to uncovering and penalizing fraud would be devoted to detection activity. For a discussion of this point, see Jack Hirshleifer, "The Private and Social Value of Information and the Reward to Inventive Activity," *American Economic Review* 61 (1971): 567–74.

politicians should be subject to myriad advertising regulations, but at the same time it would be interesting if politicians were allowed to warranty their campaign promises and statements in office. As surely as there are incentives to defraud consumers in the market for products, there are incentives for politicians to use advertising to defraud voters.

The fundamental problem is how best to handle deceptive advertising. We believe that consumer power in the marketplace arising from the authority of the consumer to choose generally provides the best response a free society can offer to this problem. Improvements may be made in our economic environment so that we may deal more effectively with this issue. It is not clear, however, that society should substitute the arbitrary interpretations of courts, lawyers, and bureaucrats for free consumer choice. The arguments for the desirability and effectiveness of free choice far outweigh the other alternatives, in terms of both economic efficiency and personal freedom.

ADVERTISING AND THE BUSINESS CYCLE

The possibility that advertising is a *macroeconomic* determinant of the business cycle has not escaped the attention of economists and other social scientists. The essential question, posed in the wake of the Keynesian revolution, is whether advertising has a stabilizing or destabilizing effect on the economy. The earliest charges, led by Neil Borden and Alvin Hansen, were that advertising was *pro*cyclical in effect, i.e., that it *caused* aggregate spending to change, and that it could be regulated countercyclically by government in order to help iron out swings in cycles of business activity.[16] Presumably, such regulation would take the form of taxation of advertising expenditures during periods of inflationary booms and subsidization in recessionary downturns of business activity.

There is no doubt that total advertising expenditures are well correlated with the business cycle, although the relationship may be complicated by lags of such expenditures in relation to consumption or income. But the existence of a large and procyclical mass of advertising expenditures is irrelevant from the point of view of economic stabilization. Further, simple logic and tests of the hypothesis reveal

16. Neil H. Borden, *The Economic Effects of Advertising* (Chicago: Inwin, 1942); Alvin Hanson, *Economic Issues of the 1960's* (New York: McGraw-Hill Book Co., 1969).

that the countercyclical regulation of advertising is preposterous. Consider why this is so.

In the first place, the procyclical nature of advertising outlays has long been well known,[17] but there are good reasons why they are procyclical. Businesses typically determine current advertising outlays on the basis of *past* sales. In serious downturns, there is a simple lack of funds with which to finance advertising. Given this practice, advertising expenditures are expected to be procyclical. Indeed, such outlays *must* be procyclical. This fact hardly indicates that public economic policies should be designed so as to dampen advertising's procyclical impact. It would make as little sense to regulate or counteract the procyclical impact of any other expenditure that happens to be procyclical in nature, e.g., the employment of labor or the leisure and recreation industries.

Support for the countercyclical regulation of advertising must depend on the proposition that such expenditures cause or determine aggregate consumption spending (the major component of aggregate demand) in a positive manner. The crucial question is whether, because of advertising, increases in consumption occur at the expense of consumers' savings or at the expense of demand for other goods and services. Alternatively stated, do higher advertising outlays *cause* increases in consumption or does increased consumption spending (increasing sales) cause an increase in advertising? Advertising must *determine* consumption if it is to be the subject of macroeconomic regulation. A relatively small body of evidence has grown up around the proposition. These studies have employed a variety of data and methods.

In an initial study of the question, Verdon, McConnell, and Roesler (1968) concluded that (a) advertising was procyclical in nature and (b) that advertising had a positive influence on GNP (income) and on industrial production (though no consistent pattern was shown).[18] In a critique of this study, which was also an initial assessment of the design of advertising—business cycle tests, Ekelund and Gramm (1969)

---

17. David M. Blank, "Cyclical Behavior of National Advertising," *Journal of Business* 35 (1962): 14–27; C. Y. Yang, "Variations in the Cyclical Behavior of Advertising," *Journal of Marketing* 28 (1964): 25–30.

18. W. H. Verdon, C. R. McConnell and T. W. Roesler, "Advertising Expenditures as an Economic Stabilizer, 1954–64," *Quarterly Review of Economics and Business* 8 (1968): 7–18.

argued (a) that Verdon *et al.* avoided relating consumption to advertising and therefore employed the wrong independent variables (income and industrial production) since advertising can affect the business cycle *only* through consumption, and (b) that all simple tests of the hypothesis were suspect owing to the fact that advertising was not only a possible determinant of sales but that sales were *also* a determinant of advertising; that is, the direction of causation between the two variables was difficult if not impossible to detect because advertising was *endogenous* to the system.[19] This means that advertising is not independent of other variables in the system as it must be in order to correctly and adequately gauge its statistical impact on consumption. Utilizing simple methods and various lagged relationships, however, Ekelund and Gramm were unable to detect any relationship between advertising and aggregate consumption.

More elaborate tests of the advertising-consumption hypothesis followed in the 1970s and early 1980s. Taylor and Weiserbs (1972)[20] found that advertising had a significant effect upon consumption, although their results relating to the direction of causality were brought into question by the research of Schmalensee (1972) and Clark (1976).[21] In an excellent and elaborate econometric study, Ashley, Granger, and Schmalensee (1980) used a commonly accepted definition of consumption and concluded that there is no evidence that advertising causes consumption, but that some evidence suggests that consumption causes advertising.[22]

These studies show that carefully executed economic-empirical investigations cannot establish an unambiguous causal connection between advertising and the business cycle. In a day when Keynesian countercyclical fiscal policies are being discredited on both academic and political fronts, this conclusion may not seem so important. It is perhaps worth remembering, however, that the proposal to regulate

19. Robert B. Ekelund, Jr. and William P. Gramm, "A Reconsideration of Advertising Expenditures, Aggregate Demand, and Economic Stabilization," *Quarterly Review of Economics and Business* 9 (1969): 71–77.

20. L. D. Taylor and D. Weiserbs, "Advertising and the Aggregate Consumption Function," *American Economic Review* 62 (1972): 642–55.

21. Richard Schmalensee, *The Economics of Advertising* (Amsterdam: North-Holland Publishing Co., 1972); D. G. Clark, "Economic Measurement of the Duration of the Advertising Effect on Sales," *Journal of Marketing Research* 13 (1976): 345–57.

22. R. Ashley, C. W. J. Granger and Richard Schmalensee, "Advertising and Aggregate Consumption: An Analysis of Causality," *Econometrics* 48 (1980): 1149–67.

advertising as a macroeconomic determinant of the business cycle originated within the economics profession among the Keynesians. A long-term recession may revive interest in the proposal but, as the above discussion suggests, logic and statistical evidence could be marshalled against this kind of regulation.

ADVERTISING AND FREE SPEECH

A final issue is at the core of a free society, which is philosophical but amenable to economic analysis. The issue is freedom of speech and expression, but it would be beneficial to contemplate the discussion in terms of a much broader class of activities. These activities are those founded upon the personal freedoms many of us are lucky enough to be born with, but sometimes take for granted.

The issue of freedom of speech and expression can be analyzed in part with economic theory and can be best understood by considering the markets for two characteristically different yet conceptually similar commodities. These markets are the *market for goods* and the *market for ideas*.[23] Everyone is familiar with the market for goods or products. The market for ideas can be considered to encompass the exchange between individuals and groups of expression and opinion in both writing and speech. Why is there a distinction? Apart from the obvious characteristic differences of the two commodities, is there any aspect of the two markets that sets one market uniquely distinct from the other? Suppliers of products, and suppliers of ideas, expression, and opinion both exist. There are demanders in both markets, and exchange between demanders and suppliers occurs in each market (though price is more exact and easier to observe in the market for goods). What, then, is the real distinction and dichotomy of the two markets?

The answer to these questions lies in how a large proportion of people feel concerning how, and to what degree, governmental policy or regulation should be applied in the two markets. On the one hand, it seems that a proportion of the population believes that, as far as the goods market is concerned, consumers lack the ability to make wise, informed choices. Consumers are either irrational and do not

23. Ronald Coase, "The Market for Goods and the Market for Ideas," *American Economic Review* 64 (1974): 384–91.

frequently act in their own self-interest, or are so ill-informed so as to make choices that are in their self-interest difficult if not impossible. Government, or the proper bureaucratic arm of government, is viewed as competent, informed, and efficient in the game of regulating the goods market. Hence, ill-informed consumers are protected by the benevolent, efficient regulator. The goal of regulating the products market is desirable for consumers.

When analyzing the market for ideas and expression, these same individuals tell a different story. Far from expounding the virtues of large-scale government regulation and intervention in the ideas market, the opposite occurs. Consumers in the idea market (the very same consumers as in the goods market) are presumed to be discerning and cognitive. They are well-informed, able to make fine distinctions, and can choose among competing options. No irrationality exists in the economic sense and, in this scenario, government is characterized as inefficient at regulating ideas. Furthermore, even if government were an efficient and successful mechanism in regulating ideas, the results of this activity would be viewed as extremely undesirable and socially destructive. What newspaper editor, reporter, or TV commentator would invite, with open arms, the establishment of a Media Bureau at the Federal Trade Commission?

This distinction between goods and ideas and the proper role and degree of government regulation in each market—active regulation in one market, no regulation in the other—is not a creature of the twentieth century. It appears to egress from decades of authors concerned with the moral, ethical, and cultural development of men and women.

Philosophically, following the medieval-scholastic tradition, writers have generally considered the spiritual and intellectual side to be somehow more important than that side of us that seeks to satisfy material wants. The "primacy of the market for ideas" emerged.[24] John Milton best espoused the primacy of ideas and expression when, in a defense of freedom of the press in 1644, he noted: "Give me the liberty to know, to utter, and to argue freely according to conscience, above all liberties. . . . We must not think to make a staple commodity of all the knowledge in the land, to mark and license it like

---

24. Ronald Coase, "Advertising and Free Speech," in Allen Hyman and M. Bruce Johnson, eds., *Advertising and Free Speech* (Lexington, Mass: Lexington Books, D. C. Heath and Co., 1977).

our broadcloth and our woolpacks."[25] Much later Adam Smith observed this phenomenon in examining certain legal aspects of nineteenth century England. Smith remarked that general warrants were widely denounced, especially by the intellectuals, yet very few objections were seen in print to the laws of settlement that severely restricted the mobility, and therefore the wage, of labor.[26] The distinction held today between the markets for goods and ideas has been held for many centuries.

Advertising presents a difficult logical paradox to those who hold the view that there are differences between products markets and ideas markets. Consider, for example, advertising as it pertains to what have been called experience goods whose qualities can be ascertained only after one purchase. Advertising of these goods provides little, if any, direct information other than that the goods exist. These are advertisements for the "juiciest" hamburger, and so on. Advertising of this nature is usually a prime candidate for regulation by the government, but is it not also the case that advertisements of this nature are an *expression of opinion,* albeit of the sellers of the goods?

It is paradoxical and inconsistent that those individuals who most staunchly oppose government regulation of opinion and expression are quite frequently those individuals who ardently favor government regulation of advertising. They hold that the consumer is at once discerning enough to assimilate information and make wise choices but somehow is totally lacking in this ability when it comes to evaluating opinion or expression embodied as advertising. Advertising seems to be the lone exception to the rule of no government interference in the ideas market, an exception steeped in illogical and contradictory argument.

Milton saw the value and desirability of competition in the ideas market almost 350 years ago: "Let [truth] and falsehood grapple; who ever knew Truth put to the worse in a free and open encounter."[27] It is easy to appreciate the value of competition in the ideas market. How many administrations have been voted in and out of office in the national competition of ideas that Democrats and Republicans wage?

25. John Milton, *Areopagitica, A Speech for the Liberty of Unlicensed Printing.* Edward Arber, ed. (London: E. Arber, 1868), pp. 25–28.

26. Adam Smith, *An Inquiry into the Nature and Causes of the Wealth of Nations* (New York: Modern Library, 1937).

27. Milton, *Areopagitica,* p. 58.

There have been deceptive political and campaign promises. Such promises have been evaluated by voters (consumers) and choices have been made. We as individuals may or may not agree with those choices, but who can deny them to be rational choices? There is no validity in the notion that consumers can properly evaluate proposed national policies when selecting officeholders but are somehow unable to choose between and evaluate the merits of two different cans of beans.

The crucial point is that advertising is an expression of opinion in addition to being factually informative. For personal and individual freedom to exist in a society, government cannot regulate or suppress the free exchange of opinion between free people, be it news, literature, editorial commentary, or advertising. Individual freedom is eroded once governmental regulation and control of the market for ideas is imposed. In some cases it vanishes quickly. In other cases it erodes slowly. In either case, it ceases to exist.

CONCLUSION

The intriguing issues considered in the present chapter are illustrative of contemporary debate in the economics of advertising. Some matters, such as the proposal to regulate advertising in countercyclical fashion, are directly testable using economic-statistical tools. Other contemporary criticisms of advertising, e.g., that it permits fraud or that it is a tool of economic imperialism, are not easily tested. This does not mean that economists cannot evaluate such criticisms. The simple economic logic and analysis presented in earlier chapters of this book make clear that the new neoclassical or neo-Austrian concepts of basic economics have clear and definite answers to these questions.

9

CONCLUSION: ADVERTISING AND THE COMPETITIVE PROCESS

This book utilizes an emerging conception of the competitive market process to evaluate the role and function of advertising. We conclude that, from a dynamic competition perspective, the role of advertising is pivotal. It is admittedly a minority view founded partly upon the rejection of the traditional static notion of competition by neo-Austrian writers and partly upon new inventions in the microeconomics of consumer and firm behavior in areas such as information theory. But the emerging view has gained force, especially in the past twenty years.

The modern view has gained momentum in both the academic community and in the arena of public policy. Evidence for the modern view of advertising, especially in the area of market concentration, barriers to entry, and the effects of advertising on prices, seems to be an important contributing factor for the steady emergence of this view. But more importantly in our assessment, a new definition of competition underlies the upheaval in economists' opinions on the role of advertising. The *process* of entry or threat of entry has come to *define* competition in an increasing number of economic applications.

Furthermore, the theoretical and empirical literature on advertising as a barrier to entry and as a creator of monopoly—what we have called the traditional view—tends to lose cogency under the microscope of competitive dynamics. A static notion of competition as a situation has enjoyed much use as a method of organizing thoughts about markets and as a ground for more modern concepts of market processes. The traditional notion of competition and of advertising's role in it is the one most amenable to mechanical description and to a taxonomic view of the economic world. This view has proved useful in a number of theoretical situations, but its unqualified application to the role of advertising and to public policy has led to naive, illogical, and untoward results.

A problem for the static conception arises when competition is characterized as a rivalrous process of entry and exit and when information itself is regarded as a good. In these modern and developing conceptions advertising becomes an essential tool of the competitive process and, indeed, the notion of competition and market freedom has little cogency without it.

Strong indications of a shift in public policies toward advertising may also be observed. Federal Trade Commission advertising regulation, for example, appears to have moderated since the late 1970s, as some of the cases considered in this book (Chapter 7) reveal. The advancing theoretical and empirical literature of information-cost theorists and the neo-Austrians have unquestionably provided a foundation for the changing regulatory climate. At the very least, "public interest" and "consumer" groups' charges are no longer taken as *prima facie* evidence of fraudulent, misleading, or "harmful" advertising. While outright fraud may be a problem in a limited number of cases, legal remedies have materialized in some instances which supersede administrative regulation of advertising.

A growing problem in the realm of public policy is the increasing attempts by the states to regulate advertising through a variety of means. Such regulation and proposed regulation rests upon motives related to "consumer protection" (to counteract the perceived laissez faire attitude at the federal level), while other states are simply attempting to expand the tax base. The state of Texas, for example, has either engaged in or contemplated both kinds of regulation. Under pressure from the Texas attorney general and the Center for Science in the Public Interest, a consumer protection group, Dart and Kraft, Inc. withdrew ads calling Cheez Whiz "real cheese" since the product only contains one-half cheese. Over recent years, Texas has also contemplated a tax on ad agency commissions to bolster declining oil tax revenues. Other states are reviving interest in a variety of advertising taxes and restrictions.

The position of the U.S. Supreme Court on state advertising restrictions, enunciated in 1980, permits states (and other government entities) to regulate fraudulent *and nonfraudulent* advertising. States may regulate advertising as long as regulatory officials have a "substantial" cause and do not institute restrictions that are "too extensive." All cases are subject to judicial review, of course, although recent Supreme Court cases leave little doubt that consumer paternalism is not ruled out by the Court's 1980 decision.[1] In general, commercial speech, including advertising, is protected by the first amendment, although it receives less protection than other kinds of speech.

Yet another avenue for the state and federal regulation of advertising has been through the so-called problems of externalities. A negative externality is often said to be created by billboard advertising in that such advertising reduces or eliminates enjoyment of scenery. Supporters of this view assume that there is no trade-off, however, and that the *net* costs to society of such regulation are negative. Vermont, for example, is a beautiful but irritating state to visit. The state's prohibitions of roadside advertising may create benefits for *some* citizens, but it also creates information problems for *all* consumers. Information costs to both residents and travelers are increased dramatically by federal, state, or local restrictions on billboard advertising. Indeed, such restrictions discriminate most severely against travelers—those who most highly value information.

The theoretical and empirical underpinnings of the modern conception of advertising—those discussed in this book—should create a climate of extreme skepticism concerning the economic efficacy of all such proposals to regulate advertising. Fraud may pose a problem in some markets (e.g., credence goods markets), but the competitive system responds to fraud. There is no evidence that regulation responds to fraud more rapidly or in less costly fashion than do market responses.

---

[1]In a five-to-four vote in 1986, the Supreme Court upheld Puerto Rican regulations barring gambling casino advertisements targeted at local residents. (Casino advertisements aimed at tourists were and are permitted.) The decision, written by Justice William Rehnquist, noted that it was in the Commonwealth of Puerto Rico's purview to allow gambling but to reduce demand through selective restrictions just as states limit liquor advertising.

The connection between free economic choice and free political choice is also a real and important one. We hold, with Ronald Coase, that the market for goods and the market for ideas are logically equivalent, but would go further to argue that control of the market for products may be a giant step toward establishing control in the idea market. The emerging economic conception of advertising stresses the value of advertising in increasing economic benefits. But the important corollary of the new assessment is surely that large-scale measures to control advertising could initiate a process within which political freedom as well as economic benefits could be diminished.

SELECTED BIBLIOGRAPHY

Adelman, Carol. "Closing the Book on Infant Formula Fears." *The Wall Street Journal* (June 19, 1983): 30.

Akerlof, George A. "The Market for Lemons: Qualitative Uncertainty and the Market Mechanism." *Quarterly Journal of Economics* 84 (1970): 488–500.

Albion, Mark S. and Paul W. Farris. *The Advertising Controversy: Evidence on the Economic Effects of Advertising.* Boston, Mass.: Auburn House Publishing Co., 1981.

Armentano, Dominick T. *Antitrust and Monopoly: Anatomy of a Policy Failure.* New York: John Wiley & Sons, 1982.

Asch, Peter. "The Role of Advertising in Changing Concentration, 1963–1971." *Southern Economic Journal* 462 (1979): 288–97.

Ashley, R., C. W. J. Granger, and Richard Schmalensee. "Advertising and Aggregate Consumption: An Analysis of Causality." *Econometrica* 48 (1980): 1149–67.

Ayanian, Robert. "Advertising and Rate of Return." *Journal of Law and Economics* 18 (1975): 479–506.

Bachman, Jules. *Advertising and Competition.* New York: New York University Press, 1967.

Bain, Joe S. *Barriers to New Competition.* Cambridge, Mass.: Harvard University Press, 1956.

Benham, Lee. The Effect of Advertising on the Price of Eye-Glasses." *Journal of Law and Economics* 15 (1972): 337–52.

Benham, Lee and Alexandra Benham. "Regulating Through the Professions: A Perspective on Information Control." *Journal of Law and Economics* 18 (1975): 421–47.

187

Blank, David M. "Cyclical Behavior of National Advertising." *Journal of Business* 35 (1962): 14–27.

———. "Television Advertising: The Great Discount Illusion, or Tony-pandy Revisited." *Journal of Business* 41 (1968): 10–38.

Bloch, Harry. "Advertising and Profitability: A Reappraisal." *Journal of Political Economy* 82 (1974): 267–86.

Boddewyn, J. J. "Tobacco Advertising in a Free Society." In R. Tollison, ed., *Smoking and Society*. Lexington, Mass: D. C. Heath and Co., 1986.

Borden, Neil H. *The Economic Effects of Advertising*. Chicago: Richard D. Irwin, Inc., 1942.

Boyer, Kenneth D. "Information and Goodwill Advertising." *Review of Economics and Statistics* 56 (1974): 541–48.

Brozen, Yale. "Bain's Concentration and Rates of Return Revisited." *Journal of Law and Economics* 14 (1971): 351–69.

———. "Is Advertising a Barrier to Entry?" In Yale Brozen, ed., *Advertising and Society*. New York: New York University Press, 1974.

———. ed. *The Competitive Economy: Selected Readings*. Morristown, N.J.: General Learning Press, 1975.

———. "Competition, Efficiency, and Antitrust." In Yale Brozen, ed., *The Competitive Economy*. Morristown, N.J.: General Learning Press, 1975, pp. 6–14.

Cady, John F. *Restricted Advertising and Competition: The Case of Retail Drugs*. Washington, D.C.: American Enterprise Institute, 1976.

Center for Science in the Public Interest. "Omnibus Petition for Regulation of Unfair and Deceptive Alcoholic Beverage Advertising and Marketing Practices." Docket No. 209–46 Before the Federal Trade Commission, 1984.

Chamberlin, Edward H. *The Theory of Monopolistic Competition*. Cambridge, Mass.: Harvard University Press, 1933.

Clark, D. G. "Econometric Measurement of the Duration of the Advertising Effect on Sales." *Journal of Marketing Research* 13 (1976): 345–57.

Coase, Ronald. "The Market for Goods and the Market for Ideas." *American Economic Review* 64 (1974): 384–91.

———. "Advertising and Free Speech." In Allen Hyman and M. Bruce Johnson, ed., *Advertising and Free Speech*. Lexington, Mass.: Lexington Books, D.C. Heath and Co., 1977.

Comanor, William S. and Thomas S. Wilson. "Advertising, Market Structure, and Performance." *Review of Economics and Statistics* 49 (1967): 423–40.

———. *Advertising and Market Power*. Cambridge, Mass.: Harvard University Press, 1974.

———. "Advertising and Competition: A Survey." *Journal of Economic Literature* 17 (1979): 453–76.

Darby, Michael R. and Edi Karni. "Free Competition and the Optimal Amount of Fraud." *Journal of Law and Economics* 16 (1973): 67–8.

Demsetz, Harold. "Accounting for Advertising as a Barrier to Entry." *Journal of Business* 52 (1979): 345–60.

Dorfman, Robert and Peter O. Steiner. "Optimal Advertising and Optimal Quality." *American Economic Review* 44 (1954): 826–36.

Edwards, Franklin R. "Advertising and Competition in Banking." *Antitrust Bulletin* 18 (1973): 23–32.

Ehrlich, Isaac and Lawrence Fisher. "The Derived Demand for Advertising: A Theoretical and Empirical Investigation." *American Economic Review* 72 (1982): 366–88.

Ekelund, Robert B., Jr. and William P. Gramm. "A Reconsideration of Advertising Expenditures, Aggregate Demand, and Economic Stabilization." *Quarterly Review of Economics and Business* 9 (1969): 71–77.

———, and William P. Gramm. "Advertising and Concentration: Some New Evidence." *Antitrust Bulletin* 5 (1970): 243–49.

———, John D. Jackson, David S. Saurman, William F. Shughart II, and Robert D. Tollison. "Exclusive Territories and Advertising Restrictions in the Malt Beverage Industry." (manuscript, 1988): 1–26.

———, and Charles Maurice. "An Empirical Investigation of Advertising and Concentration: Comment." *Journal of Industrial Economics* 18 (1969): 76–80.

———, and Robert D. Tollison. *Mercantilism as a Rent-Seeking Society: Economic Regulation in Historical Perspective*. College Station, Texas: Texas A & M University Press, 1981.

Ferguson, James M. *Advertising and Competition: Theory, Measurement, Fact*. Cambridge, Mass.: Ballinger Publisher Co., 1974.

———. "Advertising and Liquor." *Journal of Business* 40 (1967): 414–34.

Galbraith, John K. *The Affluent Society*. Boston: Houghton Mifflin Co., 1958.

———. *The New Industrial State*. Boston: Houghton Mifflin Co., 1967.

Gerschenberg, I. "The Performance of Multinational and Other Firms in Economically Less Developed Countries: A Comparative Analysis of Ugandan Data." Discussion Paper 234. Nairobi: Institute of Development Studies, 1976.

Goldschmid, Harvey J., H. Michael Mann, and J. Fred Weston, eds. *Industrial Concentration: The New Learning*. Boston: Little, Brown and Co., 1974.

Grabowski, Henry. "The Effects of Advertising on the Interindustry Distribution of Demand." *Explorations in Economic Research* 3 (1976): 21–75.

Greer, Douglas F. "Advertising and Market Concentration." *Southern Economic Journal* 38 (1971): 10–32.

Haas-Wilson, Deborah. "The Effect of Commercial Practice Restrictions: The Case of Optometry." *Journal Of Law and Economics* 29 (1986): 165–186.

Hailey, Gary D., Jonathan R. Bromberg, and Joseph P. Mulholland. "A Comparative Analysis of Cosmetic Contact Lens Fitting by Ophthalmologists, Optometrists, and Opticians." *Report of the Staff of the Federal Trade Commission*. Washington, D.C.: Bureau of Consumer Protection and Bureau of Competition, Federal Trade Commission, 1983.

Hansen, Alvin. *Economic Issues of the 1960's*. New York: McGraw-Hill Book Co., Inc., 1969.

Hayek, Fredrich A. "Economics and Knowledge." *Economica* 4 (1937): 33–54.

———. "The Use of Knowledge in Society." *American Economic Review* 34 (1945): 519–33.

———. "The Nonsequitur of the Dependence Effect." In E. Mansfield, ed., *Microeconomics: Selected Readings*. New York: W. W. Norton and Co., 1979.

Higgins, Richard and Fred S. McChesney. "Truth and Consequences: The FTC's Ad Substantiation Program." *International Review of Law and Economics* 6 (1986): 151–68.

Hirshleifer, Jack. "The Private and Social Value of Information and the Reward to Inventive Activity." *American Economic Review* 61 (1971): 567–74.

———. "Where Are We in the Theory of Information." *American Economic Review* 67 (1973): 31–9.

Huff, Darrell. *How to Lie With Statistics*. New York: W. W. Norton and Co., Inc., 1954.

Hyman, Allen and M. Bruce Johnson, eds. *Advertising and Free Speech*. Lexington, Mass.: Lexington Books, D. C. Heath and Co., 1977.

Jacobs, William W., Brenda W. Doubrava, Robert P. Weaver, Douglas O. Stewart, Eric L. Prahl, William R. Porter, Nathaniel Greenspun, and R. Dennis Murphy. "Improving Consumer Access to Legal Services: The Case for Removing Restrictions on Truthful Advertising." *Report of the Staff to the Federal Trade Commission*. Washington, D.C.: Cleveland Regional Office, Bureau of Economics, Federal Trade Commission, 1984.

Kaldor, Nicholas. "The Economic Aspects of Advertising." *Review of Economic Studies* 18 (1950): 1–27.

———, and R. Silverman. *A Statistical Analysis of Advertising Expenditure and Revenue of the Press*. Cambridge, England: Cambridge University Press, 1948.

Kamerschen, David R. "The Statistics of Advertising." *Rivista Internazionale di Scienze Economiche e Commerciali* 19 (1972): 1–25.

Kelly, Thom and Alex Maurizi. *Prices and Consumer Information: The Benefits from Posting Retail Gasoline Prices*. Washington, D.C.: American Enterprise Institute, 1978.

Kessides, Ioannis N. "Advertising, Sunk Costs, and Barriers to Entry." *Review of Economics and Statistics* 68 (1986): 84–95.

Kindleberger, Charles. "Size of Firm and Size of Nation." In John H. Dunning, ed., *Economic Analysis and the Multinational Enterprise*. New York: Praeger Publishers, 1974.

Kirzner, Israel. *Competition and Entrepreneurship*. Chicago: University of Chicago Press, 1973.

―――. "Advertising." In Tibor R. Machan, ed., *The Libertarian Alternative*. Chicago: Nelson-Hall, 1974.

―――. *Perception, Opportunity, and Profit: Studies in the Theory of Entrepreneurship*. Chicago: The University of Chicago Press, 1979.

Laband, David N. "Advertising as Information: An Empirical Note." *Review of Economics and Statistics* 68 (1986): 517–21.

Lall, Sanjaya. "Financial and Profit Performance of MNC's in Developing Countries: Some Evidence from an Indian and Columbian Sample." *World Development* 4 (1976): 713–24.

―――. "Transnationals, Domestic Enterprises, and Industrial Structure in Most LDC's: A Survey." *Oxford Economic Papers* 30 (1978): 217–48.

Lambin, J. J. *Advertising, Competition, and Market Conduct in Oligopoly Over Time*. Amsterdam: North-Holland Publishing Co., 1976.

Leffler, Keith B. "Persuasion or Information? The Economics of Prescription Drug Advertising." *Journal of Law and Economics* 24 (1981): 45–74.

Levine, Bruce C., Donald G. D'Amato, Edward T. Popper, and Donald Keenan. *Memorandum to the Federal Trade Commission* on Omnibus Petition for Regulation of Unfair and Deceptive Alcoholic Beverage Advertising and Marketing Practices, 1985.

Mann, H. Michael, J. A. Henning, and J. W. Meehan, Jr. "Advertising and Concentration: An Empirical Investigation." *Journal of Industrial Economics* 16 (1967): 34–45.

Marshall, Alfred. *Industry and Trade*. 3d ed. London: Macmillan and Co., 1920.

―――. *Principles of Economics*. 8th ed. London: Macmillan and Co., 1920.

Maurizi, Alex R. "The Effect of Laws Against Price Advertising: The Case of Retail Gasoline." *Western Economic Journal* 10 (1972): 321–29.

McGee, John S. *In Defense of Industrial Concentration*. New York: Praeger Press, 1971.

Meade, Emily F. "The Place of Advertising in Modern Business." *Journal of Political Economy* 9 (1901): 218–42.

Metivally, M. M. "Product Categories That Advertise Most." *Journal of Advertising Research* 20 (1980): 25–31.

Milton, John. *Areopagitica, A Speech for the Liberty of Unlicensed Printing.* Edward Arber, ed. London: Edward Arber, 1868, pp. 25–28.

Nelson, Phillip. "Information and Consumer Behavior." *Journal of Political Economy* 78 (1970): 311–29.

———. "Advertising as Information." *Journal of Political Economy* 82 (1974): 729–54.

———. "The Economic Consequences of Advertising." *Journal of Business* 48 (1975): 213–41.

———. "Comments on Advertising and Free Speech." In Allen Hyman and M. Bruce Johnson, ed., *Advertising and Free Speech.* Lexington, Mass.: Lexington Books, D. C. Heath and Co., 1977, pp. 1–32.

Nerlove, Marc and Kenneth J. Arrow. "Optimal Advertising Policy Under Dynamic Conditions." *Economica* 29 (1962): 129–42.

Ornstein, Stanley I. *Industrial Concentration and Advertising Intensity.* Washington, D.C.: American Enterprise Institute, 1977.

———, J. Fred Westen, Michael Intriligator, and Ronald Shrieves. "Determinants of Market Structure." *Southern Economic Journal* 39 (1973): 612–25.

Packard, Vance. *Hidden Persuaders.* New York: D. McKay Co., 1957.

———. *The Waste Makers.* New York: D. McKay Co. 1969.

Peles, Yoram. "Economies of Scale in Advertising Beer and Cigarettes." *Journal of Business* 44 (1971): 32–37.

Peterman, John L. "The Clorox Case and Television Rate Structures." *Journal of Law and Economics* 11 (1968): 321–422.

Presbrey, Frank. *The History and Development of Advertising.* New York: Greenwood Press Publishers, 1968.

Rao, Ambor G. and Peter B. Miller. "Advertising-Sales Response Functions." *Journal of Advertising Research* 15 (1975): 7–16.

Ratner, Ellis M., John F. Hellegers, Grace Polk Stern, Randell C. Ogg, Sandra Adair, Lawrence Zacharias, Dennis McNeill, Teri Freundlich, and Julie Neimasik. *FTC Staff Report of Television Advertising to Children.* Washington, D.C.: U.S. Government Printing Office, 1978.

Reekie, W. Duncan. "Advertising and Market Share Mobility." *Scottish Journal of Political Economy* 21 (1975): 143–58.

Resnik, Alan and Bruce L. Stern. "Information Content in Television Ads." *Journal of Marketing* 41 (1977): 50–3.

Robinson, Joan. *Economics of Imperfect Competition.* London: Macmillan and Co., 1933.

Rosenthal, G. "The Rule of Private Foreign Investment in the Development of the Central American Common Market." Guatemala, 1973. (Mimeo.)

Scheidell, John M. *Advertising, Prices, and Consumer Reaction: A Dynamic Analysis*. Washington, D.C.: American Enterprise Institute, 1978.

Schmalensee, Richard. *The Economics of Advertising*. Amsterdam: North-Holland Publishing Co., 1972.

―――. "Brand Loyalty and Barriers to Entry." *Southern Economic Journal* 40 (1974): 579–88.

―――. "Advertising and Profitability." *Journal of Industrial Economics* 25 (1976): 45–53.

―――. "Product Differentiation Advantages of Pioneering Brands." *American Economic Review* 72 (1982): 349–65.

Schneider, Norman. "Product Differentiation, Oligopoly, and Stability of Market Shares." *Western Economic Journal* 5 (1966): 58–63.

Schumpeter, Joseph A. *Capitalism, Socialism and Democracy*. 3d ed. New York: Harper & Row, 1950.

Sherman, Roger and Robert D. Tollison. "Advertising and Profitability." *Review of Economics and Statistics* 53 (1971): 397–407.

Simon, Julian L. "Are There Economies of Scale in Advertising?" *Journal of Advertising Research* 5 (1969): 15–20.

―――. *Issues in the Economics of Advertising*. Urbana: University of Illinois Press, 1970.

―――― and George H. Crain. "The Advertising Ratio and Economies of Scale." *Journal of Advertising Research* 6 (1966): 37–43.

Smith, Adam. *An Inquiry Into the Nature and Causes of the Wealth of Nations*. New York: Modern Library, 1937.

Steiner, Robert L. "Does Advertising Lower Consumer Prices?" *Journal of Marketing* 37 (1973): 19–26.

Stigler, George. "Monopoly and Oligopoly by Merger." *American Economic Review* 50 (1960): 27.

―――. "The Economics of Information." In G. Stigler, ed., *The Organization of Industry*. Chicago, Homewood, Ill.: Richard D. Irwin, Inc., 1968.

―――, and Gary S. Becker. "De Gustibus Non Est Disputandum." *American Economic Review* 67 (1977): 76–90.

Strickland, Allyn D. and Leonard W. Weiss. "Advertising, Concentration, and Price-Cost Margins." *Journal of Political Economy* 84 (1976): 1109–21.

Sutton, C. J. "Advertising, Concentration, and Competition." *Economic Journal* 84 (1974): 56–69.

Taylor, L. D. and D. Weiserbs. "Advertising and the Aggregate Consumption Function." *American Economic Review* 62 (1972): 642–55.

Telser, Lester G. "Advertising and Competition." *Journal of Political Economy* 72 (1964): 537–62.

————. "Some Aspects of the Economics of Advertising." *Journal of Business* 41 (1968): 166–73.

————. "Another Look at Advertising and Concentration." *Journal of Industrial Economics* 18 (1969): 85–94.

Tollison, Robert D., ed., *Smoking and Society*. Lexington, Mass: D.C. Heath and Co., 1986.

Tuerck, David G., ed. *Issues in Advertising: The Economics of Persuasion*. Washington, D.C.: American Enterprise Institute, 1978.

Verdon, W. H., C. R. McConnell, and T. W. Roesler. "Advertising Expenditures as an Economic Stabilizer, 1954–64." *Quarterly Review of Economics and Business* 8 (1968): 7–18.

Vernon, John M. "Concentration, Promotion, and Market Share Stability in the Pharmaceutical Industry." *Journal of Industrial Economics* 19 (1971): 246–66.

Von Mises, Ludwig. *Human Action*. Chicago: Henry Regnery, 1966.

Weiss, Leonard W. "Advertising, Profits, and Corporate Taxes." *Review of Economics and Statistics* 51 (1969): 421–30.

Willmore, L. "Direct Foreign Investment in Central America Manufacturing." *World Development* 4 (1976), pp. 499–517.

Wittink, Dick R. "Advertising Increases Sensitivity to Price." *Journal of Advertising Research* 17 (1977): 39–42.

Worcester, Dean A. with Ronald Neese. *Welfare Gains from Advertising: The Problem of Regulation*. Washington, D.C.: American Enterprise Institute, 1978.

World Advertising Expenditures. 17th ed. Mamaroneck, N.Y.: Starch Inra Hooper Group of Companies, 1985.

Yang, C. Y. "Variations in the Cyclical Behavior of Advertising." *Journal of Marketing* 28 (1964): 25–30.

INDEX

ABOUT THE AUTHORS

Robert B. Ekelund, Jr. is currently Liberty National Professor of Economics at Auburn University. Professor Ekelund received the M.A. degree from St. Mary's University (San Antonio) in 1963 and his Ph.D. in economics from Louisiana State University in 1967.

He is a member of the American Economic Association, the Southern Economic Association and the Assocation for Social Economics. Professor Ekelund is Associate Editor of *History of Political Economy*, the *Review of Social Economy, Social Sciences Quarterly,* and the *Review of Austrian Economics*. He is listed in *Who's Who in Economics* (edited by M. Blaug) and received the Book Award from Auburn University for *Economics,* First Edition 1987.

Professor Ekelund has co-authored several books, among them *The Evolution of Modern Demand Theory; A History of Economic Theory and Method;* and *Mercantilism as a Rent-Seeking Society: Economic Regulation in Historical Perspective*. His articles have appeared in *The American Economic Review, Economica, Economic Inquiry, Journal of Law and Economics, The Journal of Political Economy,* the *Southern Economic Journal,* and the *Quarterly Journal of Economics*.

David S. Saurman is currently a Lecturer in the Department of Economics at San Jose State University in San Jose, California as well as President and Director of Research for Ekelund & Associates, Inc. He earned a B.A. in economics from Albion College in 1974

211

and his Ph.D. in economics from Texas A & M University in 1979.

His fields of specialization include monetary theory, international economics, and industrial organization. He is a member of the American Economic Association, the Southern Economic Association and is a charter member of the National Association of Forensic Economists.

Dr. Saurman has published articles in the *Journal of Money, Credit, and Banking* and *Public Finance Quarterly* and has served as a referee for several journals. He has also served as a consultant and expert witness in numerous legal proceedings.

PACIFIC RESEARCH INSTITUTE FOR PUBLIC POLICY

The Pacific Research Institute produces studies that explore long-term solutions to difficult issues of public policy. The Institute seeks to facilitate a more active and enlightened discourse on these issues and to broaden understanding of market processes, government policy, and the rule of law. Through the publication of scholarly books and the sponsorship of conferences, the Institute serves as an established resource for ideas in the continuing public policy debate.

Institute books have been adopted for courses at colleges, universities, and graduate schools nationwide. More than 175 distinguished scholars have worked with the Institute to analyze the premises and consequences of existing public policy and to formulate possible solutions to seemingly intractable problems. Prestigious journals and major media regularly review and comment upon Institute work. In addition, the Board of Advisors consists of internationally recognized scholars, including two Nobel laureates.

The Pacific Research Institute is an independent, tax exempt, 501(c)(3) organization and as such is supported solely by the sale of its books and by the contributions from a wide variety of foundations, corporations, and individuals. This diverse funding base and the Institute's refusal to accept government funds enable it to remain independent.

OTHER STUDIES IN PUBLIC POLICY BY
THE PACIFIC RESEARCH INSTITUTE

For further information on the Pacific Research Institute's program and a catalog of publications, please contact:

PACIFIC RESEARCH INSTITUTE FOR PUBLIC POLICY
177 Post Street
San Francisco, CA 94108
(415) 989-0833

Winning Elections

A Handbook of
Modern Participatory Politics

Dick Simpson
University of Illinois, Chicago

HarperCollins*College*Publishers

Acquisitions Editor: Leo Wiegman
Developmental Editor: Shari Lampert
Project Editor: Tom Kulesa
Printer and Binder: R. R. Donnelly & Sons
Text and Cover Design: Heather A. Peres
Electronic Page Makeup: Joanne Del Ben
Cover Photo: © Bill Stamets/Impact Visuals

Simpson, Winning Elections

ISBN: 0-673-98078-2

96 97 98 99 00 9 8 7 6 5 4 3 2 1

TABLE OF CONTENTS

PREFACE

In 1968, I was campaign manager in the 9th Congressional District of Illinois, and later, state campaign manager for Eugene McCarthy's bid for the presidency. In the 9th Congressional District primary, McCarthy delegates received only 20 percent of the vote; in the entire state we elected only two of the 22 McCarthy candidates. As a direct result of losing campaigns such as these, McCarthy lost the nomination at the Democratic National Convention. Many people, disappointed or bitter about their experiences in 1968, decided to abandon electoral politics as a means of bringing change in the United States.

For me, McCarthy's defeat three decades ago was a profound experience. Our goal of revitalizing American politics was sound, but we did not know enough about campaigning. In the 1968 McCarthy campaign, our energies were directed toward change at the top of the power structure, but there are other ways of winning elections and other bases of power in this country. Instead of starting at the top, we could have built from the bottom a strong, determined reform movement in local communities throughout the nation. Along with others who shared this belief, I resolved to learn what it meant to develop such a grass-roots constituency.

This book is a distillation of our successes and failures over a number of years. It is a continuation of strategy meetings in dozens of campaigns and of seminars in practical politics. Those of us drawn into politics in 1968 have had a hand in transforming Chicago politics. This transition still continues with various local and national victories, as well as a virtual revolution in campaign styles and technologies since the 1960s.

Similar changes are occurring in other parts of the country. The general dissatisfaction with traditional political parties and local elites continues everywhere. New officials—left, right, and center on the political spectrum—are elected without yet being able to institute a new political system, either locally or nationally.

While *Winning Elections* may provide information and self-confidence, the commitment to elect honest, responsive political leaders and to open up the political process is an individual commitment. If the commitment is there, this handbook can suggest how to translate abstract beliefs into positive action. If this commitment is lacking, neither rules nor advice will help. Practitioners of effective participatory politics must begin with a strong faith that people can have an important voice in governing themselves.

Winning Elections is about a participatory politics in which citizens find candidates they want to elect to office and then, with or without party support, put together a voluntary campaign that will win. Participatory politics differs from traditional politics, because it focuses on issues critical to constituents and candidates who are free from the control of party bosses, wealthy contributors, or narrow special interests. It depends upon a large number of volunteer supporters rather than on patronage precinct captains or exclusively on paid media ads, professional campaign staffs, direct mail, or public relations firms. Participatory campaigns are distinctly different from either campaigns controlled by party machines or high-tech campaigns meant to manipulate the voters.

Winning Elections is meant to serve as a guide to folks like you who are considering running for political office, serving as campaign staff members, or becoming political reform strategists or campaign volunteers. It will be useful to those of you who are like the naive hero in the classic movie, "Mr. Smith Goes to Washington". It will be equally useful in providing new ideas to hardened veterans of political wars. Whatever your level of experience, it is meant to provide you with a keen appreciation of the problems of our political system and the possibilities of new democracies being created around the world.

Both women and men are candidates, staff members, volunteers, and voters so I have tried as much as possible to write to "you" the reader. At other times, in referring to political activists, I have had to resort to "he" or "she" and "him" or "her". In the even numbered chapters, I have used feminine pronouns, and in the odd numbered chapters, masculine. In future editions of *Winning Elections,* better means may be found to overcome this linguistic awkwardness.

ACKNOWLEDGMENTS

I wish gratefully to acknowledge that much of what I know about participatory politics I learned in some dozen campaigns working with local leaders John Kearney, Sherwin Swartz and Robert Houston. Further, had Eugene McCarthy not dared to run for President in 1968, I might never have become involved. Most of all, had hundreds of volunteers not continually renewed my faith by their sacrifices, I would not have maintained my own commitment so steadfastly.

Chapter 6 was carefully corrected and greatly improved in earlier drafts by Don Rose, former editor of *Hyde Park-Kenwood Voices* and campaign strategist for many independent campaigns. Jim Chapman, former executive director of the Independent Precinct Organization, suggested specific elaborations and the proper emphasis for the chapters on campaign structure and precinct work. Many of the campaign forms used in this book were originally developed by Barbara O'Connor.

In the years since the first edition was published, I have greatly benefited from the reaction of my students in classes at the University of Illinois at Chicago, from practitioners who have attended dozens of election workshops, and from the tough tests of countless campaigns throughout the country.

This edition of the book has gained much from the ideas of the staff of my two campaigns for congress and especially from the contributions by Tom Gradel, Jerry Jaecks, John Chester, Rich Means, and Jim Wise. It has been greatly improved by careful reading and editing by Sarajane Avidon, Shari Lampert, and Jeff Olson.

Despite this help, *Winning Elections* may still have errors of syntax, fact, and analysis. For these I take full responsibility. I hope, nonetheless, that this handbook will help many people to better understand the great potential of participatory politics.

FOREWORD

By U.S. Senator Carol Moseley-Braun

Dick Simpson was my teacher at the University of Illinois at Chicago. He helped inspire me to go into politics. In the 1970s he was elected twice to Chicago's City Council and over the years has helped run many other successful campaigns. He became one of Chicago's outstanding aldermen and his municipal reform proposals are still being adopted more than twenty years later.

In 1992 he ran for Congress, and when he lost in the primary, he helped coordinate my U.S. Senate general election campaign on the Northwest side of Chicago.

The earlier version of *Winning Elections,* which Professor Simpson published in the 1970s has become the standard handbook for participatory campaigns in Illinois and around the country. Simpson's new handbook shows how up-to-date, high-tech campaign technologies can effectively augment essential grassroots activism. His analysis of the abuses within the current electoral system and his proposed reforms to improve the electoral process need to be heeded. *Winning Elections* is the definitive guide for citizens in their battles for a better future.

Simpson's *Winning Elections* distills decades of experience in hard fought political battles. I recommend it for candidates, campaign workers, students and citizens.

Chapter I

THE BEGINNING

A campaign is composed of individuals and their decisions. A candidate decides to run; leaders and participants decide to work; the candidate and campaign leaders decide which public stands to take on some issues while ignoring others; a campaign theme and basic principles are selected; and each voter decides whether to vote for a candidate. Each choice has consequences for both the person making the decision and for the outcome of the election. A campaign is won or lost by specific decisions made by individuals.

A campaign handbook must inevitably focus on mechanical and generalized aspects of running a winning campaign. But whether a campaign is a local campaign for city council or school board or a national campaign for congressman or president, it is composed of individuals and their choices. To reach a fuller understanding of elections, this introductory chapter focuses upon the difficult personal decisions that breathe life into an otherwise mechanical process and make each campaign unique.

Everyone in a campaign makes a decision to devote time, talent and money to the campaign. For the candidate and key campaign leaders, this decision is of a different magnitude than that required of other volunteers, workers, and contributors. Not only do the candidate and key leaders risk more of their time and fortune, they risk more of themselves. Ordinary citizens provide the support necessary for victory, but the candidate and campaign leaders must launch the campaign.

Your candidate risks his name, must pay debts incurred in the campaign, and may be ridiculed by the opposition. Most of all, your candidate asks people to elect him to office. He may find it distressing to stand in front of stores shaking hands or to go to friends and associates asking for money for himself. Yet, candidates are their own best fund raisers and workers. A candidate must learn to ask people to support him if he is to run a good campaign. For many candidates, this is the most painful lesson of the campaign.

No candidate is drafted. Friends or citizen groups may ask if a candidate is interested in running, but he must decide that he will run and begin to seek the help and support necessary to win. If he decides to run, the campaign is launched. If he refuses or hesitates, the campaign is lost and someone else steps forward. The decision of one person—the candidate—to risk all on the bid for public office is the most important of the campaign and one that only the candidate can make.

Concrete reasons not to run are many—Running will mean time lost from a candidate's family and may take him away from the career that he has spent years building. It will cost a lot of money. The positive reasons to run seem terribly abstract. His election will give the community a strong representative and spokesperson, he can make government more efficient, and he can pass legislation to improve our communities. In addition, he can bring integrity, leadership, dedication, and experience to public office.

Personal ambition and ego also enter into the decision. A candidate may run in order to serve as a spokesperson, to get into the limelight, or to prove to himself that other people really love him. These motive may seem shallow or selfish, but some combination of public and private reasons must overcome the practical reasons not to run. Once the decision to go ahead is made, decisions about how to mount the most effective campaign are much simpler.

Key campaign personnel also face difficult decisions. A staff member must decide to take a leave of absence or interrupt their career to work on the campaign full time. Like the candidate, staff must expect endless hours of work and separation from their families. They struggle with the questions of whether they can do the job and whether they are willing to make the necessary sacrifices. Supporting a candidate is one thing, giving a few hours or donating a few dollars is easy, but serving as a campaign leader requires dedication and personal commitment to the candidate.

The sacrifice required of others is in many ways the greatest burden a candidate undertakes. A campaign disrupts the lives of many people and requires their contributions of work and money. This places on your candidate, the responsibility of conducting the campaign in a fashion that will make it worth these sacrifices and of continuing the campaign even though he may sometimes wish to back out. Everyone who takes a leadership position in a campaign undertakes a collective action with great consequences both for themselves and for their community.

Once the decisions to run or to support a candidate are made, campaign leaders must still decide upon a general theme and take positive actions that will symbolize to the press and to the community what the campaign represents.

In my first campaign for Chicago alderman in 1971, my proposal of a citizen ordinance in the city council to limit the power of the mayor in school board appointments made it clear that I would not be a rubber stamp alderman for Mayor Richard J. Daley. Such actions help create the enthusiasm and support necessary to win. Thus, you must find creative ways of dramatizing the campaign. Unless you do, neither personal appearances by the candidate, nor paid political ads nor precinct work will be sufficient. Existential choices, controversial issues, and bold action are some of the human stuff of campaigns. Campaign structure and hard work in the precincts provide a base, but good campaigns embody issues and actions which cannot be completely planned in advance. They require the same personal courage and careful decision-making as the original decision to stand for election and to staff the campaign.

CASE STUDIES

Although *Winning Elections* draws from campaigns around the country, I will focus specifically on my own campaigns in Chicago for alderman and congressman. Obviously, I know my own campaigns in greater detail than others.

My campaigns in the 1970s and 1990s were fought in a difficult political environment. In my successful aldermanic campaigns of 1971 and 1975, I defeated the Chicago machine during the heyday of the legendary Richard J. Daley. In my later campaigns to unseat incumbent Congressman Dan Rostenkowski, I unsuccessfully fought not only his reputation and million dollar, PAC-supported campaign budget, but also President Clinton who endorsed him, the failure of the Justice Department to indict him speedily, members of the local business, labor, political, and media elites, and a machine army of precinct workers under Mayor Richard M. Daley's orders to deliver.

Furthermore, in focusing on my Chicago campaigns, I can also show what it takes to elect a mayor or county board president in smaller cities. As Finley Peter Dunne's Mr. Dooley put it, in Chicago politics ain't beanbag.[1]

Examples from my own campaigns will provide a consistent story line enabling me to illustrate the feel of campaigns from the inside. Of course, no book is a substitute for experience. In the appendices, I also provide a listing of films, videotapes and workshop exercises to demonstrate what participation in a campaign must be like. Most of all, I recommend that after reading this book that you work in a major campaign—*preferably a winning campaign*. When you reread this book afterwards, you will understand many elements that eluded you the first time through.

Moreover, while I will discuss how to use computers, public opinion polls, paid political advertisements, phone canvassing, and other high tech methods of campaigning, I make two basic assumptions: 1) As this is a handbook for participatory politics, a large number of volunteers are involved in your campaign. 2) The candidate you support is well-qualified for the position and has a genuine platform on which to run.

THE NEXT STEP

The only way to achieve as an end to poverty and racism in the United States is to reform the entire political system so that freedom, justice, equality, and effective citizen participation become the primary goals. To do that, leaders who support these goals must be elected to office and, even more important, a large constituency must be developed not only to support these leaders but also to pressure for maximization of these ends.

Instituting new values, electing new leaders, evolving new procedures of greater participation, and developing a constituency of conscience certainly can be pursued at the national level. The ultimate success of such strategies, however, depends on creating an informed constituency and selecting capable leaders in local communities.

This handbook presents its information in a way that encourages maximum learning in the briefest period of time. It provides an introduction to innovative campaigning which is useful to political scientists and students of politics. In the last several decades, we have divorced political science from real politics to an extent that the profession offers little in the way of advice and only a limited understanding of political activities such as campaigning.

To understand politics, the study of politics needs to include the study of political action along with the more accepted study of political analysis and political philosophy.[2] While this handbook does not present political action systematically with formal political action propositions, it should evoke the excitement and fun of campaigning, as well as show that campaign activity is not arbitrary.[3] Without employing the formal methodology involved in political action propositions, recommendations for winning elections, achieving goals within the existing political system, and altering the political system to make democratic goals more easily and regularly achievable are stressed. *Winning Elections* is an introduction to the study of electoral politics in the United States as it is practiced and as it can be improved.

Because your campaign will take place in a particular community and with its own special laws governing campaigning, you will have to adapt what you learn here to those special conditions. This handbook is a distillation of what we have learned in Chicago about running campaigns from city hall to Congress. It sets out the requirements for a winning campaign against strong opposition. Its message is simple: You can fight city hall and win.

Chapter II

CHOOSING UP SIDES

$\mathbf{A}$s the journey of a thousand miles begins with a single step, major political reform begins when a single citizen commits herself to winning elections, changing public policies and opening up the political process. Reform begins with each of us fighting campaigns in our own communities and winning our own victories. Many of your neighbors, co-workers, and people you have met only casually feel the same way you do about the need to reform politics and government. They are waiting for someone to take the first step—to offer viable candidates and proposals for new government policies.

GETTING INTO POLITICS

Politics is such a dirty business! You are too good to get involved with all those liars and cheats! In a position of responsibility like yours', you just cannot afford the time. And you do not know anything about politics, anyway.

Friends and family will use this and similar arguments to dissuade you from major political involvement. We have come to consider citizenship a passive thing—read the paper, watch television news, gripe to friends, vote on election day, decry the results. Many of us believe it is the duty of a good citizen to vote, but few of us believe it is also our duty to undertake those actions necessary to make the electoral process meaningful by actually participating.

Of course, the opposite ideal is just as absurd. Not everyone can be involved passionately, completely and only in politics. There are many aspects to life. The artist more dedicated to politics than art becomes a social realist or a reactionary demagogue. Workers more concerned with politics than their vocations often become patronage workers, employed for the sake of their work done in precincts at election time.

Participating actively at some stage in our lives is important. There is a strong relationship between non-participation and a weak ego, alienation, anomie, and cynicism, just as there is a relationship between participation and positive traits such as a sense of political efficacy and personal effectiveness.[4] People with a greater sense of the latter and less of the former are more likely to participate actively in politics, which in turn reinforces their positive personal attitudes. For the ancient Greeks, the quality, as well as quantity, of activity was considered crucial to personal development. As Pericles said of Athens:

> *Our citizens attend both to public and private duties, and do not allow absorption in their own various affairs to interfere with their knowledge of the city's. We differ from other states in regarding the [person] who holds aloof from public life not as quiet but as useless. . . .*[5]

There are good reasons to become involved in politics in our time. We need to renew the entire political process from top to bottom, to reorient personal and societal priorities to place the value of people before property and concern for our fellow citizens on par with concern for ourselves. If we lose this battle, our society will deteriorate into a closed one, an eternal battleground of ever more violent factions, or a fat, complacent, greedy culture.

Few people join politics for such generalized reasons, however. They get into politics because of a candidate they want to elect or defeat. They may want to support or oppose an issue. Their friends may be involved in a campaign or they may find a movement they wish to join. More than any other single factor, most people get into politics because someone they respect asks them.

In addition to altruistic reasons for political involvement, there are also personal reasons, such as the status or honor of being an elected public official. Some desire future appointment to government jobs. Others have a more modest desire to be leaders within a community or political organization. Some people want to be recognized for making a legitimate and important contribution to the political process.

We all like to be recognized and honored for what we do, and desire the respect and esteem of our fellow citizens. In this sense, those of us who go into politics have political ambitions. There is nothing shabby or immoral about such ambitions, but politics has an amazing ability to corrupt. The desire for to serve the community is legitimate. Expecting a "payoff," especially an immediate and tangible payoff, because of political involvement is wrong.

Becoming a legitimate political person is difficult. To be political, a feel for the use of power is necessary, but not enough. A politician must first and foremost be a person of honor, sensitivity, integrity, and creativity responsive to needs and concerns of others. An outstanding political leader must first be an outstanding person. Max Lerner has put the point this way:

> *I don't hold it against a [person] that he has spent his mature life in politics, provided there is more to him than politics. The question about Richard Nixon is whether there is this added dimension (as he likes to call it) or whether the politician has eaten up the man.*[6]

Thus, both personal and altruistic reasons—self- interest and honest concern for the community—for political involvement must coincide. Only then will the political leaders necessary to the creation of a modern participatory politics emerge.

JOINING A POLITICAL ORGANIZATION OR CAMPAIGN

Individuals decide to join a political organization or back an individual candidate based on their particular situations. Most people begin by backing a candidate that they admire and want to see elected. They then go on to join a more permanent political organization or party. In any case, I recommend that you do not begin by running for office yourself. Work on another candidate's campaign and learn the craft of politics. After you have direct campaign experience, you will be able to make wise judgments about how to run your own campaign.

As a general rule, even wealthy candidates without political experience do not govern well, even if they have the resources to buy the best staff to run their campaign. No matter what your personal circumstances, start first by working in other campaigns to learn about politics, then get elected to local offices to learn how to govern. After these experiences, you will be ready and qualified to run for a major office.

People back candidates and work in their campaigns for a various reasons. Campaign volunteers gave four reasons for backing Bernie Weisberg, a very qualified candidate for delegate to the Illinois Constitutional Convention:

> *. . . because he is independent, which is especially important to me in a city like Chicago where the Democratic machine is so strong. (Student)*

> *. . . There are people in this world that are not getting a fair shake— black people, poor people, young people. I am trying to help remedy that situation. (Journalist)*

> *. . . I got sick and tired of having other people make the decision for me. I wanted to have a hand in making the decisions that affect my life, myself. So I became involved in independent politics. (Professor)*

> *. . . As a private citizen, I have to do more than just gripe about bad government. We all have to work very hard to change it. I have added personal reasons in that I am a clergyman. If I really take seriously my concern for people and human problems, then I have to do more than preach sermons on Sunday, so I am getting involved. What I am most pleased about is that large numbers of my parishioners are beginning to take seriously what it means to be religious people and do something about their government by working for a good candidate such as Bernie Weisberg. (Catholic Priest)[7]*

These campaign volunteers were attracted by their concern for other people, dismay at the failures of the political system, and a desire to be a part of those crucial decisions affecting all our lives. There are, however, many reasons why people work in campaigns. Some hope to get a job if the candidate is elected, or else they have a direct self-interest in getting a particular law enacted or repealed. Many others join up because campaigns are a great way to meet people, expand their social lives and make new friends. Campaigns can be very exciting, and people will join because of that excitement. Of course, a sense of civic duty, of being a good citizen, and of paying back to the community some of what you have been given by society, also play a role.

You must decide which combination of ideological and personal motivations cause you to get involved. But to recruit others successfully, you have to learn to sell the campaign to them. Their reasons may not be the same as yours.

WORKING IN ELECTIONS

Because participatory politics is so issue-oriented, many people want to dive immediately into issue battles waged separately from campaigns. Paradoxically, the best way to deal successfully with issues may be through electoral campaigns. Beginning with a clear-cut and exciting election is easier than fighting a separate issue battle. With an election, it is known well in advance that the decisive event will be held on a certain date and that the result will be determined by a majority of the votes cast. The date for citizens to register to vote, the rules of campaigning, and the myriad procedural details are not only established but also accepted. The public sees participation in elections as a familiar and proper activity.

In an issue campaign, it is hard to know who can make the decision you desire, much less the rules by which the decision is to be made. Major business and political leaders with decision-making power are relatively isolated from the public; thus, it is difficult to pressure them directly. Issue campaigns are possible. However, they are harder to fight and harder to win.

In my first campaign for alderman, I raised the issues of better and fairer delivery of city services, an end to machine domination or boss rule in Chicago, and the right of citizens to have a direct voice in decisions made by the local government. In my congressional campaigns, congressional reform, abortion rights, defense budget cuts, national health care reform, economic development, and saving jobs in the district were raised. When your candidate wins an election, she can clearly have an effect on issues like these. You can then work with the official you have elected. She can easily get publicity and introduce appropriate legislation to address these problems. So begin with elections, then turn your attention to the many issue battles that need fighting.

During the campaign, your candidate can address critical issues while articulating her perspective on current problems. However, if your candidate takes stands, especially extreme stands, on every issue facing your community, she will make too many enemies, be counted an extremist and defeated at the polls. Instead, during the campaign, she can dramatize two or three concrete issues to demonstrate the steps she would take if elected. In a community where no issues have previously been debated or resolved, this action is not a limitation but a major beginning.

Certain electoral themes or issues will be more basic to the outcome of the campaign than others. In my first campaign for alderman, I developed a general appeal that transcended ethnic and interest groups by running as an independent against a democratic machine candidate. I pledged that, if I were elected: 1) citizens would receive their government services as a matter of right rather than as partisan favors, because I would open a full-time aldermanic office to serve all the people; 2) citizens would have a representative in City Council who would vote according to his conscience and his constituents' interests rather than simply rubber stamp the mayor's legislation; and 3) citizens would have an opportunity to participate directly in government policy-making through the creation of a ward assembly with representatives from every precinct and every community organization. The ward assembly would hold monthly meetings open to the public, rather than continue policy-making by a handful of party leaders. My stand in favor of a more participatory and fairer system of local government in the machine-run Chicago of 1971 placed the issue of the type of government we should have squarely before the electorate. Such stands on issues, by themselves do not attract enough voters to win an election, but they point up the importance of an election to both workers and voters. They illustrate the kinds of issues that ought to be at stake in all elections.

A final warning. Some people will encourage your candidate to run an educational campaign. They mean that she should take strong stands on issues even though she will lose heavily. Such candidates make beautiful speeches and slowly begin the political education process in your district. Unfortunately even though education campaign enthusiasts are right about such campaigns being educational, they fail to understand what is taught. When a candidate gets only ten or twenty percent of the vote, *the electorate concludes that backing such a candidate or cause is useless because votes are simply being thrown away.*

When politicians see such results, far from being convinced to take a more courageous stand, their belief that they should not heed such political radicals is reconfirmed since candidates taking such stands have no support in the community. A campaign should be run to win, thereby educating the electorate to the fact that good people can be elected. If you have a good candidate, organize well and work hard, winning should be possible. You will not win every election, but you must make a creditable try. A winning campaign, to a much greater extent than any educational campaign, will convince more people to pay attention to issues, join in the political process and bring about desired policy changes.

INITIATING CANDIDACIES

Initiating a viable campaign is easiest at the local level, especially if you are part of the dominant party in the local community. An open endorsement session is held where would-be candidates present their credentials. Party members then vote for the candidate who best represents their political views and has the best chance of winning the election. Parties are inevitably pragmatic about this. They are in the business to win but usually reward political loyalty; if a long-time party worker and a newcomer both ask to be slated, party leaders will trust and endorse their fellow party worker.

Existing political party organizations can support reform candidates and participatory campaigns do develop in support of such candidates in addition to the regular party efforts. Too often, however, existing party organizations represent the status quo and are not open to greater citizen involvement.

CREATING A CITIZENS' SEARCH COMMITTEE

In a new group or a party faction, the process of initiating candidacies is necessarily different. For instance, in Chicago, potential candidates might not be part of the dominant regular Democratic party machine. In suburban communities, potential candidates might not be part of the regular Republican party organization. In these circumstances, the best way to launch a successful campaign is to create a citizens' committee to screen local candidates for city council, school board, county board, or state legislature. A strong citizens' search committee will both locate a worthy candidate and lay the foundation for a broadly based coalition capable of mounting an effective campaign.

A citizens' search committee should consist of leaders from all community, economic, ethnic, political, and religious groups that might support a reform candidate. Community leaders or citizens who have not been active in politics before may hesitate to oppose incumbent office holders or the dominant political party. They will worry about alienating other significant community officials on whom they rely for cooperation and support. For them to consider another political process in place of the usual nominating process by the two established parties is a major step. They will do so only when they are angered by current officials who fail to respond to their needs and when the dominant parties neglect their communities and the issues that they care about deeply. Then they might be convinced to support a reform candidate who opposes the status quo policies of the government in power.

Two to three months before candidate petitions must be filed, 60 to 70 people should be invited by the leaders of the strongest community group or independent political organization, out of whom fifty may actually attend. They should be informed that the committee will interview candidates who are interested in running for a specific office, such as a seat in the city council or in the state legislature.

In convening the search committee, special care must be taken to ask potential candidates and members of their families not to participate as committee members. Otherwise, the charge will be made that the committee was rigged.

Community leaders, meeting together, will discover that they have common interests and common problems. They can be convinced that a citizen-based campaign can be won and that by electing a public official they could begin to solve community problems.

The citizens' search committee process is relatively uncomplicated with two or three meetings required for the task to be completed. Before the first meeting, the conveners should make a list of 20 or 30 people who might be interested in running for office. The meeting should open with by a discussion of community problems, the upcoming election, ideal characteristics of an officeholder, and the feasibility of running a successful campaign. Additional candidates are added to the conveners' list, and all potential candidates are discussed. Through this discussion, the list is shortened to the five or six potential candidates the committee would like to interview.

Potential candidates are invited to the next meeting and questioned about their willingness to run and the type of campaign they would wage. After having made their presentations and departing, the potential candidates are discussed. The search committee then arrives at a consensus or agrees to take the names of several of the strongest contenders back to their own groups for possible endorsement. A straw vote may be taken to indicate preferences, but the object is to reach a consensus including as many community leaders as possible. Since some leaders are not empowered to act on their group's behalf, a binding vote is not possible. Each group will follow its own endorsement procedures. Later, if most groups have endorsed the same candidate, many of the original search committee members will join the candidate's own citizens committee to work in the campaign.

A search committee thus tests a candidate's ability to mount a strong campaign in the community. If the leaders of groups whose support is crucial to success oppose the available candidates, then a campaign had best not be attempted. On the other hand, the search committee often helps an acceptable candidate begin their campaign early enough to have a chance to win. Last of all, the search committee initiates a winning coalition by insuring that like-minded groups consider the same contenders in making endorsements. By the time the search committee process is finished, a general consensus to back one or two candidates has usually emerged, which also serves to deter new reform candidates from entering the race and splintering the reform vote.

LAUNCHING A CANDIDACY

When you run for a higher office than city council or school board, campaigns are launched differently. For a city, county, state or national campaign, a citizens' search committee does not work. Of course, a political organization may assemble a coalition of leaders and organizations to create a slate of candidates or draft a candidate. However, this is the exception rather than the rule.

In deciding to launch a campaign, a few people—the candidate, some advisors, and friends—determine if a campaign is feasible. Factual considerations are involved. For example, how many votes did it take to win the last several campaigns for this office? How much money was spent? By what margin did the incumbent or dominant party candidate win? In most districts, only 60 to 70 percent of the potential voters are registered. Of those, probably less than half vote. And the winning candidate gets only 50 to 60 percent of the votes cast. Therefore, in a district of 60,000 people, a candidate can win election with only 8,000 votes. In a congressional district with 571,000 people, a candidate can win the primary election with 10,000 to 50,000 votes depending upon which party primary is entered. Thus, some simple facts must be examined in deciding whether to run.

This process of deciphering election statistics is called by Lawrence Grey in his book "How to Win a Local Election," picking your target number.

> The election statistics will tell you the results in the last four or five elections, the total number who voted, the number who voted in your race, the number who voted in similar races. With this information, you come up with an average number of people who are likely to vote in your race. Divide that by two, and you have your target number.
>
> Once you have picked your number, you have to sit down with your campaign people and decide how you are going to get that number, precinct by precinct.[8]

In addition, to voting patterns, the demographics of a district and public opinion poll information can help determine whether a particular candidacy might be viable.

After picking a target number, studying demographic and public opinion poll information, and developing a general strategy, two other principal facts must be considered. First, winning an "open" seat is easier than running against an incumbent. Second, if there is an incumbent, running a successful campaign is easier in a newly redistricted constituency than in a district that has elected the same incumbent numerous times. Obviously, an incumbent has greater name recognition than a challenger, and citizens who have voted for a candidate before are more likely to vote for her again.

Suppose after collecting the facts and consulting with advisors and knowledgeable campaign leaders, a candidate still wants to run for office. How should she proceed?

Before rushing to announce a candidacy, it is critical to determine that a viable campaign can be run and key resources raised. These resources include: 1) campaign leaders and staff, 2) endorsements by recognized political or community leaders to lend credibility to the campaign, and 3) money.

The number of paid staff members in a campaign varies by the level at which it is run and by its budget. A low- key campaign for a suburban school board member will have no paid staff and a budget of only a few thousand dollars. A campaign manager will serve without pay or with minimal reimbursement.

In larger local campaigns, such as for city council, for state legislature or for citywide offices in smaller cities, there will be at least three paid staff members. These will usually be a campaign manager, an office and volunteer manager and a public relations coordinator. Often the budget for this type of campaign will range from $50,000 to more than $100,000. (The most expensive aldermanic campaigns run in Chicago to date was in the 43rd Ward in 1991, when both the incumbent and the challenger spent more than $250,000.) A congressional, county or major mayoral campaign needs at least six staff members and a campaign budget of over $500,000. Campaigns at different levels demand that different resources be raised.

At the most local level, a sufficient base of support might be a knowledgeable campaigner to serve as campaign manager. Then, the endorsement of a handful of key community leaders and, perhaps, the endorsement of a local political or community organization involved in such elections will be sufficient. These are the easiest offices for which to run, but some minimal level of support is still necessary. These minimal resources must be committed before a campaign is launched.

Middle level campaigns (for city council or state legislature) require the commitment of at least one experienced staff member and several thousand dollars to begin. Then, the endorsements of at least a couple dozen campaign activists, political officials and community leaders are needed. If that level of commitment cannot be raised before beginning the petition drive to get on the ballot, the resources necessary to win will not be raised later. It is better to withdraw and back the best of the other candidates who have the requisite resources than to lose by a wide margin.

By the time a candidate decides to run for Congress, she should won a local election and served in government. She should begin with several key campaign staff members or campaign consultants signed up to run the campaign, $10,000 to $20,000 in the bank, the firm commitment of several dozen experienced campaigners to coordinate different aspects of the campaign, and the endorsement of a number of elected officials. A party endorsement would also be helpful, but these endorsements often have to be won in party primaries or caucuses as a part of the campaign. Party leaders help, but they are less likely to support reformers proposing to reform the political process and government.

Before deciding to launch a candidacy, establishing basic resource goals is important. If minimal resource goals can't be met in the beginning, they are unlikely to be met later. Once the campaign is begun an exact fundraising plan, public relations program, and voter contact plan need to set forth targets for later stages of the campaign. If early resources are present, you will be able to mount a solid campaign with a chance to win.

CREATION OF A CAMPAIGN CITIZENS COMMITTEE

Separate from any search committee process which may have been used to find a qualified candidate, the campaign needs a Citizens Committee to endorse, support, and legitimize a candidate in the eyes of the media and the voters. It also needs a Finance Committee to help raise money. In a small campaign there may be only a single committee with both functions. In larger campaigns there will probably be at least two distinct committees with subcommittees for fundraising events.

The campaign citizens committee headed by the Campaign Chair (and, perhaps several well known Honorary Chairs) is simply a list of people who have given written permission to use their names as having endorsed the election of your candidate. Certainly, every endorsement which might convince other voters to vote for your candidate will be collected and used in some fashion, even if it is only in letters and cards mailed to the endorser's home precinct. A citizens committee often consists of hundreds of people and may never meet as a committee during the entire campaign. Yet, all campaign literature and advertising will have a box to check off like the following:

_____ Yes, you may use my name on the Smith for School Board Citizens Committee.

A finance committee is even more critical to the success of the campaign, as it must raise the funds necessary for a winning campaign. Since most people do not like to raise money, one of the difficult jobs in beginning a successful campaign is convincing supporters to take on this task.

A final test for campaigns is the ability to recruit campaign and finance chairs and the other key volunteer campaign leaders. In addition to the staff and candidate, volunteers must be willing to commit significant time and money. If they are not recruited early, the campaign will probably fail.

DECISIONS OF CANDIDATES AND THEIR FAMILIES

A good candidate decides to run more readily if there is a chance to win, and a good candidate runs independently of political parties only if independent organizations provide a base from which to launch the campaign. Any candidate needs financial resources to win. If raising the money or recruiting experienced staff and volunteers is not possible, a realistic candidate decides not to enter the race.

The candidacy of Bill Singer for alderman on the north side of Chicago illustrates the importance of resources. A citizens' committee was formed to search for a candidate, and Singer's name was one of many suggested. At the same time, the Independent Precinct Organization (IPO) needed to raise enough money to sustain itself. Bill Singer and 10 other folks were called together at a luncheon and asked if they thought an aldermanic race was possible. They were then asked to write out checks to keep IPO alive until the election and a significant sum of money was raised. When Bill Singer saw money raised so easily, he knew a tough campaign could be financed. When 50 representatives of community organizations showed up at citizens search committee meetings, he knew community support could be found. When IPO workers went door-to-door with petitions to get him on the ballot, he knew a campaign organization could be built. Raising those resources convinced this able young lawyer to run against a democratic machine candidate in a district in which no independent had ever been elected. Good candidates want to know that the race, if they enter, will be a serious one and that they will get enough support to wage the kind of battle necessary to win.

Bernard Weisberg, a candidate for Illinois Constitutional Convention delegate, said that even though a man may hold a position of considerable prestige in his profession, even though many sacrifices may be required, saying no if a group of citizens asks him is difficult:

I never thought of running for office and I could easily see that becoming involved in the campaign would involve kind of a major disruption in my working life as a lawyer, my family life; and I wasn't sure that I really had an appetite for it. The more I thought about it the more negative I was, really. I could see it taking a tremendous amount of time, costing a pretty substantial amount of money and I was pretty much on the verge of saying definitely no until, I suppose, really two things began to weigh in my consideration. One was that I felt I really wouldn't feel very good saying no for the reasons that I mentioned already because it seemed to me that those weren't consistent with the idea of having some share in the responsibility that we all have really about government. And secondly, the more I thought about it, the more I was impressed with the suggestion...that running for office can be an educational experience which you really cannot get in any other way.[9]

Yet, even if a potentially great candidate knows that the minimal resources are present to run a strong campaign, there are still other very real considerations. First of all, you should not run for an office you do not really want just for the sake of positioning yourself for some higher office. There is always a significant chance of losing. And if the candidate wins, serving in an office which she hates could be a terrible experience.

Second, candidates should not run for any significant elected office if they are afraid of possible negative campaigns by their opponents. Once in office, criticism by opposition political leaders and common citizens who believe every public official is a crook is inevitable. If there are major skeletons in a candidate's closet, she should not enter the public arena unless she is willing to have them exposed. Even if a candidate has nothing to hide, desperate opposition candidates will distort her background and positions on issues.

Third, the pressures on candidates and their families are immense and they usually intensify if they are elected. For six months to two years, a candidate has to campaign day and night. The pressures of campaigning, winning and serving in a high profile office, are enough to weaken or destroy marriages. Campaigning means not being around much as a parent, which is especially hard with young children. So any decision to campaign must be an informed family decision. This step is not to be taken lightly.

VOTER DECISIONS

Traditionally, a voter's decision as to whether to vote and for whom has been influenced by socioeconomic position and identification with a political party.[10] Sometimes, but less often, a voter decision is determined by a candidate's character, personality and stand on issues. Thus, one of the primary tasks of participatory politics is to reorient voters toward voting for the person and the issues, not party label and economic self-interest. Unless more people get involved in politics, find qualified candidates and build strong campaign organizations capable of fielding an army of volunteers to talk with the voters, political parties and powerful special interest groups will continue to control our decisions. Political reform begins with a single citizen's commitment. Political stagnation continues only because we fail to act.

CHAPTER III

ORGANIZING A CAMPAIGN

Recruiting, funding and organizing an "army" of volunteers is the first priority of a participatory campaign. It begins with the citizens' committee that selects the candidate, is augmented by a candidate's own resources, enhanced by the wise selection of leaders, shaped by the evolution of a campaign structure, and completed by direct personal solicitation, political coffees and campaign events. Every campaign activity must help to raise the hundreds of volunteers and the thousands of dollars necessary for success. If a volunteer army can be raised and equipped, election battles can be fought and won. If not, a political war is over before it begins.

Each participatory campaign differs from all others, yet many principles and techniques remain the same. Three sets of Chicago campaigns will illustrate the decisions and choices that must be made in running a campaign: my successful campaigns for alderman in 1971 and 1975; Harold Washington's winning campaigns for mayor in 1983 and 1987; and my unsuccessful campaigns for Congress in Illinois' 5th Congressional District in 1992 and 1994. Other campaigns from state legislative races to presidential campaigns will provide additional examples of campaign techniques and demonstrate the differences between campaigns at various levels of government.

In the last chapter, we examined the decisions which a candidate and a candidate's supporters must make to determine whether to run in a particular election. In this chapter, we want to consider how a campaign has to be organized to succeed. I begin with the story of my own aldermanic campaigns and those of other independent candidates fighting the democratic party machine for control of Chicago's governments during the 1970s. Just as schools teach the basics in reading, writing and arithmetic before moving to sonnets and calculus, smaller campaigns should be studied before leaping to the high-tech, expensive methods of congressional and presidential campaigns.

In 1971, I ran for alderman. A citizens' search committee like those described in the last chapter had been looking in the 44th Ward for a strong aldermanic candidate. The 44th Ward is a community of 60,000 people and about 30,000 voters on the north side lakefront of Chicago. The search committee had been unsuccessful in locating a suitable candidate. I met socially with several of the committee members, and they asked if I would be willing to move from the neighboring 43rd Ward to run as an independent, anti-Daley candidate. After discussing the race with my wife, we met with the entire search committee of about 50 people. They were enthusiastic and pledged to work in the campaign and raise some of the money necessary to begin it.

It was nearly Thanksgiving in 1970 when my campaign began. Petitions to get on the ballot had to be filed in a few weeks, and the election was less than three months away. Thus, at least two rules of campaigning were violated in my first campaign: 1) run only in an election district where you have lived for some time; and 2) build a successful base of campaign support slowly over months, if not years. On the other hand, I had two major advantages. I was running for a vacant seat in a district without an incumbent and in a district that had a current history of electing independent candidates for alderman, constitutional convention delegate and state legislator. Thus, a base of campaign volunteers and voters had already been established by previous campaigns.

In 1971, Richard J. Daley was still the boss of the last great city machine. The 1968 Democratic National Convention in Chicago, with its police riot, had demonstrated how authoritarian his reign had become. So in the 1960s and 1970s, the political battle lines were drawn between pro-Daley and anti-Daley forces. The lakefront liberal wards were breaking free of machine control election by election. My campaign was an additional frontal assault against the power and control of Mayor Daley; therefore, the machine would do all it could to defeat me.

CAMPAIGN STRUCTURE

Candidates cannot be the manage their own campaigns. They must turn over campaign direction to paid staff members and trusted volunteers. Alderman Bill Singer, who ran two successful Chicago aldermanic campaigns, a valiant race for mayor in 1975 to defeat Richard J. Daley, and who has since served on the Chicago School Board, discovered this in his first campaign.

> *The candidate must have confidence in the staff's ability to run the campaign, as he cannot run it himself. Likewise, the staff must have confidence in the candidate and his ability to see the issues and the problems of the campaign. The candidate is not going to be able to select all of the campaign personnel, and this should be particularly the job of the campaign manager who will select the persons responsible for running various aspects of the campaign. Of course, the campaign manager should consult the candidate on these selections. But the can-*

didate should and must select a few key persons upon whom he is go-
ing to have to place great reliance, and this must be done early in the
campaign. From that time on the most important thing for the candi-
date is exposure and personal contact. This can't be done from his of-
fice or on the telephone working out campaign problems. [11]

Many campaign workers play important roles in a participatory campaign.
Because of the nature of participatory politics, a dilemma arises. Decisions
must be made quickly and instructions must be followed exactly if a campaign
is to be successful. On the other hand, campaign workers have a right to participate in decisions that they are going to be called upon to implement, and they
can make perceptive contributions to campaign decision-making. A balance
must be struck between the authority of campaign leaders and the right of workers to be a part of the decision-making process. Creating a more participatory
democracy in society can begin within the campaign itself. Key campaign leaders and staff members will undoubtedly meet in executive sessions several times
a week, but the total campaign leadership should meet at least once a week.
While immediate decisions sometimes must be made by key staff, long-range
planning involving such areas as publicity, precinct work and fund raising
should be discussed in the larger weekly meetings, and the advice of campaign
workers should be heeded as often as possible.

There is no perfect organization chart or set of job descriptions for campaigns, because the structure varies according to the size of the campaign to be
undertaken, the skills and experience of the leaders, the time volunteers can
devote, the number of workers available and the personal relationships that exist
or develop among members of the campaign organization. However, the organization chart of my aldermanic campaigns can serve as example of a good campaign structure for medium-sized campaigns (see chart on the next page). I ran
in 1971 and 1975 in a district with roughly 30,000 voters, on budgets of $25,000
and $35,000, and with three paid staff members. Today, with inflation and the
costs of new technology, comparable campaign budgets are at least three times
as expensive. My campaigns also involved about 500 people in some volunteer
capacity. Recruiting that many volunteers in the 1990s is much more difficult.

The full-time, paid staff members in my campaign were the campaign manager, office manager and public relations coordinator. All the campaign officials
listed immediately beneath the campaign manager (along with the candidate
and campaign chair) formed an executive or strategy committee, although other
campaign leaders also had major responsibilities in their own areas of work.

All leaders in my campaign had more or less explicit functions and were
directly connected to the workers necessary to carry out these functions. While a
need for an explicit, hierarchical structure exists to complete the mammoth tasks
of the campaign in time for the election, considerable communication and coordination both within and between structural units is also necessary. The structure
should allow for speedy communication within given functional areas, so the
precinct coordinator, for example, can relay instructions to precinct workers and
receive precinct-by-precinct reports on the progress of the campaign. Weekly or

SIMPSON ALDERMANIC CAMPAIGN ORGANIZATION CHART

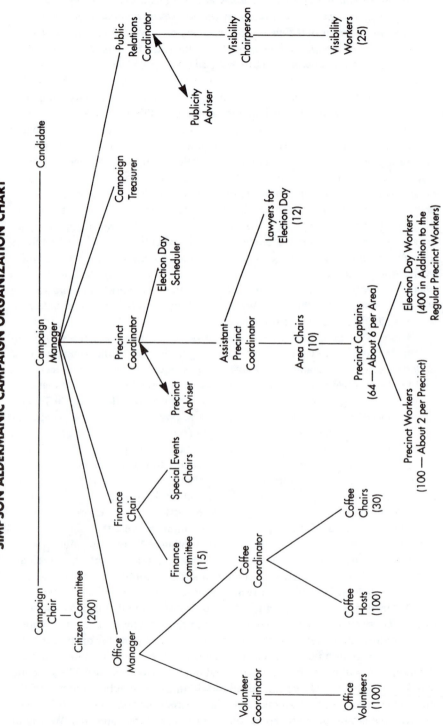

biweekly reports by precinct workers are critical in reminding workers of the tasks they have promised to perform, in allowing for effective campaign strategy and informed decision-making, and in providing for better control and potential corrective action.[11] Communication and coordination are needed between sections of the campaign as well. That is the reason for frequent strategy sessions, weekly leadership meetings, and occasional sessions with all campaign workers from the early months of the petition drive until election day. These structures, meetings and reports are meant to promote creativity.

What jobs must be done? What do the people whose names are entered on an organization chart agree to do?

Campaign Chair

The chair is head of the Citizens Committee, chair of weekly leadership meetings and an important fundraiser. However, the job can be much more, as can any job in a campaign. Donald Page Moore described his tasks in the Bernard Weisberg for Illinois Constitutional Convention delegate campaign this way:

> *The role of the campaign chair is not really definable. You have got to do a little bit of everything. You are in charge of hiring and firing people and finding people to do the multitude of tasks that have to be done. I have been involved in public relations, lawsuits, hiring a campaign manager, hiring an office manager, fundraising takes a lot of my time, recruiting lawyers to do poll watching on election day. I have done everything from sweeping out the headquarters to holding press conferences.[12]*

Unless the campaign chair has the time to oversee the day-to-day operations of the campaign, the campaign manager has the principal task of running the campaign while the campaign chair helps the candidate with raising resources and getting other members of the campaign to work hard. Sometimes the campaign chair replaces the candidate in chairing internal campaign meetings or in meeting with important people that the candidate cannot meet personally.

Campaign Manager

A campaign manager coordinates the efforts of all other workers in the campaign, designs a winning strategy in consultation with other campaign leaders, insures that the material needed (such as campaign brochures) arrive on time, and makes the daily operational decisions. As campaign managers jokingly say, a campaign manager works sixteen hours a day instead of the fourteen hours put in by volunteers.

While the candidate may maintain veto power over certain key decisions about the campaign message, spending and debt, the campaign manager should have authority to make, approve or reject almost all other campaign decisions. A wise campaign manager will encourage each of the other staff and key volunteers to make their own decisions about details of operation. He will also obtain the advise of professional campaign consultants or experienced volunteers on fundraising and public relations. Although subject to being overruled by the candidate, the campaign manager must have the authority to run the campaign.

The campaign manager must make sure that campaign strategy is consistent, that each element of the campaign fits with all other parts, and that responses to changing campaign conditions are quick. A campaign manager becomes a general of the army of campaign workers, even in a participatory campaign.

In *How to Win A Local Election* the role of a campaign manager is described as follows:

> *The candidate is out front—meeting and talking to people and listening to them. . . . The campaign manager is doing the things behind the scenes that have to be done to assist the candidate . . .*
>
> *The campaign manager is involved in all of the aspects of planning—budgeting, research, the campaign theme, mailing, radio, fundraising. Once the plan is decided upon, however, his duties shift from being a thinker to being a doer.*[13]

The campaign manager supervises all aspects of the campaign, conducts the regularly scheduled staff meetings, and works with the candidate and campaign chair to make sure that the campaign is proceeding smoothly. Any changes which need to be made because someone is not doing their job, something is not working or actions by opponents are the responsibility of the campaign manager.

In hiring a campaign manager the candidate looks for someone with prior experience in winning campaigns. Your campaign manager should be familiar with field operations, fundraising, a campaign office, and public relations. He may not have done all these things personally, but he should have observed these operations first hand before undertaking to direct them. Joseph Napolitan in *The Election Game* offers the following advice:

> *My advice to candidates is to look long and hard before selecting a campaign manager, and when you do settle on the person you want, to give him the authority to do the job properly, and this includes expenditure of funds. . . .*
>
> *The worst choice any candidate can pick for his campaign manager is himself. No one—repeat, no one—can do a competent job in a major campaign if he tries to serve both roles.*[14]

A candidate and his advisers may have agreed upon the message of the campaign before he hires a campaign manager. If the manager likes the candidate and agrees with the message, then he signs on.

The job of the candidate is to meet people, to get votes and to raise money. The job of the campaign manager is to help design and to implement the campaign plans. A major campaign is governed by the tyranny of the calendar. There is one date on which the nominating petitions should be filed, a last day voters can register, and only one election day. If printing rates are to be kept reasonable, copy must be delivered to the graphic designer and the camera-ready copy to the printer on specific dates. There must be enough time to prepare for a campaign benefit properly. The campaign manager cracks the whip and makes sure that work is done well and on time. It is not always a popular job, but it is indispensable.

Precinct Coordinator

The precinct coordinator, or field director, plays an essential role in any participatory campaign. This man or woman puts the precinct organization together, conducts training sessions, constantly receives workers' reports, and coordinates collection of petition signatures, voter registration drives, voter canvasses, and election day activities. Local elections are won or lost by efforts in the precincts, which in Chicago contain about 350 voters each. Even in national campaigns such as Bill Clinton's 1992 presidential campaign, precinct work can be the key to victory from the first New Hampshire primary to the general election. Precinct coordinators direct the personal voter contact that changes votes and motivates voters to go to the polls.

Finance Chair

The job of finance chair, treasurer and purchasing officer are sometimes combined and sometimes separated. The tasks are raising the money, determining what expenses can be afforded, and locating the cheapest suppliers of buttons, flyers, printing, posters, and other commodities necessary to the campaign.

With the change in financial disclosure laws, the job of finance chair has focused more on fundraising and the role of the treasurer has focused on reporting expenses. Often the treasurer is now a certified public accountant working pro bono for the campaign. The treasurer signs the official campaign disclosures, which report the campaign's large contributors and major campaign expenditures. In larger campaigns, a bookkeeper may be added to the structure or the office manager may assume the responsibility of recording individual contributions and expenditures.

The treasurer does not develop the finance plan or raise the money. The volunteer finance or fundraising chair, or in larger campaigns, the fundraising staff member develops the fundraising plan and helps the candidate obtain the necessary contributions.

Public Relations Coordinator

The public relations coordinator or press secretary supervises the production of all publicity, including brochures, buttons, bumper stickers, posters, news stories, and television and radio appearances and commercials. June Rosner, the Weisberg publicity chairman, summarized her job thus: "Basically my job is to get the candidate's name familiar with the voters and build the sort of image for him that will make workers enthusiastic to work in the campaign."[15]

In larger campaigns with substantially larger budgets, several people (staff members, volunteers and consultants) may be involved in the public relations activities. A public relations coordinator, sometimes called the press secretary, provides strategy and coordination. A graphic artists designs all the printed campaign materials (logo, buttons, stationery, brochures, posters, and bumper stickers). Media strategy may also be proposed by a public relations consultant or a public relations firm and television or radio advertisements essential to major campaigns are often developed by a separate media advisor or agency. Thus, in larger campaigns the public relations staff becomes larger and the candidate, campaign manager, campaign chair, and public relations coordinator become the client if outside professional firms are involved.

Office Manager

The office manager is responsible for work done in the campaign headquarters. This includes keeping records of all potential workers, supervising mailings, photocopying or printing campaign literature, typing letters, purchasing supplies, preparing for rallies and training sessions, directing telephone banks, and answering the ever-ringing campaign telephones. The office manager also supervises the computers and trains staff and volunteers in computer use.

Ideally, the campaign will have a separate volunteer coordinator to recruit volunteers for the campaign. Potential volunteers who sign pledge cards upon meeting the candidate at campaign events are called and recruited. After the volunteer coordinator does the recruiting, the office manager greets the volunteers when they arrive, plans the necessary work, assigns volunteers to their specific tasks, answers questions and coordinates all the office activities necessary for winning a campaign.

Coffee Coordinator

A good coffee coordinator or team of coordinators will, by the end of the campaign, have convinced over one hundred families to host a coffee in a district of more than 30,000 voters. In a political campaign, a coffee is a social event organized by volunteers in their homes, to which they invite their neighbors and friends. The candidate speaks and attempts to convert those who attend into becoming campaign supporters. Because coffee and cookies are often served, they are called coffees even when other refreshments are provided.

The coffee coordinator sees that the appropriate campaign materials, including instruction sheets and invitations, are delivered to the hosts. Finally, they have to recruit and train dozens of coffee chairs, develop the schedule and brief the candidate for each appearance.

These hundred or more campaign coffees are critical to recruiting volunteers, raising money and meeting voters. In some campaigns a separate coffee chair coordinator recruits, assigns and trains the chairpersons to run the coffees.

Visibility Chair

Because name identification is so important, a visibility crew, often made up of high school and college students, is created to insure that hundreds of posters are placed in windows of homes and stores, and that yard signs are placed on suburban lawns. They also make sure that lampposts throughout the district are covered with stickers or small posters (attached with wire for easy removal when the campaign is over),and that as many people as possible are induced to wear campaign buttons or place campaign bumper stickers on their cars. This hardworking crew is coordinated by the visibility chair. They work week by week throughout the campaign, and then on Election Eve they do a complete blitz, hanging posters near all the polling places in the district.

Area Chairs

The critical middle managers of participatory campaigns are the area chairs. Each chair coordinates four to six precincts. The chairs recruit many of the precinct workers; provide the workers with materials, instructions and assistance with problems in the precinct; and collect reports from all precincts under their supervision. Area chairs are the key communication links in the campaign. At the weekly campaign leadership meetings, their reports and suggestions are relied upon in making decisions to alter the direction of the campaign, to intensify the effort, or to proceed with current plans if the campaign is effective.

RECRUITING WORKERS

In West Africa there is a saying that nothing can be done without money. Whether a road needs to be built, a marriage contracted or a chief elected, the answer is always the same. In participatory politics a more appropriate saying would be that nothing can be done without workers. If there are no workers, there is no campaign. Since volunteers are necessary to a successful campaign, recruiting them is a major concern underlying every campaign activity.

Three methods of recruitment are most frequently used. The first, which often goes unnoticed, is direct personal contact. Campaign workers tell their friends and acquaintances about the campaign and sign them up as volunteers. Person-to-person recruiting is used more systematically by the campaign leadership. Whether you are an area chair recruiting 20 precinct workers to canvass the precincts you supervise or a coffee coordinator signing up 100 coffee hosts, you begin with a list of prospective workers. These lists are garnered from supporting organizations, prior political campaign files, friends and acquaintances, and people who have already volunteered but have not yet been given a specific task.

Each prospect is called and assigned specific responsibilities. If the original lists are insufficient, going door-to-door or phoning all registered voters in an area may be necessary to find enough volunteers to get the job done. In addition to direct contact of friends and prospect lists, coffees and social events make ideal occasions for citizens to meet and evaluate a candidate and be converted into volunteers.

Coffees

Coffees have been used so often and so effectively that a more or less explicit formula for success has been developed. They begin with the host or several hosts inviting their friends and every registered voter in one or more precincts. Although printed invitations (see below) are mailed or placed in the mail boxes of voters, it is essential that the host personally phone and invite as many potential guests as possible. Of those who receive only the printed invitation, one or two out of a 100 will appear, but as many as 25 percent of those invited by phone may come. Therefore, the telephone calls are essential to a good coffee.

Cover of Coffee Invitation

You're invited for coffee and to meet

Dick Simpson

Inside Text of Coffee Invitation

Dick Simpson, former 44th Ward Alderman, is an Associate Professor of Political Science at the University of Illinois at Chicago. In the Chicago City Council, he sponsored and passed legislation to curtail redlining by banks, to reduce C.T.A. fares for senior citizens and to improve the city's housing program. Most recently, he served on the transition teams for Mayor Jane Byrne, Mayor Harold Washington, County Clerk David Orr and State's Attorney Jack O'Malley.

Simpson is running against Dan Rostenkowski in the new Fifth Congressional District.

Dear Neighbor,

On _____, _____

at _____ , I'm having some of our neighbors over for coffee and to meet Dick Simpson who is running for Congress. I'd like you to meet him, and he would like to discuss with you the issues you think important.

My address is_____ .

I look forward to seeing you and any friends you'd like to bring along.

Sincerely,

RSVP _____ .

To quote Bob Houston, an expert coffee chair, "No coffee is ever a failure."[16] If only the host and one other person show up, at least the neighbors in the area have been invited and know that the candidate has been in neighborhood to meet with constituents. Moreover, the host and guest can both be signed up to do precinct work, which can affect hundreds of voters. Regardless of how many people attend a coffee, maximizing the results is important. Coffee results are measured precisely by the number of volunteers and the contributions collected at the end of the evening.

To achieve the best results, a coffee chair is assigned to cover the event. He need not come from a specific precinct or neighborhood, but he will most often

WHAT EVERY GREAT COFFEE CHAIR HAS TO KNOW

1. Call the coffee host the night before the coffee to let him or her know that you are coming.

2. Get to the meeting promptly, preferably 15 minutes before the announced time.

3. Introduce yourself and, while awaiting the gathering of the group, remind the host or hostess to have all the guests sign the sign-in sheet as they come in. Set Simpson literature out on the table and give it to guests as they arrive.

4. Call the meeting to order in time for introductory remarks before Dick arrives. (This should usually be done about 20 minutes after the announced time of the coffee.) These are the principal points to cover:

5. Background on Dick:
   • After redistricting of wards from the 1970 census, he beat Democratic Machine candidates to become 44th Ward alderman, serving two terms during which he created the 44th Ward Assembly, Community Zoning Board, and Asemblea Abierta;
   • Founder of the Independent Precinct Organization in 1968 which merged with the Independent Voters of Illinois to become IVI-IPO in 1979;
   • Associate Professor of Political Science at UIC, where he has written and published numerous studies about voting patterns of City Council and County Board members and City and County budgeting processes;
   • Former executive director of CALC (Clergy and Laity Concerned), an interfaith peace and justice organization.

6. Dick will be running in a new Northwest Side Congressional District, which will be created containing the area from about Diversey on the

be from the district in which the campaign is being waged. As the guests arrive, the coffee chair and the host have them sign an attendance sheet, introduce them to the others in the group, and hand them campaign literature to read. Usually about 20 minutes after the announced time of the coffee, the chair will call the meeting to order, and they discuss the background of the candidate briefly and review facts about the election such as the date of election, how many candidates citizens may vote for, who the candidates are, and how citizens may register to vote.

Then, the guests are asked what particular issues concern them or which ones they would most like the candidate to discuss. The candidate arrives about

---

south, Ashland on the east, and the city limits on the west and north. He will run against either Congressman Rostenkowski or Annunzio.

7. One key issue on which Dick is running is the need to reform Congress by limiting terms of members of Congress, providing public financing of congressional campaigns, and requiring more accountability from representatives.

8. Go around the circle asking guests what particular issues concern them most about the district and what issues they would like Dick Simpson to cover.

9. When Dick Arrives (45 minutes after the time for which the meeting was set), stop. The host or hostess should introduce him to the group individually, and he should shake each person's hand. Briefly tell Dick what issues are uppermost in the group's mind. After he speaks, he will answer questions until it is time for his next meeting. Generally, he should not stay more than 30-45 minutes. You may have to help him stop and get on to his other commitments.

10. *YOU, NOT DICK SIMPSON, ARE THE CLIMAX OF THE EVENING.* When, after answering all questions, Dick leaves, take over. Do not let the group drift apart. Make a pitch for **workers, money, and more coffees** to help wage a successful campaign. Use the volunteer cards to do this.

    To make a successful pitch: after you pass out the pledge cards to everyone, say that you are not here to persuade anyone to do anything to elect Dick, but to explain what they can do if they want to get him elected. Then explain what each item on the pledge card means.

11. Collect all of the pledge cards, contributions, and attendance sheets. We need them returned to 2501 W. Lunt, Chicago, IL 60645 by the next day so we can follow up on potential workers. Use any left over materials at future coffees or return them to campaign headquarters.

12. Thanks and congratulations. If you have any questions or need additional materials, call our coffee coordinator, Coralee Kern, at 472-8116 or campaign headquarters at 338-1992.

45 minutes after the beginning of the meeting, and the host introduces him to each guest. Unless the crowd is too large, he shakes hands with each guest as he is introduced. The chair will present the candidate with the questions that interest the group. He speaks, and then answers more questions for about half an hour. In a very complicated campaign like the election of delegates to rewrite the state constitution candidates sometimes spent slightly more time at critical coffees, but it is terribly important that they not stay until all the fire has gone out of the meeting.

A candidate can do three to five coffees a night if he keep his remarks brief and to the point. A candidate's exposure can be multiplied by carefully timed coffees. In larger districts, coffees can even be organized around a candidate's television appearance, thus maximizing a candidate's exposure to a number of voters by multiple, simultaneous coffees. Better financed campaigns will even produce a short campaign video to show at coffees if a candidate cannot attend or by precinct workers to interested voters and their families in their homes.

The chair, however, not the candidate, is the climax of a successful coffee. The pitch is crucial. The coffee chair explains why help is needed, what needs to be done, and urges people to make up their minds by filling out a pledge card (see next page) and turning it in before they leave. It allows voters to indicate how they are willing to contribute to the campaign. A coffee chair must remember to thank each person who commits him or herself and he can judge a coffee's success by how many workers sign cards and how much money is raised.

The pitch can be very hard sell. Although the people in the room are voters, they do not have to like the chair, which is one of the reasons the chair makes the pitch rather than the candidate.

An example of such a pitch is the one given by Campaign Chair Donald Page Moore at a Weisberg for Illinois Constitutional Convention delegate coffee:

> *The [Chicago democratic] machine is tough and we beat one machine candidate by 1600 votes and the other beat us by 115 votes [in the primary]. . . . So if we are going to win, we can only do it in a couple of well-recognized ways. One, we've got to have money and we can't shake the money out of people the way the county assessor's office does. It's going to cost us $35,000 [in 1970] to run a decent campaign for Bernard Weisberg. And this leaves us with about $20,000 to raise in the next six weeks. I don't see any point in making a secret about it, those are the facts. We've got fifteen in and we've got twenty to go. And if we don't get the money, we can't win the election because we can't run an effective campaign without money. . . . Precinct work and election day work are fundamental. They're vital. They can be fun. You can be part of something that really means something for the future of this town. And we can't do without it. We can't get by with 850 workers on November 18th. If we've only 850 workers on the street we're going to get buried. . . .*

Volunteer Pledge Card
(Front)

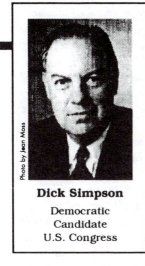

Photo by Jean Moss

Dick Simpson

Democratic
Candidate
U.S. Congress

Elect Dick Simpson to Congress!

Dick Simpson, a candidate for Congress in the new 5th District, is challenging the scandal-ridden incumbent, Dan Rostenkowski, in the Democratic Primary on March 15. As 44th Ward Alderman from 1971-79, **Dick Simpson** passed legislation to reduce CTA fares for senior citizens, to curb redlining by banks, to make rental buildings safer and to fund public art. **Dick Simpson,** a political science teacher at the University of Illinois at Chicago, has served on the transition teams of Cook County Clerk David Orr and State's Attorney Jack O'Malley. **Dick Simpson,** age 52, his wife, Sarajane, and their two children, ages 17 and 21, live in the Lincoln Square neighborhood of Chicago.

Dick Simpson will work hard for:
- local economic development to create jobs
- increased funding for schools
- neighborhood team policing
- national health care

To reform Congress, **Dick Simpson** will introduce and support:
- Congressional term limits of 12 years
- public funding of campaigns and spending caps
- a law requiring Members of Congress to hold open meetings with voters in their districts at least 6 times a year

(Back)

Simpson
for
Congress

3740 W. Irving Park Rd.
Chicago, IL 60618-3116
312 / 866 - 1994

Printed on Recycled Paper
With Soy Ink

® 215 *WBE Certified*
Paid for by Simpson for
Congress Committee,
3740 W. Irving Park Road,
Chicago, IL 60618-3116,
312 / 866 - 1994,
Thomas J. Gradel,
President;
Allen Hochfelder, Treasurer.
A copy of our report is, or
will be, available from the
Federal Election Commis-
sion, 999 E Street, NW,
Washington D.C. 20463.

Yes, I will help with Dick Simpson's campaign. Please add my name to the Simpson for Congress Citizens Committee.

(PLEASE PRINT)

NAME   OCCUPATION

ADDRESS

CITY, STATE, ZIP CODE   WARD

(   )   (   )
DAY PHONE   EVENING PHONE

You can also count on me to:

☐ Do precinct work   ☐ Make phone calls

☐ Work in the office   ☐ Host a coffee

☐ Other

☐ Make a contribution of $_____

(Please make checks payable to **Simpson for Congress**)

And don't listen to this talk that Weisberg's got it in the bag. All that means is we're running up front. We've got a whale of a chance and they can beat the daylights out of us if we don't keep up the momentum. Now we can do it, but it is not in the bag and we need help desperately.

We need 1500 workers on the street election day, working in the polling places, passing out literature, helping run the pluses [voters favorable to Weisberg], helping make the phone calls, everything that has to be done on election day.

We need at least 1,000 precinct canvassers working in between now [and then], in the odds and ends of their week: on the weekends a few hours, in the evening a few hours. We've got to have it. If we don't have it, we get beat. And all these months and months of work and dedication and hope and all the rest of it go right down the drain. A dying machine is going to get a terrific shot in the arm and independent politics on the Northside lakefront of Chicago is going to get a kick in the tail that will set it back for five years. . . .

It's terribly, terribly important. People all over this city . . . people in city hall, people in political headquarters all over this city are watching this and one or two other races in the city of Chicago to see what happens. To see if the independents can make it stick or are they going to run out of gas after a couple of cheap wins. That's what they are asking themselves and the political future of this state to some extent [depends on the outcome] . . .

Let me just put it to you, will you help? Will you take some personal responsibility to help us here? I've got some cards that I'd like to pass out. They've got blanks for your names and addresses, squares you can check off if you are willing to work in a precinct, if you are willing to work election day, if you are willing to work in our headquarters between now and election day. This is in your spare time. It can be a tremendous experience.

Please join with us. If you can't give time, give money. If you can't give money, give time. If you can, do both. If you can't do either, vote for us.[17]

The third means of finding volunteers is by making every campaign event as a recruiting effort. Each member of the citizens' search committee should be called and asked to serve in some capacity with the campaign, or at the very least, to lend their name to the campaign citizens committee and their money to the campaign effort. Not only should people be recruited to work in the petition drive, every person who signs a petition to get a candidate on the ballot should receive a personally signed thank you letter from the candidate, along with a pledge card and a request to join the campaign.

Every time precinct workers go door-to-door to register people or get their vote, they should look for potential campaign workers. Every curious headquarters visitor should be put to work in the office immediately and later convinced to help out in the precincts.

When your candidate shakes hands at bus stops or supermarkets, he should take pledge cards to sign up new workers on the spot. Every campaign effort, from stories in the newspapers to rallies in the park, should pay off by recruiting volunteers and by affecting as many individual voters as possible.

ORGANIZING A WINNING COALITION

Campaigns occur at many levels. One is creating a winning coalition, beginning with an electoral coalition. If the candidate is endorsed by the dominant political faction or party in a particular district, he usually wins. Political scientists have discovered three main reasons why people vote for a particular candidate: party identity, candidate personality, and overriding issues (usually economic issues).[18] In general elections where party labels are clear, in the absence of other information on candidates running for lower offices (because they get minimal press attention and cannot afford a media blitz of paid television and radio advertisements), democrats vote for democratic candidates and republicans vote for republican candidates. So in any election, building support of political groups is important.

Links between race, ethnicity, social economic status, and political party identity are also clear. Inner-city African-American districts tend to elect democrats and wealthy, white suburbs tend to elect republicans. Thus, the party identity of your candidate is often key to winning elections. Building the proper political coalition to gain the dominant party endorsement is critical to winning an election.

In thinking about coalition building, it is important to remember that a candidate only has to win a majority of votes cast on election day—not gain the support of a majority of citizens, or registered voters. Any political coalition is assembled by appealing to group self-interest. One of the first questions to ask when deciding whether to support a candidate in a particular district is what groups must support that candidate to win and what is the likelihood of gaining their support. That is one reason why a citizens' search committee is used in smaller district races and a campaign citizens committee is assembled in larger campaigns. Public endorsement of community leaders from either committee indicates the breadth of group support for a candidacy and makes appealing to those groups of voters easier.

In considering coalitions beyond strictly electoral coalitions, the distribution of race and ethnicity in a district is important. Generally speaking, an African-American candidate cannot win in an all-white district, and a white will not win in an African-American district. Other ethnic and social divisions are less absolute but still important.

I was elected alderman in Chicago's 44th Ward even though as a white Anglo-Saxon Protestant, I represented none of the major ethnic or religious groups in the ward. The 44th Ward was heavily Jewish and moderately wealthy on the east side, Hispanic and Catholic in the middle, and German working class on the west side, but I was acceptable to all of these groups. I won heavily on the east side because of my liberal stands on social and political issues, as well as my opposition to Mayor Richard J. Daley. I gained support in the middle of the district from the new young professionals moving in and from Hispanics because I paid close attention to the issues of the Latino community. While I did not win the west side, I also got votes there because I was not as threatening as a black politician would have been in the conservative, older German community.

In any district, campaigns begin by assembling the political organizations, former campaign workers and community leaders opposed to the incumbent or dominant political forces. You try to get diverse groups and leaders to support your candidate. Once your base is solidified, then you reach out to other constituencies. Your candidate meets with various groups and their leaders, and he takes stands on the issues that concern them. Specific ethnic groups often form community organizations to which your candidate can appeal for support. And, just as with other groups, ethnic communities have special channels through which they can be reached. Chicago, for instance, has a daily Korean newspaper, several Spanish radio stations and many other media reaching specific cultural groups. You can use these media conduits to ask for the support and participation of these voters in your campaign.

When a campaign contacts an ethnic group through their community organization and community leaders, it attempts to understand what issues the organization considers important. Just as you would not assume that a labor organization represents the political view of all working people, do not assume that a Chinese Mutual Aid Association speaks for all citizens of Chinese descent among the constituency. It may also be necessary to produce campaign literature in the language of the groups you hope to reach, using someone fluent in the language to translate it.

In appealing to different groups it is important not to make contradictory promises or play to racism or bigotry of a particular group. Groups have to know that while a candidate is sensitive to their issues and concerns that he can be trusted—that he is not telling one thing to one group and then changing his position when talking to another.

An old political saying in Chicago goes: "Politics is about addition not subtraction." You have to pick political enemies so it is clear what you stand for, but politics is basically about adding the support of different groups and individuals together, not in factionalism and splintering support.

Campaign strategy is not only about contacting voters individually, but also about assembling a winning coalition. Some of these coalitions may last for decades only to be replaced by new alliances. The assumption that white southerners would always vote democratic was destroyed by republican party victories in congressional and gubernatorial elections across the South. Other coalitions are as easily destroyed. When in power, coalitions must be carefully nurtured and maintained. When out of power, coalitions must be carefully and consciously built group by group.

STARTING A CAMPAIGN OFFICE

When an election is still a year or more away, a campaign office might be set up in the basement of a candidate's home, in a home office of an exploratory committee staff member, or in a supporting organization's office. A campaign may also be run from the offices of several campaign staff members or consultants in a larger campaign.

Even in these humble beginnings, a campaign office has to have at least one paid staff member (even if only part-time), a phone with at least one dedicated number, an answering machine, a computer, and a fax machine or fax modem. Such a small office can be adequate to launch a campaign. Strategy meetings can be held, fundraising calls made, and early press relations handled with these limited facilities. Research on the district, campaign position papers, press releases, and the first campaign literature can also be produced here.

These limited facilities would be adequate as the sole campaign office in only the smallest local campaigns—a local referendum, suburban school, zoning, library board, or town council race. For all other campaigns, this start-up office and its operations are meant only to launch the larger campaign. The limited facilities are used to keep costs down until actual campaign offices can be opened with full staffing. If the computer is donated and the rent is free, this start-up office, including part-time staff salaries might cost only about $2,000 a month.

The "real" campaign office is large enough to house the candidate, at least three paid staff members (campaign manager, office manager and public relations coordinator) and three or four volunteers. It should also be large enough to hold strategy meetings with the staff, key volunteers and precinct coordinators. When newspaper photographs are taken there or a television crew interviews the candidate, it should look like a winning campaign headquarters. Generally speaking, it will be more than 1,000 square feet with smaller cubicle offices for staff in the back and a larger open area for volunteers and meetings in front. Campaign offices for a presidential or statewide candidate take at least a floor of a downtown office building and house many more staff and volunteers.

In a full campaign office, at least three computers will be needed. Instead of a single telephone line, now there will be at least four. There will eventually be a leased copier, a fax machine, as many desks as staff members, some big tables at which volunteers will work, a coffee maker, and a refrigerator. The walls should be freshly painted and decorated with maps of the district, campaign literature and newspaper clippings about the race. The office must be staffed by friendly, professional campaign officials who will seek to recruit everyone who wanders in the door to volunteer.

An ideal office is a storefront centrally located in the district, on a major street near a public transportation line, with plenty of parking nearby. Obviously, the rent should be inexpensive so that the campaign's money is spent on reaching the voters. However, since staff and volunteers will be working there at least from 10 a.m. to 11 p.m., the office must be comfortable and attractive. A run down slum cannot be rented because either too much money and time will be spent on renovation, or it will be so unappealing that the staff and volunteers will not want to work there.

The best way to plan all aspects of a campaign is to envision what you need to win the election and plan so you can comfortably grow into that vision. If you need 500 volunteers to go door-to-door or call voters on the phone, then you have to be set up to coordinate that many people from the office and have the facilities to provide them with precinct lists, phone lists, instructions, and campaign literature. The campaign will need several phone lines, plenty of tables or chairs, room to store boxes of campaign brochures, and so forth.

To design an office, plan for the office(s) you will need by the end of the campaign. While you may start up with a single staff member, at the end you may have from three to seven or more. While one telephone line may be enough in the start-up office, a phone bank with ten lines or more may be needed at the end of the campaign.

You need to plan so that each new resource becomes available just as the campaign requires them. For instance, new phone lines take weeks to be installed after they are ordered, so you must order them well in advance, not in the last few weeks of the campaign. In planning the office, using the latest technology that you can afford is also important. Modern campaigns utilize some very fancy high-tech methods. It is necessary to understand what is possible, what it costs and how each new tool can be used to win the election. Since campaign support services change very quickly, it is impossible to provide here the names of the best software programs or providers. But I will review what is possible in 1996, confident that later changes mostly will be newer versions of the same techniques.

Most high-tech campaign technology has six main uses:

1. Research
2. Office work
3. Fundraising and financial reporting
4. Press relations
5. Campaign literature
6. Voter contact

1. Research. Early assessment of the district mostly involves collecting prior election statistics, census data and the like. Storing the information on disk and creating a simple data file to manipulate the numbers for strategy and planning may be necessary but most of these documents are readily available in a paper form at libraries, Boards of Election commissioners' offices, and universities. Little special equipment is required to determine if the race is winnat to plot general campaign strategy.

In the next few years election statistics will be available on the Internt 486 or better computer, modem, Netscape software, and internet connection will be necessary to get this data. Census data will be used in a CD-ROM format. The type of data that will become available more uniformly is represented by the 1994 California election data, which can be viewed on the internet currently at the following address: http:\\www.election.ca.gov\

Once a decision to undertake the campaign has been made, a good researcher, a research director (who is often the campaign manager or the public relations coordinator), and sophisticated computer equipment will become necessary. Voting records of opponents are most easily studied in a computerized form. Their previous campaign contributors (which may give clues to conflicts of interest) will often be filed with the Federal Election Commission, state Board of Election Commissioners, or County Clerk. These data are usually available in an electronic format. Issue research on data like factories that have closed or serious crimes in the district may develop into important campaign issues and press conferences. Sometimes this data can be purchased from private companies specializing in compiling voting records, campaign contributions, and plant closing or crime statistics. In any case, manipulating this data and producing tables and charts as illustrations for press conferences, press releases or campaign literature requires a computer and data software programs like Quattro Pro or Lotus.

2. Office Work. There is an endless amount of office work which can be made easier with computers. Some campaigns try to link all their computers into a local area network. Usually this is a mistake because, it takes a sophisticated level of maintenance which most campaigns can not support to keep the system from crashing all the time. Many volunteers (and even staff members) will be barely computer literate. If they make a mistake on a single machine, usually the damage is minimal. But if they are working on a network, they can crash the entire system, depriving the campaign of working computers for the number of days it takes to get a computer specialist to get the system running again. To date, most campaigns use the "sneaker network" and a single printer. A staff member or volunteer simply copies work onto a disk and walks over to the another computer, puts in the disk and loads the work onto the screen for the next person to use. Sneaker networks have the advantage of never crashing. In a campaign, the level of technology should be appropriate to skills of your campaign workers and their tasks instead of newer, fancier technology which requires more experience and competence.

The schedule for the candidate and the campaign will be kept on computer (usually by the office manager). There are fancy scheduling software programs available, but none of them work perfectly for campaigns. Most campaigns create an all-purpose scheduling form on the computer and print copies on which staff members fill out scheduling requests (see the request form on the next page). Once the office manager, candidate and campaign

Simpson for Congress
Scheduling Request

Event Date: __ / __ / __   Day of week: Su   M   Tu   W   Th   F   Sa

Event Start: __ : __ am / pm   Candidate Arrival: __ : __ am / pm

Event End: __ : __ am / pm   Candidate Departure: __ : __ am / pm

Event Name: _____

Event Type: _____

Place: _____

Address: _____

Directions: _____

City: _____ State: _____ Zip: _____

Inviter: _____ Home Phone: _____

Inviter's Title: _____ Day Phone: _____

Organization/Company: _____

Contact: _____ Phone: _____

On Site Contact: _____ Phone: _____

Candidate's Assignment: _____

Surrogate: _____

Driver: _____ Phone: _____

Coffee Chairman: _____

Staff Assigned: _____

Also Assigned: _____

Media Expected: _____

Notes: _____

_____

_____

FOR OFFICE USE ONLY

Originator: _____ Phone: _____

Scheduling approved by: _____ Date: _____

manager agree on the requests, the daily schedule is generated with standardized information.

Office computers are used to make agendas for staff and strategy meetings, and to draft letters and instructions for volunteers. These word-processing demands make it advisable to employ similar computers and the same word-processing software. At the current state of the technology, the computers should all be IBM clones (with the exception of the campaign graphic artist who will probably use an Apple computer). Either WordPerfect or Word for Windows is usually the standard word-processing software. Nothing can be more frustrating than having more than one staff member or volunteer unable to work on the same projects because their computers or their software will not talk to each other. Have the office manager and campaign manager make a choice of computers and software, and then make it the standard for the campaign.

3. Fundraising and financial reporting. Campaigns have come a long way in the last few years. Formerly, potential contributors were kept entirely on handwritten 3 x 5 cards and financial reports required by the government were typed by hand on government forms. Now both functions and much more are accomplished by software programs. These programs are expensive (often costing $750 to $1000), but higher level campaigns cannot live without them.

For congressional campaigns, specialized campaign software programs like "Hannibal" store and sort information on voters, volunteers and contributions. These programs produce personalized letters, envelope labels and the critical financial reports to the Federal Election Commission.[19] They allow the addresses and phone numbers of fundraising prospects to be entered, individualized letters to be generated, information on all contributions and expenditures to be kept, individual thank you letters to be written, potential precinct walk sheets to be created, lists of volunteers to be kept, as well as financial reports to be generated. For state campaigns, there are private corporations in each state which provide software tailored to the required state financial report forms. Soon campaign software will be available for local campaigns with their less stringent requirements. These software programs also work with standard word-processing programs like WordPerfect or Word for Windows.

In larger campaigns, a staff member will be assigned to fundraising and in smaller campaigns a volunteer will be in charge. But in either, they will use the new computerized methods to keep track of prospects, donors and financial reports.

4. Press relations. The public relations coordinator or campaign press secretary will need, at a minimum, a phone to call the press, a computer to write press releases and memos, and a fax machine to deliver these instantly to the news media. A preprogrammed fax machine with the fax numbers of the media, a list of e-mail addresses, and an internet hookup are becoming more standard. Setting up a home page on the World Wide Web for campaign news releases and announcements will soon become a standard means of communicating with the press, campaign supporters, opinion leaders, and interested voters.

5. Campaign literature and commercials. The production of campaign literature often occurs outside the campaign headquarters at the office of professional media consultants. Campaign brochures are usually designed on Apple or Macintosh computers by a professional graphic artist after the copy is developed by the campaign manager and public relations coordinator. After the necessary photographs are taken, the brochure will be printed out camera ready (in the old days it was typeset), and the photos "dropped in." The firm printing the brochures then provides the proofs of the work for approval by the artist, campaign staff and candidate.

A different technology is employed to make radio or television commercials. Although the copy may be written at the campaign office or on the consultant's computer, a video camera and a television or radio recording studio must produce the finished product. Because the public expects high production values in television and radio commercials, professionals must be employed in all aspects of production. A home video camera held by your inexperienced brother-in-law and an amateur script written by mom simply will not do. While immense amounts of money can be saved if the studio or talent donate their time, commercials must be made professionally. The equipment involved will be rented because, no campaign can afford to buy the equipment owned by media professionals and recording studios.

6. Voter contact. A key decision for any candidate and campaign is whether to spend as much as $10,000 of scarce resources for voters to be contacted individually door-to-door, by telephone or by direct mail, or whether this money should instead be spent on another round of mass media ads in the newspapers or on radio and television. The decision has both ideological and practical consequences. Participatory campaigns will nearly always opt for individual voter contact, because convincing voters to support your candidate is easier if volunteers directly persuade them and answer their specific questions.

As in other areas, however, major advances in the use of technology have facilitated effective contact with the voters. These applications of technology are obvious in a high-tech campaign, because much of the work is accomplished in the campaign headquarters itself.

The five principal methods of voter contact used in campaigns are direct contact by the candidate, door-to-door contact by campaign precinct workers, direct mail, telephone, and news coverage and advertising in the mass media. Very soon these methods will be joined by contact through the computer Internet and interactive television through videotapes, CD-Rom, or cable television.

Currently, creating direct voter contact with the candidate requires the least high-tech effort, although computers are used to schedule the candidate's appearances. A candidate can meet voters at public transportation stops, factory gates, supermarkets, and parades. He can also go to coffees, attend community meetings, candidate forums, and debates. Last of all, he can appear at campaign rallies and fundraising events. The scheduling will be handled by a scheduling request form developed by the office manager in a computer word-processing program. Staff and volunteers request that the candidate appear at various events, and the office manager in consultation with the staff, campaign manager and candidate produces a weekly and daily schedule. In all campaigns the candidate, key staff and volunteers get a weekly copy of the schedule. The candidate and his driver get a detailed daily event schedule. In larger campaigns, a public schedule is given to the new media once a week or upon request.

Door-to-door contact is labor-intensive because of the need to prepare maps, voter lists, training and report sheets for volunteers, not to mention the hours put in by the precinct workers actually contacting the voters door-to-door. As in so many other areas, computers have changed this process. Each campaign headquarters will now have at least one high-powered computer (486 or better) and will purchase from government election authorities or private firms data on computer disks or CD-Rom, which provide a list of all voters in the district, their addresses and phone numbers by precinct, how often and in which elections they voted, social characteristics such as age and their party identification.[20]

This information immediately tells the precinct worker which people are registered and likely to vote, their party affiliation, their address, and their phone number. Getting this data is expensive. The computer will cost at least a couple of hundred dollars a month to lease, the software and voter data for a congressional district will cost from $2,000 to $4,000 to purchase, and a staff member will have to spend 50 percent of their time supervising volunteers in printing data on the voters. However, any direct effort (door-to-door precinct work, phone banks or direct mail) to contact individual voters in a large district, is worth the costs.

Incumbent office holders have the additional advantage of computer software to track all service requests by constituents, so they can add to their voter data information such as Mary Jones requested a pothole to be filled in 1993 and was satisfied with the response from their office. This data can be added to the information sheets along with the names, addresses and phone numbers that campaign workers use in contacting the voter door-to-door, by mail or by phone.

Three alternatives exist for local campaigns that cannot afford high-tech expenditures to facilitate direct voter contact. First of all, in smaller campaigns involving fewer voters, there are cheaper ways to assemble the information. For an election run in a single city ward, small town or suburb in with fewer than 30,000 voters, preparations of voter information can be assembled by hand from free maps and poll lists from the local Board of Elections and reverse phone directories. Reverse phone directories list phone numbers by street address and can be used at public libraries or borrowed from certain types of businesses which purchase them. Often a real estate agent will even donate the previous year's directory. By cutting and pasting information from these various sources, voter lists can be compiled for volunteers in as many as 50 precincts.

A second alternative for a smaller campaign is to hook up with a bigger one. A candidate running for congress, mayor or state legislature may be willing to provide smaller campaigns computerized lists in return for simultaneously distributing their campaign literature.

Third, a political organization or group of campaigns can purchase the necessary computer equipment, data, software, and staff jointly. As a twist on this approach, I encouraged a number of judicial candidates to share the cost of a mailing that I wanted to send to voters in my campaign for congress. They could not afford the computerized lists to do direct mail on their own, but together our joint campaign mailing reached more voters than any one campaign could afford.

Some campaigns now rely entirely on direct mail, public relations and mass media ads as their principal method of campaigning. If a campaign makes the purchase of the computer, data and software which produces machine readable lists, it can cut it's direct mail costs dramatically. First of all, it can do targeted mailings using volunteers. For instance, you can mail a pro-choice mailing to women in the district below 40 years of age or send senior citizen mailings to every voter in the district older than 50. This means that you can tailor your campaign message for particular voters with hot button issues most likely to win their vote on election day. Similarly, with these computerized lists a campaign can mail to wealthier sections of the district with a contribution pitch, pledge card and return envelope. The money a campaign gets back from such mailings can help finance other mailings in the district. A computerized list of voters also lets you send only one letter per household even if five voters live there, and it will let you personalize the letter for each voter.

A final form of voter contact used effectively by more and more campaigns is contact by telephone. Once again it means having as much information about voters as possible so you can target who to call. Either a professional telemarketing firm can be hired to do the work, or as with most participatory campaigns, volunteers can do the calling. The problems with campaign workers doing the calling is that a phone bank (consisting of from four to ten phones) must be set up, volunteers must be trained and supervised by a staff member, a careful pitch must be written, and the phone numbers must be generated. This campaign operation is expensive.

The best phone campaign is coupled with other campaign efforts. A direct mail letter to the voter should be followed by a phone call pitch. This double contact is often more successful than either the mail or phone call alone. Because voters are solicited all the time commercially, they now resist campaign phone solicitations. They know this is not just a friend or neighbor calling to chat. Professional telemarketing firms have found more and more answering machines and an unwillingness of people to answer the phones. Some have switched to Friday evening and weekend calling in an attempt to reach people at home. If you want to reach the voters and do not have the precinct workers to reach each of them at their door (or if you cannot get into high-rise apartment buildings with security guards), then a phone canvass may still be the best alternative.

ORGANIZING YOUR CAMPAIGN

Campaigns look so much simpler and more glamorous in movies than in real life. In *The Candidate,* Robert Redford makes a few speeches, gets covered by television, and wins the election. The problems of coordinating staff and volunteers, the tension and personality conflicts within a campaign, and the thousands of hours of hard work behind the scenes, is not conveyed in this movie version of campaigning.

Organizing a campaign with the right staff members, campaign reporting structure, the right equipment, and the right support services is a poorly understood part of winning elections. The task of recruiting hundreds of volunteers one by one is not seen by the voters or the media. This is a part of the nuts and bolts of the master plan, put into effect months and even years before the successful candidate finally makes his acceptance speech on election night.

Chapter IV

RAISING MONEY

Raising money, like recruiting workers, is done through personal contact, intimate social gatherings and campaign events. Before much money can be raised, you have to know how much is needed. To know that, you have to know something about campaign expenses and budgets.

The beginning point for fundraising is a campaign budget (see Table 4.1 on the next page). For illustrative purposes, I present three campaign budgets: Jim Konstantelos' losing 1995 aldermanic campaign in Chicago, Chicago Alderman Joe Moore's 1995 winning reelection campaign, and my congressional campaign budget of 1994.

These three budgets provide a sense of the costs encountered at different levels of campaigns. All three campaigns were run well with distinct strategies for winning participatory campaigns with a large number of volunteers. All of them had to raise significant sums of money. Generally speaking, staff costs, office expenses, printing, advertising, and direct mail consume most of any participatory campaign's budgets. The amount each requires, differs according to the type of campaign, spending of opposing candidates and the cost of media buys in a given media market, but these are usually the main categories of expenditures. The exact choices about whether to rely on direct mail, volunteer-delivered campaign brochures, radio, newspaper, or television advertising will be decided depending on the type of race, funds available and the most effective method of getting the campaign's message to the voters. In current elections, the cost of targeted direct mail has increased all campaign budgets dramatically.

A local election with a volunteer staff may be run for a few thousand dollars. A contested aldermanic election in a city like Chicago or a race for a state legislative seat will cost from $75,000 to $250,000. State legislative races in particular are increasingly more costly. Herbert Alexander in his book "Reform and Reality" decries the skyrocketing costs of state and local campaigns, noting that in California state legislative races now sometimes cost more than $500,000, and even in rural Vermont the median cost of a state Senate race jumped 50 percent from 1984 to 1988.[1]

Table 4.1
Sample Aldermanic and Congressional Campaign Budgets*

Category	Konstantelos for Alderman Campaign		Moore for Alderman Campaign		Simpson for Congress Campaign	
	Description	Amount	Description	Amount	Description	Amount
Staff	Campaign Manager; Office Manager; Four Field Coordinators; Staff and Volunteer Expenses	$10,000	Campaign Manager	$8,700	Campaign Manager; Public Relations Coordinator; Office/Computer Manager; Fundraising Staff (2); Field Director; Assistant Office Manager; Research Assistant	$96,898
Office Expense	Rent; Insurance; Equipment; Utilities; Phone	8,000	Rent; Insurance; Equipment; Phone Bank; Voting Contact Software	11,400	Rent; Insurance; Equipment (computers, fax, etc.); Utilities; Phone (two phone banks)	31,130
Printing	Basic Piece; Yard Signs; Buttons	6,840	Newsletters; Brochures	7,200	Campaign Brochures; Graphic Design	36,210
Advertising	Newspaper Ads; Billboards	5,000	CTA Posters, Other Posters	5,100	Posters, CTA Posters, Buttons Newspaper and Program Ads Radio Ads	11,812 1,995 11,268
Targeted Direct Mail	4 mailings	22,000		18,400	Special Mailings	19,982
Fundraising Expenses					Benefit Expenses: Invitations, etc.	14,431
Polling & Public Relations Expenses		8,200		8,200		15,500
Election Day Expenses		2,000		2,000		
TOTAL:		51,840		71,200		236,217

*Source: From the campaigns. Categories across campaigns are slightly different because of different accounting systems. Numbers do not add to totals at bottom of page because there were other minor categories of expenditure in each campaign.

Congressional races are even more expensive because the districts are larger and campaigns must rely on mass media ads and expensive high-tech methods to reach the voters. Most successful races against an incumbent Congressman since 1990 have cost $500,000 or more. The average incumbent Congressman spent $595,000 defending her seat in 1992. The cost of congressional elections continues to go up from 20 percent to 40 percent each election cycle.[2]

Just as a campaign is begun by determining the target number of votes needed to win the election, fundraising begins by setting a realistic campaign budget. In Chapter 3, the division of labor in campaign finance is outlined. The campaign manager and campaign chair help the candidate determine a realistic budget. The campaign manager spends whatever money is raised as effectively as possible. The campaign treasurer keeps the books, making certain that every campaign contribution and expenditure is legal. The campaign staff fund-raiser, volunteer finance chair and event committee chairs help the candidate raise the money necessary to win her election.

Votes cost money. There are high financial costs to get a campaign's message to voters. The first thousand votes are cheap—almost free—because 3 percent to 5 percent of the vote is won just by getting a candidate's name on the ballot. A hard-working candidate can gather from 500 to 1,000 more votes by herself. Then voters get progressively harder to reach. The next few thousand votes require a headquarters, staff and publicity. Within a few thousand votes of victory, advertising extras like bumper stickers, radio ads and direct mail campaigns must be bought. These cost much more money than early expenses such as printing petitions to get on the ballot.

Lawrence Grey in *How to Win a Local Election* describes the process of making a campaign budget as one of setting priorities.[3] First, a campaign's necessary expenses such as the rental of the headquarters, telephones and postage, salaries for staff, and office equipment must be established. It may be that some of these items can be legally supplied as in-kind gifts to the campaign. If so, you will not have to raise as much money as a campaign without in-kind contributions.

Once basic campaign expenses have been calculated, discretionary costs, which depend entirely on your strategy for delivering the message to voters— the cost of campaign brochures, direct mail, telemarketing, and radio and television advertisements—can be estimated. Optional expenses must also be determined and prioritized. If you raise $10,000 more than your basic expenses, you can execute your first priority. If you raise still more, the second priority, etc. But you have to execute each priority you can afford as completely as possible to win. As Grey emphasizes:

> *The important thing to remember is the priority given to each procedure. You may want to do a bulk mailing and radio, but what happens if you do not raise enough money to pay for both. You could do a little of each, but we do not recommend that. If your first priority is to do a mailing, do that and do it well. Spend all the money you get on the first priority item and when you have completed that, then spend whatever is left on doing as much of the second as you can.*[4]

In my first congressional campaign, we ran out of money for media advertising at the critical period of the last few campaign weeks. We began by spending our money on television buys. We got some free publicity on the television advertisements, but we could not buy enough time on the major stations to have the impact we wanted. So we switched to radio advertisements, which cost less. Altogether we spent $19,000 on media buys, but because the ads were split between the media, we did not have as big an impact as we needed. In my second congressional campaign, we spent all our media advertising money on radio ($11,000) and did not attempt to buy the more expensive television advertisements. This choice was strategically better. However, we still could not raise enough money to buy saturation air time advertising, and both my principal opponents were able to buy substantial television advertising. I lost both campaigns in large part because I could not raise enough money to carry out the plans in my original campaign budget.

DEVELOPING A FUNDRAISING STRATEGY

Once a realistic budget has established, raising the necessary funds begins. Hank Parkinson, in his book "Winning Your Campaign," quotes Iowa's Thomas Murphy as advising: "The best way to get money is to ask for it—the more people you ask, the more money you're going to get."[5] Or as Donald Page Moore, campaign chair for Illinois Constitutional Convention Delegate Bernard Weisberg put it, "If you're not afraid of losing friends, go to everybody you know—tackle them in the hall, phone them, write them a letter and then call them and simply say 'Give me money.' They will because it is right."[6]

Candidates who run for office each start with certain advantages. Some candidates like Ross Perot are wealthy and can buy the best staff and full media access. Others have the endorsement of a political party or a powerful interest group that will supply the necessary funds. But most candidates have to raise money by asking for it. So, a key prerequisite of running for office is that you are willing to ask people for campaign contributions.

The bias of participatory campaigns is to get as many contributions as possible from small contributors. Everyone who volunteers time to the campaign is encouraged to contribute as much as possible. Every piece of campaign and direct mail literature should have a coupon asking people to contribute their time and money. If elected, a participatory candidate will then beholden to hundreds or thousands of constituents and not just a few "fat cats" or wealthy PACs.

No matter how broadly based you want your campaign's contributor base to be, there are still some basic truths about fundraising. David Himes, in "Strategy and Tactics for Campaign Fund-Raising," lists these:

1. No campaign ever lost because the candidate spent too much time raising money.
2. Many campaigns have lost because they failed to raise enough money to implement a winning campaign plan.

3. No one can raise money more effectively than the candidate.
4. Do not rely on political action committees (PACs), direct mail, telemarketing, or special events with important personalities to raise money. Rely on personal solicitation.
5. Everyone loves to sit around and talk politics. But the real measure of your commitment to winning an election is the willingness to personally ask another person for a contribution.[7]

In this process, a candidate must be personally committed to spend more time and effort than she wants on this aspect of the campaign. And a campaign must have a specific fundraising plan. After the campaign budget is drawn, the fundraising plan is created. There are five principal sources of campaign funds:

1. The candidate and her family.
2. Individuals in the district.
3. Individuals outside the district.
4. Political Action Committees (PACs).
5. Political party committees.[8]

To begin the process, the candidate must decide how much she can contribute. If this race is expensive costing from $50,000 to $500,000, she might expect to provide 10 percent of the total to be raised. About half that amount will probably be needed as start-up, or seed money, to launch the campaign. The other half will probably be needed at the end of the campaign to help purchase the expensive media advertising. Often the contributions will take the form of loans to the campaign, which can be paid back if the campaign raises enough money. However, no one should make a loan which she and her family cannot afford to contribute outright. Some candidates make the mistake of mortgaging their house or going so far in debt that they end up bankrupt. Your candidate should not gamble more than she can afford to lose.

The second resource is family members, especially parents and wealthy relatives. In a federal election, each family member is limited to a maximum of $1,000 per election ($2,000 total for the primary and general election). Hopefully, several thousand dollars can be raised from family members *if they are personally asked by the candidate.* Here is the rub. Although it is emotionally hard for most people to ask their family for money, this must be done. A candidate's personal funds and contributions from her family are critical to providing the financial base of the fundraising effort. If she and her family will not contribute, getting anybody else to make a commitment will be next to impossible.

A candidate must overcome her inhibitions and "put the arm" on family, friends and complete strangers for the money to run a winning campaign. She must change her mindset about fundraising.

If she has committed herself, months of her life, her own money and her reputation, then she must be convinced that more is at stake than her own ego gratification. So asking people for money is not begging for a handout. Rather, the candidate offers everyone—family, friends and strangers—an opportunity to contribute to a campaign that will end some inequity, right some injustice, overthrow a tyranny, reestablish democracy, pass an important law, or end corruption and government waste. The reasons have been persuasive enough to get the commitment of the candidate, her campaign staff and volunteers. Now is the time to convince people to give the necessary funds. The chief job of a candidate is to ask for the money, understanding that she is offering others a chance to contribute to political change and to exercise their citizenship by contributing their money as well as their vote.

After a candidate has contributed her own money and received contributions from her family, the next step is to compile a list of other potential large contributors. In a suburban, rural or town election with a campaign budget of $25,000 or less, a large contributor may be everyone who contributes $100 or more. In a larger city, county or national race, a big contributor will be everyone who contributes $1,000 or more. For most of us who run for office, there are never enough people willing or able to become major financial contributors.

The candidate, campaign staff and key volunteer campaign leaders go through their personal address books (or computerized phone lists), and a list of every potential contributor is constructed. Those who might be large contributors are earmarked. If the candidate has run for office before, a list of previous campaigns contributors, especially those who might contribute even more this time, is pulled from previous financial report forms. These names are all organized as prospective donors, either on 3 x 5 cards or in a computer database.

The resulting list of prospective larger donors gets the campaign started. If there is a fundraising staff member (or in more local campaigns, a finance volunteer), she and the candidate religiously set aside at least two days a week to make finance calls. The fundraising staff member or office manager sees that a personalized letter with an individual salutation, candidate signature and personal note is mailed to the prospects. The prospect will then have some basic campaign information. A phone call or a personal meeting will still be necessary to get a contribution of a $100 or more. These calls are slow, hard work. All candidates avoid them if they are allowed to do so. But the price of a candidate avoiding personal solicitations is nearly always defeat.

Let us suppose a campaign starts with 100 prospects. After two weeks of phone calls and personal meetings with the few people who agree to meet personally with a candidate, only five people agree to contribute $1,000, another five give $250 and 15 give $100. You may be disappointed that you made over 100 calls and people who could afford large contributions gave only small ones or none at all. However, this is a terrific result. You have just raised $7,750! If your candidate keeps calling twice a week at this level, you will probably raise enough money to win the election. By phone calls and personal visits, your candidate probably raised more money with less cost than most campaign benefits.

Going after individual contributions systematically and consistently is crucial. Can anyone but the candidate do this? In some cases a campaign chair, finance chair, campaign fundraising staff member, and a handful of committed fund-raisers who have already made a major financial contribution themselves can make calls. Often, they can make initial contacts, but the candidate will have to "close the sale."

CONTACTING INDIVIDUAL CONTRIBUTORS

What about the people who could make a significant but not a major financial contribution? They too have to be asked. Who are they and how do you reach them?

Once again, you assemble a list of prospects. First, get a list of all the candidate's friends and friends of staff members and campaign volunteers. Then have your candidate ask for the membership or contributor list of any organization that has endorsed her. Next assemble lists of board members or contributors of any organizations to which your candidate belongs, even though they have not formally endorsed her and may be prevented from doing so by tax laws. If your candidate has run before, get the list of all the financial contributors and volunteers from those campaigns. The resulting prospect list will consist of several hundred or even several thousand names, addresses and phone numbers. Each family on the list is sent a letter announcing the campaign launch with a volunteer pledge card and a return envelope. Those who agree to contribute either time or money are entered into the campaign master database with the appropriate information about their gift or pledge. This first campaign mailing will net a profit of a couple thousand dollars even if the average gift is $25 to $50.

You can double or triple the response to almost any solicitation by having volunteers call to each prospect. They will either reach the potential supporters directly or make their pitch on supporters' phone answering service. These calls will encourage many more people to return their volunteer form along with their financial contribution to launch the campaign. Those volunteers reached directly can be invited to a press conference or campaign event where they can meet your candidate personally.

These contacts with prospects should be coupled with specific benefits, coffees and receptions throughout the campaign to increase both the volunteer and financial support. The idea is to get as many people as possible to make to make even a small commitment to the campaign, such as contributing $25, attending a coffee or working a few hours one evening at the campaign headquarters. Once they are on the campaign contributor mailing list, they can be solicited to contribute again. Often, later donations will be more generous, since the contributors will feel a part of the campaign. Some may contribute as often as every other month *if they are asked.* So, developing as large a list of supporters is critical to raising the money and the volunteers needed. Sometimes it is tempting not to contact someone who is abrasive or asks troublesome questions, but someone's pest may be someone else's donor.

CONTACT EVERYBODY

Only a very small percentage of Americans contribute to political campaigns and only a small percentage of those are major donors. Those who have contributed to previous political campaigns are much more likely to a new cam-

paign *if they are asked to do so by a candidate or someone they know personally.* So if other candidates have run before with the same general political philosophy or against the same incumbent or political faction, you certainly want
their endorsement. They can be listed in your campaign literature as a campaign
chair, honorary chair or citizens committee member. More importantly, you can
ask them for their list of contributors and volunteers. Your candidate should
contact potential major donors directly, and their other supporters can be added
to your campaign prospect list and solicited by mail and phone. Endorsements
by current elected officials are even more valuable in persuading voters to vote
for you and in sharing volunteers and contributors.

Based on the principle that prior political contributors are more likely to
contribute to a campaign, volunteers should check the financial disclosure
forms of other candidates who have recently run for office. While it may be
impractical or illegal to use the entire list of contributors, if your candidate
knows even slightly some of the individual campaign contributors on these
forms, they should be called personally because they are hot prospects. Thousand dollar contributors to another candidate may only donate $100 to your
campaign in the beginning. But they are a better prospect than someone who
has never contributed to a political campaign, and these past contributors may
well contribute more to a campaign later. Professional fund-raisers carefully
develop lists of generous contributors to past campaigns and major contributors
to charities. Your campaign must develop its own lists the same way.

Compile new lists of prospects every week. The candidate, staff members
and volunteers continue systematically to call these lists. This is how large
campaign contributions and many of the smaller ones are raised. There is no
other way.

INDIVIDUAL CONTRIBUTORS
OUTSIDE THE DISTRICT

Raising money from outside the district, other than from your candidate's family members, is difficult. As Himes writes, "If a campaign plans to raise a significant amount of cash from outsiders, it will probably have to focus on the
very wealthy or the very political."[9] If prospects live in your city or state, you
have a better chance of getting contributions.

People from other states have much less interest in what your candidate
may do as a state legislator, alderman, judge, mayor, or even as congressman or
congresswoman.

Potential contributors who live out of your district are also contacted by
direct mail and phone. Simple receptions held outside the district bring in
needed funds. In each of my races against Congressman Dan Rostenkowski, I
raised more than $50,000 from contributors outside my congressional district,
but most of these contributions were from residents of Cook County or from my
family members who lived out of state. While a few thousand dollars raised out-

side the district can help reach the financial goals of a campaign, very few candidates can win with individual outside contributions alone.

Obtaining lists and contributions from specific organizations that want to defeat an opponent or elect a candidate for her stand on key issues may be possible. For instance, because I am a political science professor, a direct mail and telephone campaign to Cook County college professors who did not live in the district allowed me to raise an additional $4,000.

Similarly, a senior citizen national organization concerned about inequities in social security payments to "notch babies" (those seniors born between 1918 and 1926) sent a mailing for me to their membership. This solicitation was financially less helpful but allowed them to urge seniors in the district to vote for me because of my position on the one issue. If an organization will provide a list, and particularly if they will pay for the mailing, a direct mail effort inside and outside the district builds support for your campaign.

A campaign can hold fundraising benefits among major donors in big cities like New York, Los Angeles, Washington and Chicago. For these to be successful, contacts in those cities must organize the event, to make it worth your candidate's time and expense to attend. Usually, such externals fundraising events are targeted to raise the last of the big bucks for radio or television advertisements.

CAMPAIGN BENEFITS

Depending on the level of a campaign, fundraising benefits can raise 25 percent or more of the budget. These days, it is not surprising when people write out $100 checks at coffees where a candidate has been particularly persuasive. At one coffee in my first congressional campaign, a neighbor of the hostess gave $1,000. In my second campaign, he and his wife gave $2,000, served on my finance committee, and hosted a successful modern art benefit at his home. Small campaign events like a neighborhood coffee can unpredictably lead to greater fundraising successes.

Most campaign benefits are larger and more formal efforts than coffees. Successful benefits must be imaginative, something people want to attend, carefully organized, and hosted by a benefit committee that agrees to sell tickets to the event—especially to friends, family and associates.

A successful benefit needs to be different. Ideally it should be something other than the usual politician's dinner. One of the most successful benefits of the Bernard Weisberg campaign was held at an architectural landmark in the district and featured a harp and piano concert at which the candidate himself played. A benefit that helped pay off the debt from my first congressional campaign was an Independence Day outing for major donors and their families featuring fireworks viewed from a suburban mansion on Lake Michigan. A larger, much less expensive benefit in my second congressional campaign was a salsa party at a jazz bar in the district, complete with dance instructor and band. Such events are much more appealing than a rubber chicken dinner with boring speeches in a downtown hotel.

Almost any event can be made financially successful if carefully planned. Here are some rules of thumb to consider in planning a benefit:

1. It should be different from any previous benefit.
2. It should only be attempted if there are at least six weeks in which to make preparations and sell tickets.
3. The main event or entertainment must be donated or inexpensive. When actors or performers are paid, the event soon costs so much that no profit is made. With donated talent, or with a big reduction in ticket prices at a theater, profit close to 100 percent is made.
4. The rental of facilities should be relatively inexpensive.
5. Special invitations, flyers and tickets should be printed for the benefit that make it seem special and worth the price (see the sample invitation on pages 55–56).
6. The price per person must be either relatively high ($50 or more) or relatively low ($25 or less). With the higher price, an audience of at least 100 should be the goal. With the lower price, an audience of a several hundred is desirable. If the lower price is settled on, more money can be raised by selling special sponsor tickets at a higher price or by selling advertisements in a program.

Every campaign will have fundraising benefits. If you keep the number of campaign benefits low, really concentrate on making those successful, leave plenty of time for preparations, and keep the overhead costs to a minimum, you can raise the money you need for your campaign.

Most money in local participatory campaigns is raised from small contributions of less than $100. Each person who contributes even $1 is likely to vote for the candidate and actively encourage other citizens to do so. So even in campaigns where more money is raised in larger contributions, small contributions and benefits are vital, and many contributors will also become coffee hosts, coffee chairs, office volunteers, or precinct workers.

Increasing the level of contributions should be a continuous process. In my first aldermanic campaign two decades ago, we worked hard to increase the number of $50 and $100 contributions through a series of luncheons. Many people who were far from wealthy were convinced at these events to make a larger contribution than they had previously given to political campaigns. During lunch, I discussed my campaign and what it meant to Chicago political reform. Then the host or luncheon chair told of our plan to get 100 $100 and 100 $50 sponsors. The host then asked those present to become a sponsor at these levels. At no luncheon did we raise less than $250 and, through a series of luncheons in 1971, we raised $3,500, or 15 percent of our campaign budget that year. Today the amount asked for might be greater, but contact with potential contributors in a social situation is still an excellent way to raise money.

Be part of the campaign's Last Big Event before the March 15th primary.

CABARET & DINNER

Sunday, February 27th. Come for the Afternoon, the Evening or Both!

Cabaret & Korean Hors d'Oeuvres at
Bando Restaurant
2200 West Lawrence Avenue 2:00 to 4:00 PM

WITH VERY SPECIAL GUEST

STUDS TERKEL

MASTER OF CEREMONIES

The Windy City Gay Chorus' very own
Bob Cooner & Michael Regier

The Artemis Singers, Chicago's
lesbian-feminist chorus

Sarajane Avidon, actor & wife of Dick Simpson,
performing a monologue as Julia Moore,
19th century poet

Larry Rand, a musical satirist who'll shed some light
on politics as we know it

Pam Morita, jazz singer & pianist

Marilyn Price, a puppetmaster, with a puppet government featuring our favorite freshman con-
gressman-to-be

Megan Vaughan, a storyteller who weaves
contemporary tales

& magic by The Amazing Michael

Dinner at
LaBocca della Verita
(The Mouth of Truth)
4618 North Lincoln Avenue
Cocktails 4:30 PM
Dinner 5:00 PM

DICK &
SARAJANE'S
FAVORITE SPOT
FOR ELEGANT
ITALIAN DINING

Featuring Owner & Chef Cesare's
specialties of the house:

Wine

Three Appetizers

Two Pastas

A choice of Three Entrees—
Chicken, Veal or Vegetarian

Dessert

Coffee & Tea

CABARET & DINNER — FEBRUARY 27th, 1994

Please make checks payable to Simpson for Congress. Reservations will be held at the doors.

☐ I'll join you for the cabaret at Bando Restaurant.

Please reserve _____ places @ $35.

Please reserve _____ places @ $60.

Please reserve _____ places @ $90.

☐ I'll join you for dinner at LaBocca della Verita.

Please reserve _____ places @ $100.

Please reserve _____ places @ $200.

Please reserve _____ places @ $400.

☐ I'll join you for both the cabaret & dinner.

Please reserve _____ places @ $125.

Please reserve _____ places @ $250.

Please reserve _____ places @ $500.

☐ I can't make it on the 27th, but I really want Dick to win!
Enclosed is my contribution for $_____.

☐ I'll be glad to mail letters to people in my precinct
encouraging them to vote for Dick. Please
bring me labels and a model letter on the 27th.

**For more information, call
Robin Epstein at (312) 866-1994.**

Name _____

Address _____

City _____ State _____ Zip _____

Phone Number(s) _____

Occupation (For the Federal Election Commission)

Employer 378

Paid for by the Simpson for Congress Committee, 2218 W. Leland, Chicago, IL 60625. Thomas
J. Gradel, President. A copy of our report is available from the Federal Election Commission, 999
E. St. NW, Washington, DC 20465.

Jonathan Abarbanel
Martha Ackerman
Sam Ackerman
Marilyn Adams
Joanne Alter
Connor Anderson
David Appel
Rena Appel
Bapu Arekapudi
Jeff Balch
Neal Ball
Jane Bannar
Lee Bannar
Richard Barnett
Harold Baron
Shelly Baskin
Elissa Bassler
Bob Bergazyn
Kay Berkson
Steve Bild
Tim Black
Zenobia Johnson-Black
Irene Blankenship
Vaughn Blankenship
Sarah Bligh
Michael Boyd
Belinda Bremner
Beatrice Briggs
Ruth Byrnes
Bob Calvin
Jane Calvin
Vicki Capalbo
Dan Casey
Lianne Casten
Lori Chacos
Gloria Chevere
Rev. David Chevrier
Tom Church
Cathy Colton
Brian Cook
Patty Crowley
Arthur Dahl
Betty Dayron
Natalia Delgado
Leon Despres
Pierre deVise
Camila Hawk Diaz-Perez
Larry Dieckmann
Scott Director
Danielle Drosdick
Joan Dworkin
Barbara Engel
Barbara England
Robin Epstein
Raymond Evans
Rhoda Feldman
Sidney Feldman
Wendy Fine
Bob Fioretti

Event Committee
(in formation)

Honorary Co-Chairs
David Orr
Miriam Santos
Marty Oberman
Joe Moore

Mark Fredrickson
Mary Gau
Ron Gibbs
Charles Golbert
Jonathan Goldman
Marsha Goldman
Michael Goldman
Jeanne Goubeaux
Kenneth Govas
Tom Gradel
Bob Green
Sue Green
Norman Guenther
Helen Gutlerrez
Susan Gzesh
Peter Handler
Bobbie Hargleroad
Buzz Hargleroad
Bob Helman
Bobbie Helman
Carole Helman
Stephen Heller
Jeanne Harley
Caroline Herbert
Myrill Hillman
Louis Hirsch
Scott Hochfelder
Katy Hogan
Charles Hogren
Michael Holewinski
Stan Horn
Bob Houston
Annette Huizenga
Tim Hulzenga
Jerry Jaecks
Sherry Jaecks
Dick Johnson
G. Alfred Hess Jr.
Michael James
Paige James
Tony Judge
Paula Kamen
Amy Keller
Margaret Kennedy
Winston Kennedy
Coralee Kern

Vartan Khachadourlan
Simi Lisa Kirsch
Steven Klein
Jewel Klein
Sidney Kleinman
Richard Kohn
Zinta Konrad
Cathy Kraus
Herb Kraus
Charles Kriesberg
John Kucera
Bill Leavitt
Cece Lobin
Peter Lortie
Edward Majeski
Edward Marteka
Kevin Martin
Rabbi Robert Marx
Lowell Mathes
Mary McCain
Bridget McGowan
Norma McLennon
Richard Means
Jerry Meltes
Ed Meyer
Vicky Meyer
Dan Miller
Michele Marie Miller
Judson Miner
Sarah Mulliken
Wiley Nickel
Afshan Noor
Rory O'Brien
Ellen Partridge
Juliet Pascual
Avlva Patt
Barrett Pederson
Wendy Pick
Bob Plotkin
Nancy Plotkin
David Protess
Joan Protess
Jane Ramsey
Bob Reed
Tobin Richter
Levy Rivers

Virginia Robinson
Stacey Ross
Jonathan Rothstein
Tina Raffaldini Rubin
Hank Rubin
Jeremy Warburg Russo
Richard Saed
Hannah Samuels
Elizabeth Schwartz
Lori Scott
Bill Seach
Donald Segal
Gail Segal
Amy Sherman
Felix Shuman
Thelma Shuman
Robert Siegel
Ruth Siegel
Kathy Slegenthaler
Wayne Slaughter
Renee Snow
Nate Snow
Mary Beth Sova
Jack Spiegel
Caryl Steinberg
Carroll Stoner
Stephen Swanson
Neesa Sweet
Jo Anne Sylvester
Denise Tennison
Kishore Thampy
Todd Thelsen
Gail Thompson
Carl Tintari
Joseph Tobias
Tom Tresser
Tom Tunney
Hal Turner
Susan Udry
Paul Vickrey
Jim Wagner
Darlene Watkins
Richard Watt
Jan Wegner
Rinda West
Dan Wheat
Ann Wheat
Fred Wickizer
Rev. Mollie Williams
Judy Wise
Jim Wise
Diane Witkowski
Susan Witz
Kevin Wolf
Stephen Wood
Nancy Worrsam
Quentin Young
Carol Zavala
Michael Zurakov

POLITICAL ACTION COMMITTEES

Obviously, political action committees provide an ever greater amount of money for campaigns. While PACs have become less critical in presidential campaigns and in those few local and state races with public campaign financing, they dominate congressional and increasingly expensive state legislative races. Normally, PACs do not fund local elections, but they may do so in the near future when local laws begin to have greater impact on businesses and interest groups.

Surprisingly, PACs provide an even greater percentage of the donations for state legislative races than they do for congressional races. Herbert Alexander, in "Reform and Reality" found interest groups funding about 31 percent of federal campaigns but as high as 74 percent of state elections (see figure on page 58).[10]

It must be decided up front whether a campaign will accept PAC contributions. In my first campaign to defeat incumbent Congressman Dan Rostenkowski, I pledged not to accept PAC contributions and used this stand to distinguish myself from him, since he was the congressional "King of PACs." In my second campaign, I dropped this absolute position and sought contributions from PACs promoting women's rights, gay rights, and liberal agendas. I did not seek support from PACs wanting tax breaks or regulatory changes for corporations. Many candidates take a similar position, although their definitions of good and bad PACs may differ radically. Despite contacting dozens of PACs, I received only $1100 in PAC money in my second campaign. If another liberal candidate had not been in the race, and my standing in the polls had been higher, I would have received another $10,000 to $20,000 in PAC money, because I had demonstrated in my first campaign that Rostenkowski could be defeated. PACs inevitably look for winners, and they fund incumbents at much higher rates than challengers.

David Himes provides the following useful advice about PAC funding:

> It is easier for incumbents to raise money from PACs than it is for challengers and open-seat candidates. . . . Nonincumbents need to plan to work very hard to get PAC money, **but they should plan on getting none.** . . . PACs will usually ask for some evidence that a candidate can or is likely to win. PACs will want information about a candidate and a campaign including committee name and address, the treasurer's name, distinct profile, voting history, primary date, opposition research, special interests group ratings, key personnel, budget, and endorsements. The campaign must give it to them.[11] (Emphasis added.)

Soliciting PAC contributions is not very different from courting individual donors. A campaign begins with a list of potential PAC contributors. At the top of the list go any PAC contributors with whom campaign leaders have personal contact. If the national PAC has a local organization or affiliate, a candidate needs the endorsement of the local organization or its leaders to get a contribution from the national group. So seek the local endorsement first, and the group will provide the name of the individual to contact at the national office. If a

Legislative Fund-Raising:
The Role of Interest Groups

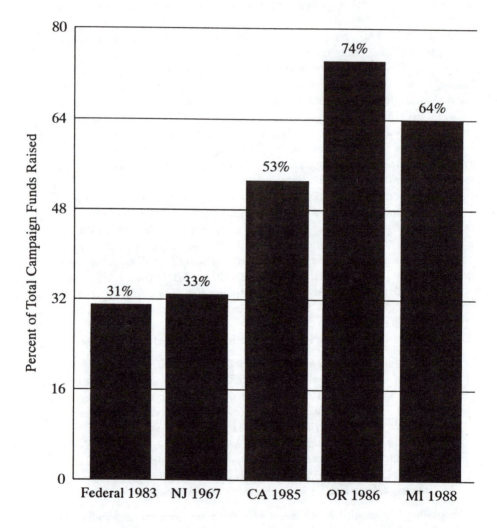

Percent of Total Campaign Funds Raised

- 31% — Federal 1983
- 33% — NJ 1967
- 53% — CA 1985
- 74% — OR 1986
- 64% — MI 1988

Sources: Herbert Alexander, *Reform and Reality* (New York: The Twentieth Century Fund, 1991), p. 20. Compiled from Federal Election Commission; New Jersey Election Law Enforcement Commission; California Commission on Campaign Financing; and Common Cause.

professional fund-raiser is hired, she should have a list of all PACs that might support your candidate.

Assemble a special packet of materials for each PAC. (Some have their own questionnaires to fill out). The packet will include a personal letter on campaign stationary selling your candidacy from their point of view; appropriate campaign position papers and campaign literature; evidence your candidate can win such as positive public opinion polls or returns from earlier elections; and a list of similar organizations which have endorsed your candidate. Then follow up with a personal phone call to the PAC staff member responsible for recommending what the PAC should do in this race.

Staff members from like-minded PACs meet with each other and frequently coordinate their contributions. So a key to success is to find at least one PAC staff member to endorse your candidate, make a contribution and agree to sell her to the other PACs being solicited by the campaign.

Our political system needs to be reformed to provide public campaign financing, set even stricter limits on PAC contributions, and prevent incumbents from being automatically reelected because of campaign finance inequities. In the meantime, many candidates will turn to PACs for contributions needed to run viable campaigns. However, if your candidate seeks PAC contributions and is not an incumbent, do not plan on receiving any PAC funds until the campaign has deposited the checks. Plan to use these funds only for discretionary spending, such as buying an extra radio or television ads. Do not depend on PACs for necessary expenses. In short, court PACs if your campaign decides it needs their support, but do not count on them to save your campaign.

POLITICAL PARTY COMMITTEES

David Himes has useful advice regarding the role of political party committees in a fundraising strategy:

> *Before any party money is included in a finance plan, all of the appropriate party committees should be contacted and asked for their criteria for making contributions to a campaign and for participating in coordinated expenditures. Typically the primary factors considered in these decisions are potential for winning, quality of the campaign, the campaign plan, extent of local party support, and extent of other local support. **Most campaigns overestimate the support the party committees can give them.**[12] (Emphasis added.)*

You will not get party funds until you have won the party primary or party nomination. Most local candidates find even then that they are expected to contribute to pay for party literature and joint advertising campaigns. Party committee funds become available only to candidates running in districts critical to the party winning control of a house in the state legislature or congress. Other campaigns often go unfunded although the general party effort to elect candidates to higher offices such as president, governor, and senator, and to get party voters to the polls may also serve in electing your candidate.

Receiving party contributions in cash or in-kind donations such as paid staff members sent to work in your campaign is great. However, most candidates must raise needed funds without much help from political party committees. Unless a firm commitment from the party is forthcoming, those funds cannot be factored into a campaign budget.

FINANCIAL REPORTS

Raising funds for a winning campaign is no longer enough. You must also file very detailed financial reports, often every few months or even every few weeks in the last days of the campaign. Your campaign is responsible for guaranteeing that all contributions and expenditures are completely legal. In addition to the moral reasons for this reporting, there are practical reasons: your opponents will carefully scrutinize your records. They can defeat your campaign if they discredit it in the media for failing to file a report on time or for accepting illegal or unethical contributions. In addition, there are heavy financial penalties, jail sentences, or forfeiture of election for violation of financial disclosure laws.

An entire section of the campaign has to be established to make these reports. The office manager or assistant office manager will record every contribution and expenditure, normally by using a special computer program geared to making financial reports, which makes printing the final report forms relatively easy. Day-to-day accounts are kept in another computer program like Quicken and then merged into the reports. But the computer does not determine if a contribution or expenditure is legal. That job rests with the office manager, candidate and campaign treasurer who signs the reports. Recruiting a CPA as your campaign treasurer whose sole duty is to insure that laws are carefully obeyed and the reports are filed on time is wise.

Candidates who have not run for office before often wait until they have raised and spent a lot of money before setting up the legal reporting system. This is a mistake. The reporting system should be in place as soon as a definite decision to run is made. The government will provide plenty of forms and copies of the regulations for campaign financial disclosure, but the campaign management must act to comply. Mistakes in raising or spending money (unlike some other areas of the campaign where mistakes are normal and expected) can cost the election.

FOLLOWING UP

When people contribute money to a campaign, they must receive immediately (within the week) a personally signed letter of thanks from the candidate (see the sample letter on page 61). For all but the largest contributions, a neatly printed letter using a computer mail-merge program is sufficient, as long as

Simpson
for
Congress

EXPLORATORY
COMMITTEE

April 22, 1993

Ms. Jane Doe
1234 Main Street
Anytown, USA 00000

Dear Jane,

Thank you very much for your generous contribution to my campaign to represent the 5th District in Congress.

Last time we didn't know where the district would be. This time we don't know when the election will be held.. Your support is crucial to our efforts to run an effective, efficient and successful campaign, no matter when it takes place.

Regardless of whether Rostenkowski resigns following an indictment and a special election is held 70 days later, or voters don't go to the polls until March, 1994, we know that we can win if we reach two key goals:

- Raising $100,000 more than last time and raising it early.
- Mobilizing 100-200 more volunteers to work the phones and precincts.

Whether I run against a weakened Rostenkowski or a group of less well-known candidates who split the Machine vote, I am clearly the front runner, which is a tremendous boost this time around.

Your contribution is helping us launch an aggressive, systematic fundraising effort. I nearly won last time. This time, with your help, we can go all the way to Washington.

Thank you again.

Yours faithfully,

Dick Simpson

2501 West Lunt
Chicago, IL 60645

the contributor's name is individually typed in the salutation. This letter must be composed carefully, updated every few weeks as new developments occur in the campaign, and signed by the candidate individually. People thanked early in the campaign can be called upon to contribute again later. Fail to thank them, and they will not contribute to the present campaign again or even to future participatory campaigns.

Your supporters will want to know how the campaign is going after you have sent the original thank-you letter. Write them at least once a month with a newsletter or solicitation letter. (A campaign newsletter can also be used in press packets, at news conferences as background material, at coffees, in letters to prospective financial contributors, and at other campaign events such as benefits.) You cannot expect a contribution of either time or money every time you contact past contributors, but if they feel they are a part of the campaign, they will help you win.

Chapter V

GETTING KNOWN

"Vote for Earl." A memorable scene from the film, *Blaze,* in which Paul Newman portrays Earl Long of Louisiana, focuses on handshaking campaign stops. Governor Long, with a police motorcade leading the way, stops at every country store greeting the voters and reminding them to vote for him. Other books and films like *The Last Hurrah* also portray old party bosses making the rounds of wakes and marching in torchlight parades. In both *Blaze* and *The Last Hurrah* candidates and officer holders are surrounded by aides, cronies, and supporters wherever they go.

Today's image of campaigning has not changed all that much. In the television footage shown during presidential campaigns, candidates address campaign rallies, take whistle-stop train tours or ride bus caravans across country. We see mayors and congressmen leading St. Patrick's Day parades or speaking at the annual conventions of organizations. So, a common perception is partially true, that campaigning is about meeting the voters, shaking their hands, being seen in parades, and speaking at large rallies.

The public expects this part of the campaign process, so it needs to be a part of your campaign as well.

THE LONG CAMPAIGN

Participatory campaigns with the greatest social impact take time to develop. Candidates may have to run more than once to get established, to convince voters of the flaws of an incumbent, and to raise major issues. In their first race they are defeated, but they come back later to win. Abraham Lincoln lost his Senate race against Steven A. Douglas, but became so well- known from the Lincoln-Douglas debates over slavery that he was elected President a few years later.

Modern presidential campaigns begin two to four years before election day. Even in local campaigns a choice must be made about timing. This choice will be determined by events as well as by strategy. Resources can either be spent in the critical weeks just before the election or used to begin a long campaign months or years in advance. Rarely, does a campaign have enough money to do both. In my first aldermanic campaign, redistricting caused me to be selected by the 44th Ward citizens' search committee only three months before the election. Successful campaigns of "reform" candidates in the ward during the two previous years gave me the base from which to wage a successful campaign in a brief period of time. On the other hand, when I ran for Congress in the 1992 election, I began in 1990 and built up my resources slowly. The downside of the long campaign is the amount spent on office, staff, mailings, and events over several years. Unfortunately, I did not have enough resources at the end for the paid media push necessary to contact voters finally focused on the election.

A long campaign, on the other hand, is an organic process. Like a plant, a campaign grows steadily from a small beginning. If a candidate can not begin with all the workers and resources needed to win, he can gradually build his base of support. It takes time to ask hundreds of people to volunteer and contribute money, and if a candidate is not wealthy or supported by wealthy interest groups, the process of reaching thousands of voters a few at a time can be very slow.

I have already outlined how a candidate decides whether to run for a particular office and described the startup office used to launch the campaign while keeping costs down. In Chapter 7, I will discuss the kickoff of the final drive, which begins with gathering nominating petitions to get on the ballot. There is a limited time when voter signatures can be legally gathered. In those months before a candidate's nominating petitions can be collected, he must decide how to campaign to build the resources for an eventual victory.

First, a candidate can raise money. Any candidate needs a lot of money to run a successful campaign. Exploratory committees are formed to provide a framework for raising early money. Your candidate, his staff and strongest supporters can write, call and meet individually with potential donors to ask them to give money to your campaign. This is always a good use of your candidate's time even though candidates never like fundraising.

A campaign research operation can also be set up early in the campaign and press conferences can be held decrying the actions of the incumbent, exposing problems in the district, and presenting legislation your candidate proposes to solve community problems. By announcing his exploratory committee and then his formal candidacy early, your candidate can become the front runner or principal contender in the race. This makes press coverage more likely and shapes news stories in a way that all other potential candidates are compared to your candidate. Once he is acknowledged as the principal contender, he will be called by the press for comments on any actions taken by others.

This beginning phase is also the time to get to know the district and to let people in district see a candidate fighting for something he cares about. In my first congressional campaign, we used a petition drive to put a referendum favoring term limits on the ballot. We did not collect enough signatures to convince the Cook County Board to put the referendum on the ballot, but it was a good way to launch my campaign. In my second campaign, we used a petition in support of a) congressional term limits, b) campaign finance reform, and c) eliminating mass mailings under the Franking Privilege during election years (see the petition on page 65).

PETITION TO THE CONGRESS OF THE UNITED STATES

We, the undersigned, qualified voters of the 5th Congressional District, State of Illinois, do hereby petition the Congress to undertake the following reforms to provide the legislative representation and fair elections provided by the Constitution of the United States:

1. To adopt a constitutional amendment limiting all Congressional terms of office to no more than twelve years;
2. To adopt a Campaign Finance Reform Act which eliminates Political Action Committee funds and provides for partial public financing of Congressional campaigns; and
3. To adopt legislation either to eliminate mass mailings under the Franking Privilege during election years or to provide equal mailing privileges for both Congressional incumbents and challengers.

Signature of Registered Voter	Print Name of Registered Voter	Print Street Address	City, Town or Village	County and State	Zip Code	Telephone Number
1				Cook County, Illinois		
2				Cook County, Illinois		
3				Cook County, Illinois		
4				Cook County, Illinois		
5				Cook County, Illinois		
6				Cook County, Illinois		
7				Cook County, Illinois		
8				Cook County, Illinois		
9				Cook County, Illinois		
10				Cook County, Illinois		

Affidavit of Circulator

STATE OF ILLINOIS) SS.
COUNTY OF COOK)

I, _____ do hereby certify that I am a registered voter and have been a registered voter at all times I have circulated this petition, that I reside atand am a registered voter
    (name of circulator, printed)

at _____, in the _____ of _____, County of Cook and State of Illinois in the 5th ongressional District, State of Illinois and that the signatures on
    (street address)   (city, town or village)   (name)

this sheet were signed in my presence and are genuine, and that to the best of my knowledge and belief, the persons so signing were, at the time of signing the petition, duly qualified

registered voters, residing in the 5th Congressional District, State of Illinois, and that their respective residences are correctly stated as above and set forth.

_____
(signature of circulator)

Subscribed and sworn to before me, this _____ day of _____, 1993 by _____

_____
Notary Public
SEAL.

SHEET NO. _____

With these petitions I went with volunteers to shopping centers, senior citizen centers and community meetings asking for support. I met voters, signed up supporters and recruited potential volunteers for what would become my future congressional campaign. Since these were popular issues, I gained the support of voters who had not met me before. The petition drive also gave me the opportunity to hold a news conference on "voter support for new laws to reform a corrupt Congress." In 1994, my opponent, Congressman Dan Rostenkowski, was an eighteen-year incumbent whom I had nearly defeated in my previous race for Congress in 1992. He had become after that election the subject of a grand jury investigation into a scandal at the U.S. House of Representatives Post Office. He was accused of converting stamps bought at government expense into cash for personal use. At the press conference on my petition drive to reform Congress, I was able to label Rostenkowski a "corrupt congressman" and to review the evidence in the post office scandal and as well as other newspaper investigative reports that Rostenkowski had converted up to $600,000 of government and campaign funds to personal use.

My press conference was held in August, eight months before the March primary at a time when no other candidates were active. Thus, I used the petition drive and resulting press conference to stake out my position as the principal challenger to Congressman Rostenkowski.

We also used the petition drives in both my congressional campaigns to create a field operation of precinct volunteers who could later carry my campaign's nomination petitions. Thus, we began to recruit through these early efforts the volunteer army necessary to fight the later, critical campaign battles in the precincts and neighborhoods of the district. For these reasons, issue petition drives are a good device for beginning the field operations of a long campaign. They provide a logical reason for recruiting volunteers and contacting voters many months before the actual election.

PERSONAL APPEARANCES BY THE CANDIDATE

In this modern era of mass media and targeted direct mail, a candidate still must make personal appearances to be elected, especially a candidate running for the first time or as an underdog. He not only needs to be seen by as many of the voters as possible, but he also needs to meet and talk directly with them to learn about the people he is seeking to represent. A candidate needs to learn about voters in ways that public opinion polls and electronic manipulation of voter registration data can not teach him. Voter contact will teach him about particular local problems that matter to voters in different sections of his district. These issues may differ from those which the office he is seeking has authority to resolve, but this direct knowledge will make him a much better representative of the voters.

As in the movies, it is important that a candidate be seen by the voters in a positive light throughout the campaign. They *and the press* have expectations as to how successful candidates look and act. Any candidate must meet those expectations.

Unless there is a special reason for casual dress, a male candidate will always be dressed in public in a suit and tie. Women's attire is similarly formal. A candidate may take off his coat, throw it over his shoulder, roll up his sleeves, or loosen his tie, but he will still be formally dressed. Candidates are clean shaven, although some wear a mustache if that is their style. I have had a beard at different times in my life, but never when I was running for office. Except for the dead of winter, candidates generally do not wear hats, because hats always convey strong impressions to voters, often the wrong ones. Hats can make a candidate look foolish and news photographers and television camera persons love to capture colorful pictures which can convey unwanted images. Former Congresswoman Bella Abzug of New York is probably the only major politician who has benefited from wearing wild hats. Most candidates are wise to avoid them.

Unless a candidate is a business person or lawyer who already dresses formally for work, running for office usually requires a shopping trip to buy a more appropriate wardrobe. A candidate running for a higher office may want to obtain the advice of a style consultant on exactly what to purchase. The consultant will cost less than a $1,000 and will have useful and surprising suggestions on how to improve a candidate's image. For lower offices, the clean formal look, carefully scrutinized by the campaign manager and public relations coordinator, will be sufficient.

Dress is one of the least difficult problems regarding candidate appearances. Potentially more problematic is the candidate's entourage. A candidate *never* appears alone at a public function, whether gathering petition signatures at a grocery store, shaking hands at a public transportation stop, attending a community meeting, or speaking at a political event. To project the image of a successful candidate, there must be accompanying supporters, even if this entourage consists of only one other person. In most successful campaigns, volunteer drivers also serve as supporters at campaign stops. To draw even more attention to a candidate, a news crew with a television camera will do the trick. If this is not a press event, a campaign volunteer with a videocamera that looks professional will also attract attention and can record an event for later use.

Drivers are among the easiest campaign volunteers to recruit. The job seems glamorous. They get to go with the candidate everywhere: press conferences, television stations and major political rallies. However, few people will serve as the candidate's full-time driver. Usually, campaigns recruit a different driver for every evening and for weekend days when there are many campaign events. Other drivers are recruited for specific functions like early morning appearances at public transportation stops. Frequently, two or more drivers will be needed to cover all the stops on a busy campaign day. (A sample candidate schedule for a week is provided in Appendix II.)

If a candidate has a driver, it is easy to add supporters as needed. When he goes to an editorial interview, his public relations coordinator or press secretary goes with him. When he goes to a debate at a community organization, his supporters from that community are in the audience, as well as the driver and staff members who accompany him. When he attends a coffee, he is taken by the driver and met by the coffee chair and hosts. When he marches in a parade, he joins a particular float or group that has agreed to let his campaign signs be carried in their section of the parade. At other events his family will join him. And so it goes. A candidate in public is never alone but always accompanied by supporters who, by their presence, guarantee that this is a genuine campaign.

For instance, if a candidate is gathering petition signatures at a grocery store, he should have three or four supporters with him. Usually, there are at least two separate doors to the store to be covered. The candidate can stand with a volunteer at one door and the other two volunteers can go to the second door. As each potential voter comes by, the candidate shakes his hand, introduces himself, offers the voter a piece of campaign literature, and asks him to sign the petition, which a volunteer has on a clipboard. Volunteers at the second door point to your candidate and ask the voters if they would like to meet him as well as sign the petition. The image created by having several campaign volunteers with the candidate is that this is a strong campaign for an accessible candidate. By the way, political lore holds that anyone who shakes a candidate's hand will vote for him, unless they are dissuaded by later information from the other side. So handshakes add up to names on your petition and votes on election day.

STAGED EVENTS

The purpose of staged events like fund-raising benefits is to recruit volunteers and raise money for the campaign. A good fund-raising benefit can showcase a candidate and build necessary support. No matter what the benefit, a candidate nearly always makes an inspiring and passionate speech explaining what is at stake in the election. His talk convinces people to support his candidacy. A large crowd of several hundred people convinces those who attend that they are not alone in supporting him.

Some of the most useful staged events in a campaign are debates or candidate forums before community organizations, which include citizen councils, block clubs, school councils, civic organizations, and senior citizen clubs. A candidate can make a major impact if carefully prepared for these community debates or forums. These events have the advantage of costing the campaign almost nothing.

Long before community organizations plan to hold candidate forums, your candidate needs to visit the community using petition drives at grocery stores and hand-shaking at public transportation stops. Beyond this, he should have met privately with leaders of the community organizations to discuss neighborhood problems and the programs undertaken by community groups and government to deal with them. Ideally, he will attend at least one meeting of the community group before any forum, to be introduced and to listen to the discussion.

Making all of these arrangements takes careful staff work by both paid staff and volunteers. In local campaigns, a separate community campaign coordinator will obtain the lists of community organizations. In larger campaigns, community coordinators will specialize even more, with one coordinator handling general community groups, another dealing with senior citizen organizations, and another handling school groups such as local school councils or PTAs. The community campaign coordinator calls community groups to find out when they meet, the names of their leaders and the key issues in each community. Working with the campaign manager and the office manager, the coordinator then schedules your candidate to attend community organization meetings and sets up meetings with key community leaders. Afterwards, he calls the organization back and suggests a debate or candidate's forum. The coordinator announces the candidate's willingness to participate and the dates he is available to attend. In nearly every case, the other candidates running will also be invited to a candidate debate or forum, but your candidate can still make a major impact in that community by his presence, careful preparation and knowledge of the community.

In a participatory campaign, at least several hundred volunteers or supporters will be willing to help elect the candidate. (Recruiting them is discussed in Chapter 3.) Before the community debate or candidate forum, area chairs in the field operation for this neighborhood call precinct volunteers and other strong supporters of the candidate and ask them to attend the meeting. Volunteers attend with campaign literature and volunteer cards to recruit anyone the candidate converts during the debate. The candidate shows up with his driver and some community supporters. Whatever the debate or forum format, he makes a strong statement about why he is running, his interest in this community, his knowledge of the issues in general, and his specific knowledge of key problems in this neighborhood. If the opponents fail to show up, the candidate gets the chance to convert the entire group. If the opponents appear, the candidate presents a positive case for why he should be elected. Usually, a candidate is wiser not to attack his opponents in these settings even if they attack him. If his opponents do not show up, he can, of course, note that he wants to represent this community, that he will work with this organization, and that his opponents do not seem to have the same level of concern for them.

Several benefits come from community forums. First, a good candidate's supporters almost inevitably convert a percentage of the crowd to join them as campaign volunteers. Second, the candidate will win some votes by a positive appearance. Third, he will generally be covered at least by the community newspaper because of the nature of the event, so whenever possible he should try to announce a new program or proposal at the forum. Major media like television stations are also more likely to cover a debate rather than just another press release or a routine news conference.

While in local campaigns there will be a single community coordinator to set up appearances at these events, in state or national campaigns more people will be involved. In presidential, congressional, or city-wide campaigns, there are coordinators for various groups such as labor, senior citizens and business. "Advance people" handle the contacts and logistics for appearances. Since these events are often covered by television, the advance people must run the event so the candidate will look good on television. Richard Dinkin, in his history of *Campaigning in America,* describes the role of advance people as follows:

> The attempt to achieve precision-like campaigning brought impor-
> tance to the role of the "advance men" [and women]. . . . These were
> members of the candidate's staff who traveled to future stops on the
> campaign schedule a few days or weeks before the candidate's arrival
> to prepare for the impending event. Instead of depending entirely on
> local officials to take care of details and certify that everything would
> happen according to plan, the advance man was given the primary re-
> sponsibility. It was his or her duty to check out the route to and from
> the planned event, look into any problems involving transportation,
> and examine the site of the event itself to determine whether facilities
> were adequate. . . . The advance man . . . worked with local leaders to
> deliver enthusiastic crowds and assured that the needs of the media
> contingent would be met.[1]

The major event format is very different from community forums. During the course of a presidential, gubernatorial, congressional, or mayoral race the only debates in which all candidates appear are a handful of televised debates. Normally, in the events arranged by advance people, a candidate gives a speech, holds a press conference, or is observed by the media and the television cameras touring a plant, a toxic dump or some highly visual site. Campaign strategists design special events like walking across the state, whistle-stop tours or bus caravans to gain media attention. Rarely do candidates in major races appear at smaller community events unless they are touring a day-care or senior citizen center to demonstrate their concern about a particular issue. In national as well as local campaigns, the importance of a candidate meeting voters face-to-face and being seen doing so, remains a constant however high-tech campaigning may become.

CAMPAIGN SCHEDULES

As many as three schedules may be needed in a campaign to coordinate both candidate appearances and essential campaign activities: 1) a master cam-paign schedule, 2) a coffee schedule, and 3) the candidate's personal appear-ance schedule. In modern campaigns, as discussed in Chapter 3, these sched-ules are stored in computerized form and printed out for those who need them. The master schedule is divided into several categories such as internal campaign meetings, candidate appearances, fundraising, public relations, and field work. During the early stages, events may be listed monthly, but as elec-tion day nears, weekly and day-by-day scheduling becomes necessary. Sched-uling is important, because with proper planning costs can be greatly reduced by eliminating overtime and rush orders on printing. Good scheduling also allows logistical and clerical support by headquarters staff and volunteers to be coordinated to provide the necessary assistance for all sections of the campaign. Finally, good scheduling ensures that each campaign effort is planned adequately.

The coffee schedule and candidate's personal schedule allow the candidate to speak where needed and ensure that his time is used to the utmost effect. For instance, a candidate can attend three to five coffees a night as easily as one, if these are scheduled properly.

A good campaign schedule is molded around deadlines (petition filing and voter registration deadlines, public relations production dates and election day), campaign priorities (debates vs. shaking hands at bus stops), campaign theme (like trips into the community personally to check on school problems), and the resources available (money and workers). Campaign schedules should include the thirteen steps listed below, which occur in every campaign. Of course, each campaign will have many other steps and deadlines. An example of a candi-

---

Thirteen Steps in a Participatory Campaign

1. Bringing together a citizens' search committee and locating a good candidate.
2. Preparing a voter profile based on census, prior election figures, and public opinion polls. Choosing your "target number" of votes which are needed to win the election.
3. Deciding upon a campaign theme and candidate image, creating the campaign structure, and selecting key campaign staff members and volunteer leaders.
4. Announcing candidacy and releasing first publicity. Preparing press packets and announcement news conference.
5. Beginning coffees and direct contact with potential donors by the candidate to raise funds and recruit volunteers. Beginning issue petition drives or other activities if this is to be a long campaign.
6. Opening headquarters, hiring full-time staff, printing buttons and first campaign literature.
7. Collecting petition signatures to put candidate on ballot and influencing other groups' (including political parties') endorsements. Putting out campaign literature through blitz, direct mail, and leafleting.
8. Planning and holding rallies, benefits, special events, and training sessions for workers; sending final campaign literature to the printer.
9. Canvassing to register voters and begin sending at least three direct mail letters/brochures if they can be afforded.
10. Intensifying coffees, candidate appearances, and media exposure.
11. Canvassing to locate voters favorable to the candidate, stuffing mailboxes, and leafletting at supermarkets and bus stops. Final direct mail is sent and phone canvass supplements precinct work.
12. Scheduling and training election day workers.
13. Election day: leafletting voters on the way to the polls, insuring that voters favorable to your candidate remember to vote, and poll watching.

date's schedule in a local campaign is the Simpson Aldermanic Campaign Schedule in Appendix II.

All of these efforts (petition drives and appearances by the candidate in the district, staged events like candidate debates, and the careful scheduling of a candidate's time) are meant to introduce the candidate to more voters. In larger campaigns, the tasks will be more specialized with different individuals filling jobs like scheduler and advance person. In smaller campaigns, the general campaign staff will assume these tasks. But there is a need in every campaign to present the candidate to the press and the voters in the most favorable way possible. This does not happen by accident. Parades, coffees, hand-shaking at bus stops, and debates on television are all carefully prepared in advance.

Chapter VI

WINNING THE MEDIA WAR

Public relations play a critical role in campaigns: in every political campaign, publicity is used to get name recognition for the candidate. Public relations are employed in participatory campaigns to attract workers and money, as well as to achieve candidate name recognition. The images and theme of a participatory campaign must therefore be powerful enough to attract supporters and must be successfully disseminated through press conferences, news releases and campaign literature. All of these activities must occur within time limits set by a tyrannical campaign schedule and governed by a sure knowledge of the media.

In participatory campaigns, public relations serve three basic functions: 1) to create name recognition and a positive perception of a candidate, 2) to attract workers and financial contributions, and 3) to distinguish a candidate and her programs from her opponents. Negative campaigning is the dark side of public relations. One candidate may need to be discredited before voters will vote for the other. The negative campaigning that opponents use to discredit your candidate must be countered.

DEVELOPING A MEDIA STRATEGY

Candidate image and a clear campaign theme are inevitably developed as a part of a larger campaign publicity plan and media strategy. One way to create such a plan is to answer the following questions:

1. Who will vote for your candidate and who will vote for your opponent?
2. Beyond the existing base of support, who else might vote for your candidate and what will persuade them to do so?
3. What is the image to be projected of your candidate and her opponent?
4. What is your campaign theme or definition of the situation?
5. How can the campaign inform the electorate that there is an election, create name recognition, and sell the campaign theme to them?

6. How can an opponent's images and definition of the issues be countered?

7. Given budget constraints, how can direct voter contact, media publicity and paid media advertising be employed to get the campaign message to the voters?

If you had unlimited funding, then manipulating the media to sell your candidate to the voters would not be a problem. Joe McGinniss documented this in "The Selling of the President, 1968."[1] He provided the inside story of how Richard Nixon was sold to the voters using Madison Avenue advertising tricks. Nixon's media people carefully crafted television commercials to win that election.

McGinniss writes that television was the way to present the "new Nixon."

But not just any kind of television. An uncommitted camera could do irreparable harm. (Nixon's) television would have to be controlled. He would need experts. They would have to find the proper settings for him, or if they could not be found, manufacture them. . . .

So this was how they went into it. Trying with one hand, to build the illusion that Richard Nixon, in addition to his attributes of mind and heart, considered . . . "communicating with the people . . . one of the great joys of seeking the Presidency"; while with the other they shielded him, controlled him, and controlled the atmosphere around him. It was as if they were building not a President but an Astrodome, where the wind would never blow, the temperature never rise or fall, and the ball never bounce erratically on the artificial grass. . . .

And it worked. As he moved serenely through his primary campaign, there was . . . a new image of him on the television screen. TV both reflected and contributed to his strength.[2]

The special technique developed for the Nixon campaign was for a panel of eight "ordinary people" to question Nixon live in front of a selected audience of 300 supporters on television. The program was created and telecast in 10 different regions of the country even though Nixon's answers to questions might remain much the same each time. This strategy along with the careful controlled production of more ordinary political commercials, was the heart of the packaged 1968 Nixon campaign. Most of the time, Nixon was protected from hostile questions from his opponent and a hostile press corps.

The Nixon story has been repeated thousands of times since the 1960s. With enough money for polls and television advertising to sell candidates the same way Madison Avenue sells soaps, mass media has been manipulated to sell candidates from city hall to the state house to the White House. Voters have often made pretty good choices between candidates despite the hype. But at other times, money, polls and paid media techniques have triumphed in electing less qualified candidates.

Any candidate running for higher office must use public opinion polls, stage activities to get media coverage, send targeted direct mail, conduct phone campaigns, and spend considerable money on paid advertising in the media. So what is the difference between a "synthetic" campaign like Nixon's and a participatory campaign? More cynical readers may ask, is there any difference?

Synthetic campaigns since the 1960s have been defined by three elements:

- big money,
- public opinion polls, and
- extensive use of 30-second television commercials.

In the 1990s, two additional elements have been added to synthetic campaigns:

- negative campaigns attacking opponents in ways that cannot be answered successfully, and
- targeted communications using cable television, radio talk shows, direct mail, and phone campaigns to reach segmented audiences with particular messages.

Synthetic campaigns distort the real personalities and qualities of candidates and pander to voters with a false presentation of issues. Elections are won with inaccurate or superficial information fed to the voters through slick media ads and duplicitous targeted communications.

Participatory campaigns depend upon both grassroots support from volunteers and a receptive electorate ready to embrace change. Participatory campaigns attempt to portray an honest image of the candidate, have less money than synthetic campaigns, and depend on volunteers to get their message out. Participatory campaigns employ public opinion polls, paid media advertising and targeted communications, but this is not the heart of the campaign. Participatory campaigns at their best are about fundamental change in politics and government, and they mobilize a large number of people to help get their message to the voters.

USES AND ABUSES OF PUBLIC OPINION POLLS

In shaping a candidate's image, selecting a visual and verbal campaign theme, choosing a slogan, picking issues, and devising a campaign strategy, knowing the attitudes of voters in the district is crucial. While your candidate, staff and campaign advisors may have personal knowledge of the district, they have not talked to the thousands of voters who live there. Public opinion polls are a way of finding out what voters think about the possible candidates and important campaign issues, and how they are likely to vote on election day.

According to Gary Selnow in "High-Tech Campaigns," there are four categories of polls used in campaigns:

A benchmark poll accesses voters before a campaign is launched. It takes a broad sweep of the issues and of the potential candidates. . . .

> *Follow-up surveys pick up on dominant themes . . . and track them*
> *through a campaign. . . .*
>
> *Panel surveys . . . monitor voters' movements through a campaign*
> *by returning periodically to the same respondents . . . [to determine]*
> *how thinking evolves over time. . . .*
>
> *Tracking polls are conducted daily among small samples to sense*
> *emerging problems or helpful trends that may evolve into significant*
> *factors.*[3]

In the most sophisticated "rolling-average tracking polls," a set number of voters are interviewed every night. Their views are added to data from earlier polls. The oldest data is discarded in the new totals. The results provide a constant track of changes in the public's moods. William Hamilton characterizes them as the "Dow-Jones stock averages for campaigns."[4]

Public opinion polls obviously have a variety of uses. Benchmark polls at the beginning of a race show where the candidate and her opponents would stand if the election were held today. However, if a candidate is challenging an incumbent or running for the first time, her name recognition will be so low that the poll cannot provide a realistic idea of how the election will turn out. After months of campaigning, she will be better known to the voters, and the election results may be radically different from any early polls. Even if the horse-race statistics are often unreliable as predictors of the final outcome of the election, benchmark and follow-up surveys can be used to test name recognition and candidate image for each candidate. Campaign issues and themes can also be tested in these polls to discover a theme or issue that would win the election if exploited properly.

Unfortunately, the most sophisticated polling techniques, panel and tracking polls that monitor changes in voter attitudes, are affordable only if hundreds of thousands of dollars is spent on television advertisements or direct mail. Since polls cost as much as $15,000 each and four weeks of tracking polls will cost as much as $50,000, these funds can be better spent on voter contact, direct mail or media ads in most campaigns. Tracking polls are especially useful if the message in media ads and direct mail flyers needs to change from week to week in response to changing voter attitudes.

If a candidate is leading or has stronger voter support than expected, or if an opponent is vulnerable, public opinion polls can also be used with: 1) the media to gain credibility, 2) with interest groups (such as PACs) to win endorsements, and 3) with donors to garner contributions. Nearly all campaigns that use polling conduct a benchmark poll at the beginning of the campaign. How many more polls they purchase depends on the money available, as well as on the need for poll information to direct their advertising campaign effectively.

The problem with polling is cost. A benchmark poll with 500 valid responses from phone calls to randomly selected voters cost about $15,000 in 1994. Two polls, one at the beginning to develop campaign and public relations strategy and one at the end to fine tune the message for final media buys, cost about $30,000. Panel and tracking polls cost considerably more. Local campaigns run for less than $100,000 usually do not purchase commercial polls. The rule of thumb is that polling should not cost more than 5 percent to 10 percent of the total campaign budget.[5]

One alternative to the high cost of public opinion polls is to lower the cost. A political science or survey research professor can design your survey questionnaire. If she is a campaign supporter, she may do it free of charge. If not, she will probably charge about $1,000 for designing, supervising and interpreting the survey for you. A random dialing list of voters to poll in your district should cost less than a $1,000. If you purchase computer voter lists for direct mail, phone canvasses and precinct work anyway, volunteers can randomize them easily enough at no cost. Campaign volunteers can also be trained to make the calls on campaign phone lines or a professional service can be hired to make the calls for $5,000 or less. Instead of $15,000, a scientifically valid poll can be done for the campaign at a cost ranging from $1,000 to $7,000. The poll will even have credibility with the media (and with donors) if the professor who designed it is willing to certify that it is valid.

Many campaigns do not have the volunteers or money to devote to polling. In these campaigns, testing a candidate's popularity and the salience of important issues is still useful. The strength of a campaign can be judged by the number of voters signing petitions to get your candidate on the ballot or signing petitions in support of hot issues like congressional term limits. Recruitment of volunteers and the level of campaign donations are very good measures of how well a campaign is going. Simple, unscientific polls can also be conducted by questioning people at grocery stores on a weekend. None of these methods provide as accurate a reflection of public opinion as polls. Experience and judgment on the part of the campaign leadership will have to suffice for races without resources to conduct them.

It is important to remember that obtaining information is difficult when relying upon impressions of the candidate and staff members. Many voters like to encourage a candidate when she meets them at transportation stops, grocery stores, coffees, and campaign rallies. A candidate is likely to overestimate the support she really has, because voters are polite and do not tell her that they are planning to vote for someone else.

No campaign ever has perfect information about the electorate and about how an election will turn out. Predicting the future is always hazardous. If campaign polls are not affordable, as much information as possible about voter attitudes should be gleaned from polls taken by the news media, universities and other candidates. Such information sources may say something about the mood of the electorate even if they do not give more valuable, precise information on a particular race.

CREATING A POSITIVE IMAGE

Public relations coordinators create an image for the candidate and the campaign. This image is necessary in participatory, as well as synthetic campaigns, if they are to accomplish the practical public relations goals of raising resources, informing voters, setting forth programs of change, and countering negative campaigns of opponents. Don Rose, my public relations consultant, explains the process as follows:

> *The important thing is to establish early an identity for the candidate, a point of reference for the candidate, assuming, as with most [reformers], that this is a guy [or gal] without a broad public image or a well-known personality to begin with.[6]*

It is crucial in building a candidate's image to begin with the real person, not some ideal type. A homebody cannot be made into a swinger or vice versa. Bernard Weisberg, a candidate for Illinois Constitutional Convention delegate, was a concerned, liberal lawyer who had been long identified with the American Civil Liberties Union. Therefore, his public relations coordinator, June Rosner, stressed his capability as a lawyer and his concern for the Bill of Rights in the new constitution. Because he was running independent of the Democratic Party, the image of an honest citizen battling the corrupt Chicago machine was also used.

Don Rose described the image projected for him this way:

> *The other reality, that is, the image of a man of the people, as it were— ordinary citizen fighting against the political machine [was stressed]. It is one that is necessary. . . . You do have a constituency of active people who are going to join such a fight, and you have to make clear that this is going to be one of those fights not only for all the good things in life and for constitutional reform, but a major battle, a chance to diminish or neutralize the machine that has been oppressing [Chicago] for so long.[7]*

In my two campaigns for Congress in the Democratic Party primary, we constantly stressed the contrasts between Congressman Rostenkowski and myself. Rostenkowski, in both campaigns, was being investigated by the federal government for corruption. I therefore emphasized that I was an honest reformer who would serve with integrity running against a "corrupt Chicago Ward Boss."

Rostenkowski was portrayed in the media as an arrogant official who ignored his constituents, while I, as alderman, had worked to encourage citizen participation. This difference between us was crystallized in an answer Rostenkowski shouted at reporters who questioned him about the Congressional Post Office scandal: "It's none of your business. None of your damn business." Throughout my campaigns, I maintained that government certainly was our business. Citizens in a democracy are meant to control the government, and public officials are expected to answer for their conduct to both the press and the public.

In my second campaign brochure, the differences were highlighted in "Three Reasons to Elect Dick Simpson:"

- **Dick Simpson** will serve with integrity.
- **Dick Simpson** has a proven record of courage and dedication to government ethics and reform.
- **Dick Simpson** is tough enough, experienced enough, and practical enough to fight for change in the currently corrupt and gridlocked Congress.

Rostenkowski countered my attempts to define the campaign with a simple image: he was powerful and he could bring home the spoils. "Rosty" claimed that his district, city, state and president could not afford to lose his clout as Chairman of the Ways and Means Committee. His supporters seemed to argue that even if he were corrupt, he at least had the clout to get them government services and programs. With the endorsement of Mayor Richard Daley and President Bill Clinton, Rostenkowski's definition of the issues won the primary campaigns of 1992 and 1994. However, after his 17-count indictment in federal court for corruption, he lost to an underfunded, unknown, Republican newcomer in the general election of 1994. His loss, along with House Speaker Tom Foley's, contributed to the Republican sweep that year. After three years of scandals and attacks on his record, he was defeated. But until then, his campaign theme and strategy had been successful.

It usually takes several elections to defeat an entrenched incumbent. Voters will eventually reconsider their support of incumbents if given clear reasons and good alternative candidates, but the process is slow.

In any case, a key to successful participatory campaigns is the ability to dramatize and distinguish your campaign from other races occurring all over the state, to signal to the media, voters and potential workers that this campaign is a major political battle worth fighting. Just getting better publicity than your opponent is not enough. First, the media and the public must be convinced the election is important, that something significant is at stake. Then media coverage becomes accessible.

Bernard Weisberg distinguished himself from other candidates by filing a lawsuit charging that the Illinois Secretary of State unfairly gave friends and party regulars valuable positions at the top of the ballot, positions guaranteed to win them several hundred additional votes from voters who vote for the first name they see on the ballot.

Action attracts attention and coverage in the media. Before his campaign had barely begun, Weisberg jousted with one of the most powerful political bosses in the state. Winning his court case not only brought good publicity for months to come, but it opened up the electoral process for other candidates. Weisberg himself was moved up from fifth place to second in the drawing for ballot position. This kind of demonstrative action reinforces the image of a candidate and his campaign.

In my first aldermanic campaign, I introduced a citizen ordinance to curb the mayor's power in making school board appointments. In both my congressional campaigns, I began with petition drives to reform Congress. In developing a public relations plan, determining what image of the candidate to project is not enough. It is not enough to make clear contrasts with your opponent. You must dramatize the differences between candidates by your actions. Then press releases, press conferences and campaign literature can reinforce the image projected.

A candidate's image must also be solid and truthful enough to withstand negative attacks. Michael Dukakis' 1988 image as the governor of Massachusetts, the "Economic Miracle State," could withstand neither the Willie Horton advertisements that portrayed him as soft on criminals nor the advertisements of a polluted Boston Harbor that undermined his image as ecologically concerned. His own campaign even posed him foolishly like "Rocky the Squirrel" riding on top of a military tank in one campaign event.[8] In the face of these negative campaign attacks and his own campaign mistakes, his image as a smart, able chief executive concerned with issues that mattered to the American voters did not hold. Most political experts concluded that Dukakis should have quickly answered the negative ads from his opponent with a response in the same media. He failed to do so and lost the election.

Bill Clinton's 1992 image as a "New Democrat" governor concerned with the economy and the fate of common people withstood attacks on him as a womanizer and as a draft dodger. Despite the attacks of primary opponents and President George Bush, voters elected him. His quick response to attacks as they came is one of the reasons that his campaign prevailed.

Before developing campaign issues, a solid image for the candidate must be created and a clear definition of your campaign formulated. Shaping that image is the task of the candidate, campaign manager, public relations coordinator and public relations consultants. Failing to do so or allowing an opponent's portrayal of the candidate to go unanswered will surely lose the election.

Despite creating a positive and truthful image of your candidate, the media does not always buy it. The media mediates information, rather than bringing reality to its audience directly. In my aldermanic campaigns and in my role as alderman, I most often received positive coverage and was portrayed as a reformer. In my congressional campaigns, the media sometimes portrayed me as sure to lose because of Rostenkowski's power, and some political commentators agreed with my opponent's characterizations of me as a wild-eyed radical out of touch with this working class district. As my experiences demonstrate, media portrayal of a candidate can not be entirely controlled, but there is a much better chance of getting your message to voters if a consistent image is developed and projected clearly.

THE USES OF A CAMPAIGN THEME

A campaign theme unifies the campaign and defines the battleground. It briefly conveys information about the character of a candidate and the issues at stake. The theme may be simplified into a slogan or it may remain implicit in the campaign literature. For example, in the campaign to elect John Stevens to the Chicago City Council, his literature stressed the simple theme: "Stevens for change." In a district represented by only white, conservative representatives of the Democratic Machine, his slogan reflected that an independent black candidate was running who wanted to heal the racial breach in the ward and eliminate machine domination.

Another example of explicit campaign themes was the wording of a poster in the Eugene McCarthy campaign for President in 1968. He was running against President Lyndon Johnson in the Democratic primaries on the issues of ending the Vietnam War, promoting civil rights, and reforming the "imperial presidency" at home. His poster carried the simple inscription: "He stood up alone and something happened." The lone figure of McCarthy standing on a brick courtyard and this slogan captured Senator McCarthy's courage in putting his political career on the line to challenge an incumbent President of his own party and the chain of successful, grass-roots primary battles that had followed.

The choice of a theme is particularly important *in defining the issues so a majority of citizens identify with a candidate.* Thus, a candidate is presented to the voters as a qualified, good government candidate rather than as an idealistic radical. While a candidate may take stands on important issues, cutting the issues, and defining the alternatives, in a way that most citizens can support her is critical. A candidate should be distinguished from opponents in strongly positive terms: an honest person vs. a crooked politician; a reformer vs. a corrupt political machine; peacemaker vs. warmaker; competence vs. incompetence; a representative of the people vs. a captive of special interests.

While the stress is primarily placed upon a candidate's positive characteristics rather than on their opponent's faults, the contrast between candidates is important. Nor do these themes have to be made verbally explicit or sloganized in every case. Buttons and posters used primarily for name identification and encouragement of campaign workers often bear only a candidate's name and the office she is seeking. Even in campaign literature, verbal slogans may not be necessary to make a point, although they often will be used. If a verbal slogan is used, it should be the same phrase every time. Repetition is very important and conflicting themes undermine the entire effort.

Joel Bradshaw in "Campaigns and Elections American Style" defines a campaign theme as "*the rationale for your candidate's election and your opponent's defeat.*" He advises that there can be only one theme, not multiple themes, because, "You can get one point through to voters who think about this [election] five minutes a week or less." The best theme is your candidate's response to the question, "Why are you running?" Bradshaw concludes that a good campaign theme answering this question has six characteristics: "It must be clear, concise, compelling, connected, contrasting, and credible. It helps also if it can be communicated in an easily understandable and memorable way."[9]

The secret of a public relations plan is "the repetitive communication of your campaign theme."[10] The theme is repeated in the campaign literature, paid commercials, debates, speeches and press releases. It is like a lawyer building a case for her client, who keeps pounding it home in as many ways as possible.

Joseph Napolitan in *The Election Game* argues that there are only three steps to winning an election:

> *First, define the message the candidate is to communicate to the voters.*
>
> *Second, select the vehicles of communication.*
>
> *Third, implement the communication process. . . .*
>
> *A campaign can break down on any one of these three steps, but more likely it will break down on the first one: defining the message. Candidates often are unclear in their own minds precisely what it is they want to say to voters, or even why they are running.*[11]

The failure to define the message or campaign theme is often the underlying cause of losing campaigns. A lack of resources to communicate the campaign message is the next most likely cause of defeat.

The theme of a campaign should be expressed visually as well as verbally. While only limited control is exercised over coverage by the media, complete control over the image portrayed by buttons, brochures and posters is possible. Carefully selecting visual themes early and continuing to use them throughout the campaign for maximum effect is very important. These graphic choices include color, typeface for the candidate's name, photographs, and general design. In making decisions about visual themes several rules apply:

- Keep it simple.
- Emphasize the candidate's name.
- Make all campaign materials easily identifiable.
- Make your graphic designs distinctive but not wild.

In my campaigns for congress we used a large blue button with reverse (white) lettering. The typeface is a slightly modified Bookman Bold. To make my name just a little different, the "i" in Simpson is dotted with a star. The result is a bold, clear, easily readable button identifiable at a distance. Like

many campaigns, we used red, white and blue flag colors in various combinations in all my campaign literature and posters. However, the blue was deeper and the red was brighter and softer than American flag colors. We used only blue and white for the button and much of the campaign literature because it was distinctive and less expensive to print than three colors. In my campaign brochure, all three colors were used along with black for the photographs and some headlines. Whatever the typeface and campaign colors, they must be used consistently in all material. Colors and typeface should not be switched after the campaign begins unless the first efforts were totally amateurish and a standard is being established for the first time.

PUBLICITY

The battle to gain maximum publicity for a candidate involves two important restrictions. First, the publicity effort must be an integral part of the entire campaign, not a side activity in the hands of a single specialist. Publicity and the art of communicating through the media are simply other methods of recruiting workers and winning votes. Major publicity decisions are basic to the campaign as a whole, and often involve the entire leadership, because there cannot be one campaign theme and another set of public relations themes. The best campaigns have a single unified theme developed and exploited by publicity, as well as by other campaign efforts.

Second, in developing a publicity campaign the single most important asset, besides a worthy candidate, is good judgment as to the newsworthiness of any event or announcement. News worth only a column note should not be sent as a major press release. Press conferences should not be called when an exclusive interview with a single reporter is more appropriate. Information developed for internal campaign use or for direct contact with the voters may be inappropriate for public announcements. Nor are targeted direct mail appeals to particular voters sent out as general press releases to mass media.

The publicity effort in a campaign thus involves a series of careful judgments as to what information is worth communicating, to whom, when, and through what media. Information about stupid things your opponent has said or marvelous things your candidate has done must be released in ways that have the maximum affect in building your campaign, communicating its purpose, and winning on election day. Without a thorough knowledge of the peculiarities and potential of different media, without experience in media coverage, without the advice of a professional public relations expert, these judgments will be difficult.

Participatory campaigns are not won by press conferences alone. With thousands of campaigns occurring simultaneously and with Federal Communications Commission rules requiring equal time for candidates in many media situations, constant coverage is impossible to obtain. So public relations coordinators must also rely on the more ordinary news release, interview, column note, and letters to the editor to keep a candidate's name in the news. A model press release used in the Adlai Stevenson III campaign for U.S. Senate in Illinois is included below as an example of the proper format for a news release.

The public relations process begins long before the first press conference, even before the first story is written about a candidate. After a public relations plan has been agreed upon, the public relations coordinator assembles a press packet in an attractive folder with the candidate's name and a campaign logo on the cover. The press packet usually contains the following items:

SAMPLE PRESS RELEASE

CAMPAIGN COUNTY
CITIZENS FOR STEVENSON COMMITTEE

July 15, 1970
For immediate release:

20th STEVENSON HOME
HEADQUARTERS OPENED IN URBANA

Urbana, IL, July 15—Joe Doe, Coordinator of the Champaign County Citizens for Stevenson Committee, today announced the opening of the county's 20th Stevenson Home Headquarters.

The newest Headquarters is located in the home of Mr. and Mrs. Jack Philips of 1413 E. Jackson Ct., Urbana. The Home Headquarters is designed as a neighborhood distribution point for organizing volunteer workers for Adlai Stevenson III, Democratic candidate for the U.S. Senate.

The Headquarters "grand opening" will be Sunday, July 18, from 2:00–4:00 P.M. The general public is invited to attend.

                                    For further information:
                                    Joe Doe
                                    217-694-3215 (Champaign)

- A one-page biography of the candidate (see next page).
- A campaign button. Reporters, despite their "neutrality," are fond of collecting buttons, so one should be included. In addition, a button demonstrates that a campaign has graphic expertise, volunteers to wear the button, and the money to pay for basic campaign materials.
- A press release or full statement of your candidate's declaration of candidacy.
- Campaign literature (a brochure or campaign newsletter).
- One-page position papers on central issue(s) of the campaign.
- A black and white glossy photograph (head shot) of the candidate.

These press packets are given out at the announcement press conference and then updated with new material and newsclippings as background briefing materials for the press throughout the campaign. After the announcement press conference, the candidate and public relations coordinator meet separately with the major news media and with the political reporters covering campaigns. The public relations coordinator arranges for these visits and ensures that the reporters get press packets that provide background information and a photograph for future articles.

After political editors and reporters meet the candidate and information about their deadlines and news needs has been obtained, a steady stream of press releases, usually two or three a week, are sent (usually by fax) to the media. Any special media needs are also met. For instance, television stations need color photographs of your candidate if they are covering this race in depth.

The key to obtaining coverage by the media is to supply effective news releases. The media will only use a release if it contains "news." The best news is that someone did something provocative or original. The following are examples of the kinds of actions around which we built press releases that became news stories during my congressional campaigns:

Former Alderman Dick Simpson today called for a federal investigation of Congressman Dan Rostenkowski for making $37,750 in illegal campaign donations just before the Democratic primary election last March. . . .

Former Chicago Alderman Dick Simpson today launched a drive to collect voters' signatures on a petition calling for three new laws designed to help eliminate corruption in Congress. . . .

Former Alderman Dick Simpson today announced his candidacy for Congress and challenged incumbent Congressman Dan Rostenkowski to make full disclosure of his personal finances including what is hidden in Rostenkowski's secret "blind trust." Simpson, who today made public his income tax returns, his assets and liabilities said he was entering the campaign "not just to weed out one corrupt congressman, but also to change Congress."

Dick Simpson

In the mid 1960s at Texas A&M University, which was then a military academy, Dick Simpson was a lone protester against the cruel mistreatment of a classmate. Simpson stood his ground despite being ostracized by fellow cadets.

And throughout his career, Dick Simpson has fought against the odds for fairness, democracy and empowerment. "I want to create whatever is necessary to give people the most power over their lives...," Simpson says.

When he came to Chicago in 1967 to teach at the University of Illinois at Chicago, Dick Simpson brought with him both his ideals and the strength and savvy to bring them about.

He founded Chicago's Independent Precinct Organization (IPO) in turbulent political times. IPO quickly won major victories in key campaigns.

In his own first campaign for political office, he surprised political observers and won election as Chicago's 44th Ward Alderman, despite a well-financed opponent with an army of precinct captains.

Once in office, Simpson created the unprecented 44th Ward Assembly whose goal was empowerment of his constituency. He established the 44th Ward Service Office which handled several thousand constituent service requests each year.

As Alderman, Simpson consistently voted for and introduced reform legislation—occasionally persuading old-line aldermen to cross over as well. Results include:

- Ending salary discrimination in the city budget for women holding the same jobs as men
- A City Council resolution urging Illinois passage of the Equal Rights Amendment
- Budget amendments to provide more money for day care
- Additional budget amendments to speed the opening of day care centers
- Programs to help the homeless and the hungry

- The elimination of bank redlining
- The extension of Senior Citizen public transportation hours

Dick Simpson served the 44th Ward for two terms before voluntarily retiring in 1979. As a private citizen, he continued to work in arenas where he could put his ideals to work.

As Chair for the Illinois Coalition Against Reaganomics, he worked to keep funding for social and educational programs, including the crucial WIC programs, which provided milk and other nutritional food to women and their infant children.

From 1987 to 1989 Simpson was Executive Director of Clergy and Laity Concerned of Metropolitan Chicago. He was an organizer and spokesperson for CALC's numerous peace and justice activities.

Dick Simpson served on transition teams that advised Mayor Jane Byrne in 1979, Mayor Harold Washington in 1983, and Cook County Clerk David Orr and State's Attorney Jack O'Malley in 1990. He helped shape their positions on ethics, fair hiring practices and citizen participation.

Dick Simpson is a practical politician. He organizes, advocates and persuades. He has introduced, shaped and passed numerous pieces of legislation. He is also a political scientist who knows how to analyze and test political action.

In the past 20 years, Dick Simpson has published numerous studies of voting patterns of elected officials and of government budgeting processes. He is the author or co-author of nine books on political action, politics and ethics, including *WINNING ELECTIONS* (1972), *THE POLITICS OF COMPASSION AND TRANSFORMATION* (1989), and *CHICAGO'S FUTURE IN A TIME OF CHANGE* (1993).

In 1992 Dick Simpson ran for Congress in Illinois' 5th Congressional District on a platform of congressional reform, women's rights, universal health care, economic recovery and senior citizens' issues. In the Democratic Primary he received 42,000 votes.

Simpson and his wife, Sarajane, are the parents of two teenagers, one in high school and one in college.

Dick Simpson
2218 W. Leland, Apt. 2, Chicago, IL 60625-2006
312/413-3780 or 312/728-1110

The National Organization for Women's Political Action Committee, Cook County Democratic Women and numerous women political and community leaders have endorsed Dick Simpson for Congress for the 5th District of Illinois.

Once there is news, some action to be taken or announced, a few simple rules should be followed for writing a news release in the form most likely to be accepted by the media. Hank Parkinson in his article in *Campaign Insight*, suggests these rules for press releases:

1. *Make sure the release carries a name and phone number in case additional information is needed.*
2. *Include release instructions. (Is the editor to hold it for a day or two or can it be used immediately?)*
3. *Include plenty of white space between the release instructions and the copy start so a headline or instructions to the back shop can be jotted in.*
4. *Keep the margins wide.*
5. *Double-space. (Never turn in a release that isn't typed.)*
6. *Never continue a paragraph from one page to another. (Use the word "More" when continuing a story to the second page.)*
7. *Keep the lead paragraph under 30 words in length, and never use more than three sentences per paragraph.*
8. *End the story with the symbol: -30- (this is journalese for "The End").*[12]

After reading these simple instructions, it might seem that an inexperienced volunteer could be put in charge of publicity. But public relations is more than just calling press conferences or drafting news releases. Successful public relations results in a candidate being interviewed by reporters, appearing on television and radio programs, and campaign notes appearing in society or gossip columns. Success requires knowing members of the working press and, more importantly, knowing the way the press works. A professional public relations person is much more likely to have personal contacts and to know deadlines and normal press procedures. With lots of perseverance and hard work, a non-professional can make contacts, learn the trade and get some coverage, but it will be harder than it would be for an experienced, full-time professional in the field.

In mounting a professional publicity campaign, simple and natural techniques that can gain great exposure for a candidate should not be overlooked. As we discussed in Chapter 5, drawing an opponent into a debate is often advantageous. Begin with simple debates in front of community organizations. Many groups will be only too pleased to hold a debate. After all, they have the problem of dull meetings to overcome and holding a debate is a public service, not taking sides. Your opponents will find it difficult to turn down the request of a legitimate organization. Later, you may be able to use the debate format to get television and radio exposure.

In my first campaign to unseat Congressman Rostenkowski, he refused to debate before community organizations and turned down invitations for formal television debates, but he did agree to separate back-to- back television interviews with the same reporters. I gained considerable positive publicity and credibility from these "debates."

Letters to the editor are often overlooked as a source of publicity. A candidate or her campaign workers can write several letters to all newspapers in the district. The published letters are often read by more people than the news or the editorials. As with everything in a campaign, there are successful and unsuccessful ways of doing the job. For best results, the Stevenson for U.S. Senator campaign suggested that volunteers abide by the following rules:

Do's

1. *Use the Stevenson brochure and other materials sent to you by the Citizens Committee as your reference material.*
2. *Always be sure of your facts.*
3. *Always be polite and objective. An earnest, honest statement with the ring of conviction can draw respect even from those who disagree with its content.*
4. *Write your own letter, in your own words. Make it brief, neat, and clear. Get your point across, then stop. The best letters run between 100 and 200 words, no longer. Long letters will not be printed.*
5. *Sign your name and address.*

Don'ts

1. *Don't write hot-tempered letters, or engage in personal attacks on the editor, or reporters. Avoid extreme statements.*
2. *Don't mail any letter that is unsigned. If you can't sign it, don't send it.*
3. *Don't copy other letters. Organized write-in campaigns have no effect. They can be detected instantly.*
4. *Do not assert as a fact anything that you cannot document.*
5. *Do not attack the newspapers. They always have the last word.*[13]

NEWS CONFERENCE

The news conference is especially useful as a communications tool, because it allows television and radio coverage of your candidate. But remember that unless your candidate is the incumbent governor or President, coverage will be limited. In some campaigns, you may never develop sufficient news to call a legitimate news conference. In most major cities, where the large number of simultaneous campaigns makes the battle for media attention fierce, one or two well-covered news conferences are all that can be expected. A simple news assignment memo on campaign stationery telling the time, place and purpose of the conference should announce it. In major cities, this same information must also be sent on the local news wire and faxed to every political reporter and news assignment editor in town. Other than news conferences that require a special location such as the opening of a headquarters, most are held at a downtown hotel or in the City Hall press room. After the memo has gone out, all major media are called and reminded of the conference. At early morning news conferences, coffee and sweet rolls should be provided to those in attendance.

The memorandum prepared by Tom Gradel and Ronni Scheier of Gradel & Associates for members of the National Association of Neighborhoods covers the basic rules for conducting a news conference (see pp. 91–93). News conference preparation begins with the news judgment that something the candidate has done (introducing a citizen's ordinance on an important issue or filing suit in federal court) or has had done to her (the campaign headquarters has been bombed) is of sufficient importance to justify a news conference. In addition to preparing the news assignment memo announcing the press conference, the public relations coordinator prepares a statement to be read by the candidate and a news release written as if it were a news story about the conference. The candidate should know the content of the statement thoroughly enough to deliver it without having to read it line by line. But a detailed formal statement to the press and the public is still handed out to the reporters even if parts of it are paraphrased by the candidate in her presentation.

Immediately after answering questions of the press who attend the news conference, the candidate calls those radio stations that take news interviews over the phone. The public relations coordinator calls the television stations that fail to cover the conference and asks if they would like to interview the candidate from the campaign office or in the television studio later in the day. Television coverage is golden and usually television stations use footage made with their limited crews, so any opportunity to restage the news event for television is instantly agreed to by the public relations coordinator even if it means an extra effort on the part of the candidate.

In a news conference, the "news" aspect should be viewed from the perspective of the reporters who cover it and their editors. *Does this action affect the lives of many people?* For instance, the President, governor, or mayor announcing new taxes that they propose to enact is always news. *Is the action real or just words?* The impact of new taxes is felt by everyone, but slogans about fiscal responsibility are only words. Statements about procedural reforms of government are even less interesting to most news consumers. *Finally, is there a human interest aspect to the story?* People do not often challenge party bosses, so such a challenge is newsworthy. A real battle between two political personalities is often more newsworthy than the merits of any proposed law. It may be unfortunate that personalities are more interesting to readers and viewers than substance, but this fact must be recognized when planning to win media coverage. The human interest aspects increase the importance of a news story.

When writing a news assignment memo, the statement to be read and the news release must be built around the best "news pegs" from the perspective of the press. The strongest words and the most far reaching action must be placed in the first paragraph, even in the first sentence. The whole news conference should not be given away in the news assignment memo. And the questions of the press who call in advance to get the story for their deadlines should not be answered, if you wish to avoid an angry press corps that has been "scooped" before the press conference.

MEMO

March 3, 1990

TO: NAN News Conference Coordinators

        Ronni Scheier and Tom Gradel

FROM: Gradel & Associates

RE: March 11 News Conference

I. Advance Preparation

1. Arrange a location for the news conference that is within five or 10 minutes by car of the area of the city where most media offices are. Avoid neighborhood locations more distant—the easier it is for the media to get to the news conference, the more likely it is that they will come.

2. Choose a room large enough to accommodate about 10 reporters plus TV cameras, unless you are certain fewer reporters will attend. Don't select a space so large, however, that sound will get lost and the news conference turnout will be dwarfed.

3. Arrange for the statement to be read and questions answered at the news conference by a spokesperson for the Platform Campaign who is articulate on his or her feet and who can deal with unscripted questions. If possible, it should be someone who has some experience in dealing with the media, and who is a public figure of some news interest. The media will pay more attention if the spokesperson is someone they are familiar with, and someone who has a reputation either as a news maker or a person the community respects. And the media is more likely to use your material if the spokesperson is articulate and quotable.

4. At least three days prior to the news conference, mail the news assignment memo to news media. Address memos to TV and radio news directors, city desk editors at newspapers and political editors for both broadcast and print media. If you or anyone in your organization knows personally any other reporters or editors, make sure that they are notified also. It's a good idea to enclose a handwritten note to these personal contacts from the individual who knows them, and to have that individual make a follow-up call to ask their friend if she thinks the news organization is interested in providing coverage. *(continued)*

5. [Prepare a] news release and statement [for the press conference] ... Make enough copies of both to distribute to all the media you contacted. Also include in each packet a copy of the National Association of Neighborhood's Platform.

6. Also prior to the conference, the designated spokesperson should anticipate questions likely to be asked and prepare quotable responses. Following is an example of a quotable response, preceded by one that is dull and therefore not quotable.

> *Question:* Are the issues raised in this platform really important enough to receive the kind of priority attention from the federal government that you are talking about?

> *Dull Response:* We believe everything contained in the platform is important. We have addressed issues of great concern to all Americans.

> *Quotable Response:* No civilization can survive if life in its cities is unaffordable, or fraught with fear and destruction. It is imperative, therefore, that we build the health and safety of our communities if we hope to preserve the strength and viability of our national state.

II. The Day of the Conference

1. Early in the morning, make phone calls to TV and radio assignment desks and newspaper city desks to remind them of the scheduled news conference. If you don't have a media guide, you can reach these desks through the organization's main switchboard. Tell the desk editor that you mailed him or her a notice of the conference, explain in no more than two sentences what the conference is about, and say you are calling to make sure she knows about it and that you hope a reporter will be able to attend. Ask if the editor thinks someone will be coming. Try to get this information if you can but don't be pushy. When you talk to TV people, say that you will hold off starting until their crew arrives if you know that they are coming. And when you talk to radio editors, if they are uncertain they will be able to cover, offer to have your spokesperson call the station after the news conference to tape an interview.

2. Arrange the conference room so that there are chairs for reporters to sit in. Leave a wide middle aisle if TV cameras are expected. Place a podium or table at the front of the room for your spokesperson and for any other community leaders or notables you want to introduce (not more than five or six, if possible). Neighborhood residents and other

interested persons should be welcome, but asked to sit quietly in the audience and not actively participate. If you expect a large community turnout, make sure there are plenty of chairs. Leave a large amount of space behind the chairs for cameras and crews.

III. The News Conference

1. Arrive at least 15 minutes ahead of time to make certain the room is properly arranged.
2. Assign someone to stand at the door and pass out a release statement and a copy of the Platform to every reporter who comes in. Ask reporters as they enter whom they represent. Keep a list of reporters' names and the news organizations they represent.
3. Wait up to five minutes after the scheduled starting time if it looks as though more media may be on the way—particularly TV. Start as soon after the scheduled time as possible.
4. A staff person or clear-speaking friend should start the conference by standing at the podium and asking the reporters if they are ready to begin. That same person should then introduce any persons you want to present other than the spokesperson and announce that a short statement will be read and then questions will be answered.
5. After several minutes of questions, when the important points have been made and the conference appears to have run its course, thank everyone for coming. If you wait too long, some reporters—especially those on a close deadline—will be uncomfortable and may get up and leave, distracting the rest. If almost everyone appears finished but one or two reporters still have questions, thank the group and add that the spokesperson will be available to answer more questions at the front of the room.

IV. Follow-up Work

1. Make sure that the spokesperson calls immediately following the conference any radio news departments which couldn't attend but requested a telephone interview.
2. Hand deliver copies of the release to any other media which didn't attend. Mail the release to others with no immediate need for the news.
3. Listen to news broadcasts and buy the early editions of the papers. If there are major mistakes in the reports, call the reporter and gently point out the mistakes. They as well as you are interested in accuracy.
4. Keep clippings for guidance in holding future conferences.

Once again, if your volunteers don't have a lot of experience holding news conferences, you will be much better off hiring a professional public relations person to coordinate at least this key press event.

ADVERTISING

For local races mass media advertising may be too expensive, because the media broadcast to a much larger audience than the residents of one district and the bulk of the readers or viewers cannot vote for your candidate. One way to overcome this handicap is to advertise only in neighborhood newspapers. If your campaign also uses radio, the station(s) with the most listeners from the district should be picked and numerous 30-second spots immediately before the election should be delivered.[14] By narrowing the audience reached through the media or limiting the period in which to advertise, a campaign saves money.

Of all the mass media, radio is one of the least expensive to reach large audiences. Three to five candidates running on a similar platform can purchase joint advertisements to cut the costs. But to be effective, you must buy "saturation time" on the few stations you select. That means as many as 10 replays a week on a single station at various broadcast hours and prices. You can probably buy two weeks of spots on each station for $500 to $1,000. Advertising rates, of course, vary according to the audience of the stations. One advantage of radio advertisements is that F.C.C. regulations require both radio and television stations to play campaign advertisements so you are guaranteed that they will get on the air even if the stations have no other times for business advertisements that week. Political advertisements have priority and the least expensive commercial rates.

An example of a simple radio advertisement used to support three aldermanic candidates (who won their elections) is shown on page 96. Writing such advertisements is tricky and usually requires a specialist. The images evoked, and the phrasing, are important, and these writing tricks are not learned quickly. Only a few concepts can be transmitted in a single advertisement so a message has to be carefully crafted. A professional announcer, the candidate or a well-known figure whose voice endorsement is helpful tapes the advertisement.

Television advertising is too expensive for most participatory campaigns unless they are part of a city, county or state-wide campaign. The same is generally true of downtown newspaper ads, although those costs vary according to the size of the city or town. Most campaigns do take newspaper ads in specialized weekly and community newspapers. Even so, an ordinary campaign advertisement is a waste of money, because political advertisements look the same and appear at the same time as advertising supporting dozens of other candidates. As with every other aspect of the campaign, imagination and people should be the hallmark of the advertising. For instance, simple testimonial advertisements can be scattered throughout the neighborhood paper at modest expense but maximum effect. These smaller advertisements are not consigned to the section of the paper with the usual political advertisements. Because they appear to be statements of real citizens rather than concoctions of a public relations firm, they are read more often and their message is more convincing.

They have a simple message like the following newspaper ad within a more striking graphic layout:

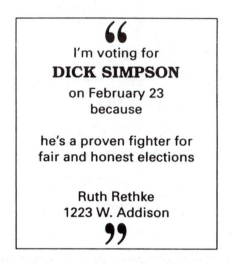

Different quotes can be scattered in small ads throughout the newspaper for less than the cost of a single standard quarter or half-page advertisement.

If a campaign is fortunate enough to have enough money to purchase television advertising, they should not look like all the other political advertisements. Bill Hillsman made the Paul Wellstone for U.S. Senator advertisements in Minnesota in 1990 (see the description on p. 97). Along with the "Ronald Reagan for President" advertisements in 1984, the Wellstone ads are often counted among the best political advertising because they reach voters at an emotional level. Hillsman's principle is, "If a political ad looks like a political ad—too preachy, too serious, too cautious, and, worst of all, dull—then it is a failure."[15] In the first Wellstone advertisement, which was called "Fast-Paced Paul," his goal was to "introduce Wellstone and give viewers a feel for his unconventional campaign, and it would warn people to look with suspicion on [incumbent Senator] Boschwitz's commercials."[16] It succeeded by being so different from standard advertising that it caught the audience's attention. Only creative advertisements like this one allow low-budget, participatory campaigns to win the advertising war against candidates with greater funds and, therefore, more television commercials.

Script for Aldermanic Election Radio Ad

I'M ALDERMAN DICK SIMPSON. THIS FEBRUARY 27TH AND APRIL 3RD CHICAGO WILL ELECT A MAYOR, CITY OFFICIALS AND A CITY COUNCIL. THE QUESTION IS: WILL WE ELECT GOOD PEOPLE, OR THE SAME OLD MACHINE? UNLESS A LOT OF PEOPLE GET OUT AND REGISTER TO VOTE, CHICAGO WILL BE STUCK WITH THE SAME OLD MACHINE. THREE HONEST, INDEPEN- DENT CANDIDATES DON'T WANT THIS TO HAPPEN. THAT'S WHY ALDERMAN MARTY OBERMAN OF THE 43RD WARD, BRUCE YOUNG OF THE 44TH, AND DAVID ORR OF THE 49TH WARD URGE YOU TO REGISTER TO VOTE. LOW VOTER TURNOUT WORKS FOR THE MACHINE BUT HINDERS THE INDEPENDENT CANDIDATES WHO PROVIDE A VOICE OF REASON IN THE CHAOS OF THE CITY COUNCIL. IF THE INDEPENDENT VOTE DOESN'T GET OUT, THE MACHINE WILL WIN OUT. YOU CAN STILL REGISTER. IF YOU'RE A NEW VOTER, OR A NEW ILLI- NOIS RESIDENT, OR HAVE CHANGED YOUR ADDRESS, REGISTER TUESDAY, JANUARY 30TH AT YOUR PRE- CINCT POLLING PLACE. ONLY IF YOU REGISTER CAN YOU HELP ELECT GOOD PEOPLE, NOT THE SAME OLD MACHINE. TO VOLUNTEER, GET REGISTRATION INFOR- MATION, OR THE ADDRESS OF YOUR PRECINCT POLLING PLACE, PHONE 555-5555. THAT'S 555-5555.

Paul Wellstone for U.S. Senate Television Commercial

The ad begins with Wellstone standing outside in short-sleeved shirt and tie. Addressing the camera, he immediately takes on Rudy Boschwitz instead of Jim Nichols, his Democratic primary opponent. "Hi, I'm Paul Wellstone," he starts, "and I'm running for United States Senate from Minnesota. Unlike my opponent, I don't have $6 million, so I'm going to have to talk fast."

Then Wellstone literally races through the commercial, stopping for a breather and a few words, such as I'll lead the fight for national health care," in front of an appropriate backdrop before he rushes off to the right and enters again from the left for the next scene. By the end of the thirty-second spot, he's running across the screen at fast-forward speed. He looks like a blurred hybrid of Harpo Marx and a Keystone Kop as he jumps into his campaign bus, which speeds away as the narrator says, "Paul Wellstone won't slow down after he's elected."

Source: Dennis McGrath and Dane Smith, *Professor Wellstone Goes to Washington* (Minneapolis: University of Minnesota Press, 1995), p. 152.

CAMPAIGN LITERATURE

Whether or not you succeed in getting front page newspaper stories or coverage on the 10 o'clock news for your candidate, you can distribute your own campaign information to all the voters in the district. You accomplish this by sending volunteers door-to-door and by direct mail.

Different types of campaign literature have different purposes. Campaign buttons and small window posters gain name identification and encourage workers. Hundreds of citizens wearing campaign buttons is more impressive than hundreds of dollars of paid advertisements in local newspapers. Buttons are among the least expensive of all forms of campaign advertising, and many campaigns recover the cost of printing buttons by selling them for a dollar each. Of course, buttons succeed only if hundreds of supporters wear them.

Small posters also have maximum effect when they go up in the windows of homes or in private yards. They demonstrate that citizens of the district support the candidate which is an impact that money cannot buy. Some campaigns augment campaign posters (see p. 98) and buttons with bumper stickers, car

Sample Campaign Poster

★Simpson for Congress

He will serve with integrity!

**DEMOCRATIC Primary
March 15, 1994**

tops and yard signs. A special visibility campaign can also put stickers on every utility pole in the district. Well-financed campaigns purchase billboard space or posters for commuter buses and trains. For local participatory campaigns, buttons, small posters and yard signs create sufficient name identification and a good campaign image. Larger campaigns employ more expensive campaign advertising as well.

Convincing supporters and campaign workers to wear buttons requires only mentioning the need for such visibility at all campaign functions. Getting hundreds of posters into windows or signs into yards is more difficult. A visibility chair or team of workers must call every potential campaign supporter listed in the headquarters' files, asking that they put up a poster or yard sign and get others to do so. Posters are dispatched immediately by car to the homes of those willing to take them, and a careful record of each poster is kept on a map of the district. As posters and yard signs go up, special efforts are made to get them into the weakest areas of the campaign and into at least one home or yard near every polling place in the district.

Buttons, stickers, posters and yard signs are primarily used to improve name recognition and create a positive campaign image. They can be very simple, perhaps containing only the name of the candidate and the office she is seeking. Literature used door-to-door, passed out on street corners, or mailed to voters must be more complete, supplying information about the candidate's history, platform and the groups endorsing her candidacy. The literature may also contain photographs of the candidate with her family, with prominent supporters and with voters to tell the campaign's story visually as well as verbally.

In my second Simpson for Congress campaign, the basic piece of campaign literature was a simple, three-fold brochure that could be mailed in a envelope, put through a mail slot, or easily handed to voters at transportation stops or grocery stores (see pp. 100–101). We created this brochure by answering a series of questions that voters might ask if they were talking to me in person.

1. Who are you and who are you running against?
2. Why should we vote for you?
3. What is your platform (or what will you do if we elect you)?
4. What have you done before running for Congress?
5. When is the election and what ballot do I have to take to vote for you?
6. Who endorses your candidacy?

The answer to all these questions and much more was provided in this single brochure. Whatever media is used to promote a candidate, the information presented will, of necessity, have to be brief. Photographs and graphic design will have to replace endless words in conveying the campaign's message to the voters.

Unlike my campaign literature, most will not picture or mention an opponent. However, since Congressman Rostenkowski already had complete name recognition in the district and a highly negative image, we attempted to contrast

Simpson for Congress Brochure
(Outside of three-fold brochure)

Dick
Simpson

OR

DAN ROSTENKOWSKI

Chicago Sun-Times

The Rostenkowski Probe

$600,000 IN QUESTIONS

The following organizations endorse **Dick Simpson** as the best candidate for Congress:

- ★ National Organization for Women's Political Action Committee
- ★ Illinois NOW PAC
- ★ Cook County Democratic Women
- ★ Independent Voters of Illinois – Independent Precinct Organization, IVI–IPO
- ★ IMPACT
- ★ Americans for Democratic Action, Northeastern Illinois Chapter
- ★ United Electrical, Radio and Machine Workers, District Council 11
- ★ University Professionals of Illinois, Local 4100, AFT, AFL-CIO
- ★ West Suburban Teachers Union, Local 571, IFT
- ★ Filipino-American Voters League
- ★ Indo-American Democratic Organization
- ★ Illinois-Hispanic Democratic Council, Northwest Cook County Chapter
- ★ Pioneer Press Newspapers

Simpson
for
Congress

He will serve with integrity!

Simpson for Congress
3740 West Irving Park Road
Chicago, IL 60618
312/866-1994

For 25 years,
Dick Simpson has fought
political corruption and government waste
in Chicago and Cook County.
Now he wants to represent you in Congress.

The choice is yours!

Dan Rostenkowski
has been in Congress for 35 years.
He likes Congress *the way it is* because
he is able to help himself and his friends.

(Inside of three-fold brochure)

He will serve with integrity!

Three Reasons to Elect Dick Simpson

1. **Dick Simpson** will serve with integrity. Unlike Dan Rostenkowski, Simpson will listen to people and vote intelligently to improve communities and neighborhoods in the 5th Congressional District.

2. **Dick Simpson** has a proven record of courage and dedication to government ethics and reform as an alderman, teacher and civic leader.

3. **Dick Simpson** is tough enough, experienced enough, and practical enough to fight for change in the currently corrupt and gridlocked Congress.

Dick Simpson's Agenda for Change:

★ Support term limits for Members of Congress

★ Honor his pledge to serve no more than 12 years

★ Work with business and labor unions to restore 25,000 jobs lost in the district

★ Strongly support a woman's right to choose an abortion

★ Fight for more funds for schools and community team policing

★ Introduce amendments to create a "single-payer" national health care plan

★ Hold six town hall meetings a year open to everyone in the district

★ Protect Social Security programs and secure equity for "Notch" seniors

★ Sponsor legislation to create public financing of Congressional campaigns and curtail special-interest PAC contributions

Vote for DICK SIMPSON for Congress • DEMOCRATIC Primary • March 15, 1994

In 1992, Dick Simpson challenged Dan Rostenkowski in the Democratic Primary and received 43% of the vote. Simpson had the courage to point out that Rostenkowski was not only a corrupt ward boss but Rostenkowski also neglected the needs of his district.

A highly effective Alderman of Chicago's 44th Ward from 1971 to 1979, Dick Simpson passed legislation to:
• curtail redlining by banks
• reduce CTA fares for seniors
• endorse the Equal Rights Amendment
• prevent overbuilding on the lakefront

Dick Simpson founded the Ward Assembly which gave real decision-making power to residents. He also donated his entire Aldermanic salary to hire two full-time staffers for his community service office.

Simpson, an Associate Professor at the University of Illinois at Chicago, has served on the transition teams of Cook County Clerk David Orr and State's Attorney Jack O'Malley.

Dick Simpson, his wife, Sarajane, and their children, August and Kate, live in the Lincoln Square neighborhood of Chicago.

the two of us in all aspects of my campaign. But the general rule remains to highlight only the positive aspects of your candidate and completely ignore opponents in campaign literature.

The best method of distributing campaign literature is door-to-door. Precinct workers talk to the voters, answer their questions, and learn their preferences. Even so, some precincts in the district will not be worked, because there are not enough campaign volunteers. Those precincts should receive a blitz, where volunteers leave campaign literature at the door or in the foyer. An experiment attempted by Byron Sistler in Evanston, Illinois indicates that just leaving literature for a slate of candidates endorsed by the Independent Voters of Illinois affected a limited number of voters. He found that in precincts not covered, an average split-ticket vote for six IVI endorsed candidates (both Democrat and Republican) was 6.1% of the total vote. In the precincts in which he left campaign literature, they received 8.2% of the vote for all six candidates across party lines. The difference, 2.1% of the total vote or about 10 votes per precinct, was effected by his literature blitz.[17]

These results demonstrate not only why personal contact is desirable, but also why blitzes and direct mail are used in otherwise unworked precincts. In the next chapter, we will discuss precinct work and direct mail campaigns in more detail, along with ways to increase the effect of voter contacts.

CHAPTER VII

SENDING YOUR MESSAGE

Your campaign could craft an outstanding image for your candidate, develop a great contrast to opponents, define campaign issues brilliantly, and lose. Your campaign could have a mediocre image, blurred distinctions, a poor definition of the issues, and win. The determining factor is often the ability to project your campaign's image, theme and issues to the voter. Your campaign message means nothing if the voters never get it.

As already discussed, candidates with lots of money have a great advantage in sending their messages. They buy their way into the voters' living rooms. They can afford radio and television commercials. For a few hundred thousand dollars, any campaign can buy enough air time to guarantee that voters will know the candidate's name and have a positive image and strong reasons to vote for him. If money is spent to hire professionals to conduct polls and to write and produce media ads, a very powerful message can be sent to voters. This effort does not guarantee that wealthy candidates always win, but money makes sending their message much easier.

Dozens of books, video documentaries and films have warned of the dangers of Madison Avenue, "synthetic" campaigns.[1] These dangers are well-known and understood. There is however, another way in which money spent on high-tech campaigns can buy access to voters.[2] Targeted, "narrowcast" campaign messages can be just as effective and just as dangerous to democracy as mass media campaigns.

We explore these high-tech campaigns in greater depth for three reasons: 1) some of their techniques can be adapted to modern participatory campaigns; 2) an opponent may use these techniques against your candidate, so they must be countered; and 3) there are new potentials and threats to our democracy in these techniques.

Gary Selnow in *High-Tech Campaigns* explains these targeted strategies of persuasion:

> *Targeting begins with the assembly of audience information— through polls and databases—and continues with data analyses that determine targetable clusters—those groups of people sufficiently like-minded that they will respond similarly to the same message.[3]*

In other words, targeted communications assemble information about the voters. Campaign strategists then use this information about subgroups such as women, senior citizens, the wealthy, and Hispanics. They select voters with specific characteristics, tailor a special campaign message with appeal to members of that subgroup, and send that message to them directly with mail appeals, phone calls or media directed at selected audiences. These narrowcast (as opposed to broadcast) media include cable television, radio talk shows, and Internet discussion groups.

> *[Public opinion] surveys tell you about population subgroups: how they think, how they behave, how they can be moved. Database analyses give you the members of these subgroups, separating them one from the other, allowing you to reach them one at a time or in small clusters. . . .*
> *This is the heart of communication targeting: the identification of audience segments and the exposition of the issues that relate to each.[4]*

These techniques are even worse than party precinct captains of the old days who promised Mr. Smith a government job, Mrs. Jones a government favor and Mr. Sullivan Irish candidates. The new technologies allow campaigns to divide voters more efficiently into very small groups, promise them limited actions on specific issues, and play to their prejudices rather than fashion a common agenda that a majority of citizens support. Voters may be deceived into believing that the campaign letter or phone call addressing them individually is a personal communication that they can trust.

These targeted communications produce what Selnow calls displacement:

> *Displacement occurs when the use of narrow channels, with special messages to special audiences, displaces communications on mass channels, with general messages to general audiences. People expect public officials to communicate with them. They once anticipated face-to-face contact, as in the ward-and-precinct system. . . . People still expect some contact with the leaders who represent them, spend their money and run their government.[5]*

Targeted communications give the illusion of meaningful contact between voters and candidates. It is easy to use this form of communication to deceive the voters into believing that their concerns have been responded to when, in fact, critical issues of government, candidate qualifications and democratic discussion have been skillfully avoided.

DIRECT MAIL AND PHONE CAMPAIGNS

For as little as $1,000, a campaign can purchase a mailing list of all registered voters in a district, their addresses and their voting history. Enriching this computer listing with voters' phone numbers and demographic data is a straightforward process. With these lists you are ready to mail material to voters or to call them on the phone, or prepare walk sheets for your volunteers to go to voters' doors. If a campaign has sufficient funds, it can hire public relations firms to write their message and direct mail companies to print, sort and mail communications. Telemarketing firms can call voters. If a campaign has even more money, public opinion polls can be used to sharpen the message. Various campaign themes and images can be tested with a sample of the voters until just the right image or issue has been found to convince voters to vote for a candidate.

Most modern participatory campaigns do not have the money to undertake a completely high-tech campaign of this sort. Expensive direct mail campaigns that ensure a message moves voters often includes seven to nine different letters and oversized postcards sent to every voter in the district. These campaigning also include targeted mail to subgroups with special issues. In direct mail campaigns, the first three or so pieces introduce the candidate, his family, background, and qualifications to establish name recognition and image.

The next mailings often vilify an opponent and are not identified as coming from the campaign that sends them other than including the minimal disclosure required by law. Direct mail can produce particularly virulent and hard-to-answer negative allegations in the weeks just before the election.

The last several pieces of mail let a candidate push a single issue, list key endorsements, and give voters a final reason to elect him.

Like expensive mass media campaigns, multiple mailings to a large district cost as much as several hundred thousand dollars. They are often reinforced with phone calls reiterating the message to voters.

Modern participatory campaigns also make use of direct mail and phone campaigns. But in contrast to synthetic campaigns, participatory campaigns make a much greater use of volunteers and avoid the worst forms of negative campaigning. For instance, a more participatory campaign might decide to concentrate on only three literature blitzes and direct mail pieces. The blitz or literature drop is done by volunteers going door-to-door throughout the district. The first piece might be a general campaign brochure introducing the candidate or even a campaign newsletter printed on newsprint. The second piece is usually mailed before the voter registration deadline, and the third is timed to arrive in the last two weeks of the campaign. These mailings may be done by volunteers. If professional mailing firms do the mailing, voter lists provided by the campaign's computer operation significantly lessen the costs involved. Phone canvasses and get-out-the-vote (GOTV) efforts can also be done from campaign headquarters by volunteers.

Participatory campaigns that successfully recruit volunteers and get good coverage in the mass media can match the paid targeted communications of wealthier opponents, especially if a candidate has charisma, the issues are strong enough to recruit both volunteers and voters, and the race is important enough to matter to the press, potential volunteers and voters. The strategic task of a modern participatory campaign staff is to decide on the proper mix of paid and volunteer efforts to send the message.

COMMUNICATIONS FROM NEIGHBORS

A personal letter from neighbors can be as effective with voters as supporters wearing buttons or putting campaign posters in their windows and yards. If supporters in a particular neighborhood or important community leaders have endorsed a candidate, they can be encouraged to send "friend of a friend" letters or postcards. However, to have any real impact this must be a systematic, well-organized campaign project. Your campaign designs a model letter (see the sample letter on p. 107) or postcard and provides a list (or computer labels) of several hundred neighbors who are voters. Supporters then sign, put on a stamp, and mail them. These letters can be sent early in the campaign to build support or mailed to arrive the last week or two before the election as a final argument presented to voters before election day.

INTERNET CAMPAIGNING

The possibilities for campaigning via the Internet are developing exponentially. For several years, campaigns have been attempting to use this new technology to reach voters and win elections. Although so far no one has made it work, campaigning on the Internet is about to become a standard tactic.

As of 1995, three principal problems remain. First, the number of voters with the access and knowledge to use the Internet are too few to swing the outcome of an election in any given district. Second, although access to the Internet is inexpensive, costing only a low monthly subscription fee and a campaign computer, the staff or volunteer time involved in setting up a home page and posting messages to different Internet discussion groups is greater than the return in votes. Third, unlike mass media ads, targeted communication and precinct work, successful techniques to win elections using this technology have not yet been invented despite several creative attempts.

None of this has kept candidates from trying to exploit the Internet. In the 1994 elections the greatest experimentation came in California, home to so many computer and software manufacturers. Election data was provided in six languages at the following address: http://www.elections.ca.gov/. While the results of the general election were tabulated, electronic updates were provided on statewide races, ballot propositions and local elections. County-by-county returns of statewide races were displayed on colored maps showing the winner in each county. Before election day, the state of California provided information on candidates and their major contributors, nonpartisan information from civic organizations and election coverage and editorials by newspapers, as well as connec-

Friend of a Friend Letter
Draft

Dear _____:

Hello. I'm your neighbor, Barbara Jones, from down the street. I'm writing everyone on the block to ask them to vote for Dick Simpson in the March 15th primary. Dick is running for Congress against Dan Rostenkowski.

First, let me say what a joy it is to live here, in one of Chicago's great neighborhoods. Chicago is built around neighborhoods, and, unlike a lot of big cities, Chicago manages to have a "small town" feel to it.

Of course, we still have big city problems. I'm more than little anxious about crime, schools, and the loss of jobs in Chicago. What angers me is that while our city is exploding with crime and poverty some congressmen are devoting their efforts to lining their own pockets. Dan Rostenkowski ought to start a Scandel-of-the-Month club.

A lot of people think Rosty brings tax dollars into the state. It's a myth, though. Illinois ranks 46th out of the 50 states in federal tax dollars returned to the state. They say our Congressman is one of the most powerful men in Washington. Powerful for whom? Insurance companies? Sure. Rich developers? You bet. Drug companies? Absolutely. You and Me? No. If he was looking out for us, he would have saved the Stewart Warner plant. If he cared about the district, we wouldn't have lost 25,000 jobs in the past decade. If he was concerned at all, he would appear in public and listen to our concerns.

Dick Simpson is both a neighbor and a friend. He is running for Congress in the March 15th primary. I have known Dick [since he was an alderman ....] I can tell you from personal experience that Dick Simpson is a man of great integrity, intelligence and compassion. His political involvement is long and distinguished.

I know you're busy, and I won't take time to list all the things Dick Simpson has done and all he plans to do. I'll let his campaign people send along that information. But I do want to personally urge you to take this letter along when you vote in the primary on March 15th. Remember the name, Dick Simpson. We have a neighbor who cares about our future. Help send him to Washington in the next election.

With warm regards,

tions to the home pages of candidates with their own biographies, press releases and position papers. California even provided evaluations of the state's congressional candidates by various interest groups. It is very doubtful that this comprehensive information changed many votes, but this California experiment provides an example of the information that state and local governments will begin to provide on campaigns. Candidates must be prepared to take advantage of this new medium of communication to the voters if they are to stay competitive.

In 1995, presidential candidates began a serious attempt to reach the 10.5 million potential constituents on the Internet. The President and the vice-president had already established a home page (http://www/whitehous.gov/) and e-mail addresses. Newt Gingrich, with great fanfare, established the new Congressional home page, "Thomas," named after Thomas Jefferson (http://thomas.loc.gov/)and his own e-mail address. In October 1995, the leading Republican candidate, Senator Bob Dole, was one of the later contenders to open a home page (http://www.Dole 96.com). It was among the most sophisticated, offering browsers the chance to volunteer or to pledge to send money directly from his home page. Some of the other Republican candidates for President with home pages were: Lamar Alexander (http:/www.nashville.net/lamar/), Phil Gramm (http:/www.gramm96.org/) and Richard Lugar (http://www.iquest.net/lugar/lugar.htm). All these candidates had their home pages up and running by the summer of 1995. As of August 21, 1995, Lamar Alexander's home page had more than 60,000 visits, Phil Gramm's, 144,000 and Richard Lugar, 25,000.[6] A general home page even allowed access to all Republican candidates (http://www.umr.edu/~sears/primary/main/html). These candidate home pages provided images, photographs, biographies, video and audio clips, and position papers. In addition, several of the candidates went to on-line chat sessions made available by services like America Online. *The Chicago Tribune* predicted in a story on May 25, 1995, that the Internet *"also could become a new venue for the most venal negative campaigning. Image being able to quickly see pictures of, and hear tapes from, Gennifer Flowers or other alleged companions of Clinton. Imagine reading about the health problems of a certain Republican candidate or the shadowy financial dealings of another."*[7]

Future candidates for major public offices will have to keep up with their opponents. At a minimum, they will need to have home pages containing their biographies, color photographs, campaign newsletters, news releases, and position papers for voters who want to get their political information from the Internet. This will mean training staff members to design home pages and text for the Internet or paying several thousand dollars for professional software companies to do the job. It will also require that campaigns update this information several times a week. As always, the newest campaign technology costs time and money.

THE PRECINCT WORK ALTERNATIVE

Staffing a field operation with leaders and trained workers able to carry out a petition drive, registration campaign and door-to-door voter canvass is still the secret of winning most elections. Precinct work provides a much more personal and less expensive way to reach voters, to register them, and to get them to the polls on election day. To succeed, this form of campaigning requires volunteers, good leaders and a clear structure for the field operation.

After a precinct structure for a field operation like the one shown on p. 110 has been established, the petition drive allows its efficiency to be tested. The registration drive allows a campaign to enlarge the constituency of voters likely to be favorably disposed toward a candidate. A final canvass allows favorable voters to be found and brought the polls on election day.

Precinct work wins or loses participatory campaigns. You can have the best candidate, good publicity, lots of money, and successful campaign events, but if you lack the workers to go door-to-door, informing and convincing voters, your campaign is doomed from the beginning. A strong precinct effort can overcome campaign problems such as having less money than an opponent or limited coverage in the mass media.

Precinct work provides the most direct and effective contact with voters. It gives neighbors a chance to talk with each other about the kind of men and women who should represent them. Translating campaign issues so that each voter can understand what the election really means to him and his community forces precinct workers to bridge the gap between rhetoric and reality and wins elections by reestablishing trust and human communication. Precinct work not only allows campaign volunteers to participate effectively, but it also prepares voters for meaningful participation on election day.

THE FIELD ORGANIZATION

Precinct work is so essential and the task so mammoth that it can be accomplished only by a highly structured and efficient organization in which each worker knows his tasks, does them well, and accurately reports his results. The success of the entire effort depends on the precinct coordinator who heads it. The precinct coordinator, like the candidate, must give hundreds of hours to the campaign, including most evenings and weekends for three or four months. A good precinct coordinator also needs to be smart, efficient and aggressive enough to get volunteers to do the hard door-to-door canvassing, hard-working enough himself to set an example for other campaign workers, but open enough to communicate effectively with workers and to encourage constructive responses and suggestions. Last of all, a precinct coordinator must have prior campaign experience, at least as a precinct worker. Locating favorable voters and getting them to the polls is the secret of success, and a good coordinator understands this principle.

Because the precinct coordinator cannot supervise hundreds of precinct workers personally, ward coordinators and area chairs are also needed. The responsibility for recruiting and coordinating precinct workers rests directly with these campaign leaders. Ward coordinators and area chairs must possess many of the same qualities as the precinct coordinator. Finding enough good

HYPOTHETICAL PRECINCT STRUCTURE

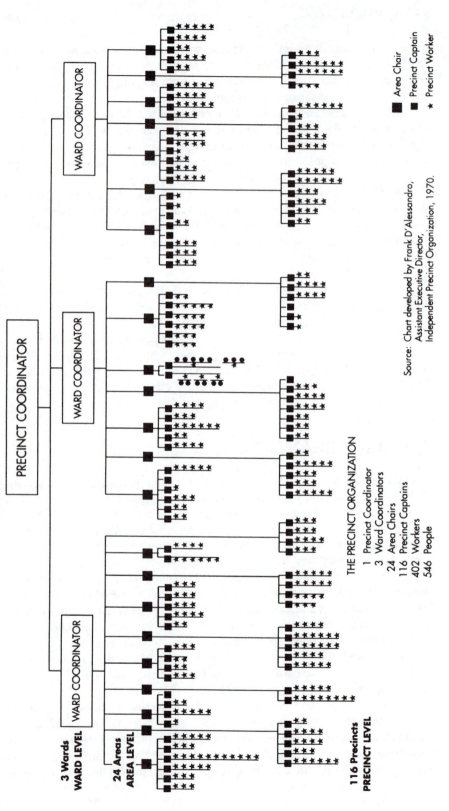

3 Wards
WARD LEVEL

24 Areas
AREA LEVEL

116 Precincts
PRECINCT LEVEL

PRECINCT COORDINATOR

WARD COORDINATOR

WARD COORDINATOR

WARD COORDINATOR

THE PRECINCT ORGANIZATION

1   Precinct Coordinator
3   Ward Coordinators
24   Area Chairs
116   Precinct Captains
402   Workers
546   People

■ Area Chair
■ Precinct Captain
★ Precinct Worker

Source: Chart developed by Frank D'Alessandro,
Assistant Executive Director,
Independent Precinct Organization, 1970.

leaders to staff these critical middle levels of the campaign is not easy. Sometimes precinct workers from prior campaigns can be promoted, but some outstanding precinct captains make bad area chairs because the two jobs require considerably different skills. A precinct worker goes personally to each voter. Campaign coordinators, such as area chairs, spend their time on the phone convincing other people to work, giving instructions, and receiving reports. If experienced campaigners are not available or would be better as precinct workers, then inexperienced volunteers will have to be appointed as ward coordinators and area chairs. Some people are natural organizers or have professions such as that of salesperson or business executive that may suit them to the task. However, there is always a risk in making someone a leader. Campaign staff must constantly check coordinator reports and check with the people they coordinate to make sure that ward coordinators and area chairs do their jobs properly.

Once volunteers have been found to serve in these critical middle management positions, they absolutely must become part of the decision-making process. Weekly leadership meetings focus on the precinct progress reports of area chairs, their suggestions for changes in strategy, and their reactions to proposals by other campaign leaders. The candidate should attend the weekly leadership meetings for at least half an hour. Staying the entire meeting would inhibit discussion and keep him from meeting with potential voters and workers. However, each week he should report on the state of the campaign to the campaign leaders and receive ideas from them. In addition to leadership meetings (unmatched for developing loyalty, enthusiasm and full discussion of the campaign), frequent letters should be sent detailing accomplishments to date, the goals of the next leadership meeting and instructions on the next phase of the campaign. Frequent communications should be sent to all campaign workers, particularly precinct workers. Many campaigns accomplish this by sending a regular campaign newsletter. Since composing such a newsletter is time-consuming; an occasional letter about the campaign, along with invitations to attend precinct work training sessions, campaign benefits and volunteer parties may be sufficient. Finally, area chairs should schedule parties and special worker meetings for those campaigners living in the area, to motivate and reward volunteers for all their hard work.

A good precinct structure for field operations comprises much more than a chart at campaign headquarters. A large group of people must work together and constantly talk about their work. The personalities, personal concerns, enthusiasm, and loyalty of the leaders and workers can be more critically important to the election results than abstract descriptions of roles they are supposed to play. Any successful structure must be flexible enough to take advantage of the unique abilities of its members, and their sense of participation and involvement must be fostered at every opportunity.

Locating hundreds of precinct workers to fill out the precinct structure may be the most difficult task of all. The existence of permanent independent organizations or political parties and a history of prior participatory campaigns in a district make a significant difference. Organizations and prior campaigns can be a major source of experienced precinct workers. New volunteers must also be recruited, but beginning with many of your precincts already covered makes it possible to concentrate on weak spots. To recruit enough workers, meetings must be held, hundreds of coffees scheduled, and every potential worker called whose name is given to the campaign. No campaign ever begins and few campaigns end with enough volunteers. Ideally, three or more workers should be based in every precinct in the district. (Precincts differ in size in different states. In Chicago, precincts consist of about 350 voters and range from a single high-rise building to three or four blocks of single family homes and duplex apartments.) Not even the best run campaigns achieve perfect precinct coverage; but the more precincts worked, the more precincts will be won by your campaign.

Political campaigns always face the reality of scarce resources: too few volunteers, too little money and not enough time. Recruiting campaign volunteers has become much more difficult in recent years. Everyone now has a full-time job, and those jobs are much more competitive and demanding. Many people also take on extra work to earn enough income to support their families. The public has become more alienated from the political process and less certain of the benefits of working for political candidates. Because of these and other trends in modern society, recruiting enough volunteers requires time and effort.

Since there are never enough precinct workers to cover all precincts completely, decisions must be made about the most effect apportionment of campaign resources. One possible choice is to depend on direct mail, mass media advertisements, and phone canvassing that can be purchased. But most campaigns will also do field work.

There are two competing principles to consider in mounting a precinct effort:

1. The maximum number of precincts possible must be covered.
2. The precincts with the greatest potential vote for a candidate must be completely covered.

Both principles are correct and neither can be ignored without jeopardizing victory.

Sometimes covering every precinct is not possible. In the 1968 campaign for Eugene McCarthy for President, 22 McCarthy delegate candidates ran in Illinois as National Democratic Convention delegates on a popular platform of ending the war in Vietnam, racial equality and curbing the "Imperial Presidency." Nonetheless, only two were elected out of 118 positions in the entire state. In the 9th Congressional District in Chicago where I was campaign manager, the McCarthy campaign tried to cover over 500 precincts and only managed to get 20 percent of the vote. Attempting to cover most congressional districts and all precincts within those districts was bigger than the McCarthy campaign organization, created only a few months earlier, had been able to handle. More selective coverage would have brought better results and seen more delegates elected.

However, this strategy may backfire. In November of the same year, Robert Friedlander, an independent Republican candidate for state Senate in the same district, wrote off 38 precincts in the near north black ghetto. The Friedlander campaign concentrated instead on Republican and potentially Independent precincts. He lost 30,000 to 27,000. Some of the precincts he failed to work voted against him by votes as great as 400 to 10. While many Republicans and Independents in other parts of the district voted for him, they did not turn out in the hoped-for numbers, and the ethnic Democratic vote killed his chances of victory. If he had not given away all the votes in those 38 precincts, he might have won.

Worker placement must strike a balance between the two principles. Every precinct in the district should be covered somehow to win at least some of the votes and to reverse the proportion by which the weakest precincts are lost, for example, from 40 to 1 to 5 to 1. On the other hand, the strongest precincts have to be worked well to obtain as many votes as possible. That means in practice covering weak precincts thinly and concentrating volunteers in the best precincts. As an added complication, people will often only volunteer if they can work the precinct where they live, so most volunteers must be left in their own precincts and only the best workers will "carpetbag" in precincts where they are most needed.

One important pool of volunteer workers is college and high school students. Sometimes students may serve as interns receiving course credit for their work, other times they simply become campaign volunteers. In my second congressional campaign, I recruited about 30 college students and a dozen high school students who were invaluable in helping staff my campaign and getting my message to the voters. Students often work more hours with more energy and enthusiasm than other volunteers. The best use of these student volunteers is to: 1) make them assistant staff members with major campaign responsibilities, 2) supplement an existing precinct organization with individual students assigned to beef up precincts that are short on volunteers, 3) send teams of students to marginal precincts where vote potential is strongest but organization is the weakest,[8] and 4) assign them to critical operations such as phone bank coordinators and callers. If students canvass for votes in weaker precincts, they can, while they are canvassing, search for potential workers to build up an indigenous precinct structure. Outside workers are best used to develop the indigenous leadership in each precinct to take over the tasks of campaigning. Then they can move on to develop new precincts.

A field operation requires careful records. At the beginning of the campaign, lists of potential workers are obtained from political organizations and from previous political campaigns in the district. These lists are transferred to a potential worker computer file with name, address, phone number, ward number, area letter (areas are lettered A-Z to avoid confusion with wards and precincts), and precinct number. This information provides the beginning of a master campaign volunteer file kept at the headquarters. A printed list of potential precinct workers by area is given to area chairs. Each area chair gives the appropriate list of potential workers to each precinct captain. When potential workers become precinct workers, this information is entered into the master campaign volunteer file, so other campaign workers do not call them in search of volunteers to help with their projects.

After the initial precinct workers are recruited, additional volunteers sign up at coffees or send in pledge cards from mailings or leafleting (see sample card in Chapter 3). The pool of potential workers is also enlarged by the recruiting efforts of area chairs and precinct workers. By the end of the campaign, the master file may number several thousand workers, potential workers, contributors and supporters.

In addition to the master volunteer file, the precinct coordinator, ward coordinators and area chairs keep their own records, including names of precinct workers and reports for each precinct showing the results at each stage of the campaign, from the petition drive to the vote count.

These precinct workers are the front-line warriors of a campaign. They go door-to-door through their precinct convincing their neighbors to support a candidate, by signing his nominating petition, registering to vote and electing him on election day. Ideally, they should be personable and well-dressed as the representative of the candidate. They should be absolutely reliable and willing to work hard. While a participatory campaign inevitably finds a use for nearly everyone who volunteers, potential precinct workers are carefully screened to ensure that they will represent the campaign well in the precincts.

PETITION DRIVE

The nominating petition drive necessary to meet the *legal* requirements to get a candidate on the ballot is not difficult. Nonetheless, many candidates fail to get on the ballot or waste this opportunity to gain other benefits from the petition effort. Candidates are frequently thrown off the ballot for failing to meet a residency requirement, failing to have a change-of-voting address properly recorded, technical errors on their petitions and statement of candidacy, and, most often, for failing to get enough legal signatures. No errors can be allowed if a candidate is to get on the ballot. However, the petition drive does more than meet legal requirements. It allows the necessary support to be mobilized at this stage to build a winning campaign.

Once a citizens' search committee has decided on the best candidate, plenty of petitions must be printed by the same printer used by the regular party candidates. This printer will use the proper forms and, since petitions cost only about $50 to print, this is no place to pinch pennies. If 500 signatures are needed to get on the ballot, at least 1,000-2,000 signatures should be collected. This means at least two hundred petitions with room for 25 signatures each. Not every worker who takes a petition gets it signed. Many workers get only 10 signatures. Some petitions get lost. A good supply of petitions should be printed to begin with and more should be printed whenever necessary.

The petition drive is important. You need the *maximum* number of signatures that can be filed, because signatures gathered by volunteers can always be challenged on technicalities such as voters who did not sign their names the same way they registered or who did not fully spell out their street address.

Signatures also provide names of potential supporters. The degree of success in obtaining signatures is also an excellent test of the fitness of a field organization. A precinct worker who turns in 25 to 100 signatures on a petition is obviously doing the job of contacting neighbors. A precinct worker who gives only excuses needs to be replaced. An area with very few petition signatures needs special attention, e.g., appearances by the candidate, coffees in the area, direct mail, or phone canvass to find precinct volunteers and build voter support. In Chicago, we expect good campaigns for alderman to collect 1,000 to 2,000 petition signatures even if less than 500 are required to get on the ballot. Good campaigns for state legislature should collect about 2,000 signatures, and solid congressional campaigns ought to gather more than 3,000.

The materials provided for a petition drive are minimal. Each worker should have instructions telling him who can pass petitions, who can sign petitions, when and where the petitions must be turned in, and when reports are expected. A worker should be given simple campaign brochures with basic information about the candidate to distribute to the voters. The worker should also have a poll list with the names of every registered voter in the precinct. In Chicago, such lists may be obtained free at the Board of Election Commissioners at City Hall. Areas of the country not as politicized as Chicago may not provide prepared lists of registered voters. In this case, the precinct effort begins by copying lists from official records or records from prior campaigns kept by political organizations. Many campaigns will choose instead to purchase a computerized list of all voters and will print out "walk sheets" for each precinct as the lists are needed. Since the petition drive takes about four weeks to complete, lists of registered voters must be prepared at least a month before the petition filing deadline.

Because most voters who sign a candidate's petition will vote for him, this process is an excellent way to begin to reach the "target number" of voters needed to win. If precinct volunteers collect 2,000 petition signatures, at least 1,200 votes are guaranteed on election day. (About 60 percent of those who signed will vote for the candidate.) The support of the rest of the voters can then be achieved incrementally and systematically. Obviously, the more valid nominating petition signatures obtained, especially from door-to-door precinct work, the closer the candidate is to the "target number" needed to win.

REGISTRATION

There may be between 30,000 and 100,000 eligible voters who are unregistered in every congressional district.[9] In every large city ward or state assembly district, there are likely to be at least 10,000 voters who could be registered. There are enough unregistered voters to change the outcome of almost every election. A campaign should establish a registration goal and work to meet it by focusing on special registration efforts such as registering high school or college students, low-income people, new citizens, or by trying to register all potential voters in the district.

The warm-up effort with petitions sets the stage for the registration drive. This stage of the campaign can be particularly useful because:

- Workers are introduced to citizens on a nonpartisan basis. People contacted during this nonpartisan effort will be more receptive when your volunteers return to solicit their vote.
- Eligible voters can be registered for the first time. The vast majority of the people registered by one candidate's workers will vote for that candidate on election day.
- Supporters are located and recruited to help with precinct work. Every worker recruited multiplies the votes for your candidate.
- Weak spots in the field operation are located and corrected before they cause the election to to be lost. Just as with the petition drive, reports of voters registered by precinct and area determine which workers are producing results and which must be replaced.

Remember that voter registration is not just a good government goal. *As many as three-quarters of the voters registered by a candidate will vote for that candidate on election day* (if they get to the polls), some out of gratitude for the service rendered and some because they registered to vote for your candidate.

In Harold Washington's campaign for mayor of Chicago in 1983, voter registration clearly made the difference between victory and defeat. Washington enjoyed his role as a congressman serving one of Chicago's inner city districts. Before he agreed to be drafted as candidate for mayor, he insisted that at least 100,000 new voters, principally from the African-American community, be registered. A grassroots effort by community and political organizations supported by a major radio campaign on African-American radio stations successfully met that goal. Harold Washington was able to motivate these newly registered voters, who provided his margin of victory in the mayoral campaign.

The arena of voter registration is changing rapidly in the 1990s. New "Motor Voter" laws are being implemented in most states. Citizens register to vote when they obtain or renew their driver's license. In the first three months after Motor Voter took effect nationally in January 1995, more than two million citizens registered to voter. In the nine states that implemented Motor Voter between 1988 and 1992, voter turnout increased from 9 percent to 12 percent by 1995.[10] As of the fall of 1995, some states like Illinois have refused to fully implement "Motor Voter" registration for state and local elections so the degree to which a campaign can plan on taking advantage of this form of registration still differs state by state.

New laws restricting the rights of immigrants to education, health and welfare benefits are encouraging legal aliens to become citizens, so they can participate in the electoral process. Many communities and states are also making it easier for volunteers to become deputy registrars, for voters to register at libraries and food stores, or to register to vote by mail. Each campaign will have to determine its exact registration drive strategy based upon these new rules of the game.

For precinct registration drives, two alternative strategies exist: 1) selective registration or 2) saturation registration. Registering voters is more than a civic good deed, it is a vital component of winning elections, so the choice between strategies must be based on the advantages of each method for the campaign.

The selective strategy is particularly appealing when a candidate is running on a party ticket in a general election and candidates from only one party are being backed. The easiest method of selective registration is doing saturation registration in the precincts that, based on past voting performance or poll data, are most likely to support your candidate.

In most participatory political campaigns, a general strategy of saturation registration is employed. In addition to expanding political participation, experience has demonstrated that most newly registered voters are receptive to reform candidates. Existing political parties already have their game down pat. As long as they can keep the players the same, they stand a good chance of winning any election. Therefore, they would prefer no one rock the boat. It is advantageous for existing groups like political parties to keep participation low. It is usually to the advantage of reformers to start a political battle and draw as many people as possible into the fight. If the fight stays small, one of the current party candidates will win. If a larger audience gets drawn in, then the outcome is in doubt. As political scientist, E. E. Schattsneider has written, "It follows that conflicts are frequently won or lost by the success that the contestants have in getting the audience involved in the fight or in excluding it, as the case may be."[11] By the very process of registering new voters, the constituency of the district is changed, and a new candidate is given more of a chance to win, as Mayor Harold Washington did in Chicago.

There are two ways to get voters to register:

1. *Lower the costs [in time and effort] of voting by making it as easy as possible to register and vote.*
2. *Increase the perceived benefits of voting by convincing potential voters of the importance of the impending electoral contests.*[12]

Providing potential voters with correct information about registration helps minimize the registration effort. Knowing the rules governing registration is essential. The following rules apply in Chicago but may differ from those in other communities:

- To be eligible to register, a voter must be a U.S. citizen, 18 years old, and have lived in the precinct for 30 days.
- Up to five weeks before the election, a voter may register in person at City Hall between 9 A.M. and 5 P.M. on weekdays and between 9 a.m. and noon on Saturdays. A voter may also be registered at special locations such as local branches of the public library or at local grocery stores by "deputy registrars" on certain weekends.
- Up to five weeks before the election, a voter who has been previously registered in Chicago, but who has moved from his previous address, may re-register by filling in the back of his voter registration card or an

Application for Transfer of Registration (change of address card) and mailing it to the Board of Election Commissioners.

* Four weeks before the election, a voter may register in person at a polling place in his neighborhood between 8:00 a.m. and 9:00 p.m.
* Voters may also be registered by deputy registrars recruited by nonpartisan organizations and given special training by the Chicago Board of Election Commissioners.

Volunteers undertake four jobs in a registration drive: 1) to delete the names of voters no longer living in the precinct, 2) to get previously registered voters to fill out change of address cards, 3) to get new voters to register in person at City Hall, at a branch of the public library or at the neighborhood polling place, or 4) to get voters registered by a deputy registrar who may be a campaign volunteer in a nonpartisan role. In none of these cases can you trust the voter. If he needs to re-register, most campaigns have him turn in a completed change-of-address card to their precinct volunteers to take to headquarters. The staff will forward the change-of-address cards to City Hall; whereas, many voters would forget to mail them on time. In my last campaign, we found this process too cumbersome and instructed the voters to mail the cards to the Board

---

VOTER REGISTRATION DRIVE INSTRUCTIONS

The registration drive of an election campaign is important because it introduces workers to citizens in a non-threatening way. People you meet now will be more receptive when you return to determine which voters are favorable to our candidate later in the campaign.

It is an opportunity to help eligible voters to register for the first time. It is also an opportunity to meet voters who are already registered and to let them know that Dick Simpson is running for Congress in the **new** 5th Congressional District against Dan Rostenkowski.

The highest priority at this time is to introduce Dick Simpson to registered voters. If we can help people to register, that is good too, but making registered voters more receptive to you when you return later is our main goal.

APPROACHING RESIDENTS:
As you walk up and down the streets of your precinct, note which addresses have registered voters listed on the poll sheet.

of Election Commissioners directly, taking a chance that the voters might not follow through. But it is better to have a campaign deliver change of address cards when possible.

If a voter has to register in person, you will have to go back and remind him: Most voters will not remember on their own. *Even on election day, voters must be reminded to vote, or as many as one-third will forget!*

The registration drive requires coordinating campaign volunteers doing exacting work. Many will not have worked in campaigns before. Therefore, a formal training session is required at which they can receive written instructions, hear an oral explanation, ask questions, meet the campaign leadership including their own area and ward chairs, be encouraged by the large number of other people working in the campaign, meet the candidate for whom they are working so hard, and pick up the necessary registration materials. This kind of formal training gives the workers a general, understanding of their job and motivation. Similar training sessions will be repeated again before the canvass and before election day. Each training session can thus be brief and focus on the job at hand at a particular stage in the campaign. The written instructions for my congressional campaign registration drive shown below explain the details of the registration drive more fully.

Knock on their door, announce that you have information about registration and the election, and introduce yourself as a neighbor. Ask if there are any registered voters in their household. If not, tell them you are a volunteer for the Simpson for Congress Campaign in the new 5th Congressional District. Tell them that Dick is running against Dan Rostenkowski. Leave the Simpson campaign literature with them and tell them it has information about registration and about Dick's candidacy. Do **not** try to convince the voter to vote for Dick at this time. That is for later.

If someone is not registered in the household, describe briefly the following methods of registering.

CHANGE OF ADDRESS CARDS:
Only for voters who were registered for the last election. If they moved from one address to another in the same election jurisdiction (Chicago to Chicago), they can re-register by completing the back of their old voter's ID card, or by completing a Change of Address postcard (which you have in your precinct worker's kit). List these names your report sheet. DO NOT TAKE THE CHANGE OF ADDRESS CARDS WITH YOU.

(continued)

VOTER REGISTRATION DRIVE INSTRUCTIONS
(continued)

WHO MAY REGISTER:

To be eligible to register to vote, a person must:

1. be a citizen of the United States on the day of registration;
2. be 18 years of age on or before March 17, 1992;
3. be a resident of the precinct on or before February 17, 1992; and
4. provide two pieces of identification, both of which must contain applicant's name and one of which must contain applicant's current address.

LOCATIONS FOR VOTER REGISTRATION:

Only for City of Chicago residents:

1. Board of Election Commissioners office (Room 308, City Hall, 121 N. LaSalle, 9–5 M–F, 9–12 Sat. Phone 269-7900).
2. Any Chicago Public Library branch (you should check which branch is closest to your precinct before you start out).
3. Area registration sites—10 locations in each ward will be open for voter registration from 11:00 A.M. to 5:00 P.M. on Saturday and Sunday, February 15 and 16.

Precinct work requires much more than an intellectual appreciation of the task to be done. It requires ringing doorbells and talking to people. Area chairs and precinct captains should supplement formal training sessions with direct help for their first-time precinct workers. Whenever possible, someone with campaign experience should accompany new workers on the visit to their first few voters, either during the registration drive or the canvass. Working with an experienced campaigner will help the new worker to understand the job, know what to say, and overcome the hurdle of the first doorbell. After this on-the-job training, the new worker will have the confidence and experience to finish the task.

The real test of a successful registration drive is the number of change-of-address cards workers collect.[13] A registration drive informs voters when they need to register in person and is used to drop voters who have died or moved from the voting lists. Voters who only need to change their voting address are the easiest to add. Deleting names from the poll list of those who have died or moved is relatively simple and often accomplished by mail inquires sent from the Board of Election Commissioners, but getting new voters registered requires talking to people. The change-of-address cards turned into campaign headquarters are physical proof that precinct workers are doing their job well. This indicator is so important, because new precinct workers are shy about

4. Deputy Registrar program. Volunteer Deputy Registrars can accept voter registration. Call the Community Services Department at 269-7851 if you want to know where volunteer registrars are located.

RECORD KEEPING:
In order for us to know how our registration drive is going, you should call your area chair or ward coordinator on **Sunday** and **Thursday** nights from now through February 16th. We will ask you for cumulative totals of:
1. How many registered voters you contacted.
2. How many change of address cards you have distributed.

Record this information on your poll sheet and report it to your area chair on Thursday and Sunday evenings.

Simpson for Congress
5th Congressional District
3534 W. Irving Park Road
Chicago, IL 60618-3220
(312) 509-1992

pushing the first doorbell. If they learn to contact voters during the registration drive, they will do a good job on the canvass. If they do not overcome their timidity during registration, they will be of little help in the election. To ensure that workers are doing the job, on carefully timed report dates the precinct workers tell their area chair, area chairs tell ward coordinators and ward coordinators tell the precinct coordinator, specifically how many change-of-address cards have been collected, how many names on the poll sheets are to be challenged, and how many voters must register in person in each precinct in the district. At least four report dates are set to allow for ample prodding of workers and to obtain complete information on the progress of the drive. In most campaigns, Thursday and Sunday evenings during the registration drive and the canvass are set as report nights.

The reports and, particularly the change-of-address cards turned in at the end of the registration drive, are hard data about the effectiveness of a precinct organization. This is the best time to strengthen the campaign structure, so the results of the registration campaign must be carefully evaluated. In areas with no reports or only reports of deletions, either the area chair must be provided with the names of more potential workers or, if the area chair has failed to recruit precinct workers or supervise their work, then he must be replaced. If few change-of-address cards are turned in, something has gone wrong. If an area chair cannot do the job, he can be made a precinct captain or, if the "demotion" would be too embarrassing, he can be kept as area co-chair. But workers who were unable to produce good results during the registration drive cannot be counted on: They must be supplemented or replaced. Failure to do so means that area will be lost on election day, and possibly the entire campaign will go down in defeat.

The petition and registration drives are the opening shots fired in the battle of the precincts. They provide the opportunity to ensure that most voters will have heard about your candidate and his issues. But these drives are only the prelude to the final battles that occur during the canvass and on election day. Registration drives provide an opportunity to recruit a volunteer army and to transform the electorate into one more receptive to your campaign. They set the stage for the final and decisive acts of the campaign.

Chapter VIII

CANVASSING THE VOTERS

A careful canvass to locate positive voters and get them to the polls wins elections, despite differences between wealthy and poor precincts, urban and rural areas, and national and local elections. The work is hard but the results on election day justify them.

The canvass takes place three to four weeks before the election. The function of this canvass is to locate all voters favorable or potentially favorable to your candidate. A secondary, but still important, function is to "mobilize lukewarm supporters."[1] The importance of locating your voters is stressed in the written instructions (see pp. 124–127) given to precinct workers:

> *Most people think of precinct workers as strong-arm salesmen. Actually, nothing could be further from the truth. The "sales" pitch is really a smokescreen to conceal the worker's true intent, which is to find out for whom the voter plans to cast her ballot on election day. Elections are won by locating and identifying the vote and, on election day, being sure that those voters who intend to vote for us actually do vote.[2]*

In practice, precinct workers affect voters as well as learn their preferences simply by providing information about the election and their candidate:

> *. . . the issue content of the canvasser's appeal is far less important than conveying the most elementary facts: first, that an election is about to take place, and second, that the name of one of the candidates is the one you are working for.[3]*

Your precinct workers also tell voters what your candidate is doing about issues that concern them, from mundane matters like street sweeping to ideological questions like freedom of speech, and they answer questions the voter may have. A precinct worker is the personal representative of the candidate.

CANVASS INSTRUCTIONS

There is no more effective way to reach a voter than talking to him/her face-to-face. While many campaigns rely on electronic media and direct mail, the personal appeal is still the most effective. When you ask a voter to support Dick Simpson and hand that voter a piece of literature, the voter is much more likely to read it. After all, you braved the cold to hand it to him/her.

We are starting early for two reasons. First, in the east end of the district we want to register voters as well as canvass. Secondly, there are areas in the district where we need to expand our volunteer base. A door-to-door campaign is the best way to recruit new volunteers.

In your kits you will find the following materials:

- this instruction booklet
- a walk sheet with sample instruction sheet;
- campaign brochures;
- voter change-of-address cards;
- window signs;
- a move-in sheet, listing people who recently moved into the precinct
- a Registration Log Sheet, for listing people who need to be registered by a deputy registrar.

WHERE AND HOW TO BEGIN

Many kits include a list of people who recently moved into the precinct. If your kit has one of these, visit these people first and register them to vote. **anyone wishing to vote on march 15th must register to vote at their new address by February 15th, 1994.**

There are several ways that one can register to vote:

- They can register to vote at the nearest public library;
- A deputy registrar can register them on site;
- They may fill out a change of address card **(provided they were formerly registered in the city of Chicago and have relocated within the city of Cchicago);**
- In suburban Cook County voters can register at their city hall.

If you are a deputy registrar work your way down the list and get everyone registered. Keep track of who you register, their address and **phone number,** so we can follow up on your work.

If you are not a deputy registrar, you may still work the list and have people fill out a "voter change-of-address card" (if, of course, they are already registered at their previous Chicago address). If they are not registered, or can't remember voting in the past four years, or are in any way confused about their registration, add their name to the provided Registration Log Sheet. Once you have finished talking to everyone on your move-in sheet, turn in the registration log sheet to your ward coordinator. This must be done by February 6th. The campaign office will have deputy registrars call to make appointments to register those voters or direct them to voter registration sites.

If you do not find a list of new move-ins in your kit you should immediately start your canvass.

HOW TO CONDUCT A CANVASS

In January you are making the first of several contacts with the voters. Even at this early date many people are focusing on the congressional race. Most voters at this stage have already decided whether they support Dan Rostenkowski or want a change. It is your job to tell them that Dick Simpson is that change.

While there are 5 candidates in the race Dan Rostenkowski is the candidate to beat. If someone tells you that they support Dan Rostenkowski don't argue; mark them down on your walk sheet as "no" and move on. If you are canvassing for a second candidate such as Ellis Levin for State Legislature ask whether they support that candidate. Mark the walk sheet Y (yes), N (no), or U (undecided), whichever is appropriate.

If someone tells you they are not voting for Dan Rostenkowski, but they don't know who they will vote for, mark them as a U. **This voter must be recontacted.**

Anyone stating that they support Dick Simpson should be marked a "Y" and asked if they want to help in the campaign.

By February 6, you should have contacted everyone on your move-in list, and given that information to your ward coordinator. By February 15, you should have gone through your precinct once and hopefully made 75% contact. Any additional people found needing to be registered should be treated as discussed above. On February 15, or there abouts you need to turn in a copy of your walk sheets to your ward coordinator.

As you work your way down the block, note buildings that you cannot get into. We will mail and phone into these buildings. Also, note people listed on your walk sheet who have moved out. *(continued)*

CANVASS INSTRUCTIONS *(continued)*

We will be planning a mailing by February 15th. We want to delete from our mailing list all of Dan Rostenkowski's supporters. We also want to delete people who have moved. **For every deletion we make we can save time and effort.** Our resources are finite, and you will help us target key voters.

You will be provided more literature on request. On February 15th start recontacting your undecided voters. By this time we expect to have data showing that Dick Simpson is the only candidate who can unseat Dan Rostenkowski. We will also have scheduled coffees in the neighborhood and you may invite the undecided voters over to meet Dick.

Finish the second sweep through the precinct by February 28. We will want you to resubmit a copy of your walk sheet to the ward coordinator. Beginning on March 1, revisit all your "Y"s and "U"s. The undecideds will now begin to tell you they support Dick Simpson.

Some Easy Ways to Win Your Precinct

1. One effective way to win votes is a "friend of a friend" letter. Enclosed is a draft of a "friend" letter. As you are out meeting people in the neighborhood, some people will want to help Dick but can't put in a lot of time. Ask them to send a "friend of friend" letter. Let us know their name and address, we will print up a letter, and they can mail it.

2. Host a coffee, or find someone on your block to host one.

3. Get everyone to put a poster in their window.

4. Work your precinct early, get to know everyone, and convince them to join a growing army of Simpson Supporters.

A Simpson Door Rap

A "Y" Voter

Knock knock.

"May I help you?"

"Hello. I'm a volunteer for Dick Simpson, who is running for Congress against Dan Rostenkowski. I live right down the street and I'm out asking all my neighbors to vote for Simpson."

"Yes, I've heard of Simpson. I voted for him last time."

"Great. Are you going to vote for him again?"

"Yes, sure."

"Well, could you help Dick out this time. The polls have Dick leading, and with a little more help we should be able to beat Rosty."

"What would you want me to do?"

"You can talk to the neighbors like I'm doing today."

"No, it's too cold."

"Would you be willing to help make phone calls in the evening?"

"No."

"Would you be willing to have a coffee then, and invite your neighbors over?"

"No."

"Would you be willing to send a letter to them asking them to vote for Dick."

"Yes."

"Let me write your name and address down, and the campaign office will help draft a letter for you. They should contact you in the next week. Oh, and here's a brochure, and why don't you hang a sign in your window where everyone can see it."

A "U" Voter

Knock knock.

"May I help you?"

"Yes. I'm a volunteer for Dick Simpson, who is running for Congress against Dan Rostenkowski. I'm out asking people to vote for Simpson instead of Rostenkowski. I'm sure you've heard all about Rosty in the news."

"Yes I have and I'm sick of him. He's got to go."

"Well, here's a brochure on Dick Simpson. He used to be alderman in Lakeview. He teaches now at UIC. He ran last time against Rosty and almost beat him. We figure Dick Simpson can win this time because people are pretty fed up with all the corruption in Congress."

"Well, I don't know this Dick Simpson, but I'm not voting for Rottenkowski."

"If you have any questions, let me know. Read the brochure about Dick Simpson, and I'll get back in touch with you."

A "N" Voter

Knock knock.

"May I help you?"

"Hello, I'm a volunteer for Dick Simpson, who is running for Congress against Dan Rostenkowski."

"No Thank You. I think I'll stick with Dan."

"Thank You. Have a nice day." Once the door closes you are allowed to mumble whatever you want.

Many voters will judge a candidate by their precinct workers. Because reformers normally represent better qualified candidates and because they ask voters to decide for whom to vote on the merits of the issues, reformers can beat regular party precinct captains and overcome mass media or direct mail appeals by opponents. But it takes hard work.

After the precinct worker talks to a voter about the candidate, she determines a voter's position on the election by politely asking, "May we count on your support for our candidate on election day?" Based on the voter's response, a precinct worker marks a plus (+), minus (-), or zero (0) beside that name on the poll list (see pp. 129–130). When she is finished with the canvass, she will have a list of *plus voters* who favor your candidate, *minus voters* who favor your opponent, and as many as one-half who are *zero voters,* because they will not say how they will vote or they have not yet decided. Unless the voter says differently, all members of the family will probably vote the same way.

Each worker develops her own way of talking with voters. Generally, a presentation will be organized around the following points:

- Introducing oneself. ("I'm Joe Smith, a volunteer working to elect Jane Doe as our state representative.")
- Handing the voter a piece of campaign literature and discussing the candidate's virtues in two or three sentences.
- Asking if the voter's support may be counted on for your candidate.
- Thanking the voter and leaving as quickly and courteously as possible.

The entire discussion with a voter should take only five minutes. If 100 families live in the precinct, a canvass of every family can be completed in less than 10 hours. With three workers in the precinct, each will have to work only slightly over three hours. You can finish the job if you:

- *Don't engage in long discussions.* If the voter has numerous detailed questions, have her call your campaign headquarters for the answers. You have hundreds of voters to see. In the hour you spend talking to a single voter you could have canvassed 20 others.
- *Don't engage in arguments.* You may win the argument, but your candidate has lost a vote and the votes of all the voters you now will not have time to see.
- *Start early.* Do not put off the job. Begin as soon as you have received canvassing instructions and materials.
- *Work systematically.* Divide the list of voters among the workers available. Divide your list so that you canvass a portion of the voters each week.
- *Recruit new workers to help.* As you go to each home, watch for potential workers. They are even more valuable than *plus voters.* If you find citizens interested in the campaign, encourage them to work along with you. After you have recruited more than two or three co-workers, turn in any extra names of potential workers to your campaign headquarters so that they can be employed in some of the uncovered precincts. In sharing your workers, remember that the point of the campaign is to win the election, not simply to carry your precinct.

PRINTED PRECINCT REGISTER — FEBRUARY, 1992

This printed list of registered voters was prepared based on the results of the Citywide mail canvass conducted by the Board of Election Commissioners for the City of Chicago. Therefore, on the basis of the canvass results, the Board certifies that the persons whose names appear on this list were qualified to vote to the addresses listed as of the time of the canvass.

It is possible that some voter or voters whose name appears on this list may not be qualified or may become disqualified before the day of election. Any registered voter who is a resident of the ward and who has personal knowledge that a person whose name appears on this list is not qualified to vote from the address listed may file an application to have the name of said voter erased from the registry. This application must be filed in person in the Office of the Board of Election Commissioners on March 2 or March 3, between the hours of 9:00 o'clock a.m. and 5 o'clock p.m. Any person may give information to the Board concerning the names of ineligible persons on this list at any time and although removal may not be legally possible before the election, any such information that has apparent validity may be used by the Board and others as the basis for challenging such person or persons on election day.

28 PRECINCT
47 WARD
CHICAGO

W CULLOM AV

- 02014 GREENE DIANE M
- 02015 GREENE ETHEL L
- 02016 GREENE RAY JR
- 02014 GREENE RAYMOND G
- 02015 GREENE RUSSELL A
- 02017 LAUREY VIVIAN
- 02018 LANNON SANDRA
- 02018 LANNON MARGARET M
- 02018 LANNON MICHAEL J
- 02018 PADHELCON DEANNE K
- 02019 SHAUDCOEUR ALENE
- 02019 DARCY MINDA M
- 02020 FLAHERTY MARIANNE M
- 02023 KRAUS WILLIANNE M
- 02023 QUEJADA GILBERTO
- 02046 RISTICH ELMA
- 02046 HUDSON SHERRY J
- 02025 WEAVER ALAN L
- 02025 WEAVER DIANE S
- 02026 BESSER CAROL ROSALIE
- 02026 SCHUEBEL ERICH E
- 02027 SCHUEBEL RUTH E
- 02027 RICHNER LINDA
- 02031 HEUCK GRETCHEN
- 02031 HEUCK OTTO
- 02031 SELFRIDGE MARY T
- 02035 SEIFRIDGE ROBERT M
- 02035 KEATING KATHERINE
- 02035 STRECKER NIKOLAUS
- 02036 CARNEY AUDREY L
- 02036 MURPHY JOHN
- 02037 MURPHY LORRAINE M
- 02037 GOODWIN ANTHONY B
- 02038 CULLEN JOANNE SRM
- 02038 FRANK LAWRENCE M
- 02039 NOESEN ROBIN J
- 02039 COHEN ROBIN J
- 02042 GOTTLIEB JOHN F
- 02042 HAWK GERALD M
- 02043 HAWK JOHN CAROL A
- 02043 RUHNKE DONALD A
- 02043 RUHNKE HELEN S
- 02048 BASURCO GABRIELA M
- 02048 BASURCO HECTOR F
- 02048 BASURCO PATRICIA

W MONTE AV (W HOYNE AV)

- +0314 MAINEY WILLIAM E
- +0316 RUMORG GREGG A
- +0318 KANNASA ROBERT C
- 0318 SULLIVAN JAMES T
- +0334 MOHR DAVID JAMES
- +0334 BUERK ELEANOR L
- +0334 BUERK JOHN
- +0338 BUERK IVER M
- +0338 MENDOZA MELANIE
- +0338 PASCUAL CYNTHIA M
- +0338 PASCUAL ELVIRA M
- +0338 PASCUAL RICARDO S II
- +0342 MUSKOVITS MARIA
- +0342 WAGNER ANNA
- +0346 MONACHINO JOSEPHINE
- +0346 SANDERS JACOMINE M
- 0346 GIKALDO CARIDAD
- 0346 GIKALDO JACQUELINE L
- +0350 PHILLIPS MARIE L
- +0350 MUENCH BRIAN
- 0350 MUENCH SONJA
- +0350 MUENCH RONALD B
- +0350 MUENCH MARIE L
- +0350 ROJAS ALEXIS

N HOYNE AV

- +0309 CAREY BARBARA
- +0309 LUNDELL ELIZABETH
- +0309 MCKINSON JEFFREY
- +0310 EGAS FINA M
- +0310 FRANCIS RICHARD M
- +0310 RANSFORD KATHLEEN A
- +0310 ROMAN JIM
- 0319 VILLALOBOS CAROLINE J
- 0320 SLAUGHTER EDNA L
- +0322 GARRABRANT MARY M
- +0322 ROSARIO RUTH
- 0322 KARUSO GEORGE T
- +0324 KENYON MILLIE M
- 0349 ALVARADO MARCO
- +0349 SHAVARADO MORENCIA
- +0349 SHAH WILLIAM M
- +0349 SHAH WILLIAM M

W HUTCHINSON ST

- 02006 TOLOMEO AUGUSTA
- 02006 TOLOMEO MICHAEL M

- -2056 SAVKOVIC DAVID
- -2056 SAVKOVIC HELENA
- -2058 BROOKS CHARLES M
- -2058 JONAS AGNES
- -2060 JONAS FRED
- -2060 VERDUZZ MARILYN
- +2060 KAPAST MANSY M
- +2064 CLASS GLADYS
- +2064 QUINN KELLY
- +2064 ROMAN CARLOS
- +2066 KELLEY CAROL
- +2066 TORO CLGAL C

N LINCOLN AV

- +4237 BUSCM MICHELLE L
- +4237 MURRAY AVRIL A
- +4239 WINNINGHAM SAMUEL R
- +4247 SCHUMACHER ELIZABETH
- +4247 SCHUMACHER HEINRICH
- +4347 BAILOG GERALD R
- +4341 BAILOG ADAM
- +4341 THOMPSON MELANO
- +4341 VERBAN NADEYDA
- +4343 FIKARI JAMES
- +4345 FIKARI JOHN
- +4345 FIKARI JOHN R
- +4345 FIKARI RUTH
- +4347 MATMOGH ERNEST
- +4347 MATMOGH ERNESTI
- +4347 MATMOGH MAUREEN
- +4351 GENRAREN ANDRES
- +4351 CERRERQ ANDRES
- +4353 DELMONTEZ PATRICIA G
- +4353 GARCIA MAGNOLIA
- +4357 BUSTER ELENORA
- +4357 BUSTER JOSEF
- +4357 BUSTER JOSEPH G
- +4357 BUSTER LAURA J
- 04363 BENITEZ RICHARD A
- 04363 BENITEZ JAVIER A
- 04363 BENITEZ PEDRO
- +4363 TRUJILLO ANNA L

W MELROSE AV

- +2111 HARJO MARIE E
- +2111 HARJO MARILYN
- +2113 HARRAHAN MARY ELLEN
- +2113 KRAHN MARLENE
- +2119 MITSUUCHI ANITA M
- +2119 MIDAS JOHN R
- 2137 ASTA HELGA T
- 2137 OLGA LOUISE
- 2137 GRCMER SHARON ROBERTA

W PENSACOLA AV

- 2017 BAILEY JAMES E
- 2017 BAILEY JOHN
- 2018 BAILEY JOYCE R
- 2018 ORALARY
- 2019 CECILLA LORAINE F
- 2019 MENAO MARIA LEONOR C
- 2019 MENAO WILLIAM
- 2022 BANK ELEANOR E
- 2022 BANK MARY PAT
- 2023 BAH RICHARD
- 2023 SEYFERTH DIETER M
- 2023 SEYFERTH NORBERT
- 2025 BASKIN THOMAS J
- 2025 DEMAEDUNE MARY A
- 2025 ROTTER LEUR
- 2029 DAVIS ELIZABETH S
- 2029 GEHRING ARNET J
- 2029 GEHART RUSSELL L
- 2029 KEEY RICHARD
- 2031 KRAEMER IRWIN C
- 2034 MALMER CLANE A
- 2034 CICEKO CHENYA
- 2035 GOFINAL DAVID
- 2035 SOUTH PARTHA E
- 2037 PISKE KAPONA
- 2037 PISKE ROBERT M
- 2038 MEJIA DANIEL
- 2038 MEJIA ALFONSO
- 2038 MEJIA CARLOS
- 2038 MEJIA LINDA L
- 2038 MEJIA LYLIA
- 2038 MEJIA MARIO D
- 2038 MEJIA RUGEN
- 2038 MEJIA RUGEN JR

The undersigned members of the Board of Election Commissioners of the City of Chicago certify that the names on this list are the names of all voters entitled to vote at the March 17, 1992 Primary Election in the Precinct listed on the top hereof and, according to the Election Code, the list is prima facie evidence that the persons whose names appear hereon are entitled to vote. This list is subject to corrections and revisions that may be published in a supplemental list subsequent hereto.

Number of names on this list: 398

Chicago, February, 1992

This symbol (+) indicates voters added to this list since April 2, 1991.

Accuracy is crucial in a good canvass. To achieve accuracy, workers must understand the +, -, and 0 symbols they mark on the poll lists and the reason for them. On election day workers will work very hard to get every one of the plus voters to vote. You will completely ignore the minus voters. Unless there are special considerations like ethnic identification with or strong support for the candidate in the rest of the precinct, workers will also ignore zero voters. Workers will work from 5 A.M. to 7 P.M. on election day to ensure that every one of the plus voters vote. To do this job effectively, campaign workers must know which voters are plus voters, which is the reason for the canvass.

Precinct workers must be careful in their evaluation of voters. Voters who can be counted on to vote for the candidate, not necessarily voters who smile in a friendly manner, are to be identified with a plus. Plus voters are only those who answer "Yes" to the question "May we count on your support?"

There are three reasons why this important task is left to the last three or four weeks before the election. First, the registration drive immediately precedes the canvass and the two cannot be done simultaneously. Second, precinct workers work best within definite time periods rather than at their leisure over several months. Without a limited time and a specific job, most workers will procrastinate. Finally, most voters do not have enough information about the candidates to make their choice until close to election day. Only in this period is media coverage great or voter interest high. Canvassing votes much earlier is a waste of time. So there is less than a month to complete the canvass and progress reports will be requested twice a week.

The canvass is the most crucial phase of the campaign. If done well, the chances of winning are good. If workers fail to contact enough voters, discern voter preferences, or be good representatives of a candidate, not enough plus voters will get to the polls on election day, and all will be lost. No candidate wins on good looks, publicity or issues alone. To win the election, your campaign workers must contact voters personally, ask for their vote, and remind them of their duty on election day. The other side will be working, too, but can be beaten if enough volunteers put in the time and if they work systematically and effectively. Over a period of several campaigns, dramatic results can be achieved by good precinct work.

While the door-to-door effort is occurring in the precincts, the candidate is not idle. She continues her schedule of three or four coffees a day to win over campaign volunteers, luncheons to raise money, news conferences to get publicity, and staff meetings to develop campaign strategy. She now adds meeting voters at bus stops each morning from 7:00 A.M. to 9:00 A.M., shopping center appearances every weekend, and walking tours of precincts in the afternoons. By talking with voters at bus stops, at stores and in their homes, the candidate demonstrates her interest in their problems and makes the job of precinct workers much easier. Word will quickly get around that your candidate personally visited the neighborhood, something that previous candidates and even incumbent elected officials might not have done.

ELECTION DAY

Election day activities complete the process of winning elections. To win, campaign workers must perform three functions in as many precincts as possible: 1) distribution of sample ballots, 2) poll watching to prevent fraud and to check on who has voted, and 3) getting plus voters to the polls. Other activities, such as troubleshooting and putting up campaign posters, support these basic functions. If a campaign's message has reached the voters and the precincts have been canvassed, a good job on election day will ensure victory.

A single day is the climax of each election. Months of effort are focused on this one opportunity to elect a candidate. A candidate's workers and those of her opponents will devote at least 12 hours to the battle on election day, and when the polls close a binding verdict will have been rendered. Any votes not obtained are lost forever. So if you don't want the hopes you have raised among the electorate to be dashed, your work on election day must ensure victory for your candidate and for participatory politics.

GETTING OUT YOUR VOTE

Other than direct mail efforts and radio and television commercials, the last hours, days and weeks of the campaign depend upon the field operation. This stage of the campaign is called "get out the vote" or GOTV.

A field operation has had three principal purposes all along. Will Robinson in "Campaigns and Elections American Style" describes them this way:

1. Repetitively move the campaign's message to key groups, areas and individuals in an effort to persuade them to support your candidate.
2. Create programs to identify the key demographic groups, geographic areas or specific individuals who are most likely to support your candidate.
3. Set up the structure and program to get those identified supporters out to vote on election day.[4]

These points are true even of national campaigns. The 1992 Clinton-Gore field operation contained all three components. They used their national field operation each week to obtain free media coverage of the campaign by rewriting themes as local press releases and using radio and television satellite feeds. Their direct mail campaigns in each state contained the same messages as their national television commercials. Their "grassroots-for- change" precinct effort provided 10 million people instructions and materials to give voters in their neighborhoods.[5]

In addition to sending a message and finding plus voters, your GOTV campaign culminates by getting plus voters to the polls. In addition, election day activities also influence uncommitted voters and prevent election fraud. Ideally, this work is divided between three different types of election-day workers, but in understaffed precincts each volunteer may have to perform several functions.

The three workers are: 1) the *distributor,* who passes out sample ballots to voters on their way to the polls, 2) the *poll watcher* or *checker,* who observes the opening, operation and closing of the polls while keeping track of exactly who has voted, and 3) the *runner* who goes door-to-door reminding plus voters to vote. Of these three functions, running is by far the most crucial to a winning campaign. Elections are won or lost on Election Day, and determined and persistent running will win the election for a candidate (see sample poll watching instructions on pp. 134–135).[6]

State and national campaigns cannot cover every precinct in such depth on election date. They organize their precincts into low-performance and high-performance precincts. High-performance precincts are those in which precinct workers have done a canvass and found a significant number of plus voters, those precincts which have voted heavily for candidates from the same party in the past, or those precincts in which voters have demographic characteristics that match the strongest supporters of a candidate as determined by public opinion polls. All voters in high-performance precincts will be visited by precinct workers several times on election day or called by volunteers or professional telemarketing firms and reminded to vote. In low-performance precincts, only plus voters are phoned and reminded to vote. In congressional, city, county, or statewide campaigns without enough workers to cover all the precincts, it is not unusual to use 300 to 500 volunteer phoners on election day.[7]

In more local campaigns with a well-developed field operation, distributors, checkers, and runners will be used in all precincts. The distributor will put up posters near the polling place and give out leaflets like the endorsement card from my congressional campaign (shown on p. 136). By encouraging each voter to vote for a candidate, the distributor can sway at least 10 to 20 votes in every precinct. If there are not enough volunteers for a distributor at each polling place all day, distributors are most effective in the hours when polls open and close, since most people vote at these times. In a close race, the few extra votes won by distributing endorsement cards in each precinct can make the difference between victory and defeat. Influencing these still uncommitted voters is important enough that the distributor will have the company of the opposing precinct captains in front of the polling place. Needless to say, they should not make payoffs to voters and workers from both campaigns should stay the same distance from the polling place.[8] (In Illinois, campaigners are required to be at least 100 feet from the polling place.)

The passer card that volunteers distribute on election day will include endorsements the candidate has received, the appropriate lever to pull on the voting machine, or the number to punch on computer punch card voting systems to vote for your candidate. Often so many offices are up for election that some voters get confused and fail to vote for candidates without this information.

Poll watchers perform dual functions on election day. They keep the election honest, and they keep track of which plus voters have voted, so the runners know which voters they still have to get to the polls. Reformers usually lose because they have not worked the precincts and have not located their *plus*

OPENING THE POLLS

YOU MUST ARRIVE AT THE POLLING PLACE BY *5:10 A.M. or you will be locked out!* Enter with the judges as soon as they arrive at 5:15. Fill out your pollwatcher's credential, sign it and give it to the judge. EVERYONE INSIDE THE POLLING PLACE MUST BE CREDENTIALED! By 6:00 A.M., the entrance to the polling place should be clearly marked by a flag and the Board of Election's sign.

All Election Day equipment and supplies are inside a large metal Equipment Supply Carrier (ESC). The judges check all items against form #21P to be sure nothing is missing. Report missing items to the Board of Elections immediately; also tell your Area Chair when s/he arrives. BE SURE THAT THE SEAL ON THE ESC IS NOT BROKEN BEFORE THE JUDGES ARRIVE AT THE POLLING PLACE.

Judges open the Transfer Case which contains the ballot pads. Count the number of ballot pads provided to the precinct (based on number of voters). Make sure the ballots are numbered in sequential order, 50 ballots per pad. Next, the Precinct Ballot Counter (PBC) is tested. Refer to the Judges' Manual (p. 7) for instructions. A blue precinct ID card inserted in to the PBC should produce a "zero tape." If the tape does not produce all zeroes in the vote count column, call the Board of Elections and Simpson headquarters immediately and tell your Area Chair when s/he arrives. If the PBC works properly, it will be packed back into the ESC until the polls close.

The judges now set up the Votamatic units. Be sure the machines are positioned so that voters have privacy. Whenever possible, machines should be set up so that the voter's back is to the wall. THE MACHINES MAY NOT BE ARRANGED TO ALLOW ANYONE TO WATCH HOW A VOTER CASTS A BALLOT. Tape should be placed on the floor two feet behind the voting machine to indicate where voters should wait in line. See the Judges' Manual (p. 9) for a diagram of polling place set-up. Be sure the judges set up their stations as outlined in the manual, insofar as possible.

The Ballot Booklet inside each voting booth must be checked for accuracy *before 6:00 A.M.* A beige demonstrator ballot is inserted into the booklet to test it. Make sure that when you vote for Simpson, the hole above #20 is punched out.

Now check the Ballot Box (ESC). You have the right to inspect it before it is sealed to insure that no votes have been cast before 6 A.M. If there are ballots in the box, call 000-0000 or 000-0000 immediately.

IMPORTANT: Before 6 A.M., be sure the judges' table is set up to allow all judges to have a good view of the entire polling place and that there is room *behind the judges' table* for pollwatchers to sit or stand so that pollwatchers may observe the signature comparison. See Judges' Manual (p. 10–11).

Completely fill out the orange Opener's Report Form; your Area Chair will pick it up around 6:30 A.M.

If there are problems, refer to the Project LEAP Guide for Solving Election Day Problems in each kit and to the Judges' Manual; consult your Area Chair or call 000/000-0000 or 000/000-0000 if you cannot figure it out. Be polite; assume that any problems are inadvertent; but insist that the law be followed. If all else fails, call the Board of Election Commissioners legal hotline: 000/000-0000 in Chicago, 000/000-0000 in the suburbs.

HOW TO CLOSE THE POLLING PLACE

The polls close at 7:00 P.M., so *you must arrive by 6:45 P.M.* to close your poll. Anyone who is voting or is waiting in line to vote is allowed to cast a ballot, but voters cannot be permitted to enter the polling place after 7:00 P.M. Make sure to record information on judges and pollwatchers on the yellow Election Results Report. Also make sure your name, phone number, and the ward and precinct are on the form. Ascertain which additional races (in italics on the yellow form) are relevant to your precinct(s).

Review the reasons for challenge in the LEAP Guide for Solving Election Day Problems, so that you will be ready to challenge any improper count procedures. As soon as you get there, and before the counting process begins, state clearly to the judges that you will want a copy of the final tape.

After the last voter leaves, the count begins with absentee ballots. The judges open the mailing envelopes and compare the voters' affidavit signatures and registration with the binder signatures. By checking the back of the binder card, you can be sure that no absentee ballot is cast for a voter who has voted in person on Election Day. The judges detach the stubs from the ballots, initial them and their ballot envelopes, and deposit them in the ballot box (see the Judges' Manual, p. 28). You should compare the signature and registration information on the affidavit with the binder information and challenge the vote if there is any inconsistency. Refer again to the grounds for challenging; challenges must be made as the ballots are being processed.

Next, the judges break the seal on the ballot box and remove ALL ballots. They should separate all write-ins and then remove the rest of the ballots from their envelopes. These ballots and their envelopes must both be initialed by the same judge; uninitialed ballots may not be counted (see manual, p. 29, step 4c).

The judges then open the Precinct Ballot Counter (PBC) and insert a blue precinct ID card to run a "zero tape" which must show zeros next to the position number of each candidate. The ballots are fed one-by-one into the PBC; the tape shows a "BLT" (Ballot) number next to each ballot cast. The last, largest number recorded is the total of ballots cast, which you should record on the Election Result Sheet.

If a ballot card won't go through the counter on the fifth try, the judges must count it as defective and repunch the numbers onto a new ballot (Judges' manual, p. 32). They must exactly duplicate the original and process the original as defective.

Make certain all ballots are properly accounted for—see p. 33, sections H and I. Fill in appropriate numbers on the yellow Election Results Report as the judges fill them in on their report.

The judges run a tape with the results of the balloting. Remind them to run the copy you asked for at the beginning of the count. Staple this copy to your yellow Election Result Form and record the numbers on the appropriate lines. Print your name and phone number on both the form and the tape. Please note that we are also taking a count for other candidates, because they are closing other precincts for us.

If at any time the judges do not comply with procedures as stated in the Judges' Manual after you have asked them to comply, call the campaign *000/000-0000 or 000/000-0000*! If you can't get through, call the Board of Elections legal hotline: 000/000-0000 in Chicago, 000/000-0000 in the suburbs.

After ballots and judges' result sheets have been sealed and locked in the transfer case, record the seal numbers and follow the locked box to the car which is transporting the ballots to the Board of Elections receiving station. Record the name of the judges accompanying the ballots and the license number of the car. If possible, follow the car to the receiving station.

Call in results ASAP to the appropriate reporting number on the pink phone number list. Bring the yellow form and tape to our office at 3733 N. Clark Street, then go straight to the victory party at Ann Sather Restaurant, 929 W. Belmont.

Passer Card (Front)

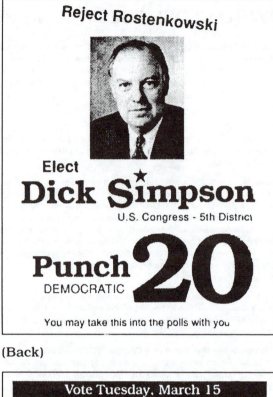

Reject Rostenkowski

Elect

Dick ★Simpson

U.S. Congress - 5th District

Punch**20**

DEMOCRATIC

You may take this into the polls with you

(Back)

Vote Tuesday, March 15

The following organizations endorse
Dick Simpson as the best candidate for Congress:

- ★ National Organization for Women's
  Political Action Committee
- ★ Illinois NOW PAC
- ★ Cook County Democratic Women
- ★ IVI/IPO, Independent Voters of Illinois
  Independent Precinct Organization
- ★ Illinois Peace Action
- ★ IMPACT
- ★ Americans for Democratic Action,
  Northeastern Illinois Chapter
- ★ United Electrical, Radio and Machine Workers,
  District Council 11
- ★ University Professionals of Illinois,
  Local 4100, AFT, AFL-CIO
- ★ West Suburban Teachers Union, Local 571, IFT
- ★ Filipino-American Voters League
- ★ Indo-American Democratic Organization
- ★ Illinois-Hispanic Democratic Council
  Northwest Cook County Chapter
- ★ Pioneer Press Newspapers

Your polling place is:

Paid for by Simpson for Congress Committee, 3740 W. Irving Park Rd., Chicago, IL 60618.
312/866-1994. Thomas J. Gradel, President

voters, but having poll watchers in every precinct ensures that no votes have been stolen from your candidate. Election results are more often incorrectly reported because of honest errors rather than through intentional fraud. But in some precincts, hundreds of votes may have been stolen. Losing by a few votes is tragic if you know that the stealing could have been prevented.

Poll watching insures that votes are not stolen. It guarantees that your opponent will not get votes she does not deserve. Most vote fraud is perpetrated by five methods: 1) stuffing the ballot box with false votes, 2) improper voter instructions and "assistance" by election judges, 3) buying votes, 4) getting voters to fill out fraudulent absentee ballots before election day, and 5) recording inaccurate election results. The best protection against such vote fraud is an alert poll watcher:

> *Poll watching is the only known means of safeguarding honest, democratic elections on election day. Your responsibility as a poll watcher is to detect and report any misconduct in the polling place.* **You, as a poll watcher, are responsible for any errors that are made in the conduct of the election in your polling place if you do not call adequate attention to them.** *Poll watching is a very serious and important job.*
>
> **You can be an effective poll watcher only if you are adequately informed.** *When you accepted the responsibility of being a poll watcher, you accepted also the responsibility of becoming informed.*
>
> *Therefore, before election day, you should know:*
> * *Correct election procedure.*
> * *Your rights.*
> * *Your duties.*
>
> *Effectiveness as a poll watcher depends upon you being more informed than the Judges of Election.*[9]

Stuffing the ballot box does not happen as often as it once did. The penalties are stiff, and it is relatively easy to detect. If the polls go unwatched, however, danger exists that this method of fraud will still be used. A precinct captain can falsely fill out voter affidavits and then punch additional votes for their candidate before the polls open, during a lull or after the polls have theoretically closed.

In the old days when paper ballots were used, a "paper ballot chain" was employed. A precinct captain stole the first ballot and marked it appropriately. She gave it to a voter, promising of several dollars if the voter would vote with it. The voter went into the polling booth and pulled the curtain. Then she took the marked ballot from one pocket and put her new unmarked ballot in the other. After voting with the precinct captain's marked ballot, she took the unmarked ballot back to the captain and received her payoff. To break the "chain," a poll watcher had to see it being used and get officials from the state attorney's office or the U.S. justice department to order an arrest.

Preventing improper use of absentee ballots is harder than preventing fraud at the polls on election day. In many states, precinct captains are now using legal absentee ballots to guarantee votes for their party's candidates before the election is held. In places like nursing homes, it is easy for campaign workers to convince voters to fill out the forms for absentee ballots and then to go back and "help" the voters fill out the ballots the way the precinct captain wants. Only legislative changes will guarantee that absentee ballots are used for the proper reasons and that the voters, not the precinct captains, do the voting. Challenging unduly large numbers of absentee ballots when they are brought to the polling place for counting is the necessary first step in curbing the improper use of these ballots.

A similar problem occurs with improper voter "assistance" by election judges on election day. Some election judges, and even some party precinct captains, simply vote for citizens under the pretext of giving them assistance. Only a handicapped or illiterate citizen may have election judges punch the computer voting cards for them, and only if there is a signed affidavit that attests to the reason this assistance is needed. Voters may ask for instructions on a voting machine model, but any such instruction must be given in the presence of at least one Democratic and one Republican judge in full view of the polls watchers. The demonstration must be given neutrally. If not carefully controlled by a poll watcher, incorrect methods of absentee voting and voter assistance can cause a candidate to lose a sizable number of votes.

Recording incorrect election results causes even greater loses (although this is less likely to occur with the newer computer counting systems). To prevent recording errors, two poll watchers are needed. One watcher stands behind the judge placing the punch cards into the counter, and the other sits with the judges recording the figures. Law suits and recounts in many elections have shown that recording errors happen frequently. Poll watchers often make sure that errors do not happen in an election and that if mistakes are made, recounts can remedy the errors.

ELECTION DAY TRAINING SESSION

Election day scheduling is a massive task requiring special coordinators who call all potential volunteers and schedule them for each precinct polling place that needs to be covered. Scheduling several hundred volunteers is not enough. They must also be trained and given their election materials.

On the weekend before the election, a training session or several training sessions are held. For each precinct, a packet is prepared with all necessary materials: plus list, additional poll lists, posters, buttons, leaflets, written instructions, assignment sheets, and report forms. At the meeting, instructions for election day work are given, the candidate speaks, and materials are handed out. If possible, poll watchers are given the opportunity to practice voting on the type of voting machine or punch-card system to be used.

Later the same afternoon or evening, area chairs may hold a party in their homes to reinforce what workers learned at the larger training session, answer questions more fully, make a final check on preparations, and give the workers a sense of being part of a team effort. Through both large training sessions and smaller area parties, morale is boosted for the final push towards victory.

THE DAY BEFORE THE ELECTION

The day before the election, precinct workers visit all their plus voters to give them an election day leaflet or endorsement card with the candidate's name and punch number. This reminds voters to vote and tells them how to vote for your candidate. Anyone who is not home can be reminded by leaving the card in the mailbox or under the door. If additional time remains after all the plus voters have been alerted, a few minutes can be spent talking with the most promising zero voters to convert them to vote for your candidate.

The night before the election in better-funded and better-staffed campaigns, a group of high school and college students are brought together to put posters up throughout the district on main streets, around polling places and at major intersections. This activity is directed by the same visibility chair who has coordinated the placement of window posters and yard signs throughout the campaign. The workers first have a pep talk by the candidate and then disperse to put up the posters. This blitz bolsters the morale of campaign workers, discourages opponents, and, by sheer visual repetition, makes voters aware of your candidate on election day. This work cannot be done before election day, because opponent's workers will tear these posters down very quickly.

ELECTION DAY

Election day begins for a handful of volunteers with the visibility blitz at 2:00 A.M. As the students finish their job at 3:00 or 4:00 A.M., the precincts remain unmanned. At 5:00 A.M. the new day begins as workers throughout the district arise and prepare to do battle. If the polls open at 6 A.M., precinct captains and volunteers arrive at each polling place in the district by 5:30 A.M. After placing campaign posters along the walks leading to the polling place, at least one of the workers goes inside, introduces herself to the judges, shows her poll watcher credentials if necessary, and watches the opening of the polls. As each machine is readied, she reads the public counter on the side of the voting machine to make sure that each counter registers 000, meaning no votes yet cast. If punch cards are to be used, she makes sure that the ballot box is empty and that the computer punch cards are still in their unopened binders. If no votes have been cast before the election begins, then the first step in ensuring a fair election has been taken.

Despite fears of election fraud, the machines usually read zero and the ballots have not been tampered with. The election begins without incident. By 6:00 A.M., five election judges (two of one party and three of the other) are seated behind the desks as voters begin to arrive. Poll watchers and precinct captains working for various contenders are also present. The election judges have complete authority over election conduct in each precinct. They should be treated with respect and courtesy, since it will do a candidate no good to have their workers thrown out of the polling place.

A poll watcher's primary responsibility is to stay in the polling place, not to be thrown out for causing trouble. Thus, a poll watcher can suggest to the judges how a situation might be handled, reinforcing their request with citations from the judge's handbook. If they fail to take a suggestion, a campaign troubleshooter (usually a lawyer or campaign staff member) is called to handle the problem, and the poll watcher continues their role of watcher.

By 7:00 A.M., the number of voters increases slightly and the distributors out front of the polling place are busy handing out literature and keeping the opposition from tearing down posters. By 9:00 A.M. most voters will have gone to work, so the number of citizens going to the polls slows to a trickle. In many precincts, a campaign volunteer will begin to visit the homes of plus voters, encouraging them to vote or leaving reminder slips if they are not at home. In other precincts, that process will not begin until 2:00 P.M. or 3:00 P.M. If the precinct has a busy bus stop, an additional volunteer may be stationed there to remind voters to vote before they leave for work.

All morning the checker or poll watcher inside the polls has been carefully drawing lines through names on a precinct poll list as each voter casts her ballot. A voter comes into the polling place, signs an affidavit that two judges check against names of eligible voters in the precinct binder. If the voter's name is found, the judges call it out so that poll watchers may also check it. If no challenge is made, the voter proceeds to the voting booth, casts her vote and leaves. During slack periods, the checker compares the precinct poll list with the plus list, which has been kept safely in her pocket until now, and makes out reminders for the plus voters who have yet to vote. These slips guide the runners as they convince voters to come to the polls. In larger campaigns for higher offices, these plus voters are called from phone banks by volunteers to remind them.

Ten hours pass. By 4:00 P.M., the number of voters increases. And at 6:45 P.M., the two poll watchers assigned to watch the count are inside waiting for the polls to close at exactly 7:00 P.M. When the last voter leaves, the ballot boxes are opened and the ballots are counted by the computer vote counters. Watchers (following instructions like those on p. 137) carefully check the count while the votes for their candidate and the opponents are read aloud, recorded, and totaled. As soon as the judges have completed and sealed their reports in long manila envelopes and the poll watchers have filled out their own reports, they rush back to headquarters to hand in their reports. If the judges make an error or their reports are later falsified, the poll watchers' records make future legal action possible.

After months of effort, a victory party can be a very exciting and satisfying experience. The spirit of camaraderie, the beer, the laughter, and the sense of accomplishment are heady stuff. Even a losing campaign is important. People have come together to participate in elections for the first time, and they see for themselves that winning is a real possibility in the next election. A successful party in victory or defeat should provide refreshments, reports of election results and a final appearance of the candidate. Win or lose, the workers need to come away from the evening with a sense of pride in what they have accomplished and a dedication to remain active in future campaigns.

CAMPAIGNS FOR MINORITY CANDIDATES

So far this handbook has treated all campaigns as if they were the same. Certain general principles apply in every case: workers must contact voters, record their preferences, and get plus voters to the polls on election day. However, campaigns in poor minority communities have special problems in accomplishing these tasks. They suffer from two liabilities: 1) lack of resources such as volunteer workers, trained staff and money, and 2) special difficulties in ascertaining voter preferences.

Many minority candidates run campaigns in minority communities, which given the realities of urban America today are often poor, racial or ethnic ghettoes. Ghetto campaigns are critical to efforts for political change because these communities are most likely to suffer from political oppression and would benefit most from new political leadership. Poor communities need the community control made possible by participatory politics. Too often, these communities are controlled by political machines. Voters are forced to support candidates who do not serve them, but rather control them through payoffs and fear. If participatory politics is to become a national political force, it must be practiced successfully in poor as well as middle-class communities.

The problem of inadequate resources for campaigns in poor communities requires a dual solution. First, more resources, particularly skilled volunteers, must be raised within the community itself. A shortage of trained staff members can be remedied to some extent if participatory campaigns outside poor neighborhoods make it a point to employ minorities on their campaign staffs, so the skills of running winning campaigns are spread as broadly as possible. This obstacle can be better overcome by running strong campaigns in poor communities themselves. It may take one campaign for a candidate to become known, for people to trust her, and for workers and staff to gain the experience necessary to win the second time around. Strong campaigns in minority communities lay a sound groundwork for future transformations.

Even with trained campaign leaders, money remains a scarce resource. Funds raised in poor minority communities must often be matched by outside funds from middle-class communities. While most funds will have to be raised internally by the campaign, a few thousand dollars of outside support can boost campaign morale, especially if the money is used to hire adequate staff, open a campaign headquarters, and print campaign literature.

Fundraising within poor communities differs considerably from fundraising in middle-class communities. Facilities and services are provided by institutions such as churches, which play a more neutral, nonpartisan role in wealthier neighborhoods. Even so, campaigns in poor communities still must raise funds from individual contributors. Small donations are raised from events like dances and potluck dinners. The same creativity is needed as is used to plan standard campaign fundraising events. Fundraising in wealthier communities is also part of the financial plan for campaigns in poor neighborhoods, and it is often quite successful.

The other problem for campaigns in poor communities, obtaining honest responses from the residents, is not easily resolved. Since many ghetto dwellers live at a bare subsistence level and depend on various forms of public assistance, they often believe they are at the mercy of regular party precinct captains. These party officials may threaten to terminate voters' welfare payments or to have them thrown out of public housing or fired from government jobs. So, many poor folks are very cautious about opposing the party in power.

For practical reasons, many residents of poor communities support regular party candidates. Even more problematic is that many residents will not tell canvassers the truth about how they plan to vote. After all, why should they make an enemy when they can just say they will vote for your candidate?

Canvassers sometimes return with 400 plus voters on their poll lists, no zeroes, and no minuses. Their precincts therefore cannot be worked effectively on election day, because the task of getting all voters to the polls is too large to accomplish in a single day and because too many voters will vote against your candidate. The only remedy for the unwillingness of voters to tell precinct workers their true preferences is well-trained workers who carefully probe the voter's initial response to be sure that most of those they mark with a plus on the poll list will really vote for your candidate on election day. At least volunteer precinct workers going door to door will guarantee that the campaign information reaches every voter which will gain your candidate some support.

Because of the shortage of precinct workers in most campaigns in poor communities, hiring people who say they have worked in previous campaigns is a great temptation. Usually these folks will take the money, but bring in no votes. It is much safer to hire only members of the central campaign staff or pay workers only for the time taken from their regular job to work on election day. Participatory politics depends on voluntary participants. Highly paid, mercenary armies of workers are no substitute.

Despite these problems in canvassing poor minority communities, plus voters must be located and brought to the polls. Sound trucks, posters, campaign literature, public relations, and talking to the voters will not win elections, but an effective voter canvass will, even in the most difficult political situations.

More and more frequently, minority candidates run in races beyond the boundaries of racial and ethnic ghettoes. They must appeal to voters from other ethnic groups. Similarly, white candidates often need African-Americans, Latinos, Asians or American Indians to vote for them. The goal for such candidates is to mobilize a solid vote of their own racial or ethnic group, without alienating voters from other ethnic and racial blocs.

In his 1983 and 1987 races for mayor of Chicago, Harold Washington used these techniques very effectively. In the 1983 primary campaign he ran against the incumbent, Mayor Jane Byrne, and the son of Chicago's most famous mayor, States' Attorney Richard M. Daley. The two white candidates split the white machine vote and Harold Washington won with an unified African-American vote and the support of progressive whites and Hispanics.

Harold Washington was drafted primarily by political activists and community organizers in the African-American community. Because of his years in public office, independence from the machine, wit, and charisma, Congressman Washington was the most popular possible black candidate, as demonstrated by a series of informal polls taken in the African-American community. He agreed to run on the condition that at least 100,000 new voters be registered. A broad-based alliance was put together under the rubric of POWER (People Organized for Welfare and Employment Rights) and their voter registration drive was funded by Edward Gardner, president of Soft Sheen Products. The money allowed "radio commercials, eye-catching posters, and bumper stickers that spread the registration message—'Come Alive October 5' [voter registration day in the precincts]—across the black community."[10]

This massive drive registered 125,000 new black voters.[11] The Washington campaign thus began with the most successful voter registration drive in the city's history. Fueled by anger at Reaganomics and by the racially insensitive mistakes of Mayor Byrne in failing to appoint blacks to high-level city government positions, an entirely new voter support base had been created even before Washington formally became a candidate.

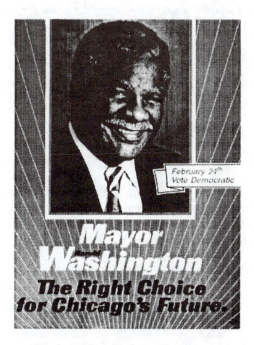

Washington Campaign Poster

Very early in his campaign, Washington met with some progressive leaders of the Mexican and Puerto Rican community, who pledged to endorse his candidacy and to work for him in their communities. These Hispanic leaders saw in the Washington campaign an opportunity to build their own political base and political power as a third force in city politics. If Washington were to be elected, his administration would vastly increase the number of Hispanics appointed to top jobs and positions of authority in city government. Liberal whites and their political organizations like the Independent Voters of Illinois-Independent Precinct Organization (IVI-IPO) also endorsed Washington and provided a campaign structure in the white wards of the city.

William Grimshaw describes the Washington campaign as three campaigns rolled into one:

> *First, there was the formal campaign organization, which was structured and conducted along conventional campaign lines. Full field operations were mounted in over half of the city's fifty wards, including all the black, Hispanic and white lakefront liberal wards. Partial operations existed in another dozen wards. . . .*
>
> *The campaign also contained an elaborate network of interest groups that worked largely outside of the formal structure . . . from Artists for Washington to Women for Washington to just about everything else in between. . . .*
>
> *The campaign's third principal component was . . . a group of black nationalists, whose idealistic, "separatist" goals clashed with the more practical and "integrationist" goals of the formal campaign. . . . The nationalists' preferred form of communication was the spectacular event: big rallies and large parades that drummed up a powerful emotional response.[12]*

Harold Washington's campaign theme was "reform" but this reform had three different meanings to his different supporters:

- Good government reform—efficiency, openness, and honesty in government.
- Affirmative action—more minorities and women in positions of political power.
- Community control—participatory democracy in local government, including more government money given to neighborhood groups, neighborhood government and decentralization of government by creating local school councils with authority over local schools.[13]

As Grimshaw puts it, "Washington thus campaigned as a reform candidate for mayor as well as a messiah for the black community. Without the capacity to encompass both roles, he could not have won."[14] The campaign contained not only the normal election effort but became a crusade as well.

Mayor Byrne's campaign unwittingly helped the Washington do an even better job of mobilizing the black community. Three days before the election,

Democratic Party Chairman and Byrne ally, Alderman Edward Vrdolyak, spelled out the Byrne's campaign message and the ballot choices in racially charged language: "A vote for [Richard M.] Daley is a vote for Washington. . . . It's a racial thing. Don't kid yourself. I am calling on you to save your city, to save your precinct. We are fighting to keep the city the way it is."[15] The Byrne campaign attempted to gain the white vote by racists appeals, but media reports of the Vrdolyak statement mobilized the black community, progressive whites and Latinos behind Washington instead.

When the primary was over, Washington won with 37 percent of the vote to Byrne's 33 percent, and Daley's 30 percent. Washington received 80 percent of the black vote, which was 92 percent of his citywide total. On the other side, 78 percent of Byrne's vote and 90 percent of Daley's vote was white.[16] Washington did what minority candidates must do: mobilize their racial or ethnic support base and appeal sufficiently to other racial and ethnic voters to guarantee the extra votes needed for victory.

CAMPAIGNS FOR WOMEN CANDIDATES

In 1992, the election of Senator Carol Moseley-Braun from Illinois provided a slightly different pattern from Mayor Washington's campaign. Rather than running only as an "African-American candidate," she ran primarily as a "women's candidate." At a time when women were outraged at the confirmation of Clarence Thomas as Supreme Court Justice and the treatment of Anita Hill, who testified against Thomas at the Senate's confirmation hearings, Moseley-Braun had powerful appeal for the electorate. She convinced many Republican and Independent voters, including white women from the suburbs, to abandon their party or conservative leanings to vote for her (see her campaign brochure on p. 146).

Carol Moseley-Braun was a former state legislator and Cook County Recorder of Deeds at the time of the campaign. She began her campaign with a coalition of liberals, pro-choice supporters and women. She mobilized enough diverse ethnic and racial support throughout the state to defeat the popular, white male incumbent, U.S. Senator Alan Dixon.

Similar to the 1983 primary in which Harold Washington was elected, Braun benefited from having two white opponents in the primary race, the incumbent Alan Dixon and millionaire Chicago lawyer, Albert Hofeld. Thomas Hardy in the Chicago Tribune analyzed both the primary and Braun's early lead in the general election against Republican challenger Richard Williamson this way: "Braun's enviable favorability rating reflects both the publicity she reaped after the primary and an above-the-fray style that managed to keep her from being caught in the crossfire between her two better-financed primary opponents. . . ."[17] While Albert Hofeld used his considerable campaign war chest to run negative television ads against Dixon, Braun was able to run a positive campaign. Dixon and Hofeld divided the white, Democratic party vote. This allowed Moseley-Braun to win with a very diverse

Sample Campaign Brochure

Send a message of
change to Washington

Send a Senator
for the people
of Illinois

From the moment you meet Carol,
you know she'll be a new kind of
Senator.

Her smile brightens the room.
She listens. She cares about people.
And she fights passionately
for their rights.

The Senate doesn't need another
millionaire. The Senate needs Carol
Moseley Braun – someone who lives
in the real world.

Someone who knows what it's like to raise a teenager,
care for a disabled parent and hold down a
full-time job.

As a Senator, Carol will spend money at home before
shipping funds abroad. She'll fight for a fairer tax system,
comprehensive health care, quality public education and
job-producing programs. And she'll support business
incentives to spark a sluggish economy.

Carol knows how to cut through red tape and make things
happen. During ten years as a Representative in the Illinois
General Assembly, she led major reforms in education and
human services. As Cook County Recorder of Deeds, she
won national acclaim by cutting patronage, streamlining
operations and returning twice as much money to the
County as the department spent.

Born the daughter of a Chicago law enforcement officer,
Carol worked her way through school attending the
University of Illinois and graduating from the University of
Chicago Law School. She entered public service in 1978
because she believed she could make a difference.

Now it's your turn to make a difference.

Elect a woman who'll challenge the status quo. A woman
who'll bring fresh ideas and innovative leadership.

VOTE CAROL MOSELEY BRAUN

A Senator for the people of Illinois

Vote on Tuesday, November 3rd

Chicago: 312-541-9292   Springfield: 217-523-1992

Authorized by and paid for the U.S. Senate Committee, Carol Moseley Braun.
Paid for by the Democratic Senatorial Campaign Committee.

voting coalition in addition to nearly unanimous support in the African-American community.

In the general election, Moseley-Braun took a strong pro-choice position on abortion while Williamson, the Republican candidate, flip-flopped on the issue. In desperation, Williamson tried to portray Braun as a liberal, tax-and-spend politician. He used hard-hitting radio advertisements during the summer that targeted her "liberal record." She responded that these attacks were unfair, while her allies assailed them as racist. The ads ended up creating negative opinions of Williamson more than they hurt Braun.[18] The Chicago Sun-Times' critical analysis of the media commercials concluded:

> *This negative spot makes dubious use of a 1979 resolution Braun sponsored while a state representative praising [Gus] Savage—before he was a congressman—as a way of linking her to the lame-duck representative's racially inflammatory politics. The spot does not mention when the resolution was adopted. In 1979 Savage was a newspaper publisher and civilrights leader. Years later, he became controversial because of his views regarding Israel and Jews. . . .*
>
> *Earlier Williamson spots mentioned the pay and tax hikes and [Jesse] Jackson (Braun was a Jackson delegate to the 1988 Democratic convention). The taxes were backed by Republican Governor James R. Thompson. The pay raises were recommended by a legislative commission.*
>
> *By bundling the welfare bill, Jackson and Savage together, the commercial uses a not-so-subtle approach that exploits race.*[19]

Moseley-Braun did not win on favorable publicity alone. Her campaign, like Harold Washington's, had one of the most extensive field operations in Illinois history. The campaign's statewide base of 4,000 volunteers was used to register voters and bring them to the polls. With the endorsement of party officials after the primary, the Moseley-Braun campaign integrated her independent base of support with the forces of the Illinois state Democratic Party. Minority candidates must do this type of coalition building to run in a state-wide race in which the African-American population is a small percentage of the total voting population.

Despite victories like Carol Moseley-Braun's, political science researchers conclude that women remain "the most underrepresented major social group in America."[20] However, this is beginning to change. Women hold 23 percent of the positions on city councils and 21 percent of the seats in state legislatures. But, as of 1994, they held only 11 percent of the positions in the U.S. House of Representatives and 7 percent of the U.S. Senate.[21] This underrepresentation is caused by a number of factors. For instance, women have traditionally been barred from prestigious education and occupations or admitted only in limited numbers. The greatest barrier to more women in power remains not their education or rank in professions but the incumbency of men currently in office. Political scientists R. Darcy, Susan Welsh and Janet Clark conclude in their book "Women, Elections, and Representation":

> *The political system and cultural milieu no longer present barriers to women state legislative candidates they may once have. If more women run, more women will be elected. And as more women begin gaining tenure in legislatures, the pool of women candidates for higher office [like Carol Moseley-Braun] will also increase.*[22]

The political parties have failed in the past to support women candidates fully and fundraising has been much more difficult for women, but these barriers are being eliminated. Generally speaking, women candidates run campaigns in the same way as men candidates, and they will continue to have greater success as term limits and voter anger against incumbents opens up more seats for newcomers in politics.

CANVASSING HIGH-RISE BUILDINGS IN CITIES

At the opposite end of the socioeconomic spectrum exists a different set of problems. Upper middle-class and wealthy citizens in major cities often live in large, high-rise apartments. In suburbs, many are starting to live in restricted "gated communities" with guards at entry points. Both high-rise buildings and gated suburban communities are "common interest developments," the various forms of which include condominiums, cooperatives, town houses, and single-family communities closed to the outside world.

Some mammoth high-rise buildings contain over 1,000 voters. Restricted, gated suburban subdivisions are growing rapidly. These communities contain so many voters that they cannot be ignored. Yet residents of high rises and gated communities are surprisingly isolated. Seldom do they know their next-door neighbors, and even more rarely do they know residents in other parts of the building or in the outside community. Their privacy is zealously protected by watchful doormen, apartment managers and security guards.

The first problem for a participatory campaign in reaching these voters is finding volunteers living in these buildings or restricted suburban compounds. Holding coffees allows the residents to meet the candidate. Alternatively, many of these communities are willing to sponsor candidate forums. But if you do not have workers in the building or housing compounds, sponsoring coffees or arranging for forums is difficult. In such cases, area chairs or coffee coordinators must call their own contacts, friends of campaign volunteers or list of registered voters until a willing hostess can be found. Then all residents must receive a coffee invitation and be personally invited to attend. Even after these efforts, attendance may still be very disappointing. Hopefully, enough resident workers can be signed up to work their own building or the other homes in the community.

In a city district with dozens of high-rise apartments, holding successful coffees or candidate forums in the high rises will not be possible. The remaining buildings will have to be worked by outside volunteers. Obtaining entry into high-rise buildings or residential compounds to canvass will be difficult. Four practical methods of gaining entrance are: 1) to have a contact who lives in the building let the canvasser in, 2) to walk in at the same time as someone who lives in the building, 3) to call people listed on the precinct poll list over the speaker system until someone willing to talk about the election lets the canvasser in, and 4) to walk up to the doorman, say hello and act as if he is expected to open the door, and often he will.[23] If none of these techniques work, ask the building manager for admittance or at least permission to place campaign literature in the mailboxes.

After trying every trick, a canvasser may obtain entry in the building or gated community only to find irate residents calling the manager to have her thrown out. Three tactics remain to be tried. Five or more workers can enter the building or community to canvass different floors or sections simultaneously. By the time the management throws them all out, the bulk of the building or community will have been canvassed. A door-to-door canvass may be replaced by a direct mail piece, followed by a telephone canvass. The results are less desirable but superior to no canvass at all. A successful telephone canvass is best preceded by leafleting or mailing campaign brochures to each resident. Then the telephone numbers for each registered voter in the precinct are found in a reverse telephone directory, where they are listed by address or in the computer listing you have purchased for campaign use.

As in a door-to-door canvass, the campaign worker introduces herself to the person she calls, gives a brief statement of the candidate's virtues, finds out the voter's preference, and marks the appropriate symbol on the poll list. In phone canvassing, as in face-to-face canvassing, the critical element is the kind and quality of interaction between the worker and the voter. Most voters will vote for a candidate if they feel that her campaign worker is trustworthy and well-informed. The worker must sell herself to sell the candidate. Her own good judgment, politeness and helpfulness will win over many voters.

In this regard, relying on a standard script is absolutely self-defeating. It makes you seem insincere and uncaring, as if you were only going through the motions of canvassing. Your most difficult job will be to maintain your own authenticity, to continue to be yourself, time after time, call after call. Your own genuineness and spontaneity, whether quick and enthusiastic, serious or bashful, are your strongest assets. Of course the voter will want you to listen to their views as well, respond appropriately, and answer their questions.

Even without volunteers for a telephone canvass, a direct mail or literature blitz can still be made, although limited results can be expected, as reported in Chapter 6. As discussed in Chapter 7, direct mail is likely to be most effective if more than one piece of mail is sent. So the unworked high-rise or gated suburban community needs to be part of the direct mail campaign as early as possible for the best results.

RURAL CAMPAIGNS

Rural campaigns differ from those run in either cities or suburbs, but the intent is the same: Voters must be contacted personally. The differences between urban and rural campaigns are: 1) money, 2) tools for campaigning and 3) distances. James Kessler reports spending less than $3,000 in a successful primary battle to become the Republican candidate for state senate in a rural district in Indiana in 1963. Half of the funds were his own and half were raised from 38 contributors.[24] The cost of state legislative races even in rural areas has multiplied many times since then. While it is still generally true that rural races cost less than contested races in major cities, they are becoming increasingly expensive.

The campaign tools and political information easily available in urban districts may be completely lacking in rural areas. In this case, the first task of the campaign will be to develop a list of registered voters, determine their party affiliation from assorted public and private records, find precinct maps and canvassing routes, and assemble the necessary kits of registration information and campaign literature. All of this must be done before the registration drive or voter canvass.

Greater distances involved in rural canvassing require more automobiles and create transportation problems not faced in urban districts. Canvassing voters also takes longer. Much coordination and planning is required in scheduling and holding meetings in the larger districts and in transporting the candidate. Time becomes a scarce commodity just because it takes canvassers, the candidate and campaign personnel so long to traverse the district.

Recruiting sufficient volunteers to canvass rural areas is also difficult unless there are colleges within the district. Volunteer canvassers in rural communities produce good results despite the legendary rural distrust of outsiders. The regular parties also tend to be weaker in rural districts and hold voters by primeval rather than modern ties. In Bloomington, Indiana, McCarthy for President Democrats won contested races for precinct committeeman by canvassing all the voters. Many rural voters, just like those in urban areas, have never been visited by a campaign worker before. Their votes are available almost for the asking, but reaching them to ask requires great effort.

Finally, rural communities frequently are very conservative. The organized antigovernment movements in the rural areas of some western states and the conservatism of the rural South are two examples. In any campaign, the attitudes of the constituents must help to shape any effective campaign platform. Nonetheless, liberal, populist candidates often do very well in rural areas if they campaign on important issues affecting the lives of these constituents.

WINNING PARTY CAUCUSES

In many states, party nominations for higher offices are won not by direct elections but by party caucuses and conventions, as illustrated by the well-publicized Iowa caucuses in presidential campaigns. Caucuses are also used in other states. Paul Wellstone's campaign in Minnesota for U.S. Senate in 1990 is a classic participatory campaign within the caucus system. Paul Wellstone was a political science professor at Carleton College, a liberal, a labor union supporter, cochair of Jesse Jackson's campaign for President in Minnesota in 1988, and member of the Democratic National Committee. He won the party nomination over the opposition of many Minnesota state party leaders, who thought he was far too radical to defeat an incumbent Republican senator.

The process within the caucus system is similar to that of any election, but the electorate comprises only voters who show up at precinct caucuses. Precinct caucuses elect delegates to higher level party conventions, who then vote upon party nominees for key offices.

The Wellstone campaign began by contacting voters, local Democratic party leaders and interest groups like labor unions. These grassroots contacts from meetings, coffees and door-to-door canvassing created a list of several thousand potential supporters throughout the state. The Wellstone campaign then followed up with a massive phone canvass. Dennis McGrath and Dane Smith in their excellent monograph, "Professor Wellstone Goes to Washington," describe the phone canvass this way:

The phone callers would ask people who they supported in the Senate race and note the answer on the computer printout of names and phone numbers using a rating system. [This is a variant of the +, -, 0 system.] A person who was solidly behind Wellstone was rated five, a person leaning toward him was assigned a four, an uncommitted person was given a three, a person leaning toward another candidate was given a two, and a person strongly supporting another candidate was awarded a one. To the people who were uncommitted or were favoring another candidate, the volunteer would make a short pitch for Wellstone. "If someone was uncommitted, we would try, if we had money in the budget that week, to send a piece of literature. . ."[25]

While the phone callers were finding Wellstone supporters to attend precinct caucuses, the campaign staff recruited a network of precinct coordinators.

In addition to being responsible for one night of phone calling every week, the [precinct] coordinators were asked to organize their neighborhoods, get supporters to the caucuses, . . . and then lead the formation of Wellstone subcaucuses that night.[26]

By the night of the caucuses, the campaign had about a thousand precinct coordinators signed up. On the weekend before the caucus, several thousand of the identified Wellstone supporters received at least one phone call urging them to attend the precinct caucuses. On the basis of the campaign's straw poll of 207 precincts, Wellstone won a major victory with 43 percent or the delegates to his opponents' 14 percent and 7 percent respectively.[27]

Wellstone's campaign returned to the phones and called as many as they could of the 40,000 delegates and alternates elected to the county and legislative district conventions. Finally, they out-organized their opponents on the floor of the statewide convention, whose delegate votes choose the Democratic Party nominee for U.S. Senate along with a number of other offices.

Wellstone's campaign was a case of field operations and grassroots efforts winning over party officials who preferred other candidates. He was also a candidate with a message and a cause. As McGrath and Smith describe it,

> *Wellstone laid out a program featuring a demand for universal health care, much heavier tax burdens on the wealthy, more spending on education and social programs, tough new environmental and energy standards, and radical reforms of the money-polluted political campaign system. And he delivered this vision to Minnesota voters with a new attitude—anger and good-humored irreverence and hope all at once. . . . Wellstone claimed to be offering real change and not just accommodation. . . .*[28]

Committed, ideological factions often win when they organize in caucus states. Barry Goldwater and Ronald Reagan proved this within the Republican Party and Eugene McCarthy and Paul Wellstone, in the Democratic Party. In Wellstone's case, he also went on to win the Senate seat with the same type of grassroots organizing and creative television commercials like the one described in Chapter 6.

The most important advice to participatory campaigns, whether engaged in primaries, nonpartisan elections or caucuses, is to *organize*. A volunteer army must be trained and deployed in the precincts and on the phone contacting voters. Free news coverage, paid media ads and direct mail campaigns are necessary, but systematically canvassing voters in person and by phone has to be the campaign focus. This is a hard, but certain, road to victory.

Chapter IX

CAMPAIGNING FOR CONGRESS

In 1990, after discussions with a number of community and political activists, I decided to run for Congress. All the districts would be redrawn in 1992, and I suspected that the 8th and 11th Congressional Districts would be merged to create a new district on the northwest side of Chicago (see map of the newly created 5th District on p. 154). I did not know if I would run against incumbent Frank Annunzio or Dan Rostenkowski, so I fashioned a campaign for either case. In October 1991, after months of delay, the courts finally created a new 5th Congressional District that included territory from liberal lakefront wards, the conservative northwest side and the heavily Republican northwest suburbs. Frank Annunzio was forced out of the race and I faced Dan Rostenkowski in a head-to-head contest in the primary of March 1992.

Congressional incumbents have great campaign advantages, often achieving a 95 percent or higher reelection rate. This truism was upheld in 1992, and even with the "Republican Revolution" of 1994, more than 90 percent of House incumbents who sought reelection, won.[1] Because of the small likelihood of success, candidates opposing incumbents are often unknowns who have not held previous elected office, have little campaign experience and less name recognition, and have limited funds. I had some advantages because I had served as an alderman for eight years on the Chicago City Council and had considerable campaign experience, but the odds against my defeating a powerful incumbent like Congressman Rostenkowski were still high.

In 1992 and again in 1994, I decided to challenge these odds with a reform-oriented, volunteer-based campaign. My campaign, and those of other congressional challengers in these years, tested the degree to which such reform-based participatory campaigns could succeed. We challengers assumed that 1992 and 1994 were sufficiently different from the usual easy reelection years that successful campaigns were possible. Term limits were being passed by voters in

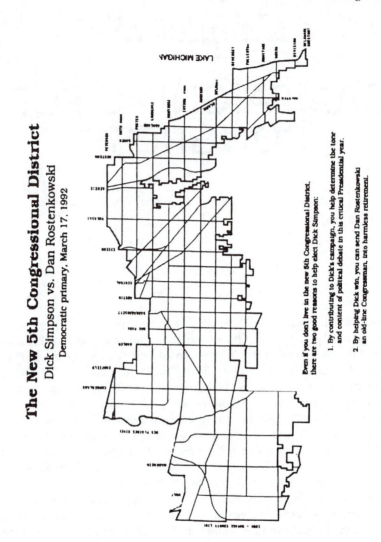

The New 5th Congressional District
Dick Simpson vs. Dan Rostenkowski
Democratic primary, March 17. 1992

LAKE MICHIGAN

Even if you don't live in the new 5th Congressional District, there are two good reasons to help elect Dick Simpson:

1. By contributing to Dick's campaign, you help determine the tone and content of political debate in this crucial Presidential year.

2. By helping Dick win, you can send Dan Rostenkowski, an old-line Congressman, into harmless retirement.

nearly every state in which referendums were held and the anti-Congress and anti-incumbent spirit was high among the electorate. Congressional scandals abounded: House Bank scandals in which many congressmen cashed checks on insufficient funds, the House Post Office scandal in which congressmen redeemed government stamps for personal cash, and the "Keating Five" scandal in the Senate in which U.S. Senators repaid a campaign contributor, Charles Keating, by interfering in federal investigations of his failing Savings and Loan. The public was also becoming more aware of the widespread misuse of Political Action Committee (PAC) funds by congressmen. I hoped that volunteers and modern campaign technology would allow my campaign to succeed despite the many advantages of Congressman Rostenkowski.

My congressional campaigns were designed to test the proposition that candidates who are neither independently wealthy nor endorsed by the dominant party organization could win under seven conditions. They must:

1. be highly qualified for the office;
2. be selected by a citizens' search or supported by a campaign citizens committee composed of leaders of major groups in the district;
3. attract a large number of campaign volunteers through candidate appearances and coffees;
4. "cut the issues" in black and white and project themselves and their issues through the mass media by use of news releases and news conferences;
5. develop a precinct or field operation to collect petition signatures, register voters and canvass for supporters;
6. have enough volunteers on election day to poll watch to limit vote fraud and to get supporters to the polls;
7. and form a permanent political organization after the election to contest future elections more easily.

These approaches work effectively in smaller districts for local elections to the city council or state legislature. They apply less well to elections to congressional, county or statewide offices, particularly in the 1990s with changed political ideologies, weakened party loyalties, major technological developments in campaigning, and changes in the media's coverage of politics.

In March 1992, when I ran against incumbent Dan Rostenkowski in the Democratic primary in the newly redistricted 5th Congressional District, all my assumptions about participatory campaigns were tested. The race was difficult because Rostenkowski was one of the strongest congressmen in the county. In previous Democratic Party primary elections, he frequently had no opponent. In the 1990 general election, he had won reelection, with an overwhelming 79 percent of the vote. In my two election campaigns, I completely reversed these trends.

On March 17, 1992, I received 43 percent of the vote in the Democratic primary: Rostenkowski won 56,059 votes and I received 41,956. Rostenkowski was permanently weakened, winning only 57 percent of the vote against a weak Republican candidate in the November general election.

In 1994, I ran once more against Rostenkowski. Early polls of a head-to-head contest between us showed me leading with as much as 60 percent of the vote. However, in a complicated field of five candidates in the Democratic primary, the results turned out differently. Rostenkowski was lowered to 50 percent of the vote (an increase over what the polls had shown until the week before), but I came in third. State Senator John Cullerton's direct mail negative attacks against me had moved him to second place and lowered my vote.

In trying to explain why I lost these elections and why so many challengers continue to lose their bids for Congress, I will describe my campaigns according to my proposals for winning participatory campaigns discussed in earlier chapters.

STARTING EARLY

My decision to run for congress in 1990 was made under conditions of considerable uncertainty. I had previously lived and served as alderman in the 9th Congressional District represented by Congressman Sidney Yates. I had decided many years ago not to run against him, because there was little ideological difference between us. We were both liberal democrats, although I believed more strongly in participatory democracy than he did.

When I married in 1987, I moved with my new family into Congressman Frank Annunzio's 11th Congressional District. In 1989, I decided not to run against him in the 1990 election because the district appeared too conservative and too controlled by the Chicago Democratic Machine to be winnable.

In 1991, however, I correctly anticipated that the old 8th District of Rostenkowski and 11th District of Annunzio were likely to be combined because of the state's loss of population and the need to preserve three African-American districts while creating a new Hispanic district to meet court challenges.

I had to decide whether to run without knowing if I would face Rostenkowski or Annunzio, or even the final shape of the district. At a more personal level, I thought that running for Congress would allow me to make a greater contribution than my teaching and writing at the University of Illinois at Chicago. I was convinced that the country and the world faced major crises to whose resolution I could make a contribution. Part of the problem we faced as a nation was congressional gridlock and corruption. Both Congressman Annunzio and Rostenkowski had been portrayed in the press as involved in major corruption scandals. By November 1990, I decided to run if a sufficient base of support existed to make winning the election possible.

Throughout the winter of 1990 and 1991, I held a series of meetings with more than 100 possible supporters, volunteers and staff members from the north and northwest sides of Chicago. From these meetings, I determined that I could recruit staff, campaign leaders and enthusiastic volunteers. I could also raise enough money to mount a major campaign. Without actually running, I could not judge if I could raise the $350,000 campaign budget necessary to win, but it was clear from early individual commitments that I could raise more than $100,000.

In the winter of 1990 and 1991, I worked with a number of aldermanic campaigns and gave major assistance to three candidates running races in or near the new district. This participation gave me access to new potential staff, supporters and activists who would make mounting the congressional campaign in the nearly 600 precincts more feasible.

During this period, response to newspaper stories that I was considering the run was positive. My campaign was being treated seriously by both the press and political leaders.

In the spring of 1991, I held several news conferences before becoming an official candidate. In them I endorsed aldermanic candidates and released a study of how the congressional redistricting would protect incumbents at the cost of destroying neighborhood representation. I also wrote a newspaper article on a proposed Marshall Plan of aid for Poland based on my trip there in March 1991. Since a large voting bloc in the district was Polish, my familiarity with the current problems of Poland would prove useful.

I launched my campaign on May 20, 1991, with a well-covered news conference announcing the formation of an exploratory campaign committee. At the same time, I proposed a congressional reform program, issued a detailed study of congressional malfeasance, and attacked Rostenkowski and Annunzio's provision of $10 million in tax breaks and exemptions from low-income housing provisions in the federal financing of the defaulted $159 million luxury apartment complex called Presidential Towers. To emphasize my point, I held my announcement news conference in front of Presidential Towers.

While starting a reform campaign a year early to allow time to let issues sink in and change public opinion is desirable, and while building a volunteer army takes time, finding the resources to run a long campaign is hard. In the beginning, I had only one part-time staff member who ran a public relations business from his home. We used our two home offices to begin the campaign to keep expenses down. We did not open a formal campaign office for several months.

From March to June 1991, we spent an average of $3,000 a month on the campaign, nearly all of which went to public relations and the design and production of early campaign literature, buttons and press packets. By the winter of 1992, I was spending at least $10,000 a month on staff and another $3,000 in basic office costs, funds that simply had not been available in the beginning.

In the early months of the campaign, I needed a way to meet people, recruit volunteers, speak to groups, and make news. I could not do that as a candidate for office in an unknown district against unknown candidates, since the congressional redistricting process was still tied up in the state legislature and after that in the courts. So after the first round of news conferences on a widening Presidential Towers scandal, I launched a congressional term limits petition drive. The petition requested the County Board to put an advisory referendum on the ballot in the March 1992 election. Eventually we collected more than 2,500 signatures at grocery stores while passing out flyers on congressional reform and my candidacy, all of which allowed me to meet voters and recruit volunteers.

I campaigned throughout the summer before the new congressional district boundaries were drawn. Although I was unsuccessful in getting a majority of the county commissioners to agree to put the referendum on the ballot, the term limits petitions allowed me to build the resources that were necessary for my own campaign.

Most candidates were waiting for the state legislature, redistricting commissions and courts to finalize district boundaries before deciding to run. I had a big advantage of being the only candidate running during this period. At events like IVI-IPO's annual Independents Day Dinner and Bruce Dumont's "Inside Politics" radio talk show, my campaign was the most visible and I was able to recruit supporters and obtain free media coverage. My campaign was the strongest and most visible of the challengers in the state, and I benefited accordingly.

In retrospect I should have opened a full-time, staffed office even sooner. I added an office manager and a part-time fundraiser to my public relations staff in August, but the office itself did not get opened until late September. I added my first campaign manager in late October. My final full-time campaign manager came aboard in December when I also switched from a part-time to a full-time fundraiser. Assembling the final staff this late in the campaign did not leave enough time to build as strong a campaign as I needed.

In Chicago, there had not been in recent years many challenges to incumbent Democratic congressmen, so there were not a large number of experienced campaign staff members with previous congressional campaign experience. Nationally, most consultants who could otherwise have been recruited as campaign managers and fundraisers were unwilling to work for an opponent of Rostenkowski because his power and influence might keep other clients from hiring them. But the single biggest problem in my first campaign was an early shortage of funds that prevented me from building an effective campaign. My general strategy of allowing the campaign to grow naturally as resources became available seemed the only possible choice. But to win these elections, I needed to raise more money up front before beginning the campaigns. At a minimum I needed four staff members (campaign manager, office manager, fund raiser, and public relations person) and a campaign office from the beginning. But by March 1991 I had raised only $3,500. By June, this figure had increased by only another $6,500. I should have already been spending from $10,000 to $13,000 a month at this stage. My campaign was not as strong as it should have been because of my difficulty in raising money.

The campaign's financial problems were even more acute at the end of the campaign. I could not raise the $100,000 to $150,000 needed for radio and television commercials during the last month before the election. It is almost certain that if we had had the advertising money we needed, I would have won the first time out. In the end, we raised $215,500. However, $37,500 was from my personal contributions or loans and another $40,000 was campaign debts, which I paid off only after the primary was over.

My campaign difficulties were partially created by the perception that an incumbent like Rostenkowski could not be beaten. Overcoming that perception took time as did making it clear to the press, contributors, volunteers, and voters that it was possible to win. Raising the large sums of money needed even for a less expensive, participatory campaign for congress is difficult until large donors are convinced you have a chance of winning. This perception is a fundamental problem that every challenger faces. It affects news coverage, recruiting staff and volunteers, and fundraising.

In my second campaign in 1994, I did not have the same problems. I had proven in 1992 that a shift of only 7,000 votes would have defeated Rostenkowski. His electoral base was continuing to deteriorate, and it was becoming clear that either I, or some other candidate, might well defeat him in this election.

After the March 1992 primary election, too late to switch the few thousand votes necessary for me to win, the U.S. Department of Justice announced its investigation into the House of Representatives Post Office scandal. One of the witnesses who pled guilty testified that he had converted thousand of dollars of government stamps into cash and given the money to Rostenkowski. So Rostenkowski was publicly accused not just of corruption or malfeasance, but of theft of government funds. After the March, 1994 Democratic primary, he was indicted by a Grand Jury on 17 separate counts of misuse of campaign and government funds. His court case was still pending in 1996 while attorneys on both sides contest and appeal various aspects of the indictment.

After my 1992 defeat, I returned to my university teaching and writing career. In 1993, I consulted my original supporters and determined that most of them were still willing to contribute to my campaign. I talked to other community leaders, assembled a new campaign staff, and successfully raised campaign contributions from people who had not contributed to my last campaign. Essentially, my 1993 to 1994 campaign picked up where we had left off a year earlier.

This time I had a better fundraising plan, knew the district boundaries, knew who the constituents were, and had the experience of previously running a full-scale participatory campaign in this district. Unfortunately, there were still some uncertainties, just as there had been when I had run in 1992. The Justice Department's investigation had been going for a year. Few doubted Rostenkowski would be indicted on felony charges, but it was not known whether he would be either indicted or forced to resign as part of a plea bargain before the 1994 primary.

These uncertainties created doubt about my opponents. If Rostenkowski did not run, three state legislators and two Chicago aldermen who represented different sections of the district were prepared to enter the race.

I decided to run a second time based on my assumption that if Rostenkowski were not indicted and decided to run for reelection, then all other major candidates would be forced out of the race. He and I would run head-to-head once again, and I believed that I had an excellent chance of winning this time. If he dropped out of the race, then I would be the front runner and could more easily raise the necessary resources, including money. I also stood an excellent chance of winning in a field of four or five new candidates, each with his or her own base of support in the district.

Timing is everything in politics, but the decision to run must be made before you know whether this is the time of change, reform and transformation. If you wait until you are sure, it will already be too late. Wallace Stegner in his wonderful novel, "Angle of Repose," writes of an engineer in the West struggling to bring about major physical transformations with the same issues of timing:

> *As a practitioner of hindsight, I know that Grandfather was trying to do, by personal initiative and with the financial resources of a small and struggling corporation, what only the immense power of the federal government ultimately proved able to do. That does not mean he was foolish or mistaken. He was premature. His clock was set on pioneer time. He met trains that had not yet arrived, he waited on platforms that had not yet been built, besides tracks that might never be*

laid. Like many another Western pioneer, he had heard the clock of his-
tory strike, and counted the strokes wrong. Hope was always out ahead
of fact, possibility obscured the outlines of reality.[2]

As often happens in politics, the assumptions that I and my campaign strategists made based on the best information available did not turn out to be completely accurate. Rostenkowski wasn't indicted until after the March 1994 primary, and he chose to run for reelection. After all he would have much more clout as an incumbent congressman, chairman of the powerful Ways and Means Committee and congressional ally of the President. From his position of power, he was more likely to beat the indictment, raise money for his defense fund from special interest groups that wanted to influence legislation before his committee, and better bargain with the Justice Department than he could as a former congressman.

The Justice Department's failure to indict Rostenkowski at this time, his indecision about running, and the late announcement of his candidacy left too many other candidates in the race. Two state legislators and one alderman dropped out of the running. But one state senator and one alderman remained. State Senator John Cullerton, from a family whose members had been elected to public offices as a part of the Chicago machine for a century and who had a liberal voting record in the legislature, posed the more serious problem for me. He positioned himself in the race by attacking me first in a direct mail smear campaign. He was running as a spoiler. If Rostenkowski dropped out, then Cullerton would be the regular party candidate. If not, he would at least keep me from getting elected and becoming a strong incumbent. Only later in the campaign did he begin to run against Rostenkowski, when he and his advisers began to think he might actually win. Cullerton's credentials as a liberal state senator cost me the support of some liberal organizations within and outside the state who chose to stay neutral. His high name recognition allowed him to split the anti-Rostenkowski vote.

When the 1994 primary campaign was over, Rostenkowski won once again with 46,683 votes (50 percent). Rostenkowski's vote was down from 57 percent in the last election, but multiple candidacies made it impossible for any one of us to win. Rostenkowski would be defeated by a weak Republican candidate in the fall after he was at last indicted for corruption by a federal grand jury.

The second time around I had started my campaign in plenty of time, opened a fully staffed campaign office earlier, began full-time fundraising many months earlier, and raised money more easily. We raised $236,000, of which I supplied only $8,500. This meant we raised about $50,000 more from other contributors than in my 1992 campaign. But we were still short at least $150,000 needed to run the full mass media or competitive direct mail campaign necessary to win. Rostenkowski spent about $2,093,000 in addition to having the full backing of the Democratic machine, Mayor Daley and President Clinton, while Cullerton spent $420,000.[3] While some of Rostenkowski's expenses went to pay lawyers to fight the grand jury indictment and court case rather than the primary election campaign, his campaign expenditures dwarfed

mine and Cullerton's. Once again, the $11,000 I spent on radio ads in the clos-
ing weeks of my campaign was far too small a media buy to be competitive
against Cullerton, who spent nearly all his money in the last months of the campaign on direct mail and television commercials or against Rostenkowski who
outspent me nearly 7 to 1.

In general, *starting early is a necessary but not sufficient condition* to build
a winning base of support for a major election in a large district. The Clinton
campaigns, for instance, are "permanent campaigns," starting years before the
first presidential primary and continuing without stop from the day he was
sworn into office. In the summer of 1995, a year and a half before the next election and without any likely strong contender for the Democratic Party nomination, Clinton was already running major television commercials on prime network television shows.

Campaigns take month or years of effort. They are costly. Especially
participatory campaigns because they usually begin early. Even then, there are
no guarantees that the support and momentum necessary for victory will be
generated.

BEGINNING WITH AN ORGANIZATIONAL BASE

Since 1945, the Independent Voters of Illinois (IVI) has provided a base for
many reform campaigns in Illinois. Historically, the IVI has had its greatest
effect endorsing Democrats or Republicans in tightly contested races and helping to elect the better candidate. In 1969, I founded the Independent Precinct
Organization (IPO) in the northside lakefront wards and during the decade
before we merged with IVI, we successfully elected more than 20 independent
candidates breaking the stranglehold of the Democratic machine on the lakefront. In the 1980s, reformers backing Mayor Harold Washington's election created, in scattered wards, groups called "networks" with experienced precinct
workers to help future reform campaigns. Finally, located in the suburban sections of the 5th Congressional District were the maverick Democrats who had
attempted to defeat the Leyden Township Democratic Committeeman.

By 1991, IVI-IPO was weakened. Most of the northwest side wards where
I was running remained under the control of the Democratic machine. There
were no independent office holders in this area to help change these communities. Mayor Harold Washington received less than 10 percent of the vote in
many of these wards when he ran for mayor in 1983. I won the endorsement
and support of IVI-IPO, Network 44 (the former Washington campaign organization in the 44th Ward) along the lakefront, and reform democrats in the suburbs. But the northwest side wards in the district were a challenge, and I could
not begin my campaign there from an existing organizational base.

One of my purposes in running was to join together the scattered dissenters
and reformers and wield them into a volunteer political army. If I could do this,
I could change the political history of the northwest side and thereby effect the
political future of Chicago. From the existing political reform organizations,

I recruited key leaders to guide my precinct organization, enough workers to carry my petitions to get on the ballot, and several key staff members. But my campaign had to be built from the ground up.

A second alternative existed. I could build upon smaller election campaigns. Even though permanent reform organizations did not exist throughout the district, mayoral and aldermanic campaigns were being waged in the winter of 1991, and I worked closely with a number of these. While most of the reform challengers lost their races, the unsuccessful aldermanic candidates that I supported in liberal wards—43rd, 44th and 50th—reciprocated afterwards. They endorsed me, gave me their list of workers to recruit, and helped me with fundraising. Their campaigns provided me with an early political base. By the fall of 1991, I recruited suburban reform democrats whom I had not met before. My campaign was weakened, because I did not gain the support of aldermanic and state legislative candidates who had run on the northwest side. Several attended my campaign's strategy sessions and offered private support, but they were afraid that identification with my reform campaign would harm their political chances in the future. So in seven key wards, I had to begin with no previous campaign base.

In my second campaign in 1994, I began with the volunteer base and community contacts from my first campaign. I had better name identification and credibility in the district because I had challenged and almost defeated Rostenkowski in 1992. I had recruited volunteers in coffees and community meetings during my first campaign who had not been involved in politics before. New alliances with some of the Ross Perot supporters who favored congressional reform were forged. Senior citizens who wanted to "dump Rosty" were supporters in 1992 and willing to be involved in my campaign again.

In 1994, all of these advantages were still not enough to overturn the machine in this large district. However, after my campaign at least one new group called the Abbey Group (named because they meet at the Abbey Pub and Restaurant) was formed on the northwest side. They continue to support the campaigns of reform candidates for alderman and state legislature within the district.

Building a new political base takes years but has the enormous benefit of helping to elect many candidates to public office. It takes time to take root where reform candidates and organizations have not been successful in the past. In four years, we had laid the foundation for the defeat of Rostenkowski on the northwest side, but we could not create a permanent institutionalized base for future reform campaigns. Often reform comes in waves: nationally, the Populist wave receded to be replaced by the Progressives; the Progressives by the New Deal; the New Deal by the New Frontier; the New Frontier by the antiwar movement; the antiwar movement by the new "progressives" of our day. The same occurs locally. In Chicago, IVI was reformed by IPO, both were superseded by the Harold Washington campaigns and then displaced by the second mayor, Richard Daley. Participatory campaigns contribute best to this process of fundamental political change when they can be institutionalized as party reform or independent political organizations.

BUILDING A PRECINCT ORGANIZATION

Even with the previous summer's petition drive for term limits, we were not fully prepared for the nominating petition drive in my 1991 campaign in November. Because we did not know the new district's boundaries when I began campaigning, we could not focus on organizing only people who lived within the new 5th District. The state legislature failed to agree on district boundaries, and the courts determined them only weeks before nominating petitions were due. Many of my early supporters lived in what would become other congressional districts, especially the adjacent 9th Congressional District. My home and that of 11th District incumbent Congressman Frank Annunzio were districted out, while the 5th District was explicitly gerrymandered to include Congressman Rostenkowski's home. Because I was not legally a voter in the new 5th District (I moved into the district after the 1992 primary), I could not even carry nominating petitions for myself in the 1992 election. This boundary confusion meant I had only 40 precinct workers from the 5th District who could legally circulate nominating petitions.

We successfully collected 2,602 signatures and filed them on December 8, 1991. This was more than the 600 signatures legally required to get me on the ballot. One potential candidate, Carol Daley, filed 616 signatures but the Board of Elections Commissioners ruled that only 384 were valid signatures of 5th District voters. She was consequently ruled ineligible to run. Getting sufficient signatures on nominating petitions was a real hurdle in this election because of the redistricting.

Frank Annunzio was forced out of the race and decided not to run. (He was later appointed to a lucrative city job as compensation.) If he had run, he would have split the machine vote with Rostenkowski, and I would have won. Instead, the primary election came down to a head-to-head contest between Rostenkowski and me. Several alternate scenarios could have occurred. Rosty, as he was called in the press and the district, could have retired as he had considered doing. Legally, he could have kept as personal funds the more than $1 million that he had accumulated from unspent campaign contributions of previous years. Had he done so, I would probably have beaten Frank Annunzio, who had won his reelection in 1990 with only 56 percent of the vote.

In November of 1991, the petition drive became a crash campaign project involving the campaign manager and all key volunteers living in the district. Despite our success in getting on the ballot, the petition drive was not strong enough to jump start my campaign. As we moved to the next stage staff was rearranged, with a new campaign manager, fundraiser and office manager coming on board. My campaign gathered more money and new supporters, but we were not going to have enough volunteers to work the nearly 600 precincts in the district. We ended up with about 100 people doing some precinct work and covering more than 10 percent of the precincts and blitzing another 10 percent with campaign literature. Although we had coordinators for all the wards and areas, about 20 area chairs covered the one-third of the district which we were able to work. Having more than 500 people working on election day could not make up for our inability to work more than 20 percent of the district earlier.

Precinct work is critical. In the 1992 campaign, despite having a large number of supporters and contributors, people would not work precincts. People do not like to do precinct work, many are nervous about campaigning out on the streets especially at night, and many buildings are secured with gates and guards so that access is difficult. Yet volunteer precinct work was one of the few ways to win the election against a powerful incumbent with a $1 million war chest and endorsement of the Democratic machine. Alternatively, I did not have the huge media budget required to reach all the voters in the district by direct mail or mass media advertising.

In 1994, we started much earlier. We had a full staff and our campaign office up and running by the summer. The district was known. I could carry my own petitions (along with other volunteers) at grocery stores and public transportation centers. The summer petition drive for congressional reform blended into the fall nominating petition drive without difficulty. But we still could not recruit enough volunteers willing to work the precincts throughout the district. By January, we supplemented volunteers with college and high school students, as well as direct mail and phone campaigns. In my second campaign, we recruited 110 volunteers to canvass 150 precincts, and another 100 to telephone canvass. We made contact with more voters. But once again, we could not get enough volunteers to match the strength of the Chicago Democratic machine working for Rostenkowski nor the intense direct mail and television ad campaign for Cullerton.

Our registration campaign was negligible and our direct contact with voters was not strong enough. We had about 300 hundred volunteers working the polls on election day, but too many precincts did not have lists of plus voters. If enough volunteers are not recruited to work precincts, participatory campaigns are doomed to fail.

When major social issues are involved like the Vietnam War in the McCarthy for President campaign, racial discrimination in the Harold Washington for Mayor campaign, or pro-choice and women's rights issues in the Carol Moseley-Braun for Senate campaign, then the volunteers can be recruited. They can be used to win the election. But sometimes the issues and charisma of a candidate are insufficient to attract enough workers. Those campaigns lose.

MEDIA COVERAGE

On the whole, media coverage of my campaigns was very good. I held four nonpartisan news conferences before beginning my official campaign for congress in 1991 and two after I was announced. After I officially became a candidate, our extensive research and press efforts allowed me to hold more than 29 news conferences in a single election (see pp. 166–167). I gave extensive media interviews with local and national press and met with reporters of community and specialized publications in the district. I managed to force three television "debates" with the limited joint appearance format demanded by Rostenkowski. Because he refused full debates, I was also able to make several individual appearances on radio and television programs. In impromptu news conferences after each debate, I engaged Rostenkowski directly, and the sparks from those encounters provided additional media stories.

Positioning is the key to good media coverage. I was positioned or defined early in 1991 as a viable challenger in an important race. I played off Rostenkowski's stature and importance. I had a reputation as a former elected official who had worked in other winning campaigns in the past. I had positive name recognition even before the campaign began. In addition, the uncertainty about this election's contestants focused media attention on my campaign.

One fundamental problem with campaign media coverage today is that only a handful can be covered in depth. The rest are ignored except for round-up stories in the last days of the campaign. Much worse, the local late evening news programs have air time for only one local political story. Newspapers cover only a few more political stories each day. Thus, I was competing for media coverage not just with Rostenkowski, but with a thousand candidates for president, congress, state legislature, judge, university trustee, and many other offices.

We were successful in positioning my campaign as one of the four or five most important in the state. Presidential and U.S. Senate candidates rated more coverage. The congressional battle between two incumbents on the southwest side of Chicago, Congressmen Russo and Lipinski, was more closely watched, because one incumbent was certain to lose. My battle against Annunzio and Rostenkowski got the next best coverage until the last two weeks of the election, when the House Banking Scandal implicated Congressman Charles Hayes, and Mel Reynolds who was running in the 2nd Congressional District against incumbent Congressman Gus Savage, got shot. Coverage of the Hayes and Savage district races eclipsed my race in the 5th District in these weeks. Had I been running major television advertising and had polls started to show me defeating Rostenkowski, the positive media coverage of my race would probably have continued into these critical weeks as well.

Not only did I receive good coverage in the metropolitan Chicago media but my campaign was also covered by publications like the *New York Times, Wall Street Journal, Roll Call,* and *Congressional Quarterly.* After my second campaign in 1994, we did a search on Lexus/Nexus and found that over 2,000 news stories in various media mentioned both me and Rostenkowski. Some stories appeared in publications not read in the district, but many were seen by our voters.

My campaign had early coverage by political columnists and local publications that pronounced it winnable. Front page feature stories in the Chicago alternative press the *Reader, New City,* and *In These Times* helped define my campaign as one to watch. Because of my announcement news conference at Presidential Towers, an inside source brought me proof, including canceled checks, of illicit campaign contributions from the Towers management to congressional and county candidates. That story played for several weeks in ways that I never could have planned in advance.

Table 9.1
Noncampaign and Campaign Press Conferences

NONCAMPAIGN NEWS CONFERENCES

1/91	Endorsement of Mary Baim for 43rd Ward Alderman and Hank Rubin for 50th Ward Alderman
2/91	Radio Ads supporting Danny Davis for Mayor
3/23/91	Endorsement of Gloria Chevere, Candidate for 31st Ward Alderman
3/91	Call for Marshall Plan of Aid to Poland
6/4/91	Heartland Institute Op-Ed Piece on Redistricting
7/3/91	City Club's City Council and County Board's Report Cards on Lack of Reform

CAMPAIGN NEWS CONFERENCES

5/20/91	Presidential Towers Announcement of Campaign Exploratory Committee
6/11/91	Presidential Towers' Officials Accused of "Laundering" Campaign Contributions to Congressmen
6/18/91	Proposed Amending Commonwealth Edison Franchise Agreement and Exposing Rostenkowski's Campaign Contributions from ComEd
6/2191	Term Limit Petition Drive Launched
7/22/91	Opposing Mass Transit Funding Cuts
9/19/91	Opposing Congressional Junket to Chicago
10/19/91	Blast Rostenkowski's Tax Give-a-ways at Taxpayers Action Rally
10/22/91	Call for Universal Health Care and Revelation that Health Care Industry Gave Rostenkowski $368,000 in Contributions
10/29/91	Opposing CTA Fare Raise and Service cuts
11/11/91	Formal Declaration of Candidacy for 5th Congressional District
12/2/91	Disclosure of Rosty's PAC by which He Corrupts Other Congressmen
12/4/91	Rostenkowski/Annunzio at Fault in Congressional Check Bouncing Scam

At the end of the campaign, another inside source brought me information on Rostenkowski's conflicts of interest with a major, bankrupt savings and loan official in Miami. Unfortunately, I did not receive as much good media coverage on this story as I had with Presidential Towers. But both news stories illustrate that by taking action and obtaining news coverage, other possibilities open up.

The initial media plan and strategy had to be modified as the campaign progressed: a complete plan cannot be made until a campaign begins to unfold. There were no clear guidelines for attempting to defeat an incumbent like Rostenkowski with a grassroots campaign, which was a nearly impossible task. We did not know a lot about his conflicts of interest when we began, so the campaign had to evolve as we progressed.

12/9/91	Simpson Files Petitions First
12/12/91	Rostenkowski's Misuse of Franking Privilege
12/17/91	Opposing State Refinancing of Presidential Towers
1/7/92	Simpson Asserts Pro-Choice Position; Releases Rostenkowski Scorecard Listing 10 Anti-Women Votes
1/10/92	Rostenkowski and Bush Caused Recession
1/14/92	First Simpson vs. Rostenkowski Debate Set for Wright Jr. College
1/23/92	Rostenkowski Radio Spots on Senior Citizens a Lie
2/9/92	The Rostenkowski Money Machine
2/12/92	Rostenkowski Declined Debate with Simpson, Lost Chance to Appear on Channel 11
2/18/92	Rostenkowski Gave $119 Million in Tax Breaks to 15 Insurance Companies in Return for Campaign Contributions
2/19/92	Rostenkowski Too Cozy with Large Military Contractors; $125,000 Military Contractor Contributions
2/27/92	Release of Simpson TV Commercial
3/2/92	Rostenkowski's Insensitivity to and Simpson's Support of "Notch" Seniors; Senior Citizens Issues News Conference
3/3/92	Fight to Cut Defense Budget, Fund Jobs Programs; Simpson Endorsed by Sane/Freeze
3/9/92	25,000 Jobs Fled Rostenkowski's District Since 1980; Opposition to "Fast Tract Proposal;" Endorsement by Illinois Public Action
3/11/92	Simpson Demands Rostenkowski Support Full Disclosure of House Bank Check Bouncers
3/12/92	Rostenkowski Secret Meeting and Campaign Contributions from Failing CenTrust S&L Exec

Week of March 4, 1992: 9 TV spots on Channels 2, 5 & 7 at evening news plus Cable TV during sporting events. (More than 2.9 million viewers.)

Week of March 11, 1992: More TV spots and radio spots purchased.

We originally planned to begin with proposals for congressional reform, which would allow me to contrast my candidacy with Rostenkowski and Annunzio as long-term congressional incumbents with multiple conflicts of interest. They had served 28 and 32 years in congress respectively. Rostenkowski was responsible for the 1986 tax bill, for which he received campaign contributions from companies and individuals who benefited financially from particular tax loopholes called "transition rules." Annunzio played a major role in writing the laws that precipitated the savings and loan collapse and then received campaign contributions from S&L's, while members of his family got jobs with S&L's and S&L lobbying organizations.

After developing the congressional corruption and reform issues, I planned to move on to other fundamental issues like the economy, senior citizen programs and the failures of these congressmen to provide adequate services to their districts. I knew that I could not win a campaign based on reform of congress alone, because the issue was too abstract. But this issue allowed me to begin my campaign early and legitimately attack my opponents on their public records.

Other campaign issues were not fully developed in our initial strategy. A partial public opinion poll of the old 8th and 11th Congressional Districts provided broad outlines of voter opinions, as did past voting records of these wards and townships, but finding ways to cut the issues into a winning formula and bring those issue messages to the voters had to be developed as the campaign moved forward.

From the beginning, I decided not to rehash old personal stories about the congressmen. Rostenkowski had drunken driving arrests and his daughters had been in trouble with the law at least twice. If I had pushed these character questions, I might have won the election. But, winning on those kinds of personal attacks and smear tactics, would not have proved that the electorate was ready for reform.

In 1992, I attacked my opponents on alleged corruption, and I contrasted their issue positions with mine, but I withheld attacks on their personal lives and their families. Nor did they attack my personal life or family members, other than to circulate to the press some of my writings taken out of context to make me look psychologically unstable and politically radical, I overcame these attacks without much difficulty.

In my second campaign in 1994, the 5th District campaign was once again perceived by the media as one of the top newsworthy campaigns in the state. For the two years before the election, corruption scandals about Rosty had been front page news. The Chicago Sun-Times, had run a series of exposes charging Rostenkowski with converting more than $600,000 in government and campaign funds to personal use. In the summer of 1993, I had publicly launched my campaign to unseat him. As with my 1992 campaign, I held several dozen news conferences releasing new Rostenkowski (and later state Senator Cullerton) exposes, announcing endorsements of my candidacy by groups and officials, including former presidential candidate John Anderson, and previewing my radio media campaign. In the last weeks of the campaign, I was holding almost daily news conferences or television interviews.

In the first campaign, we planned our public relations strategy without the benefit of direct public opinion poll data, and I was hurt by Chicago Tribune polls showing me trailing Rostenkowski late in the campaign. In my second campaign, we conducted a benchmark poll in the fall of 1993 that proved very helpful. Unfortunately, we could not conduct follow-up polls or afford expensive tracking polls that would have been the most useful. Our one poll showed I would probably beat Rostenkowski in a one-on-one race at the time the poll was taken. I could also beat all potential challengers if Rostenkowski dropped out of the race, with the exception of state Senator John Cullerton. The poll also predicted the most difficult problem would be running against both Rostenkowski and Cullerton simultaneously, because Cullerton and I would split the anti-Rosty vote. This is what occurred, and Rostenkowski was narrowly reelected.

The second time around, the publicity was not uniformly positive for me. First, Chairman Rostenkowski and Mayor Daley convinced President Clinton to intervene in an effort to save Rostenkowski from defeat. Members of the President's cabinet came to Chicago to hold press events to attest Rosty's importance. The mayor held a formal news conference endorsing him. The President spoke at a school in the district and endorsed Rostenkowski's reelection. And to further demonstrate how vital Rosty was to the well-being of the state, the Defense Department donated a helicopter to the city of Chicago.

Overcoming this kind of free media publicity for an opponent is almost impossible. The message of the Rostenkowski campaign to the voters was once again that although he may be charged with corruption, Rosty's clout was important to citizens, the mayor of Chicago, and the President of the United States. In 1994 the voters bought this message, electing him in the March primary, until he was formally indicted, and then they voted him out of office in November.

State Senator Cullerton's picking up of the negative stories about me that Rostenkowski's campaign had unsuccessfully circulated in 1992 posed a significant problem for me in 1994. Using public opinion polls with questions like "What would you think if you knew Dick Simpson . . ." they fashioned a smear campaign in three direct mail pieces in ways that were hard to answer during the campaign. The mail reached 5th District voters and portrayed me essentially as a New Age religious fanatic with wild ideas. I immediately countered by calling a news conference of a dozen religious leaders of all faiths from the district who decried the smear campaign and explained that the quotes from my writing were taken out of context. Despite their testimonials to the legitimacy of my religious ideals and proven political competence, this response was not adequate. The media coverage of the news conference did not reach all the voters who had received the mailings. In the last few weeks of the campaign, we could not design a direct mail response, nor did we have the funds to send it to all the voters. As a result, Cullerton's smear campaign cost me thousands of votes, boosted him in the polls, and helped reelect Rostenkowski.

SATURATION ADVERTISING

I very much wanted to do extensive radio and television advertising. Early in the 1992, campaign we made a television commercial involving several hundred supporters, and with a different look than any other commercial on television. Instead of making a saturation buy of $100,000 or more, we spent $3500 to make an inexpensive but professional commercial but could only purchase $12,000 of air time in the last two weeks of the campaign. On the week of March 4, 1992, our television spots were shown nine times during the 6:00 P.M. news on local ABC, CBS and NBC channels. We could not afford to place our ad on the more expensive and better-watched 10:00 P.M. news. We did show them on cable television around sporting events. Theoretically, our spots were seen by 2.9 million viewers. Unfortunately, most viewers did not live and vote in the 5th District, and the advertisements could not be repeated on television often enough for maximum impact; the advertising budget was simply too small. This first commercial did not bring in enough new contributions to allow us to buy more spots, as we had hoped. Candidates and campaigns always dream that running a few ads will generate enthusiasm and contributions. Most of the time, they do not.

Originally, we had not planned to do radio spots. When our television budget did not allow us to reach enough people, we created a radio commercial and bought $5,000 of commercial time to counter Rostenkowski's saturation radio spots. Once again, our buy was too small and too late to have the desired effect on voters.

In comparison to our limited media and direct mail budget, Rostenkowski began his campaign at government expense in 1991. He sent two "franked mail" pieces to every voter in the new 5th District in November and December. (Congressmen are allowed to send franked mail on their signature without postage stamps. The federal government pays for the cost of the mailings.) The mailings to sections of the new district that he did not yet represent were ruled illegal by the Appeals Court in Washington, D.C. The justices in that case ruled that:

> *Any statute [such as the one allowing franked mail to new district constituents not yet represented by the congressman], which provides financial support to an incumbent against a major-party challenger must receive some degree of heightened scrutiny under the First and Fifth Amendments to determine whether the burden placed on the rights of candidates and their supporters is justifiable. Otherwise Congress could grant incumbents extra travel allowances or increased salary during election years. . . .*
>
> *It is no different from a provision giving every incumbent $100,000 to hold campaign rallies in the new area, which would also inform citizens. In both cases government funding of the communication promotes the incumbent's reelection, without enhancing his capacity to serve his constituents.[4]*

However, the political damage was done before the court decision was rendered a year after the 1992 primary. Rostenkowski reached every voter in the new district at taxpayers' expense before I could.

Rostenkowski's use of franked mail placed my campaign at a serious disadvantage. In the first place, it dramatically increased his visibility among voters in new parts of the district that he had not represented before and enabled him to present his position on issues. The mailings were clearly political in content (as the courts later ruled), extolling his role on economic issues and promising action on national health insurance legislation. Both issues were central to the 1992 campaign.

After his franked mailings, he sent another five mailings, paid for by his campaign, to every voter in the district. He started saturation radio commercials that played every week from January to March 1992 on many stations. And he followed his mailings and radio ads with campaign literature delivered by regular Democratic Party precinct captains.

Altogether Rostenkowski spent about $800,000 on his reelection campaign, mostly on direct mail, media and campaign consultants. He outspent me by a margin of 4 to 1, and the difference won him reelection in 1992.

As an alternative to the more expensive mass media, I had planned to use direct mail and telephone contact with the voters. However, to send a mailing to the 238,000 households in the district cost at least $30,000 in postage at the then special third-class, carrier route presort rate of $.131 per piece. Mass mail is an effective means of communicating because the literature is permanent, not ephemeral like radio and television advertising, but it is still costly.

In 1992, we did not have the money to send mailings to every household in the district, as Rostenkowski did at both taxpayer and campaign expense. I settled instead for targeted mailings to potential financial contributors outside the district and to select potential voters within. In my first campaign, I sent out about 73,000 pieces to selected voters in the district. This effort comprised:

1. A mailing to supporters and potential contributors like IVI-IPO members, contributors to my past aldermanic campaigns and supporters of recent aldermanic candidates willing to share their mailing lists.
2. A mailing of 20,000 letters to pro-choice organization mailing lists. (I was pro-choice and Rostenkowski was pro-life on the abortion issue.)
3. A mailing to all voters of the 42nd, 43rd and 44th liberal lakefront wards who lived in the 5th District.
4. A mailing to 5,000 supporters of Illinois Public Action in Northwest Side wards.
5. A mailing to all "notch" senior citizens in the 5th Congressional District.
6. An endorsement mailing from a local public official to all Leyden Township voters.

With only one or two mailings to 73,000 voters, countering Rostenkowski's seven or so mailings to all voters was hard. In the northwest side wards, where my precinct organization was weakest, I also sent the least mail. Instead, I concentrated both my mailings and precinct work along the eastern lakeshore and in the western suburbs. Paying for the mailings further spread my resources and reduced the funds available to spend on radio and television ads.

Still, the results from the mailing and precinct effort were quite positive. I received more than 45 percent of the vote in all wards or towns in which I mailed and lost the other wards. In short, Rostenkowski won wards in which he had a monopoly on mailed campaign literature and the best precinct organization; I won or came close to winning the wards in which I could compete with him.

In addition to my mailings and radio and television ads, thousands of campaign brochures were given to voters directly and several hundred campaign supporters wore Simpson for Congress buttons. We purchased posters at CTA stations, placed window posters in the homes of supporters, and bought prime space in the IVI-IPO sample ballot, which reached more than 100,000 voters. The IVI-IPO sample ballot was dispersed to voters at public transportation stops and as an insert in the *Reader* newspaper. It was also placed as an advertisement in several major daily newspapers. However, the IVI-IPO sample ballot did not target only the 5th Congressional District but was spread among voters in the entire Cook County area as an endorsement of a slate of candidates.

We had been prepared to run a direct mail and phone campaign as well as a solid mass-media advertising campaign, but we lacked the money to carry out those plans. I raised less than $200,000 before the primary and another $40,000 afterwards to pay off campaign debts. While my campaign complied with all federal regulations governing congressional campaigns, I could not hope to match Rostenkowski's war chest of more than $1 million before the campaign even began. Nor could I raise enough money early enough to purchase the additional media coverage necessary to win the election. At least another $100,000 by January 1992 was needed to mount a sufficient advertising campaign.

In 1994, we increased the number of direct mail pieces my campaign sent to voters in the district, more than doubled the radio advertising, increased the CTA posters, and dropped television advertising as too expensive. But we could not counter the nine pieces of mail sent by the Cullerton campaign (three of which were his smear campaign against me), the massive television advertising of Rostenkowski, and the substantial television ads of Cullerton. Once again, Rostenkowski vastly outspent me, and even Cullerton spent nearly twice as much in his shortened two-month campaign as I did in my second year-long effort.

RAISING MONEY

I decided in 1991 to accept no campaign contributions from PACs. Running a campaign to reform Congress, I believed that some campaign contributions corrupt congressmen and create congressional gridlock. Furthermore, a challenger running against the powerful chairman of the Ways and Means Committee would not receive many PAC contributions. Because I fell about $100,000 short of winning the 1992 primary, I modified my stand in the 1994 campaign to accept contributions from "good" PACs, those dealing with liberal, good government issues, labor, human rights, and women's rights. These groups did not supply the additional funds I needed to win in 1994. Labor PACs were still afraid of offending Rostenkowski, because his committee controlled some key labor legislation. Some liberal PACs did not contribute for the same reason. Other human rights and women's organizations wanted assurance that I would win before they would contribute. Finally, some groups were neutralized because of Senator Cullerton's presence in the race. Usually challengers cannot depend upon PAC contributions to fund their campaigns and, therefore, challengers are always at a financial disadvantage in challenging incumbents.

Given the rules governing congressional campaigns, with which I fully agree, I was also limited to maximum contributions of $1,000 from individuals. Although I had thousands of contributors in my campaigns, most could not contribute at the $1,000 level. In the second campaign, I raised much larger individual contributions from many more people, but I still could not break the $250,000 barrier. Most challengers who defeat incumbents spend at least $500,000. I am convinced that I would have won in 1992 if I had raised at least $350,000. In 1994, with two major opponents and even more money being spent by them, I would probably have needed to raise $500,000 to win. During 1991 and 1992, Rostenkowski received the third highest amount of campaign contributions among all members of the House of Representatives. From January 1, 1991 to June 30, 1992, he raised $1,402,649, at least $825,630 of which was from PACs. He began his 1992 campaign with $1.3 million and after spending more than $800,000 on the primary still had $1.6 million left.[5] In the 1994 primary campaign, he raised another $1.3 million, but only $179,000 after his indictment for the general election.[6] Altogether Rostenkowski raised over $4 million to spend on his congressional campaigns of 1992 and 1994.

Rostenkowski, like many in congressional leadership positions, also created two PACs. With one he bought support of fellow congressmen and congresswomen, to support legislation he wanted passed and to endorse and support his reelection. With his second PAC, he gave campaign contributions to the Democratic Ward and Township Committeemen in the 5th District in exchange for their support of his reelection campaign. I filed a complaint with the Federal Election Commission on the use of nonfederal campaign funds to assist his election but they ruled in his favor.[7]

In neither of my congressional campaigns did I have a strong volunteer fundraising committee. Nor could I recruit an experienced fundraising chair to head the committee as a volunteer. I had help from a committee in raising money to pay off my debt after the first campaign, and I had excellent event committees in my second campaign, but most of the fundraising efforts fell upon me and paid staff.

By the fall of 1991, I hired a good part-time fundraising staff member, and by December 1991, I had hired an experienced full-time fundraiser who increased contributions tremendously in the last months of the campaign. In my second campaign, I hired an experienced fundraising consultant from the beginning to develop a sound fundraising plan and to direct the fundraising. I also hired a full-time fundraising staff member nearly a year in advance of the election to do the day-to-day fundraising with me. Because of better staffing and a better approach to individual contributors, I raised substantially more funds in my second campaign.

In my first campaign, I began by asking early supporters and members of my family for contributions. I made an original contribution of $1,000 and loans to my campaign as needed. A series of low-key (and low-priced) benefits raised a $1,00 to $2,000 each. Personal solicitation of large donors took much of my time in the early months of my first campaign; larger donors were hard to persuade at first. A $50-per-person theater benefit capped the first six months of fundraising, and 200 people attended. From March to December 1991, we raised $81,131. During this period, I had made a $1,000 contribution and loaned $19,000 to the campaign. Fifty people had contributed $200 or more for a total of $26,000. The rest came from small contributions.

From January to June 1992, the critical election months, I raised another $138,300: $18,000 in additional loans from me and another $27,000 in individual contributions of $200 or more. The rest were all small contributions. During this period, we raised money via breakfasts for larger donors, direct mail, phone solicitation of our potential list of contributors by a telemarketing firm and by our volunteers, calls by me to potential larger donors, and fundraising benefits after the campaign to pay off the debt.

In my first campaign, we employed new campaign technology in several fundraising experiments. A professional telemarketing firm phoned our list of contributors and we also tried having them call other likely prospect lists. Having the firm call our own list proved moderately successful but very expensive. The costs were almost as great as the money raised. The cold calls to other lists were not productive enough and were discontinued. The telemarketing calls did get us a critical $5,000 in the last weeks of the campaign and that money was used to purchase media advertisements. We did not have enough volunteers to make the fundraising calls and work the precincts at the same time, so we judged the telemarketing effort modestly successful, but we did not use them in my second campaign. Instead we had a better fundraising effort from the very beginning.

Less successful in 1992 was our attempt to use a 900 phone number to solicit automatic $10 contributions. Because the system was not set up by the phone company for political campaigns, obtaining clearance from the company to use the system took a very long time. We finally were assigned our 900 number in February 1992, too late to put the number in our television or radio commercials. We could include it only in a remaining few direct mail pieces. Thus, we could not inform constituents that this was a way to contribute. Based on this experience, I would use a 900 number again only if it was in service six months to one year in advance of the election, in time to include it in all advertising and campaign publications. We lost some money on this experiment, but it proved worthwhile for Jerry Brown's presidential campaign. Its success depends on thousands of people knowing the number, because only a small percentage will contribute by this means. A television or radio station that gives out its own 900 number over the air has a great advantage over campaigns in using this technique.

In my 1994 campaign, fundraising began much earlier and with a full fundraising staff. I focused on more calls to potential large donors with more success. We organized larger event committees that made our campaign benefits much more successful. We did not repeat the telemarketing efforts to contributors (except by staff and volunteers), and we did not use the 900 number. Despite better fundraising, we still fell far short of the necessary funds. From my experience and that of the campaigns of other major candidates for whom I have worked, I am more convinced than ever of the necessity of campaign finance reform to provide matching funds for candidates running for public office. Nothing else will level the playing field.

VOLUNTEER RECRUITMENT AND PRECINCT WORK

Coffees are indeed still the secret weapon of participatory campaigns. In my 1992 campaign, I attended 150 coffees, building my volunteer and small contributor base from these social/political gatherings. They allowed me to build in a single year a major campaign from almost nothing. In 1994, I attended more than 100 coffees and neighborhood gatherings, and we increased the number of campaign benefits in different sections of the district to more than one dozen.

However, using the coffees and other campaign techniques was not enough to build the volunteer army required to defeat Rostenkowski in either 1992 or 1994. By the end of the first campaign, we had 3,398 people who had made some kind of commitment or contribution, 1,300 of whom had contributed money. Working the nearly 600 precincts in the district, however, required 1,800 people doing door-to-door precinct work. I was unable to amass that level of commitment. We worked several wards successfully, but five of seven wards on the northwest side went almost entirely unworked. We did not have the money to substitute direct mail, professional phone campaigns or expensive media advertising to compensate for this failure.

Coffees alone cannot create a winning congressional campaign. They cannot be used to recruit an entire precinct army. People are already overcommitted and therefore unwilling to do precinct work. When I coordinated the northwest side wards for Carol Moseley-Braun's Senate campaign, we did better but not well enough. Even with a popular candidate, we could work only about 100 of the 600 precincts in the district with volunteers. Since the regular party precinct captains worked for her in the general election, and since she had good media coverage and a weak opponent, she won nonetheless.

Again in my 1994 campaign, we tried to build a volunteer precinct army to cover the entire district. We continued to draw new people into my campaign; many contributed money and some worked in the office or in the precincts on election day. But even building on my 1992 campaign and Senator Moseley-Braun's, I could not recruit enough precinct work volunteers.

I have learned that a successful modern participatory campaign in a large district must depend not only on volunteer precinct workers. It must also have enough money to run a major media advertising campaign and a direct mail and phone campaign to reach voters that volunteers cannot canvass. Campaigns will therefore continue to cost a lot of money.

BROADER SOCIAL MOVEMENTS

In 1968, the Eugene McCarthy and Robert Kennedy campaigns for president based on the anti-Vietnam War movement succeeded. McCarthy achieved a suprisingly strong showing in the New Hampshire primary and went on to win primaries in a number of states. The incumbent president, Lyndon Johnson, withdrew from the election and Robert Kennedy entered the race, one of the rare times in American history when an incumbent president was forced to withdraw or defeated within his own party.

In the 1970s, we won independent, reform campaigns as part of the anti-machine fervor in Chicago. In 1983 and 1987, Harold Washington was elected mayor by a diverse reform coalition, a critical component of which was the civil rights movement.

In 1990, Paul Wellstone was elected to the Senate in Minnesota by a variety of liberal and radical groups, including students and some labor unions. In 1992, U.S. Senator Carol Moseley-Braun and other women candidates were elected by the pro-choice movement. These elections demonstrate that social movements can make the difference between winning and losing participatory campaigns. The antiwar, civil rights, student, labor, and women's movements have all had important electoral victories.

In my campaigns, we focused on six major issues and their related movements in an attempt to build a winning coalition:

1. Reform of Congress: the anti-incumbent movement,
2. Women's issues, especially abortion: the women's movement,
3. Senior citizen issues: the seniors' empowerment movement,
4. Cutting the defense budget: the peace movement,
5. Economic issues (including NAFTA): the workers' and labor union movement, and
6. Funding for higher education: the student movement.

By advocating these issues, I received support, money and volunteers from groups and organizations dedicated to them. Either these movements were too weak or I was unable to build a campaign to motivate their supporters to provide the level of support I needed to win. For instance, as a teachers' union member, I received the endorsement of my local union in both campaigns and the support of one or two other unions in each campaign, but Rostenkowski received all the major union endorsements in the 1992 campaign. After he voted for the North American Free Trade Agreement (NAFTA), he lost his union endorsements. But the unions stayed neutral in the 1994 campaign. Neither Cullerton nor I could get labor's active endorsement.

Reform of Congress and cutting the defense budget did not move enough voters in the district to affect election outcome. While I recruited the most volunteers and strong support from women, seniors and students, I could not get a majority of these groups in the district to vote for me. To change the 1992 campaign result, I would have needed at least another $100,000, another 100 volunteers to work precincts, *or a change of allegiance among the voting public.*

Social movements, movement issues and major shifts in public opinion elect reform candidates, but these movements cannot be called up or controlled by political candidates.

WINNING PARTICIPATORY CAMPAIGNS

The story of my campaigns may seem discouraging. For many reasons, I would like to report that anyone can run against entrenched public officials who are corrupt or doing a bad job and win. That is the happy ending of films like "Mr. Smith Goes to Washington," where Mr. Smith also goes on to do great good for the country. I would also like to report that candidates always survive negative campaigns by opponents as President Clinton does in the documentary film, "The War Room." Unfortunately, the truth is not so rosy.

Participatory reform campaigns are an uphill battle against formidable odds. From time to time they are won. When they succeed, the officials elected often make an invaluable contribution to public life. Even when they are lost, like the 1968 McCarthy and Kennedy presidential bids, they force major public policy changes such as shortening the Vietnam War.

To the extent that a candidate raises significant resources, including large sums of money, she is more likely to be elected by the work of the volunteers and the power of her issues. Carol Moseley-Braun, for instance, spent $5 million on her primary and general election campaigns and, as of this writing, is still raising funds to pay off campaign debts. Congressional, state, county, or citywide races require less money than U.S. Senate races, but they still cost more than can be raised by small contributions alone.

Until the laws change to provide public matching funds, modern participatory campaigns will prove difficult to run successfully. While the odds are against the participatory candidate, reform of our democracy is ultimately at stake. When the issues are powerful enough, good candidates will emerge to run the necessary, hard campaigns, and they will win.

Chapter X

WHAT TO DO WHEN YOU WIN

At the end of the movie, *The Candidate,* Robert Redford, having won an upset victory, asks, "What do I do now?" This is not a trivial question for anyone who works in an election campaign. Whether you win or lose, there are important things to be done.

After battling an election, you gain a deep appreciation of the benefits of a permanent political organization. To build a campaign organization from scratch every time an election rolls around, without any continuity and without a mechanism for selecting the best candidate, is a hopeless task. To elect consistently good people to public office, permanent political organizations are essential.

A permanent organization dedicated to promoting participatory politics does more than elect good people to office. It provides a mechanism to support those candidates and keeps open lines of communication developed during the campaign between candidates and their constituents. By mobilizing the community support and relaying constituent complaints, requests and questions, a permanent organization can help newly elected officials better represent their community.

A permanent political organization makes officials more accountable for their actions. Without such an organization, there is considerable temptation for elected officials to make too many concessions to political bosses or wealthy special interests, to insure reelection and gain the support necessary to pass legislation. Officials with a sense of obligation to the people who elected them will be more outspoken, more vigorous in their representation of the community, more independent in their voting, and more aggressive in supplying services to a district.

If you have a strong enough political organization to elect officials pledged to governmental reform, they can use their powers as elected officials to create more participatory governmental institutions. For example, when elected 44th Ward alderman in Chicago, I instituted: a full-time service office to guarantee that all citizens received government services as a right and not as political favors; a 44th Ward Assembly to direct my vote in City Council; a Community Zoning Board to decide planning and zoning matters in the community through public hearings; a Spanish-speaking assembly, Asamblea Abierta, to focus on Latino issues; and a Traffic Review Commission to direct traffic and parking improvements. If a political organization elects candidates committed to participatory government, successful election campaigns will result in creating of new instruments of participatory government.[1]

A permanent organization also has the resources to launch lobbying and issue campaigns to influence other officials whom it did not elect. Citizens can put intense pressure on government if organized to do so. With well-organized lobbying efforts, demands are more likely to be granted, and citizens will learn to participate in policy-making as well as electioneering.

A permanent organization committed to participatory democracy can be built or strengthened by well-run election campaigns. After the campaign is over, win or lose, the volunteers should be assembled and presented a carefully thought-out proposal for working in future elections and creating a permanent organization. If the time is ripe, the specific proposal is good enough, and at least 10 people will commit time and effort for one year, there will also be support for such an organization from campaign veterans. They will understand how important this step is for future election successes, as well as for reform in government.

IF THE ELECTION IS LOST

If the candidate loses her election, a series of steps still must be taken. After the disappointment of election night, the office must be closed and staff paid. Usually a candidate will need to take a vacation with her family to recover from the ordeal of the campaign. Then, *the first order of business is to pay off your campaign debt*. The candidate, her campaign manager or finance committee chair should negotiate with each individual or business still owed money. They may accept partial payment or forgive the debt. When the final debt is known, a fundraising plan to pay off the debt must be drafted.

The former candidate must write all her volunteers and contributors, thanking them for their support, giving them a breakdown of the final election statistics, and asking them to make a final contribution towards clearing the debt. After their contributions have been received, the candidate may pay off the remaining debt herself. If the debt is large, a finance or benefit committee is formed to plan a simple benefit or series of benefits to be held a few months after the end of the campaign. These can be simple affairs like theater benefits, potluck or spaghetti suppers, or garage sales. Finally, the candidate once more solicits her larger campaign contributors to sponsor the event and make larger donations to clear the debt.

As much as 20 percent of the entire campaign budget may remain to be paid after the campaign is over. A good candidate and able campaign manager will not overspend more than this amount, no matter how hopeful the campaign may look in the last few days of the election. Regardless, any remaining debt must be paid off or future participatory campaigns in your area will be unable to raise the money or credit to run effectively.

Only after the campaign debt is paid off and a permanent political organization has been formed, can a candidate consider running again. As a rule of thumb, she probably does not have a chance of winning the race next time unless she received at least 40 percent vote. Before deciding to run again, there should also be clear evidence that she can expand her base of support by finding new contributors, additional groups to back her candidacy, and more experienced staff members. If the current incumbent will not run for reelection or has alienated voters, the candidate's chances will be even better.

If a candidate is going to run again, she should remain in the news and the public spotlight. Perhaps she can serve as a spokeswoman for an organization or social movement concerned with issues of importance to the district. She can endorse candidates running in other elections and meet their contributors, staff members and volunteers. Helping other organizations and candidates provides a candidate with future access to valuable resources and demonstrates to voters that she is a person acting on their behalf.

HOLDING OFFICE

The excitement of volunteers in winning a hard-fought election and their enthusiasm for future elections is captured in quotes from some of the folks who helped elect Bernard Weisberg to the Illinois Constitutional Convention:

... *"It is going to mean new kinds of candidates. ..."*

... *"This is sort of like the beginning, I hope of a tidal wave. We are beginning to win significantly elsewhere [in other districts], not only here. ..."*

... *"It means a total reformation of politics in Chicago. It shows that the mayor [Richard J. Daley] has lost his touch with what the people of this city want. And we are on the road. ...*

... *A lot of people in this city are growing up, and people working together for principles are showing that they are mature enough and steadfast enough to build a democracy the way a democracy ought to be built. And we do not have to take the dictates of a lot of miserable patronage-style politicians who have been choking this city and wrecking this city for three generations. We are getting to be too good for them, the people of this city. We are growing up."*[2]

Still, when the cheers die down, the candidate and those who helped elect her still must face the question, "What do we do now?" One important step is to use the momentum of a campaign to form or strengthen a permanent political organization dedicated to electing more officials, passing new laws, and holding government officials accountable.

The newly elected candidate and those she appoints to government positions also have the tasks of carrying out her campaign promises, reforming the political process, and serving in an honorable and accountable way. This will make those who worked so hard to elect her proud of their sacrifices. Having campaigned on issues powerful enough to mobilize volunteers and win over voters, the candidate must now fulfill her promises. Otherwise she will set back the movement that elected her. If, on the other hand, she becomes an outstanding public official, she will win over thousands who doubted her originally.

So what should she do? If she was elected to an executive position, she should immediately appoint an able transition team to analyze the government she is to lead, appoint strong officials to her cabinet, and set forth an agenda of change and transformation.

An ideal transition team is composed of former government officials (such as members of the opposition in the legislative branch), academics from universities, executives on loan from major corporations, and heads of public interest groups. They must be loyal to the official who appoints them, but they must also be knowledgeable and creative. The transition team should analyze both the personnel who headed agencies in the former government and the operation of government agencies themselves. The team should be given free reign to make recommendations for improvements, suggest who should be replaced in government, and provide a list of nominees to replace them. They should report as soon after the inauguration as possible and their reports on government agencies should be made public.

The new executive should appoint the best cabinet members available. Some chief executives appoint only "yes" men and women, officials who will not overshadow them. This is the sure way to disaster. President Franklin Roosevelt not only appointed capable cabinet members, he purposely appointed people with strikingly different viewpoints and backgrounds, and with overlapping areas of authority, so that disputes between them would have to be brought to him for final decision.

A wise chief executive appoints the best people possible and gives them the authority to run their agencies. If they make major mistakes, they can be fired and replaced, but the best people with the authority to make dramatic changes will do the most to improve government quickly.

Finally, a candidate should propose her most fundamental changes and new laws in the first hundred days. Her agenda for change must be presented, and fought for, from the first day she takes office. In this "honeymoon" period, the legislative branch, believing that the chief executive was elected with a mandate, is most likely to support drastic changes, as was true of such different regimes as Presidents Franklin Roosevelt and Ronald Reagan. However, when Harold Washington was mayor of Chicago, the City Council mobilized a majority vote against him and blocked many of his proposals until a special aldermanic election three years later changed the balance of power. There isn't always a honeymoon in the first hundred days. Nevertheless, a chief executive elected by participatory campaigns has an obligation to set forth her agenda of change and to begin fighting for it in her inaugural address, her cabinet appointments, and her first legislative package. She will have to keep fighting for her proposals until they are enacted, whether that occurs in the first hundred days, first thousand days, or after her term is over.

If a candidate is elected to the legislative branch, her role is different. She will have only a few legislative aides to appoint. Her bigger task is to play a creative role in the city council, county board, state legislature, or Congress. A candidate should offer reform legislation and vote in ways that best represent her constituents. But the legislative role is not an academic exercise in proposing bills that cannot be passed and for which no other legislator votes. Once elected, a candidate must join a faction or party whether the legislature is officially partisan or nonpartisan. She will likely not be a member of the majority party or faction. If she is, she will be relegated to the "back bench," not to a position of party leadership, and this will make her role more difficult.

Critical decisions need to be made by the time she is sworn into office. The very first votes of any new legislative body are to elect legislative officials and appoint members to committees. These votes set the tenor of the entire legislative term. Those who vote with the opposition faction and those who vote with the majority usually continue to align with these voting blocs throughout the next two to four years. A candidate must therefore choose her party or faction immediately.

Probably a participatory candidate will become a part of a reform bloc of legislators. If she must stand alone because no other reformers have been elected to the legislature, she can at least use the floor of the legislature as a bully pulpit to criticize the government, to point up flaws in governmental proposals, and to be a watchdog for the citizens who elected her. If she becomes a member of a small reform bloc of legislators, then she becomes a part of the "loyal opposition" to the government. She can specialize in her area of concern and work with other reformers to present alternatives to government proposals. Over the years, as the number in the opposition bloc grows, these reformers create a "shadow government," offering not just individual pieces of legislation, but alternative budgets and alternatives for each major law the government proposes. When the current government makes mistakes and falls out of favor with the voters, members of the opposition bloc are available as experienced candidates for chief executive and the cabinet of a new reform government.

Changes in government do not normally occur incrementally but in great leaps forward. Opposition elected officials strive to provide a critique of government and a genuine alternative that one day will appeal to citizens so strongly that an entirely new government with a reform agenda can be elected. My role as leader of the opposition bloc in the Chicago City Council from 1975–1979 was to prepare the way for the later reform regime of Harold Washington, who was elected mayor in 1983 and 1987. His reforms in turn became the foundation for future Chicago governments.

ELECTORAL REFORM

Democracy is undermined because elections today are won by the endorsement of closed party organizations, by name recognition of current public officials, and by millions of dollars spent on 30-second television spots or distorted direct mail campaigns. The best qualified candidates with the most compelling ideas are often not elected. From the 1960s to the 1980s, in varying degrees, participatory campaigns substituted volunteers and ideas for party endorsements, fame and big bucks. But it is becoming harder to recruit enough volunteers to beat the party machine, big money and expensive high-tech campaigns. For participatory politics to triumph regularly, fundamental campaign reforms are needed.

To judge which reforms are necessary, we must consider what democracy requires. Representative democracy is based upon a paradigm of debate and discussion. Political candidates are supposed to clash and present clear alternatives. Voters choose between these alternatives and empower their elected representatives to govern. Once in government, representatives convince the majority of other representatives to vote for the best government policies. All these stages require debate, deliberation and discussion. Candidates and policies win by persuasion in a democracy.

Today, voters are alienated from particular candidates and campaigns. They lack confidence in the political system. They believe that all politicians are crooks who make promises they do not plan to keep and that individual votes do not matter. As a result, active citizen participation has been reduced to passive participation: watching the media and reading mail sent by candidates and interest groups. Less than half of our citizens vote in any given election. Often those who vote lack the information necessary to make wise decisions.

Some political scientists and journalists claim that our political system is more responsive now because political marketing requires polling the public's opinion. These polls shape candidates' positions and future government policies. Yet, most public opinion polls reflect prejudice, not debate and deliberation. For instance, public opinion polls asking whether welfare payments should be cut will always get strong agreement from a majority of respondents. If respondents are told that many of those who benefit from welfare payments and food stamps are children, their response changes. Legitimate policy decisions should be based on debate that provides information and arguments, not on uninformed public reactions.

A number of scholars have concluded that the political marketing of candidates has actually undermined democracy. Nicholas O'Shaughnessy in "The Phenomenon of Political Marketing" concludes:

> *American politics are shaped by the need to market candidates and parties as if they were soap powder, employing the techniques taken from the world of business. . . .*
>
> *The essence of marketing is reciprocity: "consumers" themselves bring something to bear on the selling; they are not passive objects and the process is an interactive one . . .*

> *Unfortunately, [t]he progress of the marketing concept through American politics has accentuated this preference of democracy for the likable leader over the strong, the smart phrase over the smart idea, the common over the elegant; it has redefined democracy's criteria further along the path antiquity most feared since it vaunts appeals to immediate satisfaction and superficial, instantly communicable indices of worth . . .*
>
> *[P]olitical marketing . . . makes politics more fickle and opportunistic.*[3]

Political marketing often depends upon television that "is especially a propagandistic medium, conveying a visual world requiring no literacy and superficial attention."[4] Similarly, direct mail mobilizes people into armchair activism by encouraging them only to vote, to write checks for financial contributions (in the case of less than 1 percent of the recipients), or to send preprinted postcards to government officials when directed to do so. Neither television nor direct mail (even when coupled with data analysis and public opinion polls) allow voters to discuss the merits of candidates or policies or to ask questions. These media do not allow for discussion or public participation in decision making in any meaningful way. Voters are manipulated into voting for the slick candidate or backing the policies of narrow self-interest.

Rather than conduct discussions, mass media and direct mail manipulate images to convince the viewer or reader to buy a product. The media commercials and mailed communications do not provide enough genuine information for a consumer to make up her mind about the merit of the product or the candidate.

Representative democracy cannot be sustained in a system of media manipulation, mass media commercials, public opinion polling, voter data analysis, and direct mail solicitations paid for by big money. When we are reduced to consumers being sold a product by slick advertising, we are no longer citizens deciding between alternative candidates and policies. The debate and deliberation essential to democracy has been foreshortened to the point that democracy is no longer possible even if elections are held and governments change hands periodically.

The villain here is not simply television advertising or direct mail campaigns. As Randall Rothenberg has written in *The New York Times,* "A true cure . . . would require more than free [media] ads and earnest narration." In his article he quotes Professor Larry Sabato as saying "You cannot improve discourse [on television by merely requiring free time or by merely applying legal restrictions]. . . . Lack of education, lack of demands by the public that a certain level of discourse be reached are the problem. That will not change with free time. That is corrected with more and better civic education starting from kindergarten."[5]

Our society and our communication media have changed in ways that profoundly affect our politics. Rothenberg writes, "The manipulative imagery that has traveled from Madison Avenue to music videos to the network newsroom has become an unavoidable part of society's background noise."[6] Network television coverage of campaigns reveals another symptom of the problem. In the last 20 years, 40-second clips have been replaced by sound bites of less than 10 seconds even for candidates running for president.[7] Television editing techniques condense longer political statements into ever shorter news stories. Thirty to 90-second news stories with only 10 seconds of actual statements by presidential candidates eliminate any possibility of meaningful political discussion and debate. News coverage of election campaigns most often focuses upon "horse race" and human interest aspects, not on the genuine qualifications of candidates or the merits of proposed government policies. Worst of all, local television news covers murders, fires and catastrophes in much greater depth than it covers local election campaigns. Most candidates for office do not even get 10 seconds to present their case to the voters.

Paid political commercials, negative advertising and cleverly packaged direct mail messages provide even less opportunity than the news media for honest discourse. Despite counter trends such as CNN and the McNeil/Lehrer NewsHour on PBS, voters do not gather enough information to make rational choices among candidates or policies.

The media's failure to promote meaningful discussion of public policies and to provide enough accurate information for voters to make wise choices is not a plot by business and political elites to remain in power. Nor is it a side effect of capitalism and an unyielding demand for higher profits by media corporations. Rather the public does not demand political information. Technological changes like digital television that will create more television channels through compression of existing baud widths, more Internet discussion groups, and newspapers delivered on home computers will not solve the problem either. As Ron Faucheux has written:

> The trouble [with free time on new television channels created by digitalization] has nothing to do with air time but **audience size.** Giving politicians free time that nobody watches is giving them wooden nickels.
>
> How many people will tune their TVs to a channel that features only candidates pitching for votes?[8]

This is a chicken and egg proposition. As voters, we need better information to make an informed choice in elections and about government policies. But we will not get better information until there is a public demand for it.

Nor can better information alone restore and revitalize our democracy. We need to encourage the most qualified among us to run for office and provide citizens with better opportunities for influencing the outcomes of elections and government policies. Currently, elections are conducted in ways that favor incumbents, party endorsed candidates, the wealthy, and candidates supported by wealthy interest groups. Changing this system will require a major social transformation. I have been struck by the fact that, although I had many more supporters and contributors in my congressional races in the 1990s, I had more volunteers willing to work precincts and contact their neighbors in my aldermanic races in the 1970s. My congressional district is 10 times the size of my former aldermanic ward but I could not attract even the same number of volunteers as before. A change of values, as well as a change in institutions, will be required before citizens again become effective participants in our system of representative democracy.

Under today's conditions, three kinds of electoral reforms have the best chance of making elections and our government democratic:

1. term limits,
2. campaign finance reform, and
3. democratizing campaigns and government through citizen agendas, televoting and town hall meetings.

TERM LIMITS

One problem endemic to American government is the advantage of an incumbent running for reelection. In most elections, we vote in a sort of referendum on the performance of officials in office. When citizens vote to defeat or reelect the U.S. President, they have enough information to cast a reasonable vote. In addition, the opposition party candidate will spend tens of millions of dollars to criticize the incumbent and present reasons for defeating her. Since there are over 580,000 elected officials in the United States and nearly half of them are elected every two years, voters often know much less about city, county and state officials in low visibility offices and much less about how well they have performed their public duties.

Incumbents have substantially greater name recognition than challengers and greater acceptance by the media, and they can move easily solicit contributions from wealthy individuals and interest groups wanting government favors. Incumbents can also spend thousands to hundreds of thousands of government dollars to contact voters in their official government capacity, for instance by sending newsletters paid for and mailed at government expense to every voter in a congressional district. Because of these advantages, many incumbents have a 90 percent or better chance of reelection, no matter how well they have performed their government job.

Even incumbents who do a good job tend to ossify in office over time. They conduct business as usual, and government tends to stagnate rather than advance. In their first years on the job, they may have been enthusiastic and filled with new ideas. By the first decade, they will have enacted most of their reforms, made any progress they are likely to make, and carried out their original platform. We would be better served by a circulation of people in power than by the 95 percent reelection rates common in Congress. Others argue that changing officials every decade or so would eliminate officials willing to make tough choices and long-term commitments of resources. My own experience in government suggests that the greater threat is that the concentration of power in the hands of constantly reelected officials causes them to disregard the public good and public opinion.

Our electoral system, stacked by election laws and the nature of modern society, cannot provide for change and genuine election contests won on the merit of candidates and ideas. Limiting the terms of officials and making open seat elections more competitive will correct some of these deficiencies.

By current court rulings, limiting terms of congressmen requires a constitutional amendment submitted by Congress to state legislatures for their approval or a constitutional convention to adopt such an amendment. Public opinion on terms limits is clear. Nearly every term limit referendum submitted to the public has been approved by overwhelming majorities. Every public opinion poll has shown approval of term limits by at least two-thirds of the public. A number of state governments have enacted term limits, and several hundred towns and cities have adopted them.

Still, enacting term limits will not be easy. Most elected officials oppose this reform since it would potentially shorten their own terms in office. One positive result, would be to elect more women and younger men to high public offices. However, the fundamental benefit would be to level the playing field so nonincumbents are elected more often, bringing with them proposals and programs that voters currently favor.

CAMPAIGN FINANCE REFORM

Campaign finance reforms is even more important than term limits. The arguments for campaign finance reforms are simple. The better financed candidate most often wins elections. To obtain the necessary funds, she has to appeal to PACs, which represent narrow special interests. Many PACs attempt to represent both their members and the public good. They also balance each other to some extent by representing different interests, such as business and labor, human rights and law and order, economic development and the environment. But some PACs give only to candidates who support their point of view regardless of the public good. The National Rifle Association gives money only to officials who agree to oppose all restrictions on guns, even machine guns and bullets that can penetrate protective gear worn by policemen. Narrower business PACs want laws and regulations that provide them monetary advantages no matter what the effect on the environment, the budget, or the health and safety of the public. Because of the need for campaign contributions, our representative democracy is reduced to representing too many wealthy special interests. These interests buy and corrupt public officials who have no alternative but to court PACs if they want to be elected and reelected.

Permutations of the PAC problem are endless. Congressional leaders like Rostenkowski form their own separate PACs funded by special interests. They use contributions from their congressional PACs to buy support of other congressmen for legislation they sponsor and support of local party officials for their reelection. Through these PACs, corruption seeps into all aspects of government and politics. The diaries of former Senator Robert Packwood demonstrate how "soft money" contributed to congressional PACs can further undermine the election process.[9]

Despite some problems and loopholes, we already have an effective method for overcoming the undue effects of big money and PACs in the presidential campaign financing system. Contributions to all campaigns should similarly be restricted to amounts of $1,000 or less (or even $100 or less). These small contributions should be matched by federal (or state and local) funds. As with presidential campaigns, strict limits need to be placed on total campaign expenditures, and the media should be required to provide free air time (or time bought with government vouchers) for candidate debates.

Legislative proposals sponsored by organizations like Common Cause have been offered in Congress and state legislatures to enact systems of public campaign finance similar to our presidential campaign system. Undoubtedly, any system adopted will develop flaws that will have to be further reformed later. For instance, PACs grew as a result of the "reforms" after the Watergate scandals in the 1970s. Yet the general principles of campaign finance reform are clear. If democracy is to be served and officials are not to be corrupted by campaign contributions, candidates will have to rely on small contributors, government funding and free media. The amount of money available to the candidates should be roughly equal and great enough to allow them to send their message effectively to the voters. The voters must get enough information to make a reasonable choice between candidates. As a corollary, the voters must become knowledgeable enough and interested enough in their government to make informed voting decisions.

A final method of insuring that voters receive a minimal level of information is to have state and local governments mail them a voter pamphlet containing similar information provided by all candidates. In the future, information on the candidates can be placed on the Internet, as California began to do in the 1994 election. If each candidate supplies the same basic material on their qualifications and positions on issues, a voter who is willing to do a minimum amount of reading and reflecting can make an informed choice.

If candidates send their message to the voters without being beholden to corrupting campaign contributions, voters will use the information to cast an informed vote. Campaign finance reform depends on the belief in this possibility. Eliminate 100,000 or more elected offices that might better be appointed and holding fewer elections so voters could focus on fewer candidates and campaigns in election would also be useful. But few public officials are willing to vote their office out of existence.

EXPERIMENTS IN DEMOCRACY

For the last several decades, a great many experiments on democratizing both elections and government have been attempted. Some experiments have returned to the older town hall meeting model. Others have harnessed modern technology—computers, public opinion polls and television—in the service of greater citizen participation and influence. Nearly every experiment that has involved citizens more directly has been effective in its limited arena, but almost none of them has yet been adopted by government, sufficiently funded, or legitimized.

I have briefly described the successes of the 44th Ward Assembly (or town hall meeting) through which I involved thousands of Chicago citizens in their local government. The decisions of the assembly were wise, our community was improved, and I became a more effective public official because of citizen advice and direction. Members of the assembly and our other units of neighborhood government felt empowered and became much more knowledgeable about their government. Neighborhood governments have continued in other cities, but they are still not dominant in the United States. Most elected officials are simply not willing to share their power with the people who elected them, and voters do not demand a greater share of government authority.

If permanent town hall meetings with governmental authority are opposed by public officials, less demanding alternatives exist. Modern public opinion polling techniques can be used to discover policies that citizens favor. There have been a great variety of experiments in public journalism, citizen agendas and televoting during the last few years.

Christa Slaton in "Televote" summarizes the results of several experiments in community television, teleconferencing and television town meetings this way:

> *These participatory democratic government affiliated projects have demonstrated the following: 1) Large segments of the population are willing to participate in ways they never have before. 2) Attempts to educate the public on issues processes and functions of government are successful. 3) Citizens not only become better informed through attempts to involve them in public discussion and interaction, but begin to understand complexities and approach issues more analytically. 4) When legislators are involved, they become better informed on problems and issues. 5) Legislators become more accountable as public awareness and sophistication grow. 6) Citizens want more, not less, access and responsibility.*[10]

In experiments in "Televoting" in Hawaii, San Jose and Los Angeles, the techniques for involving citizens in government policy-making were developed further. Representative samples of citizens were chosen using random digit dialing and asked to participate in a televote on an issue. If they agreed to participate, they were sent a packet of information and asked to discuss the issues with friends and family and then call in their vote (or they were called back and asked their opinions). Citizens were informed about the issue through television news and special television programs designed to provide additional information on the policy questions to be voted on. The process differed from normal polling by presenting citizens with further information and encouraging them to discuss the issues before voting. The results of the Televote were then presented to the public and officials charged with making the policy decisions. In each case, experiments in televoting were judged successful by the universities involved and government agencies employing them. Unfortunately, like other experiments in democracy, they have not been used widely.

A method with some similarities to televoting has been adapted to campaigns. In the Illinois Voter Project, conducted by the Illinois League of Women Voters and the University of Illinois at Chicago during the gubernatorial race of 1994, public opinion polls were taken to determine the issues most important to the voters. Voters' views were then refined through a series of focus groups. Finally, citizen panels or juries representative of the state population heard testimony by expert witnesses and developed a citizens agenda on the most important issues, along with 10 recommendations they wanted to see the candidates adopt or address in their platforms. The gubernatorial candidates were questioned about these proposals in a televised debate hosted by the League of Women Voters. This entire citizens agenda process was well-covered by the media; nonetheless, both the Democratic and Republican candidates ignored the agenda and continued to proposed their own programs and run negative campaign commercials against each other.

For the 1996 election, there are a variety of proposals for greater citizen involvement. A citizens' convention of random voters selected before the presidential primaries to screen the issues and the candidates from both parties has been proposed. Less directed public opinion polls on issues that report citizen responses more fully have been advocated to let candidates know voters' views. Academics, foundations and media organizations remain dissatisfied with current campaigns and continue to devise new options to create greater citizen participation, but it is hard to know if any of these experiments will be tried in 1996.[11]

Greater participation by interested citizens and representative samples of citizens is now clearly possible using modern technology such as computers, television and public opinion polling. Unfortunately, government officials seem unwilling to use town hall meetings, televotes, electronic town hall meetings, citizen panels or any methods of greater citizen involvement, even though these methods have demonstrated that they improve policy making and citizens' sense of efficacy.

In the years ahead, the pressure will increase to adopt term limits, reform campaign finances, and grant citizens a greater voice in government. Electing more candidates committed to such reforms is the surest road to guarantee their enactment. When we are willing to participate in the political process, significant changes occur. Modern participatory campaigns can be won when citizens are mobilized. By our work and our vote, we can demand and achieve democracy.

NOTES

Chapter 1

1. Finley Peter Dunne, *Mr. Dooley in Peace and War* (Urbana, Il: University of Illinois Press, 1988), xxiii. The longer quotation reads: "Politics ain't bean bag. Tis a man's game; an' women, childher, an' prohybitionists do well to keep out iv it."
2. I first discussed the differences between political philosophy, political science, and political action in Dick Simpson, *Who Rules: Introduction to the Study of Politics* (Chicago: Swallow, 1970, 1971, 1973), vii-12. A more detailed elaboration of these approaches to the study of politics is contained in Dick Simpson and George Beam, *Political Action* (Athens, Ohio: Swallow/Ohio University Press, 1982).
3. A description of formal political action propositions and rules governing their formulation is contained in *Political Action*.

Chapter 2

1. For a review of some of the literature relating personality traits and political participation see: Lester Milbrath. *Political Participation* (Chicago: Rand McNally, 1965), Chapter 3.
2. From Thucydides, *History*, Book II, Chapter VI, Section 40 as translated by Alfred E. Zimmerman in *The Greek Commonwealth* (London: Oxford University Press, 1966. Originally published in 1922.), 204.
3. Max Lerner, "Political Man is Needed," *Chicago Sun-Times* (August 6, 1970), 90.
4. These are direct quotes from campaign volunteers in the documentary film on the Weisberg campaign. William Mahin and Dick Simpson, *By the People: A Study of Independent Politics—Chicago, 1969* (Chicago: University of Illinois at Chicago, 1970), Reel I.
5. Lawrence Grey, *How to Win a Local Election: A Complete Step-By-Step Guide* (New York: M. Evans, 1994), 30.
6. Bernard Weisberg in *By the People*, Reel I.

Chapter 3

1. William Singer, "Reflections on Campaign Techniques" (Mimeographed paper printed by Committee on Illinois Government, Chicago, 1969), 8.

2. In *By the People*, reports being received at the campaign headquarters are shown in registration drive sequence on Reel I.
3. Donald Page Moore in *By The People*, Reel I.
4. Lawrence Grey, *How to Win a Local Election: A Complete Step-By-Step Guide* (New York: M. Evans, 1994), 106 and 108.
5. Joseph Napolitan, *The Election Game and How to Win It* (New York: Doubleday, 1972), 16-17.
6. June Rosner in *By the People*, Reel I.
7. Bob Houston, "What Every *Great* Coffee Chairman Has to Know" (Mimeographed instructions for coffee chairmen, Bruce Dumont for State Senator Campaign, Chicago, 1970).
8. Donald Page Moore in *By the People*, Reel I.
9. See Angus Campbell, *et al.*, *The American Voter* (New York: John Wiley, 1960); William Glanigan and Nancy Zingale, *The Political Behavior of the American Electorate* (Washington, Congressional Quarterly, 1994), 8th edition; and Michael Gant and Norman Luttberg, *American Electoral Behavior 1952-1992* (Itasca, Il: Peacock, 1995), 2nd edition.
10. Hannibal is supplied by Hannibal Software, Inc., 208 G. Street, N.E., 2nd Floor, Washington, DC 20002. The program is very useful, however, we had great difficulties in my campaigns with getting answers to questions and help using the program from the company. There may be newer and better software programs available, as they are continually being improved.
11. For a more complete discussion of the data that can be supplied from various sources see Gary Selnow, *High-Tech Campaigns: Computer Technology in Political Communication* (Westport, Connecticut: Praeger, 1994), Chapter 5. For a list of national firms which supply this information see Footnote 5 in Chapter 5.

Chapter 4

1. Herbert Alexander, *Reform and Reality: The Financing of State and Local Campaigns* (New York: The Twentieth Century Fund, 1991), 2.
2. James Thurber, The Transformation of American Campaigns in James Thurber and Candice Nelson, eds, *Campaigns and Elections American Style* (Boulder: Westview Press, 1995), 6.
3. Judge Lawrence Grey, *How to Win a Local Election* (New York: M. Evans, 1994), 130-131.
4. Grey, 133.
5. Hank Parkinson, *Winning Your Campaign: A Nuts-and-Bolts Guide to Political Victory* (Englewood Cliffs, New Jersey: Prentice-Hall, 1970), 77.
6. *By The People*, Reel I.
7. David Himes, "Strategy and Tactics for Campaign Fund-Raising," in James Thurber and Candice Nelson, eds, *Campaigns and Elections American Style* (Boulder: Westview Press, 1995), 62.
8. Himes, 63.
9. Himes, 65.

10. Alexander, 20.
11. Himes, 65-66.
12. Himes, 67.

Chapter 5

1. Robert J. Dinkin, *Campaigning in America: A History of Election Practices* (New York: Greenwood, 1989), 172.

Chapter 6

1. Joe McGinniss, *The Selling of the President 1968* (New York: Pocket Books, 1970). First published by Trident Press, 1969.
2. McGinniss, 34 and 39.
3. Gary Selnow, *High-Tech Campaigns: Computer Technology in Political Communication* (Westport, Ct: Praeger, 1994), 42.
4. William R. Hamilton, "Political Polling: From the Beginning to the Center," in Thurber and Nelson, eds., *Campaigns and Elections American Style*, 178.
5. Hamilton, 170.
6. Don Rose in *By the People*, Reel I.
7. Don Rose in *By the People*, Reel I.
8. See Sidney Blumenthal, *Pledging Allegiance: the Last Campaign of the Cold War* (New York: HarperCollins, 1990), 300-301.
9. Joel Bradshaw, "Who Will Vote for You and Why: Designing Strategy and Theme," in Thurber and Nelson, eds, *Campaigns and Elections American Style*, 42-43.
10. Bradshaw, 44.
11. Joseph Napolitan, *The Election Game and How to Win It* (New York: Doubleday, 1972), 2-3.
12. Hank Parkinson, "Publicity is Inexpensive and Neglected," *Campaign Insight*, (1),3 (June, 1970), 8.
13. *Stevenson of Illinois Campaign Manual* (Chicago: Adlai E. Stevenson III for U.S. Senate Campaign, 1970), 35-6.
14. Different stations reach different audiences. To determine if advertising on a particular station is worthwhile, professional public relations firms should be consulted.
15. Dennis McGrath and Dane Smith, *Professor Wellstone Goes to Washington* (Minneapolis: University of Minnesota, 1995), 148.
16. McGrath and Smith, 149.
17. Byron Sistler, "Political Action in Action," *IVI Bellringer* (March, 1969), 6.

Chapter 7

1. See, for example, Joe McGinniss, *The Selling of the President 1968*.
2. See Gary Selnow, *High-Tech Campaigns: Computer Technology in Political Communication*.

3. Selnow, 19.

4. Selnow, 102 and 106.

5. Selnow, 172.

6. "Cyber Baby-Kissers," *Time*, (August 21, 1995), 16.

7. Michael Tackett, "Candidates go on-line to net votes," *Chicago Tribune* (May 25, 1995), 1 and 22.

8. Movement for a New Congress, *Vote Power* (Englewood Cliffs: Prentice Hall, 1970), 27. See also 14-15.

9. *Vote Power*, 18.

10. Cook County Clerk David Orr, "Questions and Answers on Motor Voter" (Mimeographed document, July, 1995), 2.

11. E. E. Schattschneider, *The Semi-Sovereign People* (New York: Holt, Rinehart and Winston, 1960), 4.

12. Vote Power, 17.

13. See speech by Jerry Murray in *By The People*, Reel I.

Chapter 8

1. Movement for a New Congress, *Vote Power* (Englewood Cliffs: Prentice Hall, 1970), 28.

2. "How to Win Elections" (Mimeographed instruction developed originally by Sherwin Swartz and Barbara O'Connor of the Independent Voters of Illinois (IVI), Chicago. Used and revised many times since the 1960s including in my congressional campaigns.)

3. *Vote Power*, 29.

4. Will Robinson, "Organizing the Field," in James Thurber and Candice Nelson, eds, *Campaigns and Elections American Style*, 183.

5. Robinson, 144.

6. "How to Win on Election Day," (Mimeographed instruction sheets developed by Sherwin Swartz and Barbara O'Connor of IVI in Chicago and revised many times since the 1960s.)

7. Robinson, 147.

8. According to Illinois law, workers may campaign no closer than 100 feet from the polls. However, laws differ on election day work in other states.

9. Sandye Wexler, "So You're a Poll Watcher," (Mimemographed manual for poll watchers developed for the Bernard Weisberg Campaign, Chicago, 1969), 1.

10. William Grimshaw, *Bitter Fruit: Black Politics and the Chicago Machine: 1931-1991* (Chicago: University of Chicago Press, 1992), 163.

11. Grimshaw, 163.

12. Grimshaw, 171-173.

13. These themes are adapted from William Grimshaw's analysis in "Is Chicago Ready for Reform?" in Melvin Holli and Paul Green, eds, *The Making of the Mayor: Chicago, 1983* (Grand Rapids: Eerdmons, 1984).

14. Grimshaw, *Bitter Fruit*, 174.

15. Grimshaw, *Bitter Fruit*, 177.

16. For one of the most detailed analyses of the 1983 campaigns see Paul Kleppner, *Chicago Divided: The Making of a Black Mayor* (Dekalb, Il: Northern Illinois University Press, 1985), 165-169.

17. Thomas Hardy, "Braun builds a comfortable lead over Williamson," *Chicago Tribune* (August 30, 1992), Section 1, 18.

18. Hardy, 18.

19. Lynn Sweet, "A critical analysis of political ads," *Chicago Sun-Times* (September 15, 1992).

20. R. Darcy, Susan Welsh, and Janet Clark, *Women, Elections, and Representation* (Lincoln: Nebraska University Press, 1994), xiii.

21. Darcy, *et al.*, 30.

22. Darcy, *et al.*, 73.

23. These tactics are discussed by Ed Lawrence, Handbook for Independent Precinct Workers (mimeographed manual for IPO and IVI precinct workers in the 42nd Ward, Chicago, 1970), 3.

24. James Kessler, "Running for State Political Office," in Cornelius Cotter, ed, *Practical Politics in the United States* (Boston: Allyn and Bacon, 1969), 126. In general, very little has been written on running campaigns in rural areas.

25. Dennis J. McGrath and Dane Smith, *Professor Wellstone Goes to Washington* (Minneapolis: University of Minnesota Press, 1995), 92-3.

26. McGrath and Smith, 93.

27. McGrath and Smith, 103.

28. McGrath and Smith, xvi.

Chapter 9

1. Many political science texts and journal articles have focused on congressional reelection rates. See especially Alfred Tuchfarber, Stephen Bennet, Andrew Smith and Eric Rademacher, "The Republican Tidal Wave of 1994: Testing Hypotheses about Realignment, Restructuring, and Rebellion," (Unpublished paper presented at the American Political Science Association, September 1, 1995), 3 and R. S. Erikson, "The Advantage of Incumbency in Congressional Elections," *Polity*, (1971), 3:395-405.

2. Wallace Stegner, *Angle of Repose* (New York: Penguin Books, 1992. First published in 1971.), 382.

3. The financial data are from the Federal Election Commission, Computer Index of Campaign Activity, 1993-1994.

4. *Coalition to End the Permanent Congress, et al. v. Marvin T. Runyon, et. al. and Donald K. Anderson, et al.* A number of the facts critical to the decision in this case were provided in a deposition that I supplied on the 5th Congressional District Race in Illinois in 1991-1992. The quotes in the text are from the opinions of Justices Silberman and Randolph respectively.

5. Reports filed with the Federal Election Commission. See *Congressional Quarterly* (August 22, 1992), and the tables on pp. 2587–2589 for sum-

mary of financial data of Rostenkowski campaign, along with that of other congressmen.

6. Federal Elecion Commission, Computer Index of Campaign Activity, 1993-1994.

7. *Dick Simpson v. Dan Rostenkowski and American Leaders Fund*, Federal Election Complaint, 1993.

Chapter 10

1. For a handbook on creating neighborhood government institutions, a discussion of the philosophy of neighborhood government, and an account of seven years experience in the 44th Ward of Chicago see Dick Simpson, Judy Stevens and Rick Kohnen, *Neighborhood Government in Chicago's 44th Ward* (Champaign: Stipes, 1979). A ¾″ color video-cassette with the same title and subject matter is available from the Chicago Film and Video Availability Center, University of Illinois at Chicago (1978).

2. Comments by Dick Simpson, Mark Perlberg, Marvin Rosner, and Donald Page Moore in *By the People*, Reel II.

3. Nicholas J. O'Shaughnessy, *The Phenomenon of Political Marketing* (New York: St. Martin's, 1990), 1, 2 and 7. Two other excellent books on the effects of political marketing upon political parties are Larry Sabato's *The Party's Only Just Begun* (Glenview, Il: Scott Foresman, 1988) and Stephen Frantiach's *Political Parties in the Technological Age* (New York: Longman, 1989). See especially the concluding chapters of both books.

4. O'Shaughnessy, 10.

5. Randall Rothenberg, "Politics on TV: Too Fast, Too Loose?," *The New York Times* (July 15, 1990), Section 4, 1 and 4.

6. Rothenberg, 1.

7. Rothenbert, 1.

8. Ron Faucheux, "Leap of Logic," *Campaign and Elections* (August 1995), 5.

9. The Senate Ethics Counsel, *The Packwood Report* (New York: Random House, 1995), See especially 228 and 224–319. For a summary of Packwood's office for contributions and gifts see also Vicki Kemper, "The Other Packwood Scandal," *Common Cause Magazine* (Winter 1995), 20–23.

10. Christa Slaton, *Televote: Expanding Citizen Participation in the Quantum Age* (New York: Praeger, 1992), 113.

11. A major experiment which has been tried in the 1996 election cycle was the National Issues Convention held in Austin, Texas in January, 1996. The theory behind the convention was outlined in James Fishkin, *Democracy and Deliberation* (New Haven: Yale University Press, 1991) and James Fishkin, *The Voice of the People* (New Haven: Yale University Press, 1995). An early report of the results is in "Poll Watch" (February 13, 1996) from the Pew Research Center for the People & the Press.

APPENDIX I

CAMPAIGN TRAINING WORKSHOPS AND STUDY QUESTIONS

Winning Elections can be read alone as a general handbook on modern participatory campaigns. It can also be used in campaign training workshops and in political science classes.

The ideal format for campaign training workshops or classes on elections is probably: 1) to read *Winning Elections* in its entirety in advance of the workshop or class, 2) to show the films *"By the People"* or *"The War Room"* at the beginning of the workshop or class, and 3) to divide the workshop or class into several discussion sessions organized around key chapters of book and film(s). The campaign training workshop may be held on a single Saturday or one night a week for seven weeks. The class schedule will depend upon the amount of time allocated to discussing election campaigns. Here is a suggested timetable for teaching the material in a workshop which can easily be adapted to other settings:

WORKSHOP TIMETABLE

I. PARTICIPATORY POLITICS (Approximately 2 hours)

A. Brief introduction

B. "By the People" or "The War Room" is shown.
William Mahin and Dick Simpson, *"By the People: A Study of Independent Politics-Chicago, 1969." (Chicago: Film and Video Availability Center, University of Illinois at Chicago, 1970)*. D. A. Pennebaker, *"The War Room."* (1993). Available at most major video stores.

C. General discussion of film

II. BUILDING AN ORGANIZATION (45 minutes)

A. An experienced campaign manager or volunteer coordinator speaks to the group on campaign structure and staffing.

B. A former office manager speaks on setting up an office, office management, computerization, and record keeping.

C. Reshowing of recruitment process at Weisberg Coffee from "*By the People.*" (Optional)

D. Discussion of setting up a campaign and recruiting key staff members and volunteers.

E. Reports of various campaigns represented at the workshop on where they are in the process and new ideas they have gotten from *Winning Elections* and the films.

III. GETTING KNOWN (45 minutes)

A. Break down into discussion groups and attempt to develop theme and schedule for an imaginary or real campaign as an example. (For instance, create an imaginary candidate for 1st Ward Alderman and structure a campaign for her.)

B. Reshowing of public relations discussion in "*By the People*" or in "*The War Room.*" (Optional)

C. Have the members of a discussion group draft and discuss a news announcement and news release for a media story.

IV. FUNDRAISING (1 hour)

A. Presentation by a professional fundraising, candidate, or experienced volunteer.

B. Break down into discussion groups to develop a budget for the imaginary campaign created in the previous discussions.

C. Develop a fundraising plan.

D. Discuss methods to raise larger contributions.

E. Discuss ideas for successful campaign benefits.

V. PREPARING FOR BATTLE (45 minutes)

A. Talk by a former precinct coordinator, campaign manager, or candidate about issue petition drives, nominating petition drives, registration drives, and coalition building.

B. Reshowing of registration instructions & drive from "*By the People.*" (Optional)

C. Discussion of whether or not campaigns ought to include registration drives under current conditions.

VI. CANVASSING (45 minutes)

A. Role playing of door-to-door canvassing in small discussion groups.

B. Discussion in small groups of plus, minus, zero voter system.

C. Presentation by someone with experience with mail/phone campaigns and setting up phone banks.

VII. ELECTION DAY WORK (45 minutes)

A. Brief discussion of roles on election day.
B. Reshowing election day for the Weisberg campaign in "*By the People.*" (Optional)
C. Discussion of how to get volunteers and the materials which are needed.
D. Discussion of worker training and scheduling for election day.
E. Election law presentation by lawyer or campaign expert.

VIII. GENERAL DISCUSSION OF POLITICAL GOALS (30 minutes)

A. Discussion of difference between "synthetic campaigns" and modern "participatory campaigns." The following chart might be put on the blackboard and the workshop can fill in the boxes and discuss the differences:

Campaign element	Synthetic campaign	Participatory Campaign
Candidate		
Campaign Theme		
Public Relations		
Campaign Finances		
Precinct Work		
Use of Volunteers		

From this chart then a general definition of the differences between the two types of campaigns can be derived.
B. Discussion of what to do about "negative" and "unfair campaigning."

Such a workshop will take from six–eight hours and could be completed in a single weekend afternoon, completed as part of a longer conference or presented in seven weekly evening sessions. (Less time will be taken if the films are not used but the films usually help the learning process considerably and give everyone a common campaign they can discuss.)

Depending on which way the workshop is scheduled, appropriate breaks for meals or relaxation will need to be added. It is also useful to have an elected official speak during lunch or at some key time about the problems a candidate faces.

STUDY QUESTIONS

The individual reader may be helped by seeing if she can answer basic questions from *Winning Elections*. Or the following questions might be asked of students or workshop participants to insure that they have understood the major ideas about election campaigns. The questions below are organized by Chapter so that the reader can find material in the text to help answer the question if she is uncertain.

Chapter II

1. What reasons do you have for getting involved in politics? Knowing your own motives, how might you expect to involve others?
2. What are the advantages of an electoral campaign over an issue campaign or lobbying?
3. What are the weaknesses of an educational campaign?
4. What is a citizens' search committee, how is it created, and why is it used?
5. In deciding whether or not a campaign is winnable you have to determine the campaign's "target number." What is it and how is it calculated?

Chapter III

1. What is the difference between the roles of the candidate and the campaign manager?
2. What are some of the primary characteristics to be considered in selecting key campaign officials? Which are the key officials in a campaign? Who usually selects them?
3. Why do campaign workers and key volunteers need often to be consulted in campaign decisions? What information do they have to contribute and on what kind of decisions are they most profitably consulted?
4. What are the three key methods used in recruiting volunteers?
5. How do you start up a campaign office?
6. How can computers best be used in the campaign? What is their role in research, office work, fundraising, press relations, producing campaign literature, and in voter contact?

Chapter IV

1. Draft a campaign budget either for an imaginary candidate or for a real candidate that you are supporting in the upcoming election.

2. What are the principal categories of expenses likely to be? How much do you estimate that each will cost? What is the total budget for the campaign likely to be?
3. Fill out the following draft budget for the campaign.

DRAFT CAMPAIGN BUDGET

Category	Description	Amount
Staff	Campaign Manager (List other staff)	
Office Expense	Rent Insurance Equipment (computers, fax, etc.) Phone Voting Contact Software Utilities	
Printing	Basic Campaign Brochure (List other printing)	
Advertising	Posters Billboards Radio (List other advertising such as Newspapers & TV)	
Targeted Direct Mail		
Fundraising Expenses	Benefit Expenses (List other expenses)	
Polling & Public Relations Expenses		
Election Day Expenses		
TOTAL:		

(In planning a more complete budget you will list the costs per month and extend the right hand column into monthly columns so that fundraising plans can be coordinated to provide the money as needed.)

4. Now draft a fundraising plan. It should contain plans for raising funds by direct calls to larger donors, campaign benefits, contributions by the candidate and her family, direct mail campaigns and any in-kind or cash contributions which can be expected by organizations, PACs, and party committees.

5. Suppose you raise only 2/3's of the amount which you had projected in your campaign budget. What would you prioritize or would you spend just 2/3's as much on all the budget categories?

6. To what extent should you rely upon PACs and Party Committees to fund your campaign?

7. Who is the most important fundraiser in the campaign? Why?

8. What are the rules for a successful campaign benefit?

9. How significant are the fundraising reports required by FEC, state, or local election agencies? What must the campaign do to meet these requirements?

Chapter V

1. What are the advantages and disadvantages of a "long campaign?"

2. Why shouldn't your candidate appear in public alone? What planning and scheduling are needed to do effective candidate appearances in public?

3. What are the 13 key steps in a participatory campaign?

Chapter VI

1. Create an image for your candidate. What sort of image like "man or woman of the people," "a fighter," etc. do you want them to project? Why?

2. What are the differences between a "synthetic" and "participatory" campaigns and how does that affect their media strategies.

3. What are the differences between benchmark polls, follow-up surveys, and tracking polls and how are they used in campaigns?

4. What are some of the choices that must be made in selecting visual and verbal themes? Try the following exercise:
   a. Decide upon an explicit or implicit verbal theme for the campaign.
   b. Make a rough sketch of a possible button and a piece of literature for the campaign, being especially sensitive to the choice of color, typeface, photographs, layout, and slogan (or verbal theme).

5. What is essential in getting your news release or news conference covered by the press, i.e. what makes it news?

6. What are the mechanics of holding a news conference?

7. Why is the advice of a professional public relations expert necessary? Why can't just any volunteer do the job?

8. Radio is one of the cheaper forms of advertising and is often used by participatory campaigns. Try writing a 30 or 60-second spot for your candidate.

Chapter VII

1. How can direct mail be used most effectively to get your message to the voters? How many pieces of mail should you budget to send during the campaign? Generally, what should their content be?

2. How can you campaign on the Internet? What are the drawbacks of doing so? What is necessary to establish a Homepage?

3. Why is precinct work so essential to a participatory campaign? How is the work structured? Why can't everybody just do their own thing instead?
4. What are the two competing principles of precinct worker deployment and how should they influence your campaign?
5. What materials are needed to conduct a petition drive and what results should be expected? How many signatures should you seek on the nominating petition? Just the legal number need to get on the ballot, twice as many, or as many as possible?
6. Given the current situation in your state and the resources of your campaign should you try to run a registration campaign? Who should you try to register? Why?
7. How is the success of a registration campaign usually measured?

Chapter VIII

1. What is the purpose of the canvass and how does the use of the *plus, minus,* and *zero* system help accomplish that purpose?
2. Of the three functions of election day activities which is the most essential to a winning campaign? Why?
3. What are the chief methods of election fraud and how may they be guarded against?
4. What additional problems have to be overcome when campaigning in poor minority communities? How can they best be handled?
5. How did African-American candidates like Harold Washington and Carol Moseley-Braun win their campaigns in majority white constituencies?
6. How can voters in highrises and "gated" communities best be reached and canvassed?
7. What are the differences in running campaigns in party caucus states?

Chapter IX

1. What seven conditions make winning campaigns more likely when your candidate is not endorsed by the dominant party organization or wealthy interest groups?
2. What are the most important lessons to be learned from the Simpson v. Rostenkowski campaigns?

Chapter X

1. What are the reasons to stay together in a permanent political organization after a campaign is over?
2. What should you do if you lose an election?
3. What should your candidate do if she wins?
4. What are the problems with the electoral system today? What are three possible reforms of the system and what do you think about each of them?
5. What will you do now?

APPENDIX II

SAMPLE OF SIMPSON ALDERMANIC CAMPAIGN WEEK SCHEDULE

January 31, Sunday

10:30 A.M. Attend church and coffee afterwards
             The Parish of Reconciliation
             1655 W. School Street
12:00 P.M. Strategy meeting at campaign headquarters
2:45 P.M.   Press conference
             Sheraton Chicago
             Lake Michigan Room, 8th fl.
             (Endorsement by several former delegates to the State
             Constitutional Convention)
7:00 P.M.   George Newton (coffee)
             522 Roscoe
7:30 P.M.   Nancy Moss (coffee)
             3330 N. Lake Shore
8:00 P.M.   Canvass training session speech
             Headquarters
8:45 P.M.   Berg family (coffee)
             2915 Sheffield

February 1, Monday

7:30 A.M.   Bus stop handshaking (Roscoe and Sheridan)
10:00 A.M. Interview with Reporter David Anderson from Lerner Newspapers
             at campaign headquarters

2:00 P.M.   Walking tour in Precinct 31
7:45 P.M.   Aaron and Lois Levine (coffee)
            3147 N. Cambridge
8:45 P.M.   Alen Silberman (coffee)
            3033 N. Sheridan Road
9:45 P.M.   Mr. and Mrs. Dave Silberman (coffee)
            4150 Lake Shore Drive
10:15 P.M. Spanish meeting at headquarters (speech, photographs for
            newspaper and mailing)

February 2, Tuesday

7:30 A.M.   Diversey El Stop handshaking, meeting and greeting voters
9:30 A.M.   City Hall Election Commission press conference
10-12:00 P.M.   Teach regular class at University of Illinois at Chicago
7:00 P.M.   Isadore Schachter (coffee)
            421 Melrose
7:30 P.M.   West Lakeview Neighbors' Aldermanic Candidate Debate
            St. Luke's Church
            1500 W. Belmont

February 3, Wednesday

7:30 A.M.   Bus stop handshaking (Aldine and Sheridan)
9:15 A.M.   Mrs. Mark Baskin
            Nettelhorst PTA President
            442 Aldine
            (Discussion of issues)
10:30 A.M. Francis Parker
            (High school assembly speech)
1:00 P.M.   Meeting with Le Moyne School Principal
            851 Waveland
            (Discussion of school issues)
2–4:00 P.M. Walking tour with Father Lezak in west side precincts
6:30 P.M.   Pat Buondin (coffee)
8:45 P.M.   Bob and Kate Kestnbaum (coffee)
            442 Wellington Avenue
9:45 P.M.   Irv and Carol Ware (coffee)
            3400 Lake Shore Drive
10:30 P.M. Weekly steering committee meeting
            Headquarters

February 4, Thursday

10:00 A.M. National Organization of Women (N.O.W.) Press Conference
            201 N. Wells
            (Endorsement by National Organization of Women)

2:00 P.M.　Senior Citizens' Aldermanic Candidate Debate
　　　　　　Jane Addams Center, Hull House
4:30 P.M.　Illinois Nurses Association cocktail party
　　　　　　8 S. Michigan
6:00 P.M.　Dinner with Scott Simpson and Sarajane Avidon at L'Escargot
　　　　　　Restaurant to raise money
7:45 P.M.　Mr. and Mrs. Allen Porter (coffee)
　　　　　　703 Briar
8:45 P.M.　Mr. and Mrs. John Light (coffee)
　　　　　　3430 N. Lake Shore Drive
9:45 P.M.　Mr. and Mrs. Julius Polikoff (coffee)
　　　　　　3180 N. Lake Shore Drive
10:15 P.M.　Lakeview Citizens Council (LVCC) Board Meeting
　　　　　　St. Bonaventure Church
　　　　　　1615 Diversey

February 5, Friday

7:30 A.M.　Bus stop handshaking (Belmont and Broadway)
9:00 A.M.　Betty Garman, Principal
　　　　　　Morse School
　　　　　　919 Barry
　　　　　　(Discussion of issues)
1:00 P.M.　Betty Fossmo (coffee)
　　　　　　1223 W. George
3:30–5:30 P.M.　Walking Tour with Kerm Krueger
　　　　　　Appleton Plaza (Wellington and Ashland)
5:30 P.M.　Dinner with Bob Johnson, Tommy and Pat Timm
　　　　　　445 W. Surf
7:00 P.M.　Mrs. Bert Schenker (coffee)
　　　　　　468 Melrose
8:00 P.M.　Mrs. Edith Bukwa (coffee)
　　　　　　850 Buckingham
9:15 P.M.　44th Ward Republican Organization meeting
　　　　　　3922 Broadway
　　　　　　(Endorsement by Republican Organization)

February 6, Saturday

9–12:00 P.M.　Shopping center handshaking
　　　　　　Lincoln, Belmont, and Ashland Intersection
12:00 p.m.　Headquarters strategy meeting
1–3:00 P.M.　Del Farm Store handshaking
3–5:00 p.m.　Lincoln, Belmont, and Ashland Shopping center handshaking
2–4:00 p.m.　Walking Tour Area B
7–8:00 P.M.　Coffee at St. Alphonsus Church

8:30 P.M.   Swedish Engineering Club
            Campaign Benefit Dinner
            (Play, dinner, and film fundraiser)

February 7, Sunday

1:00 P.M.   Latino Organizations
            St. Sebastion's Church
1:30 P.M.   Spanish speaking meeting and coffee
            1032 George
2:00 P.M.   Dan Crowe (coffee)
            741 Melrose
3:00 P.M.   Bob and Sue Houston (coffee)
            817 Wolfram
4–7:00 P.M.   Mr. and Mrs. Michael Maremont
            Committee for an Effective City Council Benefit
            940 Sheridan Road, Glencoe, Illinois
            ($250 contribution presented to campaign from the
            Committee for an Effective City Council)
7:30 P.M.   Fern Zittler (coffee)
            1104 W. George
8:00 P.M.   Temple Sholom Brotherhood Town Hall Meeting
            and Aldermanic Candidates debate

AN ANNOTATED BIBLIOGRAPHY

I. Classic Studies of Voting, Participation, and Representation

Burnham, Walter Dean. *Critical Elections and the Mainsprings of American Politics.* New York: Norton, 1970.

This is an important longitudinal study of American voting, especially those critical realigning elections in which new political parties come to power, parties change internally, or power passes from one party to another. These include not only the elections of Lincoln and Franklin Roosevelt, but several less well known elections. Burnham points out that we have not had a critical election since 1932 when would reasonably have been expected to have at least one by now because of the historical 28-32 year critical election cycles. Burnham suggests that this has occurred because political parties themselves are disagregating and disintegrating. The forces which drive realigning elections must be understood if we are to plan correctly for future elections.

Campbell, Angus *et al. The American Voter.* New York: Wiley, 1964.

The first comprehensive study of voting behavior among the entire American electorate. Focusing particularly upon the 1952 and 1956 elections, the authors of *The American Voter* explain voting decisions primarily in terms of party identification, candidate images and issues, but they also consider other characteristics such as the socio-economic background of voters.

DeVries, Walter and V. Lance Tarrance. *The Ticket-Splitter: A New Force in American Politics.* Grand Rapids, Michigan: William B. Eerdmans Publishing Company, 1972.

While not as academic as many analyses of elections, these scholars-campaign consultants focus upon independent voters and those who split their votes between candidates of both parties in an effort to understand this phenomenon and to find practical ways for candidates and campaigns to win these critical votes. This analysis is helpful in providing a general understanding of these voters and their motivations.

Fishkin, James. *Democracy and Deliberation*. New Haven: Yale University Press, 1991.

> While not immediately useful in campaigns, *Democracy and Deliberation*, sets forth the philosophical arguments for the use of deliberative opinion polls in future elections. Fishkin reviews the traditional literature favoring pluralism and recommends moving towards a system in which at least a random sample of citizens plays a greater role in shaping the issues and selecting victorious candidates.

Flanigan, William H. and Nancy H. Zingale. *Political Behavior of the American Electorate*. Washington: Congressional Quarterly, 1994. Eighth Edition.

> A good summary of current knowledge in political science about electoral behavioral. Relying on the best longitudinal data available, Flanigan and Zingale focus on the major concepts of American politics. They cover political culture, voter turnout, public opinion, mass media, and the continuing effects of partisanship, issues, and candidate images on election results.

Fowler, Linda. Candidates, *Congress, and the American Democracy.* Ann Arbor, Michigan: Michigan University Press, 1993.

> Fowler summarizes the studies of candidate recruitment and the U.S. Congress. She maintains that the ambitions of individual candidates are essential to the functioning of the nation's constitutional system. She places recent changes in candidates within the broader trends and contradictions of American politics.

Key, V. O., Jr. *The Responsible Electorate*. New York: Random House, 1966.

> A major study defending the rationality of the voter. Drawing upon voting studies of presidential elections from 1936-1960, Key argues that voters decide their party and even their candidate preferences to a great extent by their stands on crucial issues of the period.

Levine, Myron. *Presidential Campaigns and Elections: Issues and Images in the Media Age*. Itasca, Illinois: Peacock, 1995. Second Edition.

> Levine describes presidential campaigns in the television age and provides the text of several dozen television ads by presidential candidates. It considers the campaigns from the preliminary period of raising resources to the general election. It is particularly good on the linkage between issues and advertising in campaigns.

Luttbeg, Norman and Michael M. Gant, *American Electoral Behavior 1952-1992*. Itasca, Illinois: Peacock, 1995. Second Edition.

> Another good summary of our knowledge about electoral behavior. Luttbeg and Gant especially focus on the change in political behavior during the last decade. They look at the interrelationship among three important trends: 1) decline of partisanship, 2) decline in political participation, and 3) decline in political trust.

Milbrath, Lester. *Political Participation*. Chicago: Rand McNally, 1965.

A summary of existing political science literature on political participation, including a model of participation derived inductively from the findings. Perhaps still the best single book available on what political scientists have learned about the subject, *Political Participation* contains a good bibliography referring to the major works in the field at the time of its publication.

Snowiss, Leo. "Congressional Recruitment and Representation," *American Political Science Review*, 55:3, (September, 1966), 627-639.

A comparison of different types of congressional representation from the Chicago metropolitan area according to type of political party organization and candidate recruitment procedures. The author's thesis is that different types of candidates emerge from the inner city, outer city and suburban areas, not only because of socio-economic differences, but because of differences in the type of party control in each area.

Slator, Christa. *Televote: Expanding Citizen Participation in the Quantum Age*. New York: Praeger, 1992.

While the author's attempt to make a parallel to quantum physics to provide an alternative theory of political participation may not appeal to all readers, his reports of Televote experiments both in the United States and abroad are helpful. This technology is not yet directly applicable to electoral campaigns but the use of Televote technology in government will affect campaigns in the future. Moreover, some of these polling techniques have been used in shaping citizen agendas for electoral campaigns and are being proposed for use in future ones.

Wayne, Stephen. *The Road to the White House 1996*. New York: St. Martin's, 1996.

The Road to the White House covers a historical overview of presidential selection, the 1992 and 1994 campaigns, the processes to be followed in 1996 and potential campaign reforms. It provides concise summaries of campaign finance requirements, strategies of different candidates in the 1992 campaign, and the accuracy of polls. It is an excellent introduction for those who have not been involved directly in presidential campaigns.

II. Political Party Machines and Party Campaigns

Rakove, Milton. *Don't Make No Waves. . . Don't Back No Losers*. Bloomington, Indiana: Indiana University Press, 1975.

This is one of the best analyses of the famous Daley Machine of Chicago, including the principles behind the machine as well as a discussion of the coalition of interests which made the machine powerful and relatively stable. There is a limited discussion of the nuts and bolts precinct work which made it effective as well.

Reum, Walter and Gerald Mattran. *Politics From the Inside Up*. Chicago: Follett, 1966. (Paperback edition by Dutton.)

A humorous book detailing twenty-five rules on how to build a successful political career. It includes how to join a party, which party to join, how to conduct your campaign, what to do once elected, and how to be elected to higher positions. Not only is it a most readable book, but the suggestions on how to succeed reveal the way a political party actually works instead of the usual "good government" explanations of how they should work.

Riordan, William. *Plunkitt of Tammany Hall*. New York: Penguin, 1991. First published, McClure, Philips & Co., 1905.

In a set of speeches made from a shoe shine stand in City Hall, Tammany Hall boss George Washington Plunkitt, gives his personal account of the Tammany machine and the philosophical principles upon which it was based. A frank account, in Plunkitt's words, of "what all practical politicians think but are afraid to say."

Royko, Mike. *Boss*. New York: Dutton, 1971.

This now classic study of machine politics in Chicago is still among the best analyses of the corruption, patronage, and power driven politics of the city during the Richard J. Daley era. While not selfconsciously analytical, it gives the best feel of machine party politics of any book yet written.

III. General Books on Campaigning

Agranoff, Robert, (ed.), *The New Style in Election Campaigns*. Boston: Holbrook Press, 1972.

This reader covers campaign management, information systems such as public opinion polling, and manipulation of the mass media (especially television) until the 1970s. An introductory essay by Agranoff describes the decline of political parties and the rise of candidate centered, technologically-oriented campaigns. It is a thought provoking collection of essays rather than a handbook for employing this style of campaigning.

Alexander, Herbert. *Financing Politics: Money, Elections, & Political Reform*. Washington: Congressional Quarterly, 1992.

This is the best short introduction to the current state of campaign financing in national elections. It includes a historical survey of campaign finance reforms and a careful look at the post-Watergate reforms of 1972. It analyses the various reforms currently proposed.

Alexander, Herbert. *Reform and Reality: The Financing of State and Local Campaigns*. New York: the Twentieth Century Fund, 1991.

Since nearly all books on campaign finance and the need for campaign finance reform have either been written about national campaigns or are a case study of campaign financing in a single state, Alexander's book on general trends in state and local campaigns is especially important. Unfortunately, the same PAC-driven financing which has bedeviled national campaigns is becoming the norm for states. It will soon dominate local elections as well. As the costs of state and local elections continue to soar, legal restraints and public funding will have to be employed or the trend of PAC-domination will continue to grow. Alexander provides a useful summary of the trends as of 1990.

Alexander, Herbert and Anthony Corrado. *Financing the 1992 Election.* Armonk, New York: M.E. Sharpe, 1995.

This is a very detailed analysis of the raising and spending of money in the 1992 election—focusing primarily, but not exclusively, upon the presidential campaigns. The authors place the 1992 spending levels at $3.2 Billion. They discuss the sources of funds, the reasons they are needed, and the attempt currently to regulate campaign finance.

Corrado, Anthony. *Creative Campaigning: PACs and the Presidential Selection Process.* Boulder, Colorado: Westview, 1992.

A specialized study of precandidacy PACs and how they effect presidential races. The Federal Election Campaign Act inspires presidential candidates to break the laws, or at least the intent of the laws, governing campaign finance. Corrado describes how "candidates...seek out creative methods of financing their campaigns outside the scope of the law [and]...how they succeed in their quest by using precandidacy PACs as shadow campaign organizations." He includes a series of reform proposals as well as an analysis of the problem.

Dirkin, Robert J. *Campaigning in America: A History of Election Practice.* New York: Greenwood, 1989.

This book provides a historical overview of election practices since the founding of the Republic. The final sections of the book cover the dramatic changes in presidential and congressional campaigns from the 1950s - 1980s when professionally managed, media-dominated campaigns became the norm.

Herrnson, Paul. *Congressional Elections: Campaigning at Home and in Washington.* Washington, DC: Congressional Quarterly, 1995.

This is the best book on Congressional campaigns. It is of use to both political scientists and campaigners. Among the topics covered are primaries, campaign organization and budget, campaign expenditures, PACs, campaigning for resources in Washington, campaign communications, electoral success, and campaign reforms. It even provides formulas for the effect of direct mail campaign expenditures by nonincumbents. It is recommended reading for anyone running or studying congressional campaigns.

McGinniss, Joe. *The Selling of the President 1968*. New York: Pocket Books, 1970. First published by Trident Press, 1969.

This volume describes attempts to manipulate the media to a candidate's advantage. In this case, McGinniss provides the inside story of the attempt to use the media to elect Nixon as president in 1968. It is not a handbook, but it gives detailed descriptions and contains an appendix of several television scripts for various political commercials.

McGrath, Dennis and Dane Smith. *Professor Wellstone Goes to Washington: The Inside Story of a Grassroots U.S. Senate Campaign*. Minneapolis: University of Minnesota Press, 1995.

Written by two reporters for the *Minneapolis Star*, this account of the Wellstone Senate campaign is important as a general guide to participatory campaigns. It is particularly useful in caucus states. Whether one agrees with Wellstone's philosophy or not, the strength of his issues, the motivation of his volunteers, and unique blend of grassroots organizing and creative media ads are excellent guideposts for any modern participatory campaign.

Napolitan, Joseph. *The Election Game and How to Win It*. New York: Doubleday, 1972.

While not a campaign manual, *The Election Game*, is an excellent book for a variety of reasons. First of all, it is a companion volume to McGinniss' account of the 1968 because Napolitan was Humphrey's strategist on the other side of the contest. He tells how Humphrey almost won the election and why. The difference in the money raised and media strategies of the two campaigns is clear. Second, Napolitan offers sage advice on choosing a campaign manager, using television and radio, and a host of other strategic campaign issues. It does not tell everything you need to know to win a modern media campaign, but it tells you mistakes to avoid. Finally, it is a window into the work and opinions of a major political consultant.

Scammell, Margaret. *Designer Politics: How Elections are Won*. New York: St. Martin's, 1995.

This is a book about political marketing of candidates in Britain in contrast to the American experience. Scammell tends to be a supporter of political marketing or high-tech campaigns and argues that they are not the threat to democracy which other authors fear. Scammell studies political marketing attempts by Conservative and Labor Parties, by Margret Thatcher and in the Post-Thatcher era. It is a book likely to be of interest to political scientists and campaign professionals. The specific tactics from British politics are not likely to translate well in the average U.S. election although Bush borrowed some expertise from the Conservatives during his 1992 campaign.

Selnow, Gary. *High-Tech Campaigns: Computer Technology in Political Communication.* Westport, Connecticut: Praeger, 1994.

This is the best general discussion to date of the role of computer databases, targeted mailings and media in modern campaigns. It is particularly useful in describing targeted direct mail and public polling techniques. Selnow's description of creating databases from various sources for direct mail and phone canvassing allows candidates and their staffs to be much more knowledgeable about the products and services which they can purchase to improve voter contact. Selnow also discusses the threat to democracy which high-tech campaigns pose.

Stavis, Ben. *We Were the Campaign.* Boston: Beacon Press, 1969.

This is the best of the books on the McCarthy for President campaign in terms of the details of campaign organization and day-to-day decision-making. It is also successful in distinguishing between the McCarthy campaign and earlier efforts, and in telling the story of the campaign from the perspective of student volunteers. Stavis also discusses the internal campaign struggles and problems.

Thurber, James and Candice Nelson. *Campaigns and Elections American Style.* Boulder, Colorado: Westview, 1995.

This book is a particularly rich mix of academic political scientists and campaign professionals writing on the same topics in back-to-back articles on designing campaign strategy and themes, campaign fundraising, media advertising, media coverage of campaigns, field work, polling, and campaign ethics. It is the best collection of essays on campaigns currently published and a must read book for both campaigners and scholars.

IV. The Nuts and Bolts of Campaigning

Atkins, State Senator Chester, with Barry Hock and Bob Martin, *Getting Elected: A Guide to Winning State and Local Office.* Boston: Houghton Mifflin, 1973.

Still a good guide for candidates who would combine the techniques of volunteer campaigns with running in regular party primaries, *Getting Elected* is particularly helpful for someone deciding whether or not to run. The principles behind each of the campaign activities from public relations to canvassing are well explained. Vignettes about six progressive candidates running for local office for the first time in different parts of the country (including the Simpson aldermanic campaign in Chicago) reassure the reader that it can be done. Certainly this is a guide well worth reading for campaign workers just getting into electoral politics. The fact that Atkins himself was elected to the Massachusetts State Senate lends considerable credibility to his recommendations.

Campaigns & Elections: The Magazine for Political Professionals. (1511 K Street, N.W., #1020, Washington DC 20005.) Subscription rate $29.95 per year.

This is the best campaign magazine currently published. It provides monthly articles on the latest polling, direct mail, and modern campaign techniques. It provides up-to-date information for scholars and campaign staff members who want to track the latest campaign developments.

Faucieux, Ron. *The Road to Victory: The Complete Guide to Winning in Politics.* Dubuque, Iowa: Kindall/Hunt, 1995.

This is a collection of the best articles from *Campaigns & Elections* magazine. It covers a wide range of topics such as media production, time buying, field operations, candidate debate training, and direct mail. It is an uneven collection without an index or the single point of view that an individual author provides. But it has good practical hints and is an excellent supplement to other campaign manuals.

Grey, Judge Lawrence. *How to Win a Local Election: A Complete Step-By-Step Guide.* New York: M. Evans, 1994.

This is an excellent guide to local election campaigns with small staffs and low budgets which rely upon volunteers. It was endorsed by the chairmen of both the Democratic and Republican National Committees. Like *Winning Elections,* Judge Grey provides information and advice on virtually every aspect of a campaign from the moment a candidate decides to run. The book's appendices provide worksheets for planing campaign strategy, schedule, and budget. It is less useful for campaigns in larger districts with paid staff and bigger budgets which need to employ high-tech campaign methods.

Movement for a New Congress. *Vote Power.* Englewood Cliffs: Prentice Hall, 1970.

Although focusing upon preparations for the 1970 Congressional campaigns, the suggested techniques are useful in any campaign. *Vote Power* emphasizes how to choose campaigns in which to work, the specific services that volunteers can perform, and how to remain politically effective after the campaign.

Parkinson, Hank. *Winning Your Campaign: A Nuts-and-Bolts Guide to Political Victory.* Englewood Cliffs: Prentice Hall, 1970.

A realistic guide to modern campaign practices and most particularly to public relations aspects such as announcing candidacy, holding press conferences, writing press releases, and campaign scheduling. It is written particularly for potential candidates, offering advice both under what conditions one should run and how to run a successful campaign. Although somewhat dated by now, it is still a good handbook for regular party candidates and of use to any candidate, campaign staff member, or volunteer.

Parkinson, Hank. *Winning Political Campaigns With Publicity.* Wichita, Kansas: Campaign Associates Press, 1973.

Parkinson's second campaign handbook concentrates on all the necessary techniques of a news-making, public relations campaign. A particularly essential book for a candidate who may not understand the media, the campaign manager who wants to sharpen his or her tools, and the volunteer or professional public relations person working their first big campaign. The book focuses generally on tactics and mechanics but inadvertently raises strategic questions as to the implications and possible abuses of this kind of campaigning.

TEN FEATURE FILMS ON CAMPAIGNING

All the King's Men. (Robert Rossen, 1949, Columbia)

Blind Ambition (Time-Life, 1982)

Blaze (Ron Shelton, 1989, Disney)

Bob Roberts (Tim Robins, 1992, Parmount)

The Candidate (Michael Ritchie, 1972, Warner Brothers)

Distinguished Gentleman (Jonathan Lynn, 1992, Hollywood Pictures)

The Last Hurrah (John Ford, 1958, Columbia)

Seduction of Joe Tynan (Jerry Schatzberg, 1979, Universal)

Mr. Smith Goes to Washington (Frank Capra, 1939, Columbia)

State of the Union (Frank Capra, 1948, MGM)

Of the various films *The Last Hurrah* and *All the King's Men* are the best films on the old style campaigning in the machine party era. *The Candidate* and *Bob Roberts* are among the best on the mass media or synthetic campaigns.

TEN DOCUMENTARY FILMS ON CAMPAIGNING

By the People (Bill Mahin, 1970, University of Illinois at Chicago)

The Best Campaign Money Can Buy (Steven Talbot, 1992, PBS)

Campaigning for the Presidency (University of California at San Diego/KPBS, 1992, PBS)

Chicago Politics: A Theater of Power (Bill Stamets, 1985-87)

Election Day Chicago Style and *Election Night With Jane Byrne* on a single tape entitled *Pugs 'n Pols* (Scott Jacobs, 1979)

The Great Upset of '48 (WETA, 1988, PBS)

The Last Party (Mark Benjamin/Marc Levin, 1993)

The Making of the President (ABC, Wolper, 1960 and Wolper, 1964)

The Race for Mayor (Howard Gladstone and James Ylisela, 1983)

The War Room (D. A. Pennebaker, 1993)

INDEX